ORGANIZATION:
A GUIDE TO PROBLEMS
AND PRACTICE

ORGANIZATION: A GUIDE TO PROBLEMS AND PRACTICE

John Child

University of Aston

P·CP

Paul Chapman
Publishing Ltd

Reprinted in this edition
by Paul Chapman Publishing Ltd
144 Liverpool Road
London N1 1LA

British Library Cataloguing in Publication Data

Child, John
Organization. — 2nd ed
1. Management
I. Title
658.4   HD38
ISBN 1 85396 014 4

Typeset by Bookens, Saffron Walden, Essex.
Printed and bound by Athenaeum Press Ltd,
Newcastle upon Tyne

C D E F G   4 3 2 1 0

CONTENTS

Part III　ORGANIZATIONAL CHANGE

Criteria for organizational design. Organization and performance. The search for universals. Considerations of contingency. The task contingency approach: relevance of environment, diversity, size, technology and personnel. Limitations of the task contingency approach. The political contingency approach: relevance of managerial preferences, market conditions and political context. Considerations of consistency. Implications for organizational change. Summary. Suggested further reading.

List of Figures and Tables

Preface to the first edition

Having been engaged on research and consultancy into organization for a number of years, I have felt that there is a need for a book which draws from available findings some guidelines for the analysis of practical problems. The problem with most books on organization is that they are written by academics for academics, and their material is presented in a way that enlightens purely academic themes.

This book is grounded on the belief that research is of great significance for the improvement of practical affairs. Research studies are in themselves usually directed to the refinement of theories, but as an eminent psychologist, Kurt Lewin, once observed, 'there is nothing so practical as a good theory'. What I have attempted here is to examine problems which practitioners will recognize as theirs. I have drawn upon my knowledge of relevant research, including my own. The book is, however, written in a straightforward non-academic manner. Each chapter closes with a short summary of its main themes. These summaries are followed by suggested further reading on the topics which have been covered. There are no academic footnotes.

This is an introduction to the field of organization. It delineates the main problems which arise in designing structures and jobs. It does not cover the field of organizational behaviour as a whole, although the interfaces between structure and behaviour are examined. Frequent reference is also made to the context in which decisions on organization have to be made.

The readers I have had in mind when writing this book include both those who are practising management and administration and those who are engaged in its study. I have had the benefit of valuable comment from my students, many of whom have been practitioners attending an advanced course of study. My personal belief, however, is that the subject of organization cannot be treated simply as a technical matter. It has a wide social relevance, affecting access to decision-making in society and the quality of life of all who work in, or have dealings with, social institutions. The more widely it is appreciated that there are many choices available to us in the organization of public, industrial and other institutions, the closer we should move towards a truly democratic society. In this light, the present book is offered to all. We should each and every one of us be concerned with how our fellow human beings and our scarce economic resources are managed.

Increasing difficulties are being placed in the way of giving time to reflection in British universities today, and it has not been an easy matter to write this book. I am therefore all the more grateful to colleagues who have both helped to relieve me of additional burdens and also found time to exchange ideas and comment—particularly John Berridge and Diana Pheysey. My debt to students is a heavy one, especially to members of the 1974/75 and 1975/76 Master in Business Administration courses at the Aston Management Centre. Miss Katie Talbot worked wonders in typing from untidy manuscripts. Above all my wife, Elizabeth, inspired perseverance and lent a critical faculty which will perhaps offset some of the faults in this work for which I alone bear responsibility.

John Child
July 1976.

Preface to second edition

This new edition of *Organization* incorporates a number of changes and improvements, while continuing to address the same purposes as its predecessor. There are new chapters on reward policies and the relevance of new technology. New material is included on job design and work structuring, control, the relation of organizational design to performance, and the relevance of political contingencies. In rewriting the book, I have reflected the important developments in thinking about organizations which have been evident since the mid-1970s. The enquiring reader can pursue these in detail through the additional reading suggested at the end of each chapter and by recourse to journals such as the *Academy of Management Journal, Administrative Science Quarterly, Organizational Dynamics*, and *Organization Studies*.

A point that requires clarification is the way I have referred to gender. I have attempted to steer between the Scylla of insensitive male chauvinism and the Charybdis of ungainly repetition (he and she, her and his) which is tedious and out of touch with ordinary idiom. Reference to any person or role in the text is to female or male without any prejudice. My intention is to employ the male and female gender just sufficiently to remind the reader of that fact but not so frequently as to be irksome.

I have again been fortunate to have benefitted from the exchange of ideas with colleagues, especially those in the Microelectronics Project and the Work Organization Research Centre at Aston University: Peter Clark, Margaret Grieco, Janet Harvey, Ray Loveridge, Chris Smith, Jennifer Tann, Marion Tarbuck and Richard Whipp. Lex Donaldson, Tom Lupton and Monir Tayeb made very helpful comments on a draft of this new edition, as did members of the 1982/83 MBA Programme at the University of Aston Management Centre—I am grateful to all. Vera Green, Beryl Marston, Monir Tayeb and Myra Wheeldon contributed to the production of the typescript, while Marianne Lagrange of Harper & Row was most helpful in fettling the rough edges of my English. As always, my wife Elizabeth offered both constructive criticism and emotional support, while the whole family patiently suffered the temperament and unsociability of the writer in their midst.

John. Child
February 1984

PART I

INTRODUCTION

CHAPTER 1

The contribution of organization

'A machine designed by geniuses to be run by idiots.' Herman Wouk,
The Caine Mutiny, *on the organization of the wartime US Navy.*

The leaders of successful companies and other institutions generally attribute a significant part of that success to good organization. The design of organization is one of management's major priorities. The problem lies in determining what 'good organization' is for each of the great variety of institutions that are engaged in very different activities on all kinds of scale within the contrasting economic, social, political and cultural settings which make up the world's patchwork. It is the purpose of this book to identify some of the choices in organization that can be made and the considerations pertinent to those choices.

The design of organization is normally understood to cover the basic framework of positions and relations between them, systems for measuring what has been accomplished by the people in those positions, systems for rewarding them, and procedures for selecting and developing them. Structure is central to all of these aspects and has to be given particular attention in organization design, especially from the perspectives of how structural arrangements can be devised which suit the purposes given to the organization and the expectations of people working within it. As Peter Drucker has put it: 'Structure is a means for attaining the objectives and goals of an institution (1974: 52).* The requirement is to create a structure which suits the need of the particular enterprise or institution, while achieving consistency between the various aspects of that structure and being able to adapt it to changing circumstances over time.

There are three main aspects to organization structure which can assist the attainment of objectives. First, structure contributes to the successful implementation of plans by formally allocating people and resources to the tasks which have to be done, and by providing mechanisms for their co-ordination. This is sometimes called the *basic structure*. It takes the form of job descriptions, organization charts and the constitution of boards, committees, working parties, task forces and teams.

Second, it is possible to indicate to the members of an organization more clearly what is expected of them by means of various structural *operating*

---

*Full references to any sources cited in the text are given as part of the suggested further reading at the end of each chapter and are also listed in the Bibliography at the end of the book.

mechanisms. For example, devices such as standing orders or operating procedures can set out the ways in which tasks are to be performed. In addition, or perhaps as an alternative when the manner of doing tasks cannot be closely defined, standards of performance can be established incorporating criteria such as output or quality of achievement. These would be accompanied by procedures for performance review. As well as control procedures such as these, other operating mechanisms include reward and appraisal systems, planning schedules and systems for communication.

Third, the ambit of structure encompasses provisions for assisting decision-making and its associated information processing requirements. These may be called *decision mechanisms*. They include arrangements for relevant intelligence to be collected from outside the organization, partly through specifying these among the duties of specialist jobs. Procedures can be established whereby information is collated, evaluated and made available to decision-makers on a regular basis and/or in response to some new development outside of the organization. The process of decision-making itself can be assisted, where appropriate, through programming, specification of stages in the process, indication of decision rules and provision of procedures for post-audit.

The allocation of responsibilities, the grouping of functions, decision-making, co-ordination, control and reward—all these are fundamental requirements for the continued operation of an organization. The quality of an organization's structure will affect how well these requirements are met.

Components of structure

The structure of an organization is often taken to comprise all the tangible and regularly occurring features which help to shape its members' behaviour. This encompasses what used misleading to be called formal and informal organization. The way in which those terms have generally been used is misleading because it fails to distinguish between the degree of formality in a structure and the separate dimension of whether it is officially sanctioned or not. The degree of formality in structure is a dimension of design which will be considered in a later chapter. On the other hand, a book like this naturally lays emphasis on structural arrangements which managers or other groups can design and which are therefore official by definition. Unofficial practices have to be recognized as part of the context of organizational design, and they often point to a deficiency in the official structure. But organizational designers do not implement unofficial structures.

There has also been a long-standing confusion as to whether the term 'organization' refers to the structure of an organized body, institution or enterprise, or whether it describes the total entity *per se*. In this book I shall use the term 'structure' whenever the sense of 'organization' would be ambiguous. Otherwise, I have conformed with popular expression and used organization to refer to structural attributes (as in 'reorganization' or 'the organization of a company'), and the term 'an organization' or similar to refer to institutions or units as a whole.

Some idea of the components of an organization structure has already emerged. Major dimensions are:

1 The allocation of tasks and responsibilities to individuals. Aspects of structure which come into play here are the form of specialization designed into jobs and the discretion attached to them.
2 The designation of formal reporting relationships, determining the number of levels in hierarchies and the spans of control of managers and supervisors.
3 The grouping together of individuals in sections or departments, the grouping of departments into divisions and larger units, and the overall grouping of units into the total organization.
4 The design of systems to ensure effective communication of information, integration of effort, and participation in the decision-making process.
5 The delegation of authority together with associated procedures whereby the use of discretion is monitored and evaluated.
6 The provision of systems for performance appraisal and reward which help to motivate rather than to alienate employees.

If any of these structural components is deficient, there can be serious consequences for the performance of an organization.

Consequences of structural deficiencies

As Starbuck and Nystrom point out in introducing their *Handbook of Organizational Design* (1981), there seems to be overwhelming evidence that very large improvements could be made to the ways in which organizations are run. Because organizations are today the most common mode of collective effort in industrial and urbanized societies, even quite modest improvements could affect millions of people. For example, the ways in which many jobs have been designed to subject their incumbents to monotony and pressure, often backed up by harsh controls, have been found to affect adversely the mental and physical health of employees. The way in which the structure of an organization is designed will largely determine what job moves and career paths are available for those employees who seek the chance to develop themselves. Our capacity to design effective organizational arrangements can also affect the speed at which technological progress is applied to the production of goods and services. A report by Scholz and Wolff to the EEC (1981) concluded, for instance, that the limited resources of organizational knowledge will slow the speed of diffusion of microelectronics and weaken its potential effects.

There are a number of problems which so often mark the struggling organization and which even at the best of times are dangers that have to be looked for. These are low motivation and morale, late and inappropriate decisions, conflict and lack of co-ordination, rising costs, and a generally poor response to new opportunities and external changes. Structural deficiencies can play a part in exacerbating all these problems.

1 Motivation and morale may be depressed because:
(a) Decisions appear to be inconsistent and arbitrary in the absence of standardized rules.
(b) People perceive that they have little responsibility, opportunity for achievement and recognition of their worth because there is insufficient delegation of decision-making. This may be connected with narrow spans of control.
(c) There is a lack of clarity as to what is expected of people and how their performance is assessed. This could be due to inadequate job definition.
(d) People are subject to competing pressures from different parts of the organization due to an absence of clearly defined priorities, decision rules or work programmes.
(e) People are overloaded because their support systems are not adequate. Supervisors, for instance, have to leave the job to chase up materials, parts and tools as there is no adequate system for communicating forthcoming requirements to stores and tool room.

2 Decision-making may be delayed and lacking in quality because:
(a) Necessary information is not transmitted on time to the appropriate people. This may be due to an over-extended hierarchy.
(b) Decision-makers are too segmented into separate units and there is inadequate provision to co-ordinate them.
(c) Decision-makers are overloaded due to insufficient delegation on their part.
(d) There are no adequate procedures for evaluating the results of similar decisions made in the past.

3 There may be conflict and a lack of co-ordination because:
(a) There are conflicting goals which have not been structured into a single set of objectives and priorities. People are acting at cross-purposes. They may, for example, be put under pressure to follow departmental priorities at the expense of product or project goals.
(b) People are working out of step with each other because they are not brought together into teams or because mechanisms for liaison have not been laid down.
(c) The people who are actually carrying out operational work and who are in touch with changing contingencies are not permitted to participate in the planning of the work. There is therefore a breakdown between planning and operations.

4 An organization may not respond innovatively to changing circumstances because:
(a) It has not established specialized jobs concerned with forecasting and scanning the environment.
(b) There is a failure to ensure that innovation and planning of change are

mainstream activities backed up by top management through appropriate procedures to provide them adequate priority, programming and resources.
(c) There is inadequate co-ordination between the part of an organization identifying changing market needs and the research area working on possible technological solutions.

5 Costs may be rising rapidly, particularly in the administrative area, because:
(a) The organization has a long hierarchy with a high ratio of 'chiefs' to 'indians'.
(b) There is an excess of procedure and paperwork distracting people's attention away from productive work and requiring additional staff personnel to administer.
(c) Some or all of the other organization problems are present.

Organizational choices

All the components of organization structure can be designed to take different forms, and they in fact vary considerably in practice. As Jay Lorsch of the Harvard Business School has put it, 'the structure of an organization is not an immutable given, but rather a set of complex variables about which managers can exercise considerable choice' (1970: 1). There is no single way of organizing; and therein lies the dilemma facing managers, or indeed anyone else participating in organizational design decisions.

The one model of organization with which we are most familiar is bureaucracy. Bureaucracy not only has a long history, its genesis reaching back to the administration of ancient civilization, but it is in a more advanced form the type of structure commonly adopted by large organizations today. For several thousand years bureaucracy has been widely accepted as the most efficient, equitable and least corruptible basis for administration. Despite some early social criticism by novelists such as Balzac and sociologists like Max Weber, it is only during the past few decades that bureaucracy has been attacked as an inefficient model of organization in the conditions of unprecedented change, complex technology and ethos of personal initiative which prevail today.

Bureaucratic structures are characterized by an advanced degree of specialization between jobs and departments, by a reliance on formal procedures and paperwork, and by extended managerial hierarchies with clearly marked status distinctions. In bureaucracies there tends to be a strictly delimited system of delegation down these hierarchies whereby an employee is expected to use his discretion only within what the rules allow. The bureaucratic approach is intended to provide organizational control through ensuring a high degree of predictability in people's behaviour. It is also a means of trying to ensure that different clients or employees are treated fairly through the application of general rules and procedures. The problem is that rules are inflexible instruments of administration which enshrine experience of past rather than present conditions, which cannot be readily adapted to suit individual needs, and which can become barriers behind which it is tempting for the administrator to hide. There is always a tension in the design of organizations between preserving control and encouraging flexibility, and bureaucracy comes down heavily in favour of the former. This is why bureacracy today has come under increasing attack on the grounds of its inability to innovate, its demotivating effects on employees and its secrecy. The search for alternative forms of organization serves to remind us that bureaucracy is only one organizational design and that other choices are available. The fundamental question is what form of organization should be selected and on what basis? The following are some of the decisions that have to be made.

1 Should jobs be broken down into narrow areas of work and responsibility, so as to secure the benefits of specialization? Or should the degree of specialization be kept to a minimum in order to simplify communication and to offer members of the organization greater scope and responsibility in their work? Another choice arising in the design of jobs concerns the extent to which the people in them should be given discretion over how to organize and perform their work.

2 Should the overall structure of an organization be 'tall' rather than 'flat' in terms of its levels of management and spans of control? What are the implications for communication, motivation and overhead costs of moving towards one of these alternatives rather than the other?

3 Should jobs and departments be grouped together in a 'functional' way according to the specialist expertise and interests that they share? Or should they be grouped according to the different services and products that are being offered, or the different geographical areas being served, or according to yet another criterion? Can the advantages of two or more types of grouping be secured through matrix or overlay arrangements?

4 Is it appropriate to aim for an intensive form of integration between the different segments of an organization or not? What kind of integrative mechanisms are there to choose from?

5 What approach should management take towards maintaining adequate control over work done? Should it centralize or delegate decisions, and all or only some decisions? Should a policy of extensive formalization be adopted in which standing orders and written records are used for control purposes? Should work be subject to close supervision? Can control also be assisted by the development of a common culture and identity within the organization?

6 What considerations should be taken into account when designing reward systems? How can these be made consistent with the general approach being adopted towards organization?

When thinking about these organizational choices, it is not possible to ignore the changes that are likely to be relevant over time. A number of questions have to be posed, which place one's analysis in a dynamic context. These are:

7 What are the changing structural requirements posed by the strategic development of an organization? What are the practical implications for the planning of change that can be drawn from research into the relation between organizational design and performance?

8 The most significant source of organizational change and development today lies in the rapid and widespread application of new technology. What are the implications for organizational design of its use, and what design choices are possible with new technology?

9 Finally, how might the need for a change in organization be recognized, and what problems commonly arise with reorganization? How can these be tackled and change implemented?

These are the main issues which managers face when thinking about the design of their organization.* They constitute the subject matter of this book. It is not possible to offer any precise answers to problems of organization structure in abstraction from the particular institution we are talking about, and from the conditions it is facing. As Drucker has also said in the article cited, 'organization is organic and unique to each individual business or institution'. What one can do, however, is to provide the reader with a constructive way of analysing his or her organizational problems and to draw attention to the kinds of alternatives he or she has available when designing a structure.

A full consideration of structural design has to be informed by the objectives which are selected for the organization. It is in this respect a political rather than a purely technical question. If the governing body and members of an organization value its present culture and way of doing things, then the preservation of these features will enter into the range of objectives of that organization. In other words, it is not just a case of asking how appropriate a structure is to do a job of co-ordination or control; it is also a matter of asking who had the power to establish the structure the way it is and what advantages do they secure from preserving it in that form? Structure, after all, also embodies a particular distribution of control, power and rights within an organization.

I wish to stress this point at an early stage because most of the literature on organizational design treats it as a purely technical matter, a question of adjusting structure to suit prevailing contingencies. These contingencies are, of course, significant and they will be discussed shortly. A recognition that organizational design should have regard to contingencies is important in drawing attention to the need to select an appropriate structure and to avoid the fallacy of thinking that there is any 'best' general model of administration. My point is, however, that in reality this choice goes even further. It incorporates the preferences which decision-makers and other influential groups have for a particular approach to management, preferences which are ultimately derived from their philosophies of mankind and/or their per-

*The term 'manager' is used in this book to denote anyone who has responsibility for the work performance of others. Managers might themselves be responsible to bodies with quite different objectives such as a capitalist industrialist, the State or a workers' council. They may also have some latitude to pursue objectives of their own choosing.

ceptions of self-interest. Consensus over such preferences and its embodiment in an accepted culture can itself have a powerful positive motivating effect, and this goes some way towards explaining a phenomenon discussed in Chapter 8, whereby successful enterprises operating under similar contingencies are found to utilize different types of organizational design.

The objectives selected for an organization are in principle translated into a strategy. Strategy refers to the policies and plans through which a management chooses to realize the objectives it has set (or has been given) for its organization, under conditions where policies carry a degree of risk (because of uncertainty and the cost of failure), and where the range of viable policies may be constrained by dependence on the support of other organizations. The policies that are implemented over the course of time will determine the tasks an organization performs, its areas of location, the diversity of its activities and the kind of people it seeks to employ. The level of success attained by the organization will determine its growth and its accumulation of resources and standing. Accumulation will in turn reduce risk and dependence, and so relax constraints on the future choice of policy. The reverse process will attend failing performance. Dynamic processes such as these generate changing contingencies for the design of organization structure (see Child and Kieser 1981). Decisions on structure are, however, major items of policy in themselves which may in practice have to be weighed against other strategic considerations. For example, in many contemporary societies the design of organization has to satisfy political expectations such as those embodied in demands for the extension of participation. Nevertheless, the impact of existing contingencies upon structure is substantial enough, and warrants some consideration at this point.

Structural contingencies

Decisions to follow a particular policy usually have some direct implications for organizational design. For example, if primacy is given in a business company to a policy of growth via acquisition then the experience of American firms indicates that the establishment of specialized acquisitions teams is normally required to carry out a thorough search for an evaluation of opportunities. If greater emphasis comes to be placed upon cost reduction and cash budgeting in order to improve profitability and use of funds, then an elaboration of financial control procedures and an expansion of financial departments may logically follow. The success with which policies have been achieved will contribute to the amount of surplus resources ('slack') available to an institution, or conversely to the degree of pressure its management feels itself to be under. A pressure situation almost invariably leads to a greater centralization of decision-making, as well as to reductions in the scale of some activities which may in turn reduce numbers of departments and the level of specialization within the organization.

The overall size of an organization has been shown in many research surveys to be closely associated with the type of structure adopted, particularly in the range up to about 3,000 employees. Institutions in many fields of business, public services, trade unionism and so forth have grown steadily larger, with the aim of expanding their field of activity, taking advantage of economies of large-scale operation and supporting the overheads of advanced research and development or a wider range of specialist support services. As the numbers employed in an organization grow so does its complexity. The number of levels of management increases, bringing additional problems of delegation and control at each level. The increase in size makes it economically possible to utilize specialist support services, which must be slotted into the organization structure. The spread of separate groups and departments across the organization also increases with growth. Additional procedures are then required for co-ordination and communication between these different units, while the contribution of new specialists has to be integrated with the activities of line management.

Size in these ways has very significant implications for organizational design, a theme which will be illustrated at many points later on. It creates so many administrative and behavioural problems that many organizations are divided into semi-autonomous units upon reaching a certain scale, especially if this coincides with diversification into different fields of activity. Hence, the relative impact of size on an organization's structure may in practice be progressively reduced beyond this stage in its development.

Many large organizations, business companies in particular, have diversified their activities into a number of distinct fields or industries. Large companies will also quite often be selling and manufacturing in several different regions of the world. Diversification is an important means of growth, through which firms move into expanding fields and avoid the constraints of legislation that discourages over-concentration in any one industry. When an organization's operations in a new field have attained a certain maturity and scale, it is normally appropriate for its structure to be divisionalized. This permits suitable personnel and resources to be allocated specifically to what is now a distinctive field of operation and for their activities to be integrated closely around it. If the proportion of a company's business in a particular geographical area reaches a significant scale, then a similar logic may justify the establishment of area divisions. Depending on the balance between product and area diversification, area divisions may be an alternative to product divisions or may be established concomitantly with them. Divisionalization is an organizational response to diversification, though it is also encouraged by the growing administrative problems of large scale. As divisions themselves grow large, and possibly diversified, pressures towards further subdivision are activated both to achieve smaller units of management and to reflect the distinctiveness of separate business areas.

Diversification extends the range of different environments in which an organization operates. These environments may also vary in their characteristics, especially the rate of change experienced in market and technological features, the rate at which they are expanding, types of competitive pressure and the degree of dependence on other institutions. These factors will serve to generate different levels of managerial uncertainty regarding new developments to which the organization has to adapt. The greater its dependence on other organizations for custom, supplies, governmental sanction or other necessary support, the more that uncertainty will be reinforced, because management's ability to ignore new developments or to control them will be correspondingly reduced. Uncertainty and dependence together place a premium upon an organization's capacity to secure and rapidly disseminate intelligence about the outside world, and to operate in a flexible manner which permits any necessary reactions to new developments that have been forecast. For example, the conglomerate ITT, which had been operating in a climate of chronic uncertainty about the future of its telephone business in countries such as Allende's Chile, felt it necessary to build up a highly developed system of political intelligence in order to provide this capacity to anticipate and adapt. Environmental conditions have important implications for the type of organization structure to be adapted.

The kinds of environment in which an organization is operating determine the tasks and production it undertakes, and these have implications for its structural design and choice of personnel. For example, a firm may be operating in a high-technology science-based industry. It will have to give special attention to organizing its research and development activities so as to encourage inventiveness while also retaining control over expenditure and commercial relevance. Seeking to utilize advanced technical knowledge, it will probably employ a broad range of occupational specialists who must be adequately co-ordinated. If a company can place its operations onto a mass-produced basis, this will speak for a different form of production organization than if it happens to be producing for a small-batch or one-off market. Much attention was paid in pioneering studies of organization to the physical technology of production as a contingent influence on effective organization, and the practical implications of these studies will be considered later on. By and large, the technology of an organization reflects the kind of environment in which its management has chosen to operate. Some complex technological processes may also only be available on an economic basis to organizations which have attained a given size. Nowadays, the application of microelectronic technology can significantly alter the organization of information processing and office work, as well as the general structure of employment.

The purpose of some institutions will reflect the nature of their membership. This is obviously true of a voluntary association like a trade union. The character of other institutions such as hospitals or universities will attract certain types of employees, most notably in these cases staff who expect to work to their own professional standards free from close administrative control. A science-based company will employ a significant body of scientists who similarly are likely to have strong preferences about how they wish to work. The proportion of the total working population accounted for by professional and highly trained personnel such as these is steadily rising. In contrast, a mass-production car assembly plant may attract semi-skilled workers who place more emphasis on relatively high pay than on conditions of work. These instances go to show that the kind of job design and working environment which is in tune with the expectations of an organization's members will vary according to who they are and why they have joined the institution.

Both from a managerial viewpoint of securing motivation and a social viewpoint of raising people's quality of working life, the type of membership and workforce an institution has provides a further important contingency to be satisfied in the design of jobs, operating procedures, career opportunities and so forth.

This brief discussion of structural contingencies permits three further points to be made at the outset of this book. The first point is that the attainment of an organization's objectives will be facilitated if two conditions are satisfied: (a) the policies it adopts are realistic in the light of prevailing conditions; and (b) its structure is designed to satisfy these policies. A simple example can illustrate this point.

The management of a small company producing good quality and rather expensive confectionery wished to expand out of its limited markets by supplying a new low-price quality line to a chain store. This line would consist of simply produced and wrapped sweets which were made from standard ingredients and varied only in flavouring. The company proved unable to supply the store at a sufficiently high rate of production, and it lost the contract.

Its structure was such that it had a director in charge of quality control ('Technical Director') as well as a director of production. Quality control was rigorously applied at various stages of production and to wrapping. The company was sufficiently small to mean that initial production of the new line used existing mixing, boiling and other plant. Also no change was made to quality control procedures or to the system of production control. Considerable conflict arose between production management and quality control who attempted to apply the normal procedures to the new line, including rules such as the placing of trays at certain distances from walls. (The higher level of volume generated pressures on storage space.) Production was seriously disrupted by batches being rejected or delayed, and by batches of traditional products holding up those of the new. At this stage, then, the company had not modified its structure to suit its new growth-oriented policies.

At a later date the company was successful in securing and fulfilling another high-volume contract. This time it revised its quality requirements for the new line, held discussions between quality control and production about the new operation and after a short while placed inspectors under the day-to-day control of production management. It also set up a formal procedure whereby decisions on conflicting batch priorities were referred to the sales manager as opposed to merely following traditional practice on the sequencing of batches. The structure had now been amended to support the shift in objectives.

The second point is that contingencies such as environment, size, type of work, and personnel employed are not the same in different divisions and departments within an organization. Accounting tasks and the kind of personalities carrying them out are not very similar to research tasks and personnel. An electronics division of a conglomerate like ITT operates in quite different conditions from its hotel chain. This means that within an institution one should expect to find variations in structure to suit its different parts. There is no merit in imposing a common form of structure on the diverse sections of an organization. That would merely represent a misplaced sense of administrative tidiness. Structural diversity, however, does mean that the integration of sections is a problem. As we see in Chapter 5, the more an organization is internally differentiated, the more its management will have to pay special regard to integrative mechanisms.

Thirdly, structural contingencies are themselves interrelated; for instance, larger companies are generally the more diversified. The particular combination of objectives and contingencies found in an organization gives it a unique character. The set of contingencies which are peculiar to that organization may also in some degree conflict, which poses a policy and structural dilemma for its management. For instance, a firm which has based its commercial success on standardized mass production employing relatively cheap and low-skill labour may find it difficult to move into more innovative and higher value-added products should market conditions require this. In 1974 British local authorities were amalgamated in pursuit of scale economies but this was at the expense of their ability to maintain close involvement with local people.

The implication of this is not that we should give up any hope of designing structures which will cope, or even forget about considering any general guidelines at all. The unique character of an institution can be identified in terms of component dimensions which can be compared with experience of other organizations along the same dimensions. Managers in practice have to take account of a multiplicity of details and attempt to reconcile the pressures of conflicting contingencies. This really means that improvements in organizational design can only proceed through a process of organizational development, which entails a painstaking working through of details with the managers and employees concerned. As I wrote some years ago, the guidelines which can be derived from our present knowledge will assist managers in working through their organizational problems. 'But, in the present state of knowledge, this working through is necessary. Particular cases have to be assessed, that is researched, virtually from scratch' (Child 1970: 388). This is, of course, what managers often attempt to do by trial and error. In many organizations today structures are constantly being adjusted, partly as operating conditions and contingencies change, partly in response to the changing balance of managerial politics.

Limitations to the contribution of structure

I have so far put forward the view that the design of organization structure must make reference to a complexity of different requirements, and that it cannot proceed on an *a priori* basis. At certain times one of those requirements may be given priority over the others, but it will not be fruitful to ignore them completely. In this section, I shall mention some of the reasons why structure, however well designed, can only be expected to make a limited, though none the less significant, contribution to an organization's effectiveness. Effectiveness is first discussed in economic terms from the standpoint of the whole organization, and then from the standpoint of the individual employee.

The performance of an organization is influenced by many factors apart from its structure. For instance, an organization structure may be effective in guiding people to perform the right tasks, in co-ordinating their efforts and in processing information, but this will not be reflected in overall performance if strategies are being followed that are not in tune with desired objectives or prevailing circumstances. As Alfred P. Sloan, former President and Chairman of General Motors, wrote: 'An organization does not make decisions; its function is only to provide a framework, based upon established criteria, within which decisions can be fashioned in an orderly manner' (1967: 466). Nor can a mere structure of organization support an appropriate pattern of behaviour if there is not the will or competence among managers and employees to perform in that manner. If skills are lacking or the climate of morale is bad, then an otherwise appropriate structure will have relatively little effect.

Certain structural features can come to be regarded as ends in themselves, whether or not they contribute to a higher level of performance. For example, provisions to allow employees or their representatives to have a greater say in decision-making were under serious discussion in Europe during the 1970s. The argument for these lies not so much in their possible contribution to economic efficiency (which could nevertheless be quite real) as in the way they can satisfy other aspirations. Family-controlled firms have often been known to persevere with a centralized system of decision-making long beyond the stage of growth at which delegation to non-family members came to be required on grounds of effectiveness. Some organizations may temper their pursuit of economic goals with social policies that cause their organization structures to be other than the most efficient. I know of one large group of companies in which a policy of plant rationalization coupled with one of declaring few managerial redundancies led to extended hierarchies within which surplus managers were lodged. These not only embodied excess manpower costs but gave rise to communication problems.

Organization structure cannot be expected to resolve political problems within an institution. There are deep-seated conflicts in many fields about the legitimate objectives of institutions, and concerning the correctness of the methods by which they are run. If objectives are in dispute between managers and employees, managers and groups outside the organization or between managers themselves, a formal structure cannot of itself resolve these differences in a way that integrates people's actions in an effective manner. At best, it can be designed to provide mechanisms, such as discussion meetings, which bring conflicts into the open and so offer some chance of reconciling them. In fact, when the ownership of an organization or the objectives that are being pursued are not regarded as legitimate by its employees or members, the structure will probably come to be regarded as a means of repressive or exploitative control and hence something to be resisted and even sabotaged.

Structure itself often becomes victim to politics, and indeed it will not be allowed to operate effectively if it does not reflect political forces within the organization. A department, for instance, will tend to ignore a restrictive procedure if it has the power to do so. Political ambitions are frequently a driving force behind structural changes. A few years ago a major programme of organizational development was initiated in a division of a large British company partly because a newly appointed production manager felt he was not occupying a viable job and wished to make his mark in time to succeed the divisional director who was due to retire eighteen months later. The development involved the regrouping of various functional support activities under his command.

Wider political and social forces in societies as a whole also limit the choice and operation of organizational structures. This is very clear in the case of state enterprises in both socialist and capitalist economies and of public service departments as well. Here the form of structure is to some degree imposed as a political rather than a purely managerial decision. The question of culture is also relevant, since it may heavily influence what kinds of structures are regarded as legitimate. Ideas about organization developed in the United States or Britain may not be wholly appropriate for, say, a traditional Islamic country. In the latter case a highly formalized structure emphasizing vertical authority relationships might most closely fit the society's customs and social precepts and thus be considered appropriate for any operational environment, while in the West such a structure does not have deep cultural roots and would not necessarily be recommended, certainly not for an organization engaged in high technology or operating under rapidly changing market conditions. Culture may determine the repertoire of organizational choices which are socially acceptable or comfortable.

It is important therefore to find ways of shaping structures in ways that accord with changing views on the correct manner of conducting relationships at work. In the West, traditional norms of authority have been challenged from many quarters and effective structures of organization have to be adapted accordingly. Whether in fact the organization of any units above the primary group size can be designed in such a way as completely to eliminate formal authority relationships is a moot point. Therein probably lies an inevitable source of conflict between managers and others, which is heightened by contemporary western notions of the freedom and responsibility necessary to the achievement of personal fulfilment. Organization structure in this respect will always appear potentially coercive to employees. In business firms and other institutions where there is a cash nexus with their members this coercion of formalized authority will be reinforced by economic conflicts of interest. Organizational design and development can only help to resolve this conflict with the individual to a limited extent, by exploring more satisfactory means of reconciling the different interests involved.

Plan of the book

In Part II, six chapters examine different organizational choices in turn. The choice of structural alternatives is discussed in the light of relevant contingencies. Much of the research literature on organization divides up the field in terms of these contingencies, since to a large extent they define the different academic interests involved. From a practitioner's point of view it is more useful to concentrate upon the specific structural choices with which he or she will have to deal, though at the same time bearing in mind their interdependent nature.

Chapter 2 considers the micro-level of structuring individual jobs, including developments in job design and work structuring. Chapter 3 discusses the hierarchical distribution of jobs in terms of management levels and spans of control. This chapter addresses the problem of vertical differentiation, which is one of finding an appropriate balance between tall and flat structures. The subject of Chapter 4 is horizontal differentiation—the ways in which jobs and departments can be grouped together and the basis on which such groupings should be divided. An important consideration in grouping people together is that this should be done in accordance with major co-ordination requirements. Chapter 5 is concerned with co-ordination and integration, and attempts to set out the main structural mechanisms that can help. Chapter 6 addresses the problem of control and considers the use of delegation, formalization and direct supervision. The main area of organizational design that is not considered at length is the specialized field of reward systems, on which an ample literature is already available. However, the last chapter in Part II, Chapter 7, considers the choice of reward policies and how the decision here relates both to the types of employees in question and also to other aspects of organizational and work design.

Part III contains three chapters that attempt to place the field of organization structure into a dynamic perspective, through giving attention to the question of change. Chapter 8 links the theme of Part II to that of Part III by reviewing evidence on how organizational design relates to performance, recognizing that conclusions about this relationship should inform policies on organizational change. The performance that organizations will be able to achieve in the future depends on how successfully they adopt and utilize new technology, particularly that based on microelectronics. Chapter 9 examines the relevance of new technology for organizational design. As organizations introduce new technology or otherwise develop, their managers naturally have to cope with various accompanying changes. Chapter 10 looks at signs which point to a need for structural change, and it also considers the practical problems of implementing change.

Summary

Organizational design aims to devise appropriate structural arrangements. Organization structure is a means for allocating responsibilities, providing a framework for operations and performance assessment, and furnishing mechanisms to process information and assist decision-making. Deficiencies in structure can give rise to serious problems.

There are many alternative structural designs to choose from. This choice is not simply a technical matter but also reflects the preferences embodied in an institution's dominant culture. In addition, contingencies such as the organization's scale, environment, diversity and type of membership need to be considered. Too much should not, however, be asked of structure and even a well-conceived organizational design cannot be expected to cope with problems such as deep-seated conflicts. None the less, the way a structure is designed makes a contribution to an organization's performance, and a book such as this can present useful guidelines which inform both practising managers and students of the subject.

Suggested further reading

The number of books on organizational design and structuring has multiplied in recent years. They divide between those written with an academic readership in mind and those which are likely to appeal to the practitioner as well.

In the first category, pride of place has to be given to Henry Mintzberg's *The Structuring of Organizations* (Prentice-Hall 1979). This is a masterly review of research organized around an imaginative analytical framework. A shortened version, supposedly addressed to the practitioner but still academic in style, is Mintzberg's *Structure in Fives: Designing Effective Organizations* (Prentice-Hall 1983). Another lively thinker, though in a somewhat drier style, is Jeffrey Pfeffer who has written *Organizational Design* (AHM Publishing Corporation 1978). The two-volume *Handbook of Organizational Design* edited by Paul C. Nystrom and William H. Starbuck (Oxford University Press 1981) contains a large number of contributions covering a wide range of topics; these are however generally academic in tone and of varying quality. Daniel Robey's *Designing Organizations: A Macro Perspective* (Irwin 1982) provides a conventional treatment but includes eleven case studies. Finally, in this more academic category, mention should be made of Peter Blau and Marshall W. Meyer, *Bureaucracy in Modern Society* (Random House, 2nd edition 1971), which is a readable guide to bureaucracies, how they operate and their significance in society.

Jay R. Galbraith, *Organization Design* (Addison-Wesley 1977) is a major contribution to the subject written for 'those people who will make the choices by which organizations will be designed', namely 'managers and employees'. John P. Kotter, Leonard A. Schlesinger and Vijay Sathe's *Organization* (Irwin 1979) contains cases and readings introduced by relatively short textual sections. Though compiled some while ago, the papers edited by Jay W. Lorsch and Paul R. Lawrence in *Studies in Organizational Design* (Irwin-Dorsey 1970) remain useful. All the books mentioned so far have come from North America. A British writer, Peter A. Clark has produced *Organizational Design: Theory and Practice* (Tavistock 1972) which is a case study of how behavioural scientists worked with a company team on the design of a new factory.

Sources referred to in this chapter but not yet mentioned were John Child, 'More Myths of Management Organization?', *Journal of Management Studies*, October 1970; John Child and Alfred Kieser, 'Development of Organizations over Time', in the *Handbook of Organizational Design* (vol. I) already noted; Peter Drucker, 'New Templates for Today's Organizations', *Harvard Business Review*, January–February 1974; Jay W. Lorsch, 'Introduction to the

Structural Design of Organizations' in Gene W. Dalton, Paul R. Lawrence and J. W. Lorsch (editors), *Organizational Structure and Design* (Irwin-Dorsey 1970); L. Scholz and H. Wolff, *Limits of Conventional Theories and New Approaches for Theoretical and Empirical Investigations* (EEC Brussels September 1981); Alfred P. Sloan, *My Years with General Motors* (Pan Books 1967).

PART II

ORGANIZATIONAL CHOICES

CHAPTER 2

The Design of Jobs and Work Structures

'I can't tell you much about my job because I think it would be misleading to try and make something out of nothing.' Worker in a cigarette factory in Ronald Fraser (ed.), Work: Twenty Personal Accounts (*Penguin 1968: 11*).

Many people seem to feel that their jobs are necessary evils: their only means to a livelihood but offering little by way of present interest or future prospects. Jobs are also a problem for employers in many of the older industrial economies who design them in the hope of harnessing human capabilities productively, but who are seeing that productivity improve only slowly. The manager may look forward to a factory automated by robots which guarantee consistent quality and quantity of production, and which do not complain. The worker may dream of the pools win that would open the door to a leisured existence. In the absence of such dramatic transformations, however, it is not surprising that a good deal of attention has been given to the design of jobs and work in the hope that ways can be found to make them more acceptable and thereby also reduce the alienation of workers from management's purposes.

This chapter examines ways of analysing the design of jobs and describes some of the experiments that have taken place in redesigning jobs and the work structures in which they are located, away from traditional models. It begins by looking at two basic dimensions of job design, specialization and discretion. There are then three sections which deal with job design and the structuring of work at the 'operative' level; that is, among routine manual and clerical jobs where the greatest problems are generally seen to arise and where most attention has been directed. The first of these provides a review of the main developments, the second considers relevant contextual factors, and the third looks at causes and criteria of success and failure in the redesign of jobs and work. Following that, there is an attempt to preserve some balance by considering the design of jobs for two categories of non-operative employees, supervisors and professional specialists. The chapter concludes with a summary of points relevant to making a decision about the design of jobs.

A number of observations need to be made at this early stage by way of qualification. First, jobs amount to a good deal more than their mere design, if by that one means the responsibilities and areas of discretion ascribed to them. For those who hold them, jobs are also properties which have attached to them certain rights and benefits including income, a status in the community, and (for the fortunate minority) the promise of progression up a career structure. Employees are likely to weigh up these rights and benefits against the effort and commitment required by management. They may well resist any changes in job design which in their eyes disturbs that equilibrium unfavourably, even though the changes offer a more intrinsically meaningful content to their jobs. This serves to remind us that jobs have people in them who bring to those jobs a whole set of attributes which will affect the translation of any intended job design and specification into actual practice—their skills, occupational values, personality and motivation. This is not to devalue the contribution that thoughtful job design can make. It is, however, to say that, while most likely initiated by management, job design is a process in which job holders are going to participate and on which they understandably have their own views, and it is wise to recognize this fact.

Second, although their jobs will always be the most important organizational point of reference for the people in them, they are not necessarily the most appropriate focal unit from a design perspective even at the most local organizational level. Individual jobs are an appropriate unit of design when such jobs are concerned with tasks that are readily identifiable and in some degree stand alone in their own right. 'Task' here means the transformation of inputs into output objects such as fabrications, assemblies, projects or complete services. Many specialist, supervisory and managerial jobs are responsible for one or more whole tasks in this sense, as are also some skilled jobs.

Often, however, it takes a group of persons, each in his or her own job, to complete a task. It is, then, logical to allocate responsibility for the task to the work group, and it becomes more sensible to select the group and its task as the unit for design than individual jobs within the group. For, given the high level of interdependence between jobs within the group, changes could not readily be made to one of them without considerably affecting the others. In this situation, if agreement is reached on the responsibilities of the work group as a whole, its members can be left to decide upon the allocation of duties to their individual jobs as they prefer, and to change this allocation between themselves over time. The term 'work structuring' is often used to indicate a design focus on the work group and its task rather than on single jobs, and it also draws attention to the fact that this task is set within the confines of a wider workflow (production) system. Hence thought has to be given to the design, or 'structuring', of the work system as a whole even though the focus is upon particular work groups. In contrast to the 'work structuring' perspective, many discussions of 'job design' have not only ignored the location of jobs within work groups but have also given little attention to the possibilities of modifying workflow systems and technology so as to open up more choice in the design of people's work. We return to the concept of work structuring later in the chapter.

A final and obvious qualification to discussions of job design concerns the problem of generalization, when such an enormous variety of jobs is to be found among organizations. It cannot even be assumed that jobs which pass under the same title, such as fitter, supervisor or accountant are necessarily similar. Some of this variation stems from the way that jobs are embedded in the different organizational arrangements, systems of work and technologies of every work unit. Job design has to be sensitive to this context, and attempts to redesign jobs that neglect to assess how far appropriate contextual adjustments are possible are almost certain to fail. However, the variation found in job and work design even under similar contextual conditions suggests that there is often a degree of choice between alternatives, with each one having certain pros and cons. In other words, the design of jobs and work does not follow automatically from the context; a conscious analysis and decision are involved.

Basic dimensions of job design

A job involves responsibility for the satisfactory completion of certain activities forming part of a task. Although this entails the use of resources such as materials, equipment and time, the person holding a job will not necessarily have much discretion over which resources to use or which methods to apply.

The extent to which jobs are specialized in the sense of being confined to a limited range of activities, and the level of discretion enjoyed by job-holders, are the two basic dimensions of job design considered in this chapter. Jobs can be shaped in different ways along these dimensions. One way of appreciating the range of possible choices and how job design fits into the way work is structured is to consider the answers you are given in different organizations when asking how particular tasks are carried out.

Take the example of dealing with customer complaints in manufacturing firms. In one company you might be told that 'Peter Jones from Quality or one of his team, and a chap from Engineering—quite often Phil Bond or Jim Dankworth—usually get together on that one. They will sort it out, and call in anyone else, as they think best.' In another company, you might be referred to page 23 of the procedures manual where it states that 'customer complaints are the responsibility of the Assistant Quality Control Manager.' This man, you are told, 'has a job description which lays down quite specifically the way he should deal with a complaint, including the maximum amount of expenditure he can incur. Should he wish to spend more, or handle the complaint in any other way, or involve anyone from another department, he must first refer to the Quality Control Manager.'

The different ways in which management in these two companies has gone about organizing the handling of customer complaints reveal the kinds of decisions that have to be made about people's jobs. One question is how specialized should jobs be? In the first organization, jobs appeared to be less specialized in that people contributed to additional tasks such as dealing with a customer complaint when they believed it appropriate to do so. Their jobs were not tightly and narrowly bounded regarding which activities they were and were not to cover. In this organization, the staff also had some discretion over how customer complaints were to be handled—less of a sharp distinction was drawn between the discretion they could exercise and that confined to their managers than in the second organization. In fact, in the first case, two departments—Quality and Engineering—had been given the responsibility for dealing with customer complaints and it was left to members of the departments to decide who would be involved with any complaint that arose and how best to deal with it. In the second case, the method for dealing with complaints was precisely laid down as were various constraints on the way the task was to be carried out. This different structuring of the work of dealing with customer complaints led to contrasts in the design of individual jobs.

The example just described draws attention to the two job design dimensions of specialization and discretion. It also suggests that jobs which combine a high level of specialization with a low level of discretion tend to be subject to rather precise formal definition by job descriptions, procedure manuals and the like. Not only is it easier to encompass such jobs in formal definitions, but definition is also a way in which management can attempt to set limits on the range of activities officially entering into the scope of a job and on the level of discretion permitted to the job-holder. As will be seen in Chapter 6, formal definition is a control device.

There are two main forms of *specialization*, which are on the whole distinguished by their different levels of discretion. The first is found in repetitive, short-cycle, routine manual or clerical operations. The second is found among those who carry out technical or professional work. The first form of specialization is one of activities within a task. Its beginnings lay in a realization by employers that tasks which do not vary greatly and which involve the application of well-understood techniques permit management to understand and to specify the necessary relationships between the basic activities entering into the task. This meant that each simple basic activity could be allocated to a different worker. Each activity could be isolated for study in its own right, and the methods for performing it standardized to a supposedly technical optimum and possibly mechanized or machine-aided. It then became feasible to employ less-skilled workers commanding only a low wage rate, who could easily be trained to proficiency in these narrowly specialized, simplified and standardized activities.

This process is a very familiar form of job specialization and is often referred to as 'de-skilling'. It involves the assumption by management of previously discretionary job content, such as deciding on the planning of tasks, on the methods for tackling them, and on the selection of appropriate tools and materials. The guidance and control which employees previously exercised over their work might also be taken over by, or incorporated into, automatic or self-correcting machinery. It is fairly easy to appreciate the economic motives of employers in fostering this kind of narrowing specialization, but the cost imposed on employees is severe. A loss of skill in jobs damages their labour market standing. It also reduces the interest available in those jobs by decreasing the variety of work, the opportunities to exercise any judgement and the sense of achieving something that is complete and meaningful.

The other form of specialization is literally that of the 'specialist'. Many technical and professional jobs in organizations are confined to an area of expertise which is quite narrow in scope but founded on a considerable depth of knowledge. Much the same characterizes a good deal of specialist manual work in Britain, such as maintenance, where tightly-bounded occupational specialisms have been defended by craft unions. However, the person employed as an organizational specialist will generally be left with considerable discretion over how to plan and conduct his or her work.

The amount of *discretion* that a person is able to exercise in his or her job is considered by writers such as Elliott Jaques (1956) to be the most significant criterion for assessing the level of work that the person is doing. Jaques and his colleagues have consistently argued that levels of pay should be based on the upper discretionary limits designed into jobs, on the grounds that there is no other way to ensure a sense of fairness about payment differentials. The reason is that differentials would then parallel the hierarchy of levels of work, which Jaques and his colleagues say is to be found in all organizations. If this is so, it is still the case that jobs can be designed to span more or fewer levels of work; that is, to be given higher or lower upper limits of discretion. The level of discretion given to the holder of any particular job will be influenced by management's general approach towards the problem of controlling the activities of subordinates. High discretion levels in a job could indicate managerial controls that are either loose or indirect; low discretion definitely signifies their presence in a tight form.

Even when considered in very broad terms as we have done so far, the two job design dimensions of specialization and discretion in different combinations serve to illustrate the wide variety of organizational jobs found in practice. Figure 2.1 provides some examples. Jobs falling into quadrants A and B in the diagram are examples of expert specialist jobs (such as hospital consultants and craftsmen) and routine manual or clerical operative jobs respectively. Although the form of specialization differs somewhat between the two categories, the main contrast lies in the levels of discretion typically accorded to job-holders. This contrast in discretion approximates to the degree of expertise or skill that people in the jobs can exercise. As we move from quadrant A to quadrant B (and the crude dual categorization of course

Figure 2.1 Examples of jobs with different levels of discretion and specialization

		discretion	
		High	Low
		A	B
specialization	High	specialist jobs	routine "de-skilled" operative jobs
		D	C
	Low	higher managerial jobs	supervisors, salesmen, assembly-line utility men, junior reporters

masks a whole range of discretion levels found in practice), so the ability to exercise personal judgement and skill in performing the job is reduced. De-skilling involves primarily a transfer of discretion and control over the process of carrying out work from the worker to management, though it can also entail an increase in specialization by reducing the range of activities performed.

Quadrant C contains a number of different jobs. These have in common a low level of specialization—in other words a wide range of duties, assignments, working situations or problems to face—which is combined with relatively low levels of discretion. For instance, many first-line production supervisors meet a considerable variety of contingencies during the course of a working day and they may physically move around quite a lot. In these respects their jobs are not specialized. On the other hand, it is usual nowadays for supervisors to be assigned little formal discretion over how to handle these contingencies if, say, expenditure, changes to production schedules or decisions on operatives' pay are involved. This is not to say that some supervisors do not assume discretion if there is no one else available to take action; it is rather to describe their jobs in the terms intended by management.

Quadrant D is a combination of low specialization and high discretion. Most higher managerial jobs would come into this category. The managers in such jobs are likely to have responsibility for a wide range of tasks performed by their subordinates: they may be in charge of several sections or departments. This low level of specialization will tend to be coupled with relatively high discretion and an ability to make major decisions, unless the organization happens to be controlled in a centralized manner by a chief executive, or other higher authority. In jobs at this level, the individual is to a large extent his or her own job designer. This is one reason why the concept of job design is rarely applied to higher management, and why instead greater emphasis is placed upon individual qualities, acceptance of corporate objectives, and regular review and appraisal in terms of achieving previously agreed targets for the departments under the manager's charge.

Most attention and research has been directed at the kind of routine operative jobs located in quadrant B of the diagram. The following three sections are each concerned with jobs at this level.

Design of jobs and work structures at operative level

Jobs at the operative level are those which contribute directly to major workflows in organization and to closely related ancillary services. This is a broader definition than simply jobs in which people 'operate' machinery or equipment, and it comes close to that of 'worker' in common parlance. The problem is that some would claim that anyone who works is a 'worker'! Excluded from our definition of operative level are jobs which are primarily concerned with supervising or managing others, specialist technical and professional jobs, advisory and administrative jobs. Examples of people in operative jobs are machining and assembly workers, maintenance workers, clerical workers processing routine documentation such as insurance policies, clerks in the buying office of a retailing company, or members of a word processing unit.

The fragmentation of operative tasks into limited specialized constituent activities and the removal of discretionary possibilities has a long history. Xenophon recorded the subdivision of labour in ancient Persia, commenting that specialization on a single activity, such as sewing in shoemaking, allowed workers to develop a higher level of proficiency. Adam Smith in *The Wealth of Nations* published in 1776 provided the famous example of the enormous increase in output which resulted from breaking down pinmaking into eighteen different jobs. Lord Shelbourne in 1766 described John Taylor's Birmingham factory in which the process of manufacturing a button passed through fifty different people, and each job had been so simplified that children of six to eight years could perform it as well as could adults. In jobs such as these there was clearly little room for the exercise of discretion or skill. They were highly repetitive and even at this early stage of industrialization were tied closely to the operation of machinery.

The scientific management movement, promoted early this century by industrial engineers such as Frederick W. Taylor and Frank Gilbreth, carried still further the subdivision of jobs and the transfer of discretion away from workers.* It also popularized this particular philosophy of job design as the means of achieving significant increases in productivity. Lenin regarded scientific management combined with socialist organization as the best basis for Soviet industrialization: he wrote, 'we must organize in Russia the study and teaching of the Taylor system and systematically try it out and adapt it to our own ends' (1918: 25). Where workers were persuaded or forced to accept the Taylor system, their rates of output were normally speeded up because of the specialization of their jobs into smaller elements and a consequent increase in repetitiveness, combined with tighter managerial control over the planning of work and over working methods. So far as repetitiveness is concerned, an often-quoted rule of thumb is that for every doubling of the number of times an operation is carried out by an individual the time taken per cycle is reduced between 10 per cent and 25 per cent—subject, of course, to certain limits.

It is not surprising that there has been such a long and persistent trend in operative job design towards specialization and the reduction of discretion, bearing in mind the advantages for the employer which have been claimed for this approach. These are listed in Table 2.1 to provide a point of reference against which to consider newer job design philosophies that turn their back on scientific management. It may be noted that some of the items listed amount to direct reductions in the cost of operations, while others have an indirect relation to productivity through enhancing the employer's control over the labour process and workplace practices. It is also apparent from the table that many of the advantages claimed for greater specialization

*Although Taylor sought to identify the basic elements in tasks in order to facilitate their method study and timing, he did not offer job specialization as a general recommendation for operative work though he did for first-line supervision. However, applications of scientific management typically involved the subdivision of jobs and de-skilling.

**Table 2.1 Advantages to the employer claimed to arise from greater special-
ization and reduced discretion in jobs at the operative level**

1 *Advantages ascribed primarily to greater specialization*
    1.1 increase in the worker's dexterity
    1.2 saving of time lost in switching from one task to another
    1.3 reduction of time lost when jigs and tools have to be changed
    1.4 ability to hire lower skilled labour which is cheaper and more readily
        replaced
    1.5 reduction in training time and the attendant wastage of materials
    1.6 development of specialized machinery is encouraged
    1.7 facilitation of the substitution of machine for manual pacing and guidance,
        and eventually the mechanization or automation of manual operations
    1.8 eases the application of 'scientific' method study based on measurement
        instead of the worker's 'rule of thumb'

2 *Advantages ascribed primarily to reduced discretion*
    2.1 permits management rather than workers to establish methods of work
    2.2 permits management rather than workers to establish standards of per-
        formance
    2.3 reduces loss of time involved in consultation and discussion with workers
    2.4 is consistent with hiring of less trained and cheaper labour

depend upon the implementation of policies which also entail giving little
discretion to workers.

These principles of operative job design are not only widely applied today,
as John Burbridge (1981) has described for British industry, but there is also
evidence (discussed in Chapter 9) that the introduction of new microelectronics-based technology is being used by some managements as an
opportunity to extend their application still further. The installation, for
example, of computer-controlled machine tools is often used as an opportunity to remove responsibilities for machine setting and adjustment from
shopfloor workers to specialist programmers. The belief among managers in
the economic advantages of following this trend is clearly strongly and
widely held, which is noteworthy when one considers how equally vigorous
and quite long-standing has been the criticism of the whole approach.
Indeed, it is not widely appreciated that the same Adam Smith who saw the
division of labour as the prime cause of economic progress, later on in *The
Wealth of Nations* (Book V) regarded its effect on the worker's mental
capabilities, judgements and sentiments as disastrous.

Three main lines of criticism have been levelled at the combination of
fragmented specialization and low discretion in job design. The first is a
Marxist critique, which really starts from a recognition that this 'de-skilling'
approach has been successful in benefiting the employer at the expense of
the worker's market value and personal well-being at work. In other words,
it is seen as an exploitation of the worker, impelled by the nature of capitalist
competition, which for a while at least is successful in reducing costs, raising

productivity and thus enhancing a rate of profit that is continually threatened by competition. The other two critiques may be called the humanistic and the managerial. They overlap to a considerable extent because many social scientists who express a concern with the quality of working life are actively engaged in consulting work for management, while some managers who have instituted reforms in job design have been encouraged by humanistic as well as economic considerations.

The humanistic critique of the fragmented specialization of manual and clerical jobs is that such jobs, tightly controlled by management through rigid procedures, close supervision or a machine technology, can no longer satisfy the aspirations of present-day employees. Many psychologists agree that jobs of this type do not afford adequate satisfaction for those in them. Research in the United States has in fact indicated that workers in machine-paced specialized assembly jobs suffer from particularly high levels of psychological strain and somatic complaints (Caplan et al. 1975). Today, unemployment and fear of unemployment have somewhat taken over as the major threats to workers' personal well-being and mental health, and deprivating jobs probably appear more tolerable as a consequence; but there is no reason to believe the deleterious effects they have will be any the less for that. It is interesting to note that the humanistic complaint has been most vociferously directed against over-specialization and less so against controls and lack of discretion. That is, attention has been focused mainly on the desire employees may have for more varied and more interesting work rather than on their desire for autonomy and responsibility. It is probably no coincidence that the latter directly challenge managerial control whereas the former do not, although it has to be admitted that, in the 'Anglo-Saxon' countries at least, managerial control and authority have generally been accepted by workers as legitimate.

Both humanistic and managerial commentators have also drawn attention to the rises in the general level of ability in the population that have accompanied educational progress. It is concluded that people now expect to be able to use their own judgement and to be stretched rather more. Highly specialized routine jobs do not make use of people's mental abilities much above the educationally subnormal level. They are therefore out of line with the expectations people have of work (especially younger people) and are frustrating. This conflict between the job as defined by the organization and by the individual may lead the latter to react by engaging in 'unproductive' activities ranging from shoddy work to literally 'throwing a spanner in the works'.

During the 1960s and early 1970s, at a time of generally high employment and tight labour markets, some employees did react against highly specialized, low discretion, repetitive work through absenteeism, rising rates of labour turnover, wildcat strikes and sabotage. It became more difficult to recruit new employees to undertake such jobs, and 'guest workers' were not always the answer. In Sweden, these recruitment problems became severe for many companies, which helps to explain their particular interest in job reform. Disruption of production and problems of recruitment can impose considerable costs on an organization which may more than offset the economies offered by a technology that is optimum from the perspective of plant engineering.

It is important, however, to evaluate carefully cases that are cited in support of the arguments just made. In the first edition of this book I joined many other writers in concluding that the costs of deprivating jobs were already cancelling out the economies of traditional mass production assembly in many car plants. I cited General Motors' Lordstown, Ohio plant as an instance. This was a triumph of the latest 1960s production engineering, with average cycle time per job pared down to 36 seconds and workers facing a new but same car (or component) 800 times in each eight-hour shift. The plant became infamous for its industrial unrest in the early 1970s; plagued by both official and wildcat strikes, go-slows and sabotage. At times, the line had to be closed down during the second half of a day in order to remedy defects emerging from assembly during the first half. I pointed to the relative youth of the labour force there and suggested, along with virtually every other writer mentioning Lordstown, that it provided a prime example of how the new generation was rejecting the policies of high specialization and low discretion.

After publishing the first edition, I had the opportunity to visit the Lordstown plant several times in 1977 and to talk with managers, union officials and workers. The plant still utilized the same technology and approach to job design, except that a minor degree of rotation between jobs was now permitted. It had the same kind of workforce, though rather smaller. The plant, however, was now quite peaceful with quality and productivity records which compared well with other General Motors plants. The change could not readily be explained in terms of job design, and further investigation indicated that the disruption during the early 1970s had been primarily due not to job design or technology but rather due to management's attempt to speed up the pace of work and reduce manning as part of an exercise to improve productivity (Child 1978). This example shows just how important it is to examine evidence closely, particularly as the deprecation of traditional and engineering-oriented forms of job design has for some social scientists assumed something of a moral crusade.

The rejection of high specialization and close control as principles for job design has been concerned in different ways to reconcile more effectively the requirements of production with the conditions for injecting greater personal control and meaning into work. The underlying guidelines have been to ensure that:

(a) each employee can again see a tangible result to his labour in the form of working on a whole product or assembly;
(b) he is made aware of the quality of this result through obtaining some direct feedback on his performance;
(c) his job contains some personal challenge in the exercise of more than purely mechanical movements;
(d) he can plan and organize his work to suit his own rhythm, pace and capabilities;

(e) while some controls on the worker are removed, he is now more account-able for his work, which should ideally be geared to performing a complete task(s).

Since the Second World War there has been a considerable amount of experimentation in various forms of job redesign aimed at moving away from highly specialized and low discretion operative jobs. Sources which review the progress of these advances in redesigning jobs are given at the close of this chapter, and I shall attempt merely to highlight some of the basic developments, their effects, and the considerations which should be taken into account when contemplating changes in the design of operative work. The term job redesign refers to changes in the design of individual jobs. It will become apparent that these usually involve further changes in the organization of work—the wider context of work restructuring. Work organization changes may include rearrangement of workflows, provision of buffer stocks, changes in supervision and so forth.

There have been two main stages in the move towards job redesign. The first involves a broadening of the tasks a worker performs, but does not re-tract that vertical aspect of specialization which, in F. W. Taylor's terms, separates thinking from doing and thereby removes a substantial amount of discretion from the worker. This stage is expressed by the two concepts of *job enlargement* and *job rotation*. In job enlargement two or more specialized jobs are merged so as to provide a worker with a wider range of tasks to per-form and hence a longer work cycle time. Job rotation does not of itself imply a reduction in the specialization of jobs, but allows workers to achieve greater variety in work through moving at regular intervals between dif-ferent jobs. The 'utility man' on motor car assembly lines has often been a sought-after position, because in substituting for absent men its occupant enjoys the variety of working at different jobs.

Pioneering experiments in job enlargement at IBM resulted in both improved productivity and greater job satisfaction. In Philips, a combi-nation of job enlargement and job rotation instituted in the early 1960s increased morale and job satisfaction among workers, but economic factors such as productivity and scrap rates showed little improvement. Experience in Sweden indicates that the association between job enlargement (a lengthening of cycle times) and efficiency depends on the type of work involved and on the people concerned. In light assembly work (such as assembly of household appliances or automobile interiors) previous cycle times were generally between 1 and 3 minutes. For the great majority of people doing this type of work, cycle times can be lengthened up to 20–25 minutes with no loss in efficiency. For a few people they can be extended up to 60–90 minutes without loss of efficiency, while for some 10–20 per cent of people efficiency drops if the original cycle times are extended at all. In heavier assembly work (such as the assembly of truck bodies or agricultural equip-ment) the maximum cycle time compatible with high efficiency has been found to rise for most people to 45–60 minutes. Most forms of job rotation have, however, been a failure in Sweden. The more successful schemes have either been those designed to provide multi-skill training or those cases where rotation has been organized spontaneously by work groups themselves.

Many authorities, such as Frederick Herzberg, Louis Davis and members of the Tavistock Institute of Human Relations, regarded this first stage of job redesign as quite inadequate. Their criticism has been twofold. First, job enlargement and job rotation do not substantially increase the intrinsic quality of a person's work. To paraphrase Herzberg, adding one Mickey Mouse job to another does not make any more than two Mickey Mouse jobs. In other words, simply adding specialized, repetitive, routine and dreary tasks to one another, or rotating around these, is not likely to create a job that is satisfying and motivating. In order to meet the aspirations it is believed many people have towards exercising judgement and assuming some responsibility, it is necessary to enlarge (or de-specialize) jobs not just 'horizontally' (adding more of the same) but also 'vertically'—adding discretion to make some decisions. This vertical enlargement of jobs is expressed by the concept of *job enrichment*, which represents a move away from *both* high specialization and low discretion. There are commonly three main elements in job enrichment: (a) enlargement of the work cycle; (b) incorporation of indirect elements (such as routine maintenance or inspection) into direct jobs; and (c) delegation of more decision-making over the planning and conduct of their activities to employees. The horizontal enlargement of jobs (de-specialization) is regarded as a necessary but not a sufficient condition for job enrichment. It is necessary because responsibility for planning and regulation of a task cannot be given to individuals whose jobs are so specialized as to be confined to only a partial aspect of the task, such as applying a single skill. Such jobs require supervision and coordination by another party who is aware of the task as a whole.

The second criticism of some early experiments in job redesign was that their focus had been on individual jobs rather than on clusters of closely related jobs forming a work group and contributing to a common task which could be distinguished from other tasks in the overall workflow or 'production' system. The *sociotechnical systems* approach developed by Trist, Emery, Rice and others drew upon the advances in small-group theory at the Tavistock Institute after World War II and married these to systems thinking and to a recognition of the dependence of work activities upon technology. The earlier sociotechnical systems research examined and experimented with possibilities of creating a social organization of work, based on cohesive and self-regulating groups of employees, within production systems which retained an unchanged technology of plant and equipment. In other words, attention was directed to the amount of choice that was available in work organization within a given technological system. The best known of these studies examined group-based forms of work organization that had arisen in British coal-mining and also moves towards group working in an Indian textile mill under the guidance of the researcher, A. K. Rice. In these cases and others, work groups undertook responsibility for production and for the allocation of individuals to jobs, which meant that their level of specialization could be determined through rotation and/or enlargement according to group members' preferences. The economic benefits of the change to work groups or teams not only included this greater flexibility of labour deployment but also higher productivity, lower absenteeism and higher job satisfaction.

The work group is today the normal unit of analysis for design at the operative level of work, where in fact activities generally depend upon the collective contribution of more than one or two individual employees. A work group is taken to be a primary group normally comprising between 4 and 20 members. Although larger groups are sometimes involved, it is argued that this is the size into which larger groups tend to subdivide spontaneously, that it is the largest unit which can be supervised effectively, and that communication and flexibility are greater within groups of this size because their members remain in close personal contact.

There are several reasons why the tasks performed by work groups should be the initial focus of design rather than individual jobs. The adequate functioning of work systems is generally the result of group activity rather than individual activity taken in isolation. The process of work design therefore logically begins by establishing the boundaries of work undertaken by groups. A group-based approach to work design also offers more scope for individual differences in competence and preference to be matched to the tasks to be done than does a job-by-job approach. These individual differences may call for the people concerned to be given varying degrees of job enrichment, and a group organization of work promises more flexibility in this respect because such decisions can be worked out within the group. Another advantage of a group-based organization is that it provides a more powerful mode of learning: it permits problems to be readily discussed with colleagues and information shared. This, of course, is an important characteristic of work organization in most Japanese companies.

The focus of design onto the work group is often referred to as 'work restructuring'. The term is somewhat misleading since the restructuring of work in any full sense would also have to include some modifications to the contingent contextual factors which are discussed in the following section. The intention is to arrive at a work group design that permits (1) the operation of certain desirable factors which are internal to the work system, and (2) the recognition of individual needs within the group. The foundations for work restructuring principles were neatly set out some years ago by Chris Schumacher and Roger Maitland, two British specialists in this field, and the essence of their perspective is presented in Table 2.2.

Sociotechnical systems theory accepts these work group design principles, where work groups can be formed. The principles themselves are compatible with the spirit of job enrichment. Job enrichment analysis began with the studies by Herzberg and colleagues of professional staff, accountants and engineers, and is more appropriate to the kinds of jobs they are likely to have (involving the application of individual judgement to a range of problems) or to jobs that are supervisory. Such jobs are neither necessarily group-based nor closely interdependent with a workflow

Table 2.2 Work restructuring principles

Factors internal to the work	*achieved by*	Work restructuring principles
Social interaction and support Recognition Discipline and leadership Opportunity for development	⟶	Team-working; i.e. forming primary work groups (4–20 people) <div align="right">(1)</div>
Use of skills and abilities Variety Challenge Sense of 'completeness'	⟶	Work group to perform 'whole' task <div align="right">(2)</div>
Responsibility Discretion	⟶	Work group to plan its own work <div align="right">(3)</div>
Achievement Identifiable objective Knowledge of results	⟶	Work group to be able to evaluate performance against standards <div align="right">(4)</div>
Individual needs within the work group Individual differences Fair treatment Flexibility	⟶	Common method of payment and conditions of service <div align="right">(5)</div>

(Adapted from an original table by P. C. Schumacher and R. P. Maitland presented to a course at the Brunel University Institute of Organisation and Social Studies.)

technology. They contrast therefore with the operative jobs to which sociotechnical systems and work restructuring analyses have normally been addressed.

Another point to note is that whereas the earlier job enrichment theorists like Herzberg did not give any significant attention to variations in individual needs, the work of Hackman and Oldham (1980) in particular has identified the strength of people's need for personal growth as a moderator of relationships between the scope of their jobs and their motivation—both in individual and work-group situations. In the group situation, to which work structuring applies, it is also likely that the reaction of the individual to changes in tasks will be influenced by established work-group cultures. If these are centred around restrictive practices and suspicion of management's intentions, then workers may not seek to have any personal growth needs satisfied through changes which they could perceive as engendering greater risk to themselves by, for instance, more readily identifying responsibility for performance or by requiring greater effort.

Various experiments in job enrichment are now available to study and evaluate, and these are described in the sources given at the end of the chapter. In Britain, for example, several categories of staff employees in ICI were given additional decision-making responsibilities—they included salesmen, qualified laboratory technicians, design engineers, craft foremen, and production operatives on shift work. In each case, the employees responded by increasing their performance and the quality of their work (at least for the few months over which results were monitored). In financial terms the company benefited at the cost of only a few days in managers' time when establishing the new arrangements.

There are examples of redesign on a group basis in addition to the Tavistock studies mentioned: some involved little or no change to technology, while others did. At Philips, employee groups were given total responsibility for assembling black-and-white TV sets and colour selectors for colour sets. The group responsible for assembling monochrome sets not only performed the entire assembly but also dealt directly with service personnel such as purchasing, stores and quality control; it communicated directly with other departments too when that was necessary. There was no supervisor acting as intermediary or expeditor. In the Philips case some additional costs were involved—in re-equipment and in training. To offset these there was a 10 per cent reduction in manhour production costs, reducing waiting times, improved quality and greater job satisfaction. In Air Canada maintenance shops, to quote a further example, employees were given the responsibility for deciding when and how to replace windows in DC8 aircraft. As a result productivity doubled over a twelve-month period and supervisory time required dropped to a quarter of its former level.

Swedish developments in job design are particularly noteworthy because they are more extensive in scale than most and have often involved changes to technology through the building of new plants or offices. The central feature in these new buildings has been flexibility—the attempt to become free from many of the constraints on the shape of jobs imposed by traditional technologies. In new factories built by companies such as Saab-Scania, Volvo, Holmens Bruk and Orrefors Glass, layout and facilities have been designed to permit the work to be done by operative groups with responsibilities for major stages of manufacture, which organize their own work as they think best. These new developments represent a synthesis of mainly American ideas on individual job enrichment with ideas on semi-autonomous group working derived largely from Norwegian experiments initiated during the 1960s in companies such as Norsk Hydro, and guided by socio-technical principles.

A significant potential for the extention of the semi-autonomous working group approach is offered by the 'group technology' concept. This began (it is claimed in Russia) as a development intended to improve throughput times and the predictability of workflow. Most applications have been in the field of component manufacture, where group technology involves a reorganization of the shopfloor away from the grouping of machines according to function (all lathes in one section, all grinding machines in another, and so forth) in favour of their grouping by contribution to a common product, usually families of given parts such as gearwheels. This change can greatly simplify problems of co-ordinating work between different functional operations, reduce the amount of work standing idle and simplify overall workflows. In principle these are comparable advantages to those claimed for a move away from a functional structure at the whole organization level, which are discussed in Chapter 4. The potential not only for job enlargement and rotation but also for increasing work group autonomy that group technology provides has come to be appreciated in recent years. For it sets up relatively self-contained working groups with work passing between different operations that are all within the group's own purview. This provides a natural base from which to increase the flexibility of manning within the group and to delegate decisions on this type of issue to the group itself.

The developments both in Sweden and in group technology involved changes in technology as well as innovations in working arrangements. Recent sociotechnical systems thinking has come to the view that there may be beneficial opportunities to redesign both workplace technologies and social systems, most obviously in situations where plant is being installed for the first time or being replaced. It is recognized that technology can impose limits on the choice of viable work structuring; also that the choice of technology is constrained by the possibility of adverse worker reactions to some of the designs engineers might put forward. This leads to the objective of striving for a joint optimization of both social and technical systems, and the need for designers to attend to both. As Louis Davis has argued in an article which outlines the stages of a sociotechnical systems design process, 'sociotechnical systems as transforming organizations achieve desired goals through the joint action of technical and social components operating under joint causation' (1979: 15).

The inclusion of technology within the scope of work design analysis is consistent with a systems perspective, which draws attention to contextual systems that interface with a work unit. In addition to the technical system these include the system of management control and supervision, the total workflow system in which the activities of particular job holders or work groups are located, and the payment system. An attempt to make changes in job or work-group design in isolation from these other systems is unlikely to succeed.

Contextual factors

1 Technology

There is considerable confusion in the use of the term 'technology'; in particular whether it refers to the workflow (or production) process or to the plant and equipment employed in that process. For the purposes of job design and work structuring it is essential to distinguish between workflow process and plant/equipment, because the former constitutes the key analytical starting-point. It is necessary to examine the workflow process in order to identify its various stages and the nature of the links between those stages. A particular stage will be identified by the presence of strong links between its constituent activities, where strength may be assessed in terms of certain criteria. These include whether: (1) only one activity can lead to another (lack of substitutability); (2) the first activity always leads to the second being performed (sequential determinism); (3) the second activity has to be performed as soon as the first has been completed (immediacy); and (4) the sequence of activities cannot be reversed so that the first task may be performed again or rectified (irreversibility). Weaker links between activities indicate where one set of activities may be said to end and another begin: where, for example, it would be possible to have buffer stocks. Identification of sets or groups of activities provides the logical basis for delineating work groups.

A problem arises when plant and equipment are not arranged in configurations that are consistent with the boundaries of groups of activities within the production process. For example, a functional organization of machine tools generally cuts right across the boundaries of clusters of activities which are closely connected with respect to producing whole components or products. This was, of course, the reason for reorganizing machining along group technology lines. In other words, the plant and equipment required for a close-knit group of activities may be dispersed physically or arranged in a way that inhibits the close communication between workers which the interdependence between their activities requires.

In cases such as these, plant and equipment inhibit the application of work restructuring principles. How, then, may technology be rearranged to facilitate the desired system of working (social system), and how costly might such changes be? A great deal depends on the closeness of human interaction with plant and equipment built into its design, and whether that interaction permits a choice of job design and work-group structuring. In labour-intensive workflows utilizing tools and light equipment (such as individual machines or desk calculators), the equipment can usually be reorganized without much cost to suit a redesign of jobs and/or work groups. In contrast, substantial costs may be incurred in rearranging or redesigning heavily capitalized plant away from a technical optimum. However, if this plant is of a process type where the main human operational involvement is monitoring, then the fact that this activity can be physically removed from the plant itself (especially via electronic monitoring) and can be organized in several ways, permits a choice of work design at little extra cost. Heavily capitalized mass production assembly plant, which is itself inherently inflexible and requires close worker involvement, has generally imposed the greatest constraint upon work restructuring, especially where production is arranged on a standard speed linear basis. The traditional automobile assembly line provides the classic example. Its technological design permits little discretion on the part of workers and the scope for reducing narrow specialization is confined to rather limited job enlargement and some job rotation.

Nevertheless, even in automobile and automative assembly, companies have invested in new types of technology in order to provide some of the conditions for an improved quality of working life via job and work redesign. These include Volvo's Kalmar car assembly plant and Renault's Le Mans axle factory. These unorthodox plants are, however, more expensive to build than are those incorporating traditional technologies. Volvo's initial investment at Kalmar is estimated to have been 10 per cent higher than that required for an equivalent plant on traditional lines, while some other non-orthodox plants are said to have cost up to 25 per cent more. With the development of robotics and the combination of assured quality and flexibility they provide, it is likely that future moves away from fragmented and pressurized mass production assembly work will be through automating-out direct human involvement.

Automation brings its own problems: it may remove some of the worst operative jobs in terms of physical strain and psychological stress, but this carries a penalty in the loss of jobs altogether. For example, the use of robots on the Austin Metro body frame welding line requires one operative as opposed to an estimated 80 operatives for a non-automated equivalent. The jobs that remain do not necessarily allow for much enrichment since, with automation, planning, programming and inspection responsibilities are usually removed to the care of staff specialists. The reduction of operative jobs to monitoring roles, while allowing for close social interaction and some responsibility, may diminish the interest and sense of achievement that are available.

2 Management control and supervision

Changes in job design or in work structuring are likely to have two effects on the rest of the organization—a 'shunt' effect upon the distribution of authority and the nature of hierarchical control, and a 'ripple' effect laterally upon relations with other jobs and work groups within the overall workflow system. If these effects are not recognized or are resisted, the policy of redesign will be threatened and even stifled. The shunt effect is considered here with reference to management control and supervision, and the ripple effect subsequently.

When the changes involve granting more discretion and allocating new tasks to operatives, there are clear implications for line managers' own jobs. With job enrichment, for example, transferring responsibility to operatives eats into the traditional role of the first-line supervisor. Indeed, some experts have envisaged that the supervisor would become redundant as operatives undertook his functions, especially if semi-autonomous work groups were established as in some Norwegian experiments. However, when supervisor-less groups have been set up the result has often been serious disagreements within the group on questions of planning, methods or individual conduct, with no one to manage the conflict. Current opinion, including that of many Swedish employers, is that job enrichment can relieve supervisors of the more trivial everyday pressures of 'firefighting', progressing work and materials, or reallocating people to machines and tasks. It should allow them instead to devote more time to major responsibilities such as co-ordinating work groups, developing their members' abilities, taking part in recruitment and dealing with important technical problems. In so far as supervisors can be relieved through job enrichment, it may prove possible to flatten the shape of organization by increasing spans of control. The advantages of this policy will be discussed in the next chapter.

Managerial control systems have a bearing upon attempts at job redesign and work restructuring. The delegation of discretion to operative employees on matters such as working methods clearly requires a reappraisal of any controls which specify in manuals of procedures and the like the methods to be followed. If the work group is to be free to decide on the allocation of activities among its members, and to have the right to change these by mutual agreement, then any existing attempts to specify individual job responsibilities via formal job descriptions will become redundant. A well-established system of job descriptions may provide so much detail as to inhibit the flexibility of perspective required for a successful exercise of work redesign. Moreover, job descriptions provide a point of reference for people, including managers, who seek to maintain things as they are. Controls and grading systems that refer to the performance and duties of individuals in specific jobs will not be suited to a group mode of working. Many management controls such as budgets, cost accounting systems, and devices to measure attendance, encourage a precise specification of who is to perform specific tasks, which could inhibit attempts to change the design of jobs and work. If close supervision forms part of management's control strategy, this too is unlikely to be compatible with the principles of job enrichment or semi-autonomous group work.

These illustrations serve to make the general point that failure to revise a management control system founded on the principles of high job specialization and low discretion will jeopardize the attempt to reject these principles in the design of jobs and work groups. Systems which assume a precise specification of individual jobs cannot co-exist with a group mode of working.

3 The overall workflow system

Although the principles of enriching individual jobs or creating semi-autonomous work groups involve the identification of tasks and groups of activities that have some degree of completeness in their own right, these are none the less still part of a wider workflow system. Thus changes made to the organization of work within one part of the system have implications for the other parts related to it—the 'ripple effect'. For example, if the right to choose different rates of working during the day or week is delegated to job-holders or to work groups (subject to their meeting an overall output standard), then it will be necessary to build up stocks to serve as buffers between the different work rates of each work unit. This preserves an overall balance within the workflow system, but requires changes in some aspects of its planning. If a group technology design is adopted then a considerable reorganization of the production system is required, involving careful identification of the families of products to be worked on.

The incorporation of indirect elements into the work of operatives engaged on direct work can improve efficiency, but it involves a substantial change to traditionally established job boundaries. For example, under the traditional specialized system operating in the British motor industry, it would not be unusual for twenty minutes to be required to rectify a machine going off its setting. An operator, his foreman, an inspector and a setter might all have to be involved. But if the operator were given a restructured 'enriched' job incorporating some inspection and setting responsibilities, this delay could be greatly reduced because all the previously specialized functions would now be incorporated into the one man's job. The ripple effect of such a change concerns the redrawing of boundaries between operator and other jobs. This can be seriously impeded if traditionally specialized job boundaries are reinforced by established demarcation lines and collective bargaining units, and comparisons such as these made by Pierre Dubois (1981) between British and French factories suggest that specialized demarcation lines are particularly entrenched in British industry. Demarcation in fact tends to be a traditional characteristic of work organization in English-speaking countries. Many managements regard the removal of demarcation as a major step towards more efficient working and would favour this aspect of job enrichment.

4 The payment system

Job enrichment involves the addition of new responsibilities over and above the requirement to achieve a certain rate of working—responsibilities such as planning and checking work. It is therefore no longer appropriate to reward the holders of enriched jobs through the individual output-linked incentive schemes they may have been on previously, or to offer rates of pay that have been traditionally attached to narrowly specialized jobs. Individual incentives are clearly not suited to a group mode of working either, whether or not the group is given additional responsibilities.

This means a change either to fixed rates or group bonuses. Changes in pay structures often meet with considerable employee and union resistance and can involve a costly 'buying out' of old schemes. In addition, Swedish experience suggests that productivity can fall off quite seriously if fixed-rate payment is adopted. For example, in 1972 the Swedish Employers' Confederation published the results of a study of 36 companies where experiments involving a change from payment by results to fixed wages had been made. In these companies there was an average fall in productivity of between 10 and 20 per cent. No compensating improvements were found in regard to quality, absenteeism or labour turnover although a 'calmer working climate' was usually reported. Evidence such as this strongly suggests that an incentive element should be retained in the payment system adopted under job enrichment, perhaps attached to the fulfilment of objectives agreed with management, or linked to the meeting of a combination of output, cost and quality standards. Where a group system of working is adopted, group or departmental bonus schemes may be appropriate.

Job redesign and work structuring are usually accompanied by rises in pay, which complement the assumption of greater responsibility by workers and are sometimes required to buy out restrictive practices. If the redesign is confined to certain employees or sections only, the selective rise in pay they receive may generate friction because of the threat to long-established differentials and comparabilities. Indeed, any change in the design of jobs which improves rewards, either intrinsic or extrinsic, is likely to be interpreted as signifying a change in the status of the workers concerned and hence have wider potential consequences within an organization. This is another example of how ripples spread across other parts of an organization as a consequence of changes in any one area.

The design of jobs and the structuring of work are, then, intimately linked to the design of organization as a whole. To be successful, changes to jobs and work require complementary modifications to other organizational systems. This has not always been appreciated in practice and is one of the reasons why some experiments fail.

Success and failure in job redesign and work structuring

The scale and scope of experiments in job redesign and work restructuring remain extremely limited (see Kelly and Clegg 1981). There are many minor developments masquerading under the label of job enrichment, but there are possibly no more than 100 or so European schemes that really enrich jobs significantly. And that is despite the investment of considerable sums in research on new forms of work organization by a number of governments and their agencies. According to surveys, relatively few experiments are under way in North America either, although certain firms such as General Motors have shown recent interest (as much in forms of participation as in job and work redesign) and the Ontario Government has established a major Quality of Working Life Centre. Pioneering companies like Philips and Saab are apparently not extending their existing schemes, which still involve only a small proportion of their labour forces. The early and best-known sociotechnical design developments in British coal-mining and in Indian textile mills did not spready widely through the corporations concerned, and indeed tended to 'regress' eventually to more conventional ways of working. Changes in work structuring are continuing but they are now usually part of an engineering-led development of more flexible manufacturing systems.

Failure in job redesign and work restructuring can take a number of forms. First, it may have proved impossible to have introduced changes at all because of opposition—it is difficult to learn of cases such as these. Second, the change may have ended up being confined to a small part of the workforce or to a local department, rather than spreading widely through the organization as was perhaps originally hoped. Third, the new ways of working may gradually erode and regress to traditional models.

Richard Hackman (1975), commenting on job enrichment failures in the United States, takes the view that the way in which projects are implemented is most frequent cause of failure. Among the common deficiencies in implementation are: (a) an inadequate diagnosis of existing jobs to see whether they are suited to enrichment and/or a failure to assess how receptive employees are likely to be to job enrichment; (b) a failure actually to change jobs at all, which is a more complex challenge than is sometimes anticipated; (c) development of unexpected side-effects, such as supervisory resistance to change; (d) inattention to systematic evaluation which leads to projects being discredited in management eyes; (e) inadequate education of the managers and staff responsible for carrying out projects to redesign jobs; and (f) an eventual reassertion of bureaucratic procedures, which stifles the additional discretion offered as part of job enrichment. Clearly, the successful implementation of changes in the shape of jobs requires careful planning, analysis of how the change can be located within the wider organizational system, the allocation of trained and experienced people to manage the change, some involvement of those affected by the change, and adequate arrangements for monitoring and evaluating the change throughout its whole life. These problems of bringing about organization change are considered further in Chapter 10.

An example of failure in the redesign of jobs due partly to an inadequate assessment of the likely receptivity of employees to the change and to its consequences for payment, occurred in a British factory producing washing machines. There was an attempt to enlarge (rather than to enrich) the jobs of female workers who assembled control systems for the machines. These workers, however, did not look for intrinsically interesting work so much as for the satisfaction of earning good wages and of having enjoyable social relations at work. Both these rewards were threatened by the redesign. The women could not reach the speed of work achieved under the old specialized and repetitive system. This led to considerable pressure from management, which in turn was seen as a threat to their levels of pay and even their continued employment, despite various guarantees. The pressure to reach target production removed the freedom the operators had previously enjoyed to leave their places of work and socialize with others. Management terminated the experiment because of the reduced level of output and hostility from the workers. It had in fact given little time and consideration to the change, and had failed to involve supervisors in its planning at all, so that their support was not forthcoming either.

Miller's (1975) re-examination over a period of up to sixteen years of the Indian textile mills in which the Tavistock Institute sociotechnical systems experiments had been conducted, also identifies management as having a key role. The failure that occurred in the new work organization could be particularly attributed to the inadequate training and preparation of new recruits and to too much variation in the input material (cotton thread). For the experiments to have succeeded, the magnitude and speed of change in input needed to be kept to a minimum by management. This experience appears to reinforce the point long made by Tavistock Institute writers that management has a key function in managing boundary conditions, and it suggests that autonomous working groups cannot readily handle high levels of uncertainty unless they receive adequate training and their members have the necessary ability.

There are several likely points of resistance to job and work redesign. Junior management and supervision will frequently resist increases in employees' responsibilities and autonomy that threaten their traditional roles and authority. Some, perhaps many, workers do not seek to assume greater responsibility or commitment to their work, regarding it in an instrumental light as primarily a means to an end. They are therefore likely to regard job enrichment with little enthusiasm, particularly in periods of economic recession when every change is feared as a pretext for eliminating jobs. As we shall see shortly, the balance of advantage over disadvantage in job and work redesign has in fact tended to favour employers rather than workers. Under more favourable conditions, however, there is evidence that most workers are inclined to support opportunities for job enrichment once they have got used to it, though, if there has been any labour shedding these will be the more fortunate people who have retained their jobs. The initial reactions of employees to changes in job and work design will depend heavily upon prevailing circumstances such as the economic situation, the climate of trust or otherwise within the organization, the values which employees attach to work, and the way in which the change is planned and implemented, including opportunities to participate in its design and guarantees offered.

The earlier discussion of relevant contextual factors leads to the conclusion that if changes in job and work design are to have lasting effects, they must be consistent with the way the organization is managed. If they are part of a planned programme of change and development which enjoys senior management's understanding and approval, then there may be an opportunity to alter contextual variables in a way that is compatible with job and work redesign. If a potentially major stumbling block such as technological constraints can be overcome, other organizational systems and practices are likely to require modification in order to give long-term effect to redesign. If employees' jobs are to incorporate new skills and responsibilities, they are likely to require some additional training and time to develop such skills. These will probably be both technical skills and also skills in handling the new working relationships that accompany redesign, such as dealing with other departments directly. Payment systems are likely to require modification for reasons already mentioned. Many people expect higher pay for more responsible jobs; incentives may have to be altered to recognize the incorporation into jobs of new ancillary tasks; if work groups and systems have been redesigned around interdependent clusters of tasks along sociotechnical lines, it will be appropriate to focus the reward system onto group performance of that cluster. Supervisors have to be helped to adjust their own job content, their use of time and their style in the light of job enrichment or work structuring. Care also has to be taken to see the new design is arranged in such a way that those employees of more limited capabilities, or who do not place a high value on additional interest and responsibility, are accommodated. This is one of the advantages claimed for the greater flexibility and 'democracy' of job allocation under group working.

Reports that the introduction of job design and work restructuring have resulted in higher performance must be treated with considerable caution. There are three considerations here: (1) adequate data are not often provided on productivity gains or efficiency improvements; (2) it is frequently unclear how much of any higher performance was due to other changes which accompanied redesign and restructuring; and (3) the criteria which are used to assess improved performance typically overlook the costs that have been incurred, particularly costs to workers.

Regarding the adequacy of data, while specific prior expectations of economic returns from redesign may be encouraged by consultants, and may be entered into project justifications if expenditure on plant and equipment is involved, the measures of actual economic returns tend to be far more vague. They are quite likely to be in the form of 'improved quality' or 'contributed to a 10 per cent rise in productivity' rather than anything more precise. This inability to add greater precision is often due to the presence of other concomitant changes, such as methods improvements.

There used to be a comparable problem with the evaluation of how much increased productivity could be attributed to the introduction of incentive payment schemes, rather than to the work study which usually went with them. Many of the job enrichment schemes in the United States have been accompanied by a clearer identification of responsibility for quality and output. This is made easier when an employee is given a more visible area of responsibility, such as compiling and verifying whole sections of a telephone directory (AT & T) or assembling a whole radio receiver (Motorola). Previously, highly specialized jobs, perhaps forming part of an assembly line, offered employees much more anonymity when it came to accountability for performance.

Some introductions of job enrichment have also linked pay more directly to performance through output bonuses, and most schemes have been accompanied by higher pay. This improved level of pay may have been an important incentive factor. To take a third example, in the widely quoted new General Foods petfood plant at Topeka, Kansas, there was an extremely rigorous screening of job applicants. This resulted in far from typical workforce and probably accounts in part for the plant's favourable level of performance. All these considerations suggest that factors other than the intrinsic job satisfaction motivators singled out by job enrichment theorists can help to account for the success it has enjoyed.

The question of the performance consequences of job and work redesign experiments moves our discussion on to a consideration of who has gained and lost from them and in what respects. John Kelly (1980, 1982) has provided a valuable review of job redesign which severely qualifies the claim that it satisfies the mutual interests of workers and employers through its provision of greater job satisfaction and improved performance. He examined almost 200 case studies and experiments in job redesign in the literature, covering the period 1950–1978. He reviewed material from 14 different countries published in 39 different journals as well as many books and reports. The scope of 'job design' in this review concerned both the individual job-oriented enrichment and the workgroup-oriented socio-technical systems approach.

Kelly's analysis repays detailed reading and only a summary can be provided here. He points out first of all that the needs and interests of workers which are involved in job redesign are not confined to 'psychological' aspects such as job satisfaction or personal fulfilment. They also extend to economic issues such as an acceptable intensity of effort, job security and levels of pay. In our present social and economic system most employees will of necessity if not of preference give highest priority to these requirements being met. Since keeping effort down, security and pay are at the sharp edge of conflict with management (which will perceive the same issues in the opposite terms of raising effort, treating labour as far as possible as a variable not a fixed resource, and keeping wage costs down), then it is appropriate to examine how the introduction of job redesign has affected this balance of interests. The conclusion is that it has generally benefited management far more than workers.

In the first place, job redesign has often resulted in a loss of jobs either in areas of direct work such as production or among indirect functions such as maintenance. In approximate terms, for every 80 jobs redesigned almost 20 have been lost. This incidence of loss is relatively high in countries such as the USA and India and low in the UK, a contrast which suggests that union membership densities and collective bargaining strategies may influence the burden of this cost of job redesign. Job losses, of course, contribute to improved productivity and this was complemented by pay increases in most but not all cases. Where job redesign leads to a fall in labour costs commensurate with a rise in wages, a mutual advantage to management and workers may arise. However, this can only benefit those workers who have retained their jobs and even then must be considered in the light of the net balance that ensues between additional pay and the demands now placed upon them in the redesigned jobs. In fact, Kelly concludes that an intensification of labour (rate of effort and time given over to productive effort) appears to be associated with job redesign, though the experience of this as a cost by workers may be mitigated by the new opportunities they are given to organize their own working time and pace. Kelly also points to the possibilities, which job redesign often provides, for a more direct and accurate assignment of accountability for work performance in so far as individuals or groups now take on responsibility for the satisfactory completion of 'whole' tasks.

In contrast, Kelly concludes that job redesign has usually provided net benefits to management, some of which are the obverse of the costs to workers just discussed. Management, however, is likely to incur several costs in job redesign: additional capital costs are entailed where technology is substantially altered; there are costs in making other adjustments such as training and revised payment schemes; and the creation of work groups may remove some flexibility in the redeployment of workers between groups. It is also unlikely that consultants writing of their job redesign work will be wholly forthcoming about the costs and difficulties managements faced. As a managerial investment, job redesign is high risk and offers an uncertain payback period. Much depends on the reaction of employees and Kelly's analysis helps to explain the suspicion that workers and their representatives sometimes have of job redesign proposals. White-collar and staff employees have often given job enrichment an almost immediate and favourable response and it is rather more consistent with their expectations of work and status; but a long period of discussion, trial and retraining may be required before it gets a favourable response from manual operatives. The technological constraints on redesigning jobs and work systems are also likely to be much more severe in manual rather than in non-manual work.

It is essential, then, to evaluate each case carefully on its merits before concluding whether or not to institute job redesign and work structuring. Although one can argue that the principle of the humanization of work is in keeping with the underlying expectations of a more highly educated population which has been exposed to values of self-expression and personal fulfilment, conditions of mass unemployment do not encourage these values to take precedence. There are also obvious dangers in making generalized statements about the development of a wide range of different jobs and work situations. The following section illustrates the latter point by briefly considering two examples of non-operative jobs.

Two examples of non-operative jobs

Although discussions about job redesign have concentrated very much on the operative level, this does not mean that problems do not exist at other levels. The two examples considered here, first-line supervisors and professional specialists, are both groups in which some members have expressed considerable dissatisfaction with their jobs, and which are often regarded as a problem by managements. Supervisors were located in quadrant C of Figure 2.1 and professional specialists in quadrant A. The particular combinations of specialization and discretion found in these jobs creates some difficulties which it may be possible to mitigate by sensitive attention to redesign options.

1 First-line supervisors

Supervision is widely regarded as a problem area in British industry and in many other countries also. The failure to find a satisfactory design for the supervisor's role in workplace management inhibits the productive use of industrial investment. In addition, the considerable unionization of supervisors in Britain since the mid-1960s, together with other expressions of their dissatisfaction, points to there being a problem of supervisors' own welfare.

Supervisors often have a wide range of shopfloor or office responsibilities to cover, though these may be relatively minor. A substantial part of their job can consist in handling a stream of different 'disturbances' in the course of keeping the workflow going smoothly, and this appears to be particularly characteristic of batch productions systems. In this respect their jobs are not normally specialized. On the other hand, their discretion has usually become very limited so that they cannot be said to be exercising managerial authority, whether this be over employees, over the planning of workflows or over technical matters. The combination of wide responsibility within the confines of their department or section, and severely limited discretion, has been found to bother many supervisors both in the United States and in situations which the writer and Bruce Partridge have investigated in Britain (1982). We concluded from our research that, while a decision on the design of supervisory jobs should be made with reference to the characteristics of the workflow system to be supervised, there was still considerable scope within technological and organizational parameters to choose between alternative models for supervisory job design according to other criteria—such as the philosophy management might have about job enrichment, and the capabilities and expectations of supervisors themselves.

There are four alternative models, one of which would abolish the role of first-line supervisor and delegate the responsibility for routine supervisory tasks to work groups. This option was discussed earlier and it was noted how problems could arise (see page 40). In fact the more need there is for someone to cope with unforeseen contingencies in the workplace, to correct problems which arise from the limitations in management organization, to manage interdependencies between different work groups, or to sort out conflicts within work groups themselves, the less plausible this model becomes. The second alternative is to clarify and generally tidy up the supervisory job as it is. This would involve clearing away the myth about supervisors being first-line 'managers' so that they might at least be encouraged to hold realistic expectations. It would reduce the level and perhaps the range of supervisors' responsibilities to suit the discretion they were permitted. This would also make it more difficult for the next level up in the hierarchy to hide their poor understanding of operations behind an unfair reliance on supervisors to keep problems from their office doors.

The third model of job design for supervisors would, in contrast, adjust their level of discretion upwards to come into line with the responsibilities placed upon them. In other words, it would seek to develop the supervisor into a full first-line manager and so move him closer to quadrant D in the diagram. This model recognizes that supervisors have a particularly close knowledge of their sections' work, its technology and its staff. They may already be meeting the challenge of keeping things going and satisfying higher management's requirements, but have the frustration of not being able to make or even share in the decisions that are required. Such decisions could well include the re-allocation of manpower between a supervisor's section and adjacent areas, or the time when a new job of work is taken onto his section. So, it is argued, why not give the supervisor this essentially managerial level of discretion?

The fourth model envisages an increase in the supervisor's specialization so as to concentrate on technical problems in his employees' work. Within this narrower band of responsibilities, the supervisor would enjoy considerable discretion. This model moves the supervisor somewhat closer to quadrant A in the diagram, and it has two main variants. The first is appropriate to the supervision of technical and scientific areas of work; the second is appropriate to the supervision of craft workers, as in maintenance work or in craft production such as quality furniture. In both cases, the supervisor will have considerable expertise in his workers' specialism, and be able to act as a technical adviser, a translator of management's requirements (and to an important extent a buffer between management and his employees), and as a coordinator between his section and others.

These alternative models of supervisory job design allow for a wide variety of possible arrangements within the framework of options they delineate. The basic choices are with respect to the *specialization* (versus range) of tasks for which the supervisor is held responsible and the *discretion* he is permitted in carrying out each task. As with operative jobs, there are a number of organizational contingencies relevant to choosing between alternative models, while factors such as the prevailing culture and climate in the organization and the attitude of the supervisors themselves would also have to be considered.

2 *Professional specialists*

An increasing number of professionally qualified people have become employees in organizations, including business companies. When working as an independent practitioner the professional person has traditionally enjoyed a high degree of discretion over the way he arranges working time and carries out his job. Although there has always been some degree of specialization in professional work, and this is tending to increase, it remains nevertheless a specialization 'in depth' based upon a considerable accumulation of knowledge and expertise. It has frequently been asked, therefore, whether the entry of a professional into employment within an organization requires a grudging submission to managerial control on the part of people for whom the stereotype of the independent 'free' professional has been the traditional point of reference. This question is considered for three professional groups commonly employed in organizations—accountants, engineers and scientists—with particular reference to the implications for their job and work design.

A number of research studies have reported on, or at least speculated about, conflict between professional specialists and management. If such conflict exists it might be due in part to the way professionals' jobs are designed, though it could also result from differences in values between the two groups and from frustration among the professionals at limited promotion prospects. The conflict of values, for example, might be particularly acute for professionals employed within business organizations where the importance they would attach to the intrinsic worth of their work and to the desirability of pursuing excellence in it could clash with commercial pressures that lead management to stress low cost, 'adequate' quality and the completion of work in the shortest possible time.

A close look at the available evidence for accountants, engineers and scientists employed in business firms suggests that the real situation is more complex and varied than is allowed for in any such simple description (see Child 1982). Conflicts are inherent in the relationship between professionals and managers, but the distance between objectives held by the two groups is not always that great, and professionals may be willing to accommodate to the tensions that remain. The problem is probably greater for scientific staff than for accountants and engineers, since many of the last two groups look to a career in management itself and, having decided to take up employment in business, are prepared to accept business objectives.

So far as job design is concerned, the challenge is to reconcile two basic requirements. The first is to retain for professional staff the freedom and time to exercise their specialist expertise and judgement effectively: in the case of scientists, for example, to permit them to carry out sound research or development. After all, such staff represent quite expensive resources which have been acquired to perform such tasks well enough to provide a company with a competitive edge—there is no point otherwise in employing them. The second requirement for the effective utilization of specialist manpower is that its activities be aligned with those of the rest of the organization. Conflict between professional specialists and managers signifies a failure to achieve this alignment, or if it stems from personal antipathies as it can with such differently socialized groups then these can jeopardize the alignment. Specialization into different groups can itself encourage conflict in so far as individuals tend to identify with colleagues in 'their' group as opposed to people in 'other' groups.

If we consider scientists and engineers working in research or development groups (because that is where the problem is generally most acute) it is possible to outline a solution which has often gone some way towards meeting these two requirements. This, in effect, retains the professional's high level of discretion where his or her expertise counts most—over the performance of the job itself—but attempts to reduce the danger of isolation from the rest of the organization, which can result from high specialization.

The job of the individual specialist is not, in this approach, closely defined or closely supervised. If suitably qualified persons have been recruited and they have been encouraged to keep up to date, then it is assumed that they know best how to carry out their tasks. Staff still in training would, of course, require some supervision. The absence of close definition and supervision will probably not be enough, however, to secure a high level of motivation from professional staff. They are likely to perform better if they feel a sense of ownership over what they are doing, if their work presents a challenge and if they are given recognition for achievement. These considerations imply that professional staff should be allowed to participate in discussions which set priorities among the tasks to be done and which set the work standards associated with those. They also imply that, so far as possible, staff have the opportunity of rotating to work on the more interesting and challenging tasks (such as more complex tests in a laboratory), and that provision is made for achievements in research to be recognized within the organization and also outside it, where relevant. Recognition within the organization may include promotion up a specialist career grade ladder offering enhanced status and remuneration, although this type of promotion can only be made available to relatively few 'stars' without introducing serious distortions into an organization's wage and salary structure.

Participation in setting work goals with members of other departments and with management also offers a way in which to encourage the integration of specialist activities and priorities with the requirements which other parts of the organization place upon their contribution. Integration is vital, and failures in new product development have often to be laid at the door of deficiencies in integration, especially between research and marketing areas. However, a participative non-coercive style of integration is the most compatible with the professional's sense of worth based on his specialist knowledge, and is therefore likely to be the most effective.

Care has to be taken to distinguish between involvement in planning and integrative meetings directly relevant to an individual professional's work and involvement in other perhaps more administrative meetings. There is little point in professionals spending their time in meetings that do not concern their work, except perhaps where this would be in a representative capacity or in cases where it was part of a broadening training exercise as a preliminary to promotion or relocation. So far as general dealings with management are concerned, the professional manager or supervisor therefore becomes the key link. For this he needs to have the respect both of his professional team and of management, and the demanding nature of this role can readily be appreciated. Finally, the problem of integrating different specialized sections within a professionally specialized function often arises, in addition to the integration of the professional activities with those of other functions. This may point to the need for a matrix structure, which is discussed in Chapter 4.

Making a decision about the design of jobs and work structures

The previous sections have reviewed some of the main considerations that have to be taken into account when thinking about the design of jobs and work structures. An initial decision is whether it is more appropriate to proceed in terms of designing individual jobs or instead to analyse design possibilities with work groups in mind. While much of this chapter has concentrated on the scope for redesigning improvements into jobs and work structures, the considerations it has raised apply, of course, to all decisions about jobs and work groups even where these result in conventional solutions.

Two major dimensions in the design of individual jobs are specialization and discretion. Among the more important considerations for decisions about job specialization and discretion are:

1 The requirements which management places upon the job and the manner in which it is to contribute to the activities of the organization as a whole. Is the job concerned with purely routine activities in which there is little variety or need to seek solutions to unfamiliar problems? Does it require little imagination, flair and creativity? Can it be relatively self-contained from other jobs? Is it relatively unchanging over time? If the answers to these questions are affirmative, then a high level of specialization and a low level of discretion are likely to be 'technically' viable job design characteristics, though whether they are considered desirable by job holders is another matter.

2 The ability of available personnel and their expectations. The greater their ability and expertise, the less (other things being equal) need a manager restrict them to a limited range of activities, unless the area of their work is so technically or professionally complex that it is necessarily highly specialized, albeit in depth. The greater are employees' abilities, the more confidence can be placed in their use of discretionary powers, assuming that they are motivated towards attaining objectives which contribute to the purposes of the organization as a whole. This is where employees' expectations are relevant, since in order to motivate people to commit themselves to their jobs, the levels of specialization and discretion in them should as far as is possible match job-holders' expectations as to what is appropriate. It has been suggested that these expectations are moving towards a desire for less specialization and more discretion in jobs.

3 The design of jobs and work structures should not only take into account the nature of the work and the characteristics of the personnel; it also has to be consistent with the philosophy of management that is being followed. The structuring of jobs needs to be matched by an appropriate design of organizational systems and an appropriate managerial style. In a sense, organizational systems represent the 'hard' context for jobs, changes in which can be effected through a specific redesign of procedures, systems and the like, whereas managerial and supervisory style represents a 'soft' permeating context, which cannot so readily be changed through specific decisions and steps. Consideration has therefore to be given to the nature of the organizational context and prevailing managerial philosophy, and to their implications for job design. If the context and managerial approach appear to reflect a successful and appropriate strategy, given the environment in which the organization operates and the type of work it does, then it may be wiser to adjust employees to the type of jobs that are consistent with contextual features, through recruitment and training policies, rather than attempt a change in job design that is incompatible with the organizational and managerial context. Consistency is probably the most important requirement here. For example, if management announces its belief in personal initiative yet continues to allow jobs to be characterized by narrow specialization and severely restricted discretion, it is inviting an unfavourable reaction by employees to what they will see as a credibility gap.*

It is possible to indicate a step-by-step procedure for setting about designing jobs and work structures in a way that takes account of their location within a context of technology, a workflow system, management control systems and payment systems. The following outline is a distillation of recommendations by several authorities and is expressed with particular reference to designing group-oriented work structures (work structuring):

1 Carry out a preliminary scanning of the unit to be analysed (a department or plant), paying particular attention to the workflow, technology and deployment of workers.

---

*The relationship of consistency to organizational performance is discussed in Chapter 8.

2 Analyse the workflow (production system) with a view to identifying the main transformations of materials or products which constitute distinct tasks. These tasks are clusters of tightly coupled activities or processes which are, or could be, more loosely coupled with the activities entering into other tasks within the total workflow. Tasks may be built into the technology of plant and equipment and they are manifest in a close-knit set of operative activities. The intention is to isolate tasks which are 'complete' in themselves, together with their constituent activities, since these provide the point of reference for allocating responsibilities either to individual jobs or to work groups.

3 The question of what might be designed into the scope of jobs or work groups leads to a consideration of the 'variances' or deviations that have to be controlled in the tasks identified, and the means of their control. Control could perhaps be built into technology (and may have to be, in which case this becomes a major design constraint), or allocated among workers, supervisors and managers. According to sociotechnical practitioners, this information on the source and type of variances and their means of control is crucial for the design of work organization since it affects both the choice of instrumentation and control processes built into the technology, and the boundaries, content and discretion allocated to jobs and work groups.

4 As well as input and output connections to the rest of the workflow and technology, other aspects of the task context need to be identified. These include support systems such as maintenance and information retrieval, and systems of managerial control, supervision and payment.

5 At this stage, a preliminary picture will have emerged of the division of workflow into its constituent tasks, the interrelationships between them, the role of technology and social system in controlling variations and disturbances, and relevant contextual factors. This should suggest some possibilities for job or work group design, both within the existing set of contextual constraints and within possible alternative contexts. In order to check out this preliminary analysis and to assess reaction to possible changes, information is required on how workers, supervisors and managers perceive the present work arrangements, their role in these, and what they think of potential rearrangements. These people will almost certainly be essential sources of data for the analysis of existing work systems, and their views and perspectives need to be incorporated into the innovative design process as well. Indeed, people at various levels in an organization will usually have developed unofficial working practices of their own, which must be recognized and talked about. This is because such practices point both to the personally unacceptable aspects of existing job and work group design and to operational inadequacies in that design. Unofficial practices often turn out to be changes that employees have made on their own initiative in order to reduce inefficiencies.

6 Once a structure for jobs and workflow groups has been discussed and decided in principle, details then have to be decided regarding the allocation of specific activities, the specification of new discretionary limits, agreed standards of performance, mechanisms for feedback and control, the role of supervision in the new design, and the method of payment. Decisions have

also to be made about any training and personal development that may be required. It is to be expected that in this whole complex process, which requires multiple adjustments and considerable goodwill for its long-term success, a number of reiterations of analysis and discussion will be required at any of the stages outlined.

Arriving at appropriate decisions about the design of jobs and work structures therefore entails quite an arduous process in which judgement and securing acceptability play important roles. There are no stereotypes that can provide ready-made solutions, though different models may furnish useful points of reference for some of the broad choices that are available.

Summary

Two basic dimensions of job design are specialization and discretion. The movement towards job enrichment and work restructuring has been concerned to reverse the trend in conventional industrial engineering practice, which has degraded jobs through narrowing their scope in regard to the range of skills utilized (specialization) and to the discretion workers are permitted.

Job enrichment focuses upon the content of individual jobs, whereas work restructuring is directed to the design of work units, which will usually consist of groups of employees each contributing to an identifiable task. The work group is the more usual unit of activity at the operative level, and in recent years there has been growing attention to ways in which work group systems and technologies can be designed together in order to enhance satisfaction, motivation, flexibility and performance.

Many attempts to redesign jobs and work structures have failed or have not been sustained over time. Several reasons have been identified for these failures, ranging from inadequate diagnosis of existing jobs and work systems to the lack of complementary adjustments in contextual systems such as control, supervision and payment. The receptivity of employees to enrichment has also to be established. These considerations need to inform decisions about the design of jobs and work structures, and it is possible to suggest a step-by-step approach that takes account of the analyses it is appropriate to undertake.

Suggested further reading

Louis Davis and James Taylor (editors), *The Design of Jobs* (1st edition Penguin 1972; 2nd edition, Goodyear 1979) is a collection of important articles particularly on the design of operative jobs. J. Richard Hackman and Greg R. Oldham, *Work Redesign* (Addison-Wesley 1980) builds on work by the authors and colleagues over the previous decade, including ways of analysing work situations, diagnostic tools and guidelines for job and work redesign. Of the many articles cited in this book, J. R. Hackman, J. L. Pearce and J. C. Wolff 'Effects of Changes in Job Characteristics on Work Attitudes and Behaviors', *Organizational Behavior and Human Performance*, vol. 21, 1978 is particularly interesting in providing quite strong quasi-experimental evidence for positive effects of job enrichment on employee satisfaction and performance. John Bailey, *Job Design and Work Organization* (Prentice-Hall 1983) presents a rather conventional treatment, which does not show much critical awareness but which gives many examples of practical applications. Two readable descriptions of the sociotechnical systems approach are Louis Davis, 'Optimizing Organization-Plant Design: A Complementary Structure for Technical and Social Systems', *Organizational Dynamics*, Autumn 1979, and Eric Trist, *The Evolution of Socio-Technical Systems*, published by the Ontario Quality of Working Life Centre, Toronto, Occasional Paper No. 2, 1981 (and also appearing as Chapter 2 in Andrew H. Van de Ven and William F. Joyce (editors), *Perspectives on Organization Design and Behavior* Wiley 1981).

There are now many accounts of experiments and developments in job redesign and work structuring. A useful review covering seven countries is provided by the International Labour Office's *New Forms of Work Organization* (Geneva 1979). *Job Reform in Sweden* published by the Swedish Employers' Confederation (English translation 1975) remains a valuable account of Swedish experience. A summary of Norwegian developments is given in Einar Thorsud's article 'Democratization of Work as a Process of Change Towards Non-Bureaucratic Types of Organization' in Geert Hofstede and M. Sami Kassem (editors), *European Contributions to Organization Theory* (Van Gorcum 1976). Robert D. Caplan et al.'s *Job Demands and Worker Health* (US Department of Health, Education and Welfare 1975) reports a detailed study into the medical evidence on stress and strain associated with different types of job. A worldwide survey of group technology experiments is the *Final Report on a Study of the Effects of Group Production Methods on the Humanization of Work* (International Labour Office 1975). The Work Research Unit, London, issues abstracts, bibliographies and occasional papers covering a wide range of topics relating to jobs and work.

A number of writers strike a cautious note about developments in operative job redesign and work restructuring. Several of the papers in Lloyd Zimpel, *Man Against Work* (Eerdmans Pub. Co. 1974) are examples, especially those by William Gomberg and Thomas H. Fitzgerald. J. Richard Hackman, 'On the Coming Demise of Job Enrichment' in Eugene L. Cass and Frederick G. Zimmer (editors), *Man and Work in Society* (Van Nostrand-Reinhold 1975) draws attention to the ways in which job enrichment is inadequately implemented. Greg R. Oldham and J. Richard Hackman discuss contextual constraints on job and work design in 'Work Design in the Organizational Context' in Barry M. Staw and Larry L. Cummings (editors), *Research in Organizational Behaviour*, vol. 2 (JAI Press 1980). John E. Kelly's 'The Costs of Job Redesign: A Preliminary Analysis', *Industrial Relations Journal*, vol. 11, 1980 concludes that workers rather than employers have borne the brunt of these costs. His subsequent book, *Scientific Management, Job Redesign and Work Performance* (Academic Press 1982) adopts a radically different view of the job redesign movement and its relation to scientific management. John Child, 'The Myth at Lordstown', *Management Today*, October 1978 questions how far the Lordstown plant of General Motors should have been used as an example of the rejection of traditional job design by the workforce.

Turning to non-operative jobs, Henry Mintzberg, *The Nature of Managerial Work* (Harper and Row 1973) reviews problems and research on management jobs. John Child and Bruce Partridge, *Lost Managers: Supervisors in Industry and Society* (Cambridge University Press 1982) discuss supervisors' jobs, while research on accountants, engineers and scientists employed in business companies is reviewed in John Child, 'Professionals in the Corporate World: Values, Interests and Control' in David Dunkerley and Graeme Salaman (editors), *International Yearbook of Organization Studies 1981* (Routledge and Kegan Paul 1982).

Other sources referred to in this chapter were John L. Burbridge, 'Britain's Counter-Productive Plants', *Management Today* (November 1981); Pierre Dubois, 'Workers' Control over the Organization of Work: French and English Maintenance Workers in Mass Production Industry', *Organization Studies* (No. 2/4, 1981); Elliot Jacques, *Measurement of Responsibility* (Tavistock 1956); John E. Kelly and Chris W. Clegg (editors), *Autonomy and Control at the Workplace* (Croom Helm 1981); V. I. Lenin, 'The Immediate Tasks of the Soviet Government' April 1918 reprinted in *On the Development of Heavy Industry and Electrification* (Progress Publishers 1962); Eric J. Miller, 'Sociotechnical Systems in Weaving, 1953–70; a Follow-up Study', *Human Relations*, vol. 28, 1975.

CHAPTER 3

The Shape of Organization – tall or flat?

'The ranks of officials mounted endlessly, so that not even adepts could survey the hierarchy as a whole.' Franz Kafka, The Trial.

One theme in Chapter 2 was that the redesign of jobs and work structures so as to devolve responsibilities should correspondingly relieve managers and supervisors. For example, the delegation to a work group of the responsibility for allocating people to tasks should save the necessity for first-line supervisors to do this, so long as the workers are able to carry it out effectively. In addition, many motivation theorists take the view that granting people greater discretion and scope for personal achievement in their jobs enhances their commitment to doing their work well. This view assumes that subordinates are willing to work towards standards and targets set by management and do not contest these. If this is the case, then it suggests a further way in which the redesign of jobs and work structures may effectively reduce the burden of supervising subordinates.

When developments in job design and work structuring are successful in these terms they make possible a shift in the content of managers' and supervisors' jobs. If managers and supervisors were previously overloaded, they should now have less to cope with. If they were not previously overloaded, they can now devote more time to other duties. Indeed, it may be possible to delegate additional responsibilities down to them and so relieve a higher level of management. Alternatively or additionally, these managers or supervisors may now have the capacity to cope with an increase in the number of subordinates reporting formally to them—an increase in their *span of control*. Whatever adjustment is made, the net result ought to be that a given amount of managerial work is now performed more economically, with fewer managers and possibly with a less extended managerial hierarchy. Modern thinking on job design and work structuring therefore has a bearing on the old debate over the choice between tall and flat organizational shapes. For it implies that it is possible to contain and perhaps even reverse the growth of long organizational hierarchies, with their problems of heavy managerial overheads and extended communications, and that this will be accompanied by the widening of managers' spans of control.

Hierarchy and span of control

This chapter is particularly concerned with the length of organizational hierarchies, and how this relates to the average span of control present in an organization. Tall and flat structures are usually identified by the number of hierarchical levels there are in an organization relative to its total size. A tall structure is one that has many levels in relation to total numbers employed, while a flat structure is one that has few levels relative to total employees. It is important for practical purposes when making comparisons between the hierarchies of different organizations to take their overall size into account, since it has been found among organizations operating in the fields of business, public service and government in various countries that the maximum length of their hierarchies varies in a predictable manner with their total size measured in terms of employment. As organizations grow from small units up to about 1,000 employees, their number of hierarchical levels generally rises from the four levels of chief executive, department heads, supervisors and workers typical of the organization employing one to two hundred persons, to about six levels at about the thousand mark. The rate of increase in levels which typically accompanies larger size is, however, a decreasing one. Even at 10,000 employees the norm is only around seven to eight levels. Number of levels is calculated here for the longest hierarchy (normally the production of operations one) in a way that counts chief executive and operative (or clerical) worker as a level each, and then adds the levels in between to these. Deputy managers are counted as a hierarchical level, but personal assistants are not. The way in which the number of levels thus calculated has been found to vary with size of organization is illustrated in Figure 3.1, which draws upon three different surveys.

Figure 3.1 Variation in number of levels with size of organisation: trends from three samples

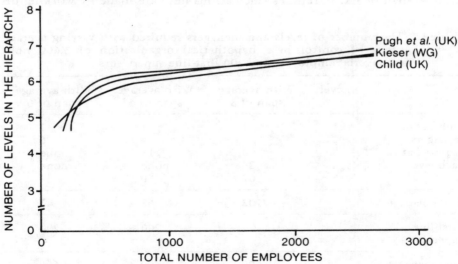

Studies by:
Professor D. S. Pugh and colleagues, 46 Midlands organizations of different types, data collected 1962–64; Professor Alfred Kieser, 51 West German manufacturing companies, data collected 1970–71; the author, 82 British manufacturing and service companies, data collected 1967–69.

Although there are reasons (discussed in Chapter 9) to expect that the introduction of new microelectronics-based information technology may somewhat reduce the number of levels of management required for a given scale of operation, evidence such as that presented in Figure 3.1 provides us with a point of reference for suggesting whether a given organization is taller or flatter than the average for its size. On this basis an organization employing, say, 3,000 people and having nine hierarchical levels from chief executive to the lowest level inclusively would be somewhat 'taller' than average. An organization of the same size having only four levels would be considerably 'flatter' than the average, which available trend lines suggest is about seven levels for an organization of 3,000 people.

Another way of making the same distinction is to say that a structure is relatively tall when it has a low average span of control, and that it is relatively flat when it has a high average span of control. Basically, there is a choice between increasing levels of management or increasing spans of control as the total size of an organization rises. For example, simple arithmetic shows that the difference between an average span of control of four and one of eight in an organization of 4,000 non-managerial personnel can make a difference of two entire levels of management and nearly 800 managers. Barkdull (1963) has produced a schema, shown in Table 3.1, which illustrates the effect of varying the size of average spans of control on the number of levels. The table shows how a hypothetical organization with 3,600 non-managerial employees, and 200 first-line supervisors, requires seven levels and 102 managers with an average span of three, six levels and 68 managers with an average span of four, and only five levels and 41 managers with an average span of six. Barkdull's calculations here are made by working up

Table 3.1 The number of levels and managers required with varying average spans of control in a hypothetical organization of 3,600 non-managerial employees and 200 first-line supervisors

	Level	With average span of 3	With average span of 4	With average span of 6
Number of	1	1	1	1
managers	2	3	4	6
required at	3	8	13	none
each level	4	23	none	none
	5	67	50	34
Total managers		102	68	41
First-line supervisors		200	200	200
Non-managerial employees		3,600	3,600	3,600

Adapted from: C. W. Barkdull (1963) 'Span of Control: A Method of Evaluation'. *Michigan Business Review,* 15, pp.25–32.

from the first-line supervisor level and rounding up to the nearest whole number of managers required with a given span of control at each level. Barkdull appreciates that in real life organizations do not build up their structures as evenly as the hypothetical organization in his table. Nevertheless, while in reality the figures might be somewhat different, the overall effect would not be substantially altered.

There is a trade-off, then, in the design of organization between the number of levels in the hierarchy and managers' spans of control. In a small organization this trade-off is not likely to be experienced as a major problem, because it will be possible to combine few levels of management with modest spans of control. It becomes more of a problem as the size of the organization increases. The shape of the graphs shown in Figure 3.1 suggests that on the whole managements attempt to hold down the increase in levels as their organizations grow and, as we shall see, there are good reasons for doing so. A policy of restraining the growth of hierarchies without necessarily restricting the growth of employment will mean that serious attention has to be given to the possibilities of increasing spans of control.

The arguments for and against tall and flat structures will now be reviewed, and it is suggested that the weight of argument comes down against tall structures. This then raises the question of what limits there are on the width of spans of control, and a consideration of these in turn brings to light some bases on which decisions on hierarchy and spans of control may be reached. A method developed by the Lockheed Missiles and Space Division provides a successful example of how judgements appropriate to a given organization's circumstances can be drawn together systematically in order to change the balance between the number of hierarchical levels and managers' spans of control.

Arguments for and against tall and flat structures

Two main considerations are advanced in favour of tall hierarchies. The first is that tall hierarchies with many levels increase employees' commitment to the organization and enhance their job satisfaction because they provide many steps for career progression. According to this argument, those employees who are given access to a career ladder (and many of course are not) can experience some degree of advancement up the many small steps of a tall hierarchical ladder, perhaps at fairly frequent intervals, whereas those in a flat structure are likely to be stuck at the same level for many years and advance up very few steps. This argument is particularly attractive for those managements that wish to create 'internal labour markets' for a core of valued employees in whom special training and close knowledge of the organization and its competences have been vested, and whose commitment it is considered particularly desirable to retain.

However, and to anticipate a point discussed shortly, the use of a hierarchy in this way to provide a sense of personal progression and recognition is to run the risk of obscuring genuine, and possibly relatively few, differences in levels of responsibility by substituting another structure containing many small differences in grading, remuneration and status. Progression in remuneration and status in order to reward performance, to recognize valued skills and experience, and to secure continued commitment, can be achieved through a separate system of gradings in which there may be several grades within a given level of authority and responsibility. Given the likelihood that relatively few employees can be genuinely promoted anyway, there is even more reason to devise a system which permits the recognition and reward of merit within a given hierarchical level. Professor Elliott Jaques (1976) has in fact concluded from his studies in industry and the public service that about three times as many pay and status grades should be provided as levels in the hierarchy of work (authority and responsibility). For several reasons, then, doubts have to be expressed about the validity of this first argument in favour of tall hierarchies.

The second argument can be dealt with briefly at this point because it is based on the claim that spans of control must be kept within certain limits. The reasoning behind this claim is discussed shortly, but its implication is that tall hierarchies will be necessary if large collections of people are to be managed as a single unit. Strictly speaking, this is not so much an argument in favour of structures that are tall in relation to the size of organization as a statement that hierarchies have to expand along with growth.

If it were not for difficulties that can arise with wide spans of control, the case against relatively tall organization structures would be overwhelming because of the problems which attend them. Tall structures involving many levels of management entail heavy administrative overheads. They can lead to communication problems and a dilution of top management control. They encourage the 'bypassing' of supervisors and subordinates. They can make it difficult to distinguish closely between responsibilities at different levels in the organization. They may reduce the scope subordinates have for exercising responsibility and so have a damaging effect on motivation and initiative. These objections to tall hierarchies are now considered.

Just as concern has been expressed over the expansion of what has, in an oversimplified manner, been called the 'non-productive' sector in the economy, so there are grounds for seeking to restrain the size of the 'non-productive' component within sectors: both the business and public sectors (Child 1978). In other words, while management and administration are in some form and to some degree essential, they are nevertheless overheads, which do not contribute directly to the production of goods and services. These overheads have exhibited a long-term tendency in both private and public sectors to rise in proportion to the numbers of people in direct employment, a tendency which is difficult to account for simply in terms of technological development and a growth in management science. Not only are managers' salaries involved in this overhead but also the associated costs of fringe benefits and pension payments, support staff, office accommodation, and the staff and time involved in effecting co-ordination between managers. The British Rank Xerox Organization, for example, recently calculated that a manager's salary only accounts for about one-third of his or her total employment cost. The potential economy in numbers of managers that can be brought about by reduction in the number of management levels and widening spans of control has already been illustrated in Table 3.1. In principle at least, the reduction in levels increases the productivity of each manager, though some of the reduced overhead may actually be achieved through delegation to direct workers (the 'productive' component). The first main argument against tall hierarchies is therefore the overhead costs that they entail.

Very often, when managers complain that they have problems of communication with operative employees and first-line supervisors one finds that they are operating with a tall structure. The ways in which communication can become distorted in passing up and down through hierarchical levels are well documented. Subordinates frequently interpret as merely advice or guidance for action what their managers had intended to be firm instructions. These instructions consequently become diluted or re-interpreted, especially if the communication is purely verbal as a certain proportion must always be. In passing information up, there is also a well-known tendency for those at subordinate levels to communicate in terms that will least offend the recipient, and indeed some communications may not be passed up at all.

The link between an over-extended hierarchy and communication problems was evident in a factory producing drinks with which I have some acquaintance. This factory employed about 1,200 employees and managers. It had nine levels in its main production hierarchy. The chief executive was keenly aware of what he called 'communication problems' between himself and the shop floor. He attempted to overcome these by somewhat unorthodox methods such as paying spot visits to the shopfloor almost every day, working some days at operative jobs, and accompanying drivers unannounced on their runs to the company's distribution depot. In themselves these appeared to have generated a high regard among employees for their chief executive—but at a cost and without solving the real problem. Production managers and supervisors disliked this approach considerably, primarily because they were apprehensive about what this persistent 'bypassing' implied for their authority. It was in any case questionable whether so much top management activity aimed at improving communications was being judiciously balanced against the time required to develop longer-term strategic policies for the business. It seemed to an observer that the net effect of the chief executive's methods was to create a diffuse feeling that status barriers were being broken down, rather than to create the conditions for precise information to be communicated effectively and on an everyday operational basis up and down the hierarchy. A reduction in the number of managerial levels would almost certainly have made a more significant contribution to that end.

A structure with many levels of management can make for difficulties in distinguishing sufficiently discrete levels of responsibility and authority between positions at adjacent points in the hierarchy. The Fulton Committee pointed to this as a problem in the British Civil Service. The Committee expressed the view that to operate efficiently large organizations including government departments need a structure in which units and individual members have clearly defined authority and responsibilities for which they can be held accountable. The Committee identified a number of typical features of civil service organization which were preventing the clear allocation of authority and responsibility. One of these was the large number of hierarchical levels and correspondingly narrow spans of control in most civil service departments. In these departments there were usually at least nine levels from Permanent Secretary down to Clerical Assistant, and spans of control averaged only between two and three.

This very narrow and tall structure meant that the same work was passing through too many hands. While this accorded with civil service traditions of multiple drafting and checking of work, it also severely restricted the scope for individual officers to exercise discretion in the pursuit of their duties. From the standpoint of administrative overheads the system was wasteful (as Parkinson (1958) had indicated long before), and from the standpoint of managerial control it made an assessment of individual performance difficult in the extreme. Part of the problem in the civil service lay in a confusion of levels of management with grades in the salary structure. As the Fulton Committee pointed out, the salary grading structure with its twenty or so grades was essentially a pay structure and was not designed to determine the actual organization of work. The Committee recommended that the organization of each section of work, and the number of working levels in it, should be determined solely by the requirements for achieving its objectives efficiently.

In the case of the pre-Fulton civil service, the personnel effects of too many levels amounted to the same as those of narrow spans of control. It is likely that within a managerial or executive structure most staff will prefer to have opportunities of exercising discretion and taking initiatives commensurate with their relatively high abilities and qualifications. In this situation, narrow differentials in the hierarchy and narrow spans of control are both likely to impair motivation. Unless the content of the work being performed is highly complex or innovative, as in a research team, this narrowness will almost certainly result in excessively close supervision or in much of the same work being gone over again by a superordinate manager. Neither prospect can readily attract the enthusiastic commitment of able employees.

The phenomenon of 'bypassing' has already been mentioned in connection with the drinks factory, and this can also readily produce anxiety, frustration and demoralization among its victims. While bypassing might be encouraged by personal factors such as loss of confidence in the abilities of the person being bypassed, or patterns of personal loyalty which have a long past and now cut across hierarchical levels, it is a regular feature of over-tall hierarchies. If there are more levels in an organization's formal hierarchy than are warranted by differences in levels of authority and responsibility, then the situation is liable to arise in which subordinates, in order to obtain a firm decision on a parameter affecting the performance of their work, are obliged either to use their immediate superior merely as a messenger or to bypass him and to go straight up to a higher level where a definite answer can be obtained. Bypassing is likely to be quicker and to risk less distortion in communications. What has happened is that for operational purposes an over-extended hierarchy containing too many levels has become truncated but probably at a cost of unease to all the parties concerned (especially the person being bypassed) because 'proper' channels are not being followed. This kind of situation, and its attendant anxiety and ambiguity, often develops around positions designated as deputy or assistant manager, which appear to constitute a distinct hierarchical level but which in terms of real responsibility and authority actually do not.

Investigations conducted by members of the Brunel University's Institute of Organisation and Social Studies, primarily in public sector organizations, led them to the conclusion that there are typically only five levels of work in organizations, and at the most, probably no more than seven (Rowbottom and Billis 1977). Level of work here denotes a distinct level of responsibility particularly with respect to the scope and significance of decisions that employees and managers are expected to make. The Brunel researchers therefore argue that these levels of work are necessary bases for designing levels in an organization's hierarchy. In an organization containing five levels of work, the highest level would be one at which the manager has responsibility for a comprehensive provision of products or services in a general field (an industrial product field such as electronic calculators or public service area such as health provision) within a broad territorial area, and including the innovation of new provisions to meet demands within that field. This is the level of chief executive or head of a major division. If this analysis is valid, and it has been built up from close and long-term contact with organizations, then it implies that any organization having a hierarchy which contains more than five levels is under suspicion as being too tall and hence liable to suffer the problems which have been mentioned.

The weight of argument is therefore in favour of restraining the increase in the number of management levels that would otherwise tend to accompany organizational growth. Indeed, for many organizations, it implies that they would benefit from a reduction in the number of levels they already have. In both cases, a widening of average spans of control is indicated. Support for this conclusion comes from a study which examined spans of control in relation to organizational performance. Lenz (1980) found in an investigation of American savings and loan associations that the better performing organizations tended to limit their hierarchies by adopting wider marginal spans of control. This relationship held after controlling for a range of environmental and strategic factors which also bear on performance.

What objections are there then to widening spans of control, and are there any limits on how far this can go?

Spans of control

It was a cornerstone of classical management theory that managerial spans of control should be limited. A figure of between three and six subordinates was usually recommended. Classical theorists such as Sir Ian Hamilton, Henri Fayol, Colonel Lyndall Urwick and V. A. Graicunas argued principally from the personal limitations of human beings—since a manager's spans of attention, memory, energy and other capacities are limited, he will be unable successfully to supervise the work of more than a few subordinates. Graicunas (1933) in a famous paper demonstrated how an arithmetical increase in the number of subordinates is accompanied by an exponential increase in the number of relationships the superior has to manage.

The classical theorists were primarily concerned with the maintenance of control from the top of an organization. They wrote at a time when relatively little was understood about the ways in which organizational design can affect human motivation or about the ways in which the demands made upon managers can vary according to the kind of work that is being undertaken. So they found themselves arguing for the general application of two principles—limited spans of control and a limited number of hierarchical levels—which were mutually inconsistent, above all in the larger organization. On the one hand, spans of control were to be limited so that it was possible to retain adequate supervisory control over subordinates, sufficient communication with them and adequate co-ordination between their activities. On the other hand, they advocated a restricted number of hierarchical levels so that loss of control down a hierarchy and the dilution of instructions before they reached the point of action should be kept to a minimum. In effect, these two principles were speaking strongly for the administrative advantages of small-scale organization.

The principle of limited spans of control has percolated widely within managerial thinking, and it is probably a major factor in the development of excessive levels in organizations. There is a school of thought that seeks to reverse this trend by widening spans of control wherever possible. It is often said that the greatest scope for widening spans of control lies in the middle of hierarchies, and several studies have found that in practice there tend to be narrower spans of control in the middle levels of management than at the top, or for that matter at first-line supervisory level.

In a small non-ferrous metal manufacturing plant where I conducted a study of managerial organization there were five levels in the production hierarchy. The plant had only about 250 employees. While the plant general manager had six subordinates reporting to him and there was an average production supervisory span of 20, there was a one-over-one relationship between a works manager and a production superintendent. There was considerable overlap between the work content of the superintendent and of the foremen who reported to him, and many of the latter were impatient at the lack of discretion this situation gave them over matters such as the planning of work. Their greatest complaint was, not surprisingly, inadequate communication up and down the hierarchy. The over-manning within the management of this particular company had its roots partly in a policy of avoiding managerial redundancies when the owning group had in the past closed or rationalized other sites.

Another circumstance in which narrow spans of control can arise in the middle ranges of hierarchies is when activities are divided up into many specialized departments and sub-departments, each having a specialist manager in charge. This may be encouraged by specialists who prefer to work with their own group and to have somebody qualified in their own field in charge. However, as well as increasing the general complexity of the management structure, this arrangement also increases spans of control of the higher level to which the managers of specialized departments report. The higher level may be a functional or divisional head, or it could be a chief executive especially in small or medium-sized organizations. If as a result senior executives become drawn into supervising and co-ordinating a large number of specialist managers, this is likely to detract seriously from the time and attention they can give to longer-term policy and to dealing with external matters of a strategic nature. Studies of chief executives' work patterns by investigators such as Mintzberg (1973) have illustrated the very real nature of this problem. Relying on administrative support staff to assist in dealings with subordinate managers may only lead to confusion as to the authority of such staff. If ways can be found whereby subordinates at this senior level need only be subject to general policy control rather than supervision in the usual sense, then wide spans of 'control' may be feasible, in which case they are really spans of 'policy control' rather than 'executive control' to use a distinction that R. C. Davis (1951) has made. The way in which top management exercises control is therefore also relevant, a point to which I shall return.

James Worthy, a sociologist who became an executive of Sears, Roebuck and Company, described in two articles published in 1950 how the company took deliberate steps to break the principle of limited spans of control at the middle management levels. This was part of a policy to reduce the centralization and complexity of management organization, and to increase efficiency and employee 'morale'. Worthy claimed that an increased degree of self-reliance was built into the retail store manager's job by increasing the number of stores that area chiefs had to look after, which now prevented them from supervising store managers too closely and spending time on matters of relatively little consequence. In turn as many merchandising managers within each store as possible reported to each store manager. The conventional intervening level of management between merchandising and store managers was abolished.

Worthy's view was that 'flatter, less complex structures, with a maximum of administrative decentralization, tend to create a potential for improved attitudes, more effective supervision, and greater individual responsibility and initiative among employees' (1950a: 179). Store managers had so many subordinates reporting to them that they were forced to delegate some decision-making authority. Giving more discretion to subordinate managers not only improved their morale, according to Worthy. It also put more pressure on them and consequently improved their performance, since they now had to make their own decisions and take responsibility for the results. By being forced to manage, these managers learned to manage. Store managers, knowing they had to delegate more authority, took greater care in selecting, training and briefing their subordinates. And, despite the wider spans of control, the abolition of one hierarchical level improved communications between store managers and their subordinates.

Worthy, of course, was arguing merely from a single case and in fact he did not present any specific details or statistics to support his conclusions. Successful examples of a similar policy have, however, been reported, such as in the Bank of America where the intention was to encourage local branch managers' initiative. Other writers have also argued in support of this policy. Suojanen (1955) pointed out that the principle of a limited span of control was first developed in military organizations (both Sir Ian Hamilton and Urwick were military men), where the requirement of operating under emergency conditions leads to a greater reliance on the formal hierarchical command structure to achieve co-ordination. In large governmental and business organizations operating conditions are different. Also, the principle was put forward before social science research had drawn attention to the ways in which informal and lateral relationships can assist co-ordination and reduce the need to effect integration through supervision by superordinate managers. Suojanen's view was that the whole idea of 'proper' span of control is meaningless and that the principle had become a 'fable'.

In response to these criticisms, Urwick (1956) reformulated the span of control principle, stating that no manager should supervise the work of more than six subordinates whose work *interlocks*. In the Sears Roebuck case, he argued, spans of control could be widened to advantage because the work of the subordinate managers did not interlock appreciably. Where there is a considerable degree of interdependence between the tasks of subordinates, the burden of supervision is increased, assuming as Urwick did that the subordinates cannot carry out the necessary degree of mutual integration themselves—an assumption that is today being challenged by methods of promoting lateral relations, as we shall see in Chapter 5. Urwick did appreciate that reducing the number of levels in an organization can improve communications and devolve more authority and responsibility onto junior managers. He took the view, however, that in industry there was too much emphasis on reducing the inefficiencies of excessive levels at the expense of ignoring the need to limit spans of control.

The problem of striking a balance between hierarchical levels and spans of control, particularly acute for the large organization, can be stated clearly enough; but the practical question is how to deal with it. The debate over span of control began to move out of the realms of the abstract when it started to refer to considerations such as the level of management concerned and the extent of interlocking between subordinates' work. It is only by locating the problem in a realistic context that some useful guidelines can be formulated. First of all, what considerations should a manager bear in mind when thinking about the shape of his or her organization?

Deciding on hierarchy and spans of control

If an organization is small its management can afford to opt for very few levels or for narrow spans of control without forcing the other dimension of shape into an unacceptable position. In the absence of strong constraints, the small organization would be advised to economize in its levels of management for the reasons given earlier. In a larger organization the trade-off becomes more acute. The question is now how far the number of levels can be limited by increasing the span of managerial supervision.

The conventional measurement of span of control as the number of sub-ordinates who report directly to a manager (or supervisor) really needs to be weighted by the time he requires to interact with each subordinate. For time is the key to the question of how wide a manager's span of control can be without overloading him, given his level of personal capacity and competence. It is important to recognize that a manager's working time is not totally available for managing subordinates. While it is difficult to draw precise boundaries between them, there are four types of activity which can take up a manager's time, the first three of which do not involve any interactions with his subordinates. These four types are: (1) 'solitary work' such as planning, problem solving, setting out procedures, doing technical work on his own, and writing reports. Although a secretary is normally involved, handling correspondence might also be placed in this category; (2) 'entrepreneurial activities' such as entertaining influential outsiders or negotiating a contact; (3) interaction with superiors and colleagues, including formal meetings with them; and (4) 'supervisory activities' which normally involve interaction with subordinates for purposes of controlling and co-ordinating their work and also advising, training and otherwise assisting them. In some ostensibly managerial jobs the amount of time that has to be devoted to one or more of the first three activities may be substantial: examples are the sales manager who continues to undertake some selling of a particularly important kind, accounting managers who carry out some direct accounting work, many research and development managers, and the head of a university department.

When approaching the question of managerial spans of control, it is necessary to establish first how much time a manager is expected to devote to activities that do not involve the supervision of his subordinates. Having in this way identified the appropriate total amount of time that is available for supervisory activities, the second step is to ask what factors are likely to affect the amount of time required per subordinate, and the extent to which these apply to the manager in question. It is possible to identify some of these factors in the light of research findings and available experience. These are the nature of the work being undertaken and the 'technology' of which it forms part (that is, the total logic of operations), the strategies of control being applied in the organization, the competence and training of managers and subordinates, and the motivation of the people being managed. I shall first discuss these factors and then look at a method which assists the process of judging how much they apply in any particular situation.

Joan Woodward (1965) found in her research on 100 manufacturing firms in south-east Essex that the more successful ones adopted a shape of organization that varied according to their main production *technology*. Among firms engaged in one-off or small batch production, the appropriate shape was one with relatively few hierarchical levels and wide middle management spans of control. Moving up the scale of complexity in production technology through mass production to process production, structures became taller and more narrowly based, with longer hierarchies and smaller middle management spans. Chief executive spans became correspondingly large. Within each category of technology, the best performing companies were those closest to the median in the type of structure adopted. At first-line supervisory level the relationship between technology and the span of control was curvilinear. That is, the largest spans of control tended to be found in mass production technologies.

Woodward's research was a pioneering effort and it has been qualified in important respects by later works. Certain of her findings have, however, been confirmed, such as the way in which first-line supervisory spans tend to vary with technology. In general, her research serves to draw attention to the technology-related factors that managers have to think about when deciding on questions of shape, especially spans of control. These factors are:

1 The degree of interaction between the personnel, or units of personnel, being supervised;
2 The degree of dissimilarity of activities being supervised;
3 The incidence of new problems in the supervisor's units;
4 The degree of physical dispersion of activities;
5 The extent to which the supervisor must carry out non-managerial duties, and the demands on his time from other people and units.

The greater the incidence of these factors, the heavier is likely to be the burden of supervision and hence the more severe the limit on the number of subordinates a person can manage without inefficiencies setting in. The ability to operate large supervisory spans of control in a mass production system (including mass production clerical work) can be appreciated in that the incidence of all the above factors is likely to be low. At the other extreme, in a unit developing prototype or one-off special order products the reverse is likely to be the case. There will be new problems to tackle, a range of specialized skills to draw upon and to co-ordinate, and probably a large call on the supervisor's or manager's time to advise on difficult technical and operational matters. Spans of control will have to be kept narrow. In process plants there may be a fairly frequent change-over of production requiring supervisory attention and, even if that is not the case, most companies prefer to retain a relatively high ratio of supervisors to employees because of the high cost of failure, damage or accident with high investment plant.

A characteristic of larger organizations, and of large mass production manufacturing units especially, is the employment of many specialist support staff. Some of these staff will be appointed to roles that are designed to relieve the supervisory burden of line managers, by taking over responsibilities for planning of work, quality control, work study, personnel, training and other matters. The use of staff personnel should therefore allow for the widening of spans of control at the levels to which they are offering direct assistance, although their presence will necessitate a broadening in spans of control at a higher level of management. If staff personnel are also able to assist in the development of standard procedures, and if the tasks of the organization are sufficiently repetitive or familiar to permit the application of set procedures, then the burden of management can be further reduced with consequent widening of spans of control.

This last point reminds us that a manager who is supervising the work of his subordinates is not doing this in a vacuum but in the context of one or more *control strategies* which are being applied in the organization as a whole. These strategies are discussed in Chapter 6. If considerable reliance is placed on maintaining control through close personal supervision of work, then this will clearly increase the burden of supervision on each manager and the time he has to spend with each subordinate. When subordinates' activities are defined through impersonal means, either because their jobs are closely constrained by the technology (plant and equipment) with which they are working or because formal procedures and definitions have been applied to their jobs, then it is to be expected that supervisory burden of their managers will be reduced. Even in these circumstances, however, managers may still conclude that they have to spend time coping with actions taken by subordinates to exercise some control of their own over how they perform their work, actions which do not comply with job definitions set out by management and which are thought to go against the attainment of management's objectives.

If it is possible to set measurable standards for the results and outputs of subordinates' work, the use of these standards for purposes of control should reduce the supervisory burden on managers who do not now have to devote so much attention to how the work is done. The burden of supervision falling on managers should also be reduced if they can successfully enlist the co-operation and motivation of subordinates and secure their willing acceptance of management's objectives, through building up shared norms and identity (what I shall call 'cultural control'). Quite close contact with subordinates and a willingness to enter into discussion with them may, however, be required in order to maintain shared norms and identity at a high level.

The *competence and training* of managers and subordinates have also to be taken into account when considering appropriate spans of control. The ability of managers to take on a wide span of supervisory responsibility varies from individual to individual. The greater the competence of subordinates, the less closely they need to be supervised and the less often does their work require review. Therefore as the competence of managers and subordinates rises, possibly over time through experience and training, so it becomes feasible to widen spans of control and to reduce levels of management. The ability to modify the shape of structure in this direction should be one of the benefits of a successful policy of management and manpower development. The chances are that it will also prove more satisfying to the people involved, since the degree of discretion being allowed to them will be tending to rise along with their competence (and in most cases their desire) to exercise it. If the situation involves the management of highly skilled or professional work then a balance will probably have to be struck between (a) the capability and wish of personnel to be left alone to carry out tasks as they see fit, applying their own judgement, and (b) the technical complexity of the overall operation itself which may require considerable consultation and integration of different specialist contributions. If the necessary degree of teamwork can be achieved without close managerial involvement (and this should be the aim) then supervisory spans can be broadened; otherwise the burden on managers is likely to be heavy and spans of control will have to be narrow.

In technically complex work, particularly that of an innovative or developmental kind where there is considerable new information to be processed and uncertainties to be coped with, a high degree of cohesion between a group of subordinates will normally be necessary. The employees concerned will have to work closely and constantly together in a problem-solving mode. Research into the conditions favourable to group cohesion draws attention to the desirability of keeping down the size of groups. As group size increases, particularly beyond seven or eight members, there is tendency for factions and cliques to form, generating conflict; the participation of individual members falls off and the number of relationships to be managed increases sharply. In effect, this research lends support to Urwick's view that wherever there is a requirement for subordinates' work to interlock—for them to work in cohesion as a team—then a significant constraint may be imposed on the size of an effective span of control. The constraint may, however, be relieved to some extent if subordinates can be organized into smaller separate groups rather than a single group.

Another consideration is that smaller groups have been found to generate greater satisfaction for their members than do larger groups. In so far as job satisfaction is an important criterion in its own right, this may appear to be an argument in favour of small spans of control in order to permit subordinates to work as small groups. But the issue is not quite so straightforward. First, job satisfaction does not itself necessarily enhance the level of employees' job performance, as was once thought. Much is likely to depend on whether they perceive links to exist between their performance levels and benefits which offer them satisfaction, and whether such satisfactions are the ones they value highly. A second related point is that although working in a small group may provide satisfactions from opportunities to participate highly in the group and from close personal working relations, other satisfactions may derive from the greater opportunities to exercise responsibility, to enjoy some autonomy, to achieve, and to secure personal recognition, which broad spans of control will tend to promote. Indeed, it was argued in Chapter 2 that the possibilities for realizing these opportunities through work restructuring depend on being able to identify 'whole tasks', the scope of which in some systems of work may require quite large groups. Up to twenty members was mentioned as a viable size. Because satisfactions associated with responsibility, autonomy, achievement and recognition derive from the level of work that is performed rather than from the nature of social relations, they may be expected to have a more direct effect upon employees' 'motivation' to do that work well (assuming that these satisfactions are valued), especially if good performance is directly remunerated.

The relevance of *motivation* has now been touched on several times. The argument here for broadening spans of control and reducing levels is, as Worthy put it, that people respond positively to the chance of exercising more responsibility and having more scope to their job. This is the cornerstone of the theory which lies behind job enrichment in general. It should be borne in mind, nevertheless, that people cannot be looked upon merely as materials which respond identically to given change in their environment. Apart from the question of different innate capabilities, it is not certain that everyone will welcome, let alone seek, greater responsibility, especially if it carries the objective cost of a greater burden of worry, of time spent on work and so forth. It depends a great deal on the nature of people's attachment and commitment to their job and their organization—why they have entered that employment and what they most seek from it.

If employees are both capable and committed, the motivational basis for keeping a small number of levels and using broad spans of control will be present. It will, however, be absent if employees cannot or will not willingly assume greater responsibility. In fact, if management is not successful in motivating employees its supervisory burden is *ipso facto* increased, and considerable judgement has always to be exercised in trying to discern whether the type of supervision is creating poor motivation by its inappropriateness or whether close supervision is a necessary response given the intrinsic qualities of the employees who are available on the labour market. A similar point has always applied, of course, to the choice of a payment system—if this is in tune with employee expectations and the task system then the burden of supervision is eased and spans of control can be wider to that extent.

I have reviewed the main considerations that a manager would be advised to take into account when assessing the shape of his or her organization or parts of it. The next step is to find a method for making this assessment as specific as possible and this entails the assignment of points in the form of a simple weighting system. In this way one systematically makes explicit the judgements that are in any case made implicitly.

A useful method was developed by the Lockheed Missiles and Space Division. The division had experienced a period of very rapid growth, which had led to a proliferation of hierarchical levels and narrow spans of control in middle management. Problems had arisen which top management and its organizational designers linked to this tall shape, notably the increasing difficulty employees and supervisors were finding in obtaining the go-ahead to get jobs done, and a rapid rise in costs. Attention therefore was focused on the span of management control and seven factors were selected as the most critical ones for its evaluation. These factors were: similarity of functions managed, geographical contiguity of functions managed, the complexity of those functions, the direction and control required by the personnel being managed, the degree to which the manager had to provide co-ordination, the amount of planning he had to carry out, and the assistance received by the manager from staff personnel. When these seven factors had been isolated, a set of point values was established for the first six, which together represent the burden of supervision placed on a manager. Provisional point values were tested against actual cases and a final set was agreed upon on the

Table 3.2 Elements in the supervisory burden of managers and their assessment

Element	Degree of supervisory burden, and points allocated				
Similarity of functions	Identical 1	Essentially alike 2	Similar 3	Inherently different 4	Fundamentally distinct 5
Geographical contiguity	All together 1	All in one building 2	Separate buildings, one plant location 3	Separate locations, one geographic area 4	Dispersed geographic areas 5
Complexity of functions	Simple repetitive 2	Routine 4	Some complexity 6	Complex, varied 8	Highly complex, varied 10
Direction and control required	Minimum supervision and training 3	Limited supervision 6	Moderate periodic supervision 9	Frequent continuing supervision 12	Constant close supervision 15
Co-ordination required	Minimum relationship with others 2	Relationships limited to defined courses 4	Moderate relationship easily controlled 6	Considerable close relationship 8	Extensive mutual non-recurring relationship 10
Planning required	Minimum scope and complexity 2	Limited scope and complexity 4	Moderate scope and complexity 6	Considerable effort required, guided only by broad policies 8	Extensive effort required; areas and policies not charted 10

From: H. Stieglitz (1962) 'Optimizing Span of Control', *Management Record*, 24, pp. 25–29.

basis of experiment, experience and common sense. The point values finally assigned are shown in Table 3.2.

The seventh factor, the amount of assistance given to the manager by the organization, was treated differently because it lightens rather than increases the supervisory burden. It was given a range of negative weightings reflecting the degree to which the burden of supervision on a manager was reduced.

In a manner similar to job evaluation, the points values for each managerial or supervisory job were then added together to produce an overall 'supervisory index'. Units that were thought to be effectively organized and managed, and where managers had wide spans of control, had their readings on the supervisory index taken as standards. These standards were then used to assess an appropriate span of control for other managerial positions. Table 3.3 shows how the supervisory index was utilized in this way to suggest appropriate spans of control for middle management positions. Different conversion standards (rates of supervisory index to span of control) were used for first-line supervisors to provide for spans of approximately twice the size. The table also shows the distribution of actual spans found for 150 middle managers who were surveyed in the first stage of the programme.

The dotted line on Table 3.3 indicates the shift of the suggested standard span of control along with changes in the index of supervisory burden. Nearly all the jobs surveyed lie to the left of the line; in other words they had narrower spans of control than the standard. The Division therefore went ahead with a reorganization in several units to increase average spans and to reduce the number of hierarchical levels. The results are impressive. For example, in one unit the average span was increased from 3.8 to 4.2 subordinates and levels reduced from five to four; in another average span was widened from 3.0 to 4.2 and levels reduced from six to five. A more dramatic change occurred in a third unit where two levels of management were

Table 3.3 Conversion of supervisory index into suggested spans of control

Supervisory index	Range of actual spans (150 middle managers)										Suggested standard spans of control
	2	3	4	5	6	7	8	9	10	11	
40–42		1	1	1							4 – 5
37–39	1	1	4	5	4						4 – 6
34–36	10	9	13		3						4 – 7
31–33	10	6	12	7	3	1	1				5 – 8
28–30	12	17	7	3	2	1					6 – 9
25–27	3	3					1	1			7–10
22–24	1	1	1			1		1	1	1	8–11
Total number of managers	37	38	38	16	12	3	2	2	1	1	

From: C. W. Barkdull, op. cit.

eliminated (reduced from seven to five), the average span of middle management increased from 3.9 to 5.9, management personnel were reduced by seven (mostly in transfers) and management payroll cut by an annual rate of over $70,000 (at 1960 prices). In those parts of the Division where changes were made, over $280,000 was saved in annual managerial payroll, to which had to be added savings in fringe benefits, secretarial assistance, office space and supplies.

The Lockheed method cannot be applied in a purely mechanical way, and in practice considerable judgement is needed in assessing the extent to which each factor is present in each manager's job, whether other factors should enter into the calculation, and in deciding whether the suggested standard span is appropriate in any given case. Here, the other considerations I have mentioned must enter into the assessment, including the individual capabilities and motivations of both managers and subordinates. It is also possible that one or more of the six supervisory burden factors, such as the need for planning, may be of sufficient importance to warrant giving them higher point values than was the case at Lockheed.

In this connection, it is of some interest that Jon Udell (1967) examined how far the factors which the Lockheed analysts and management writers had identified as relevant to spans of control were actually associated with the spans of chief marketing executives in 67 American firms. He found that the following factors predicted wider spans: (1) supervision of subordinates shared with other managers; (2) similarity of functions supervised; (3) use of personal assistants; (4) length of experience of subordinates; and (5) geographical dispersion of subordinates. The last relationship went contrary to Lockheed's assumption, but Udell found that when marketing subordinates were highly dispersed the similarity of their jobs also tended to be high and this could be the more significant influence. It is also worth noting that today modern techniques of communication such as facsimile transmission, data lines and video greatly facilitate contact and reporting over a distance. Udell found that other factors such as the degree of control and supervision subordinates were thought to need, or the application of formal procedures and definitions to subordinates' jobs, did not predict variations in spans of control. This, however, was a purely descriptive study and does not imply any optimum solutions.

I have spent some time describing the Lockheed approach because it has been applied in practice with encouraging results. The same general method (*not* its specific content) could be applied within virtually any kind of organization. However, managers would need to decide what were the most relevant factors to include in the supervisory index, and what appropriate weightings to attach to them. They would also need to consider its political acceptability, which will be much lower when redundancies may result than in Lockheed's growth situation where displaced managers could be readily absorbed elsewhere in the company. Stieglitz (1962), writing on the Lockheed method, cautioned that anyone who attempts to use it should first recognize that 'there is no really neat, packaged formula that anyone can use to determine the proper span of control for a particular supervisor. Nor is there anything close to a foolproof device for determining the proper number of levels that should exist in an organization' (p.25). None the less, given that we now have some appreciation of the considerations relevant to those decisions, a method that leads us to make a systematic evaluation of them is a definite advance on *ad hoc* implicit judgements.

A systematic evaluation of the considerations bearing on organizational design choices, such as tall versus flat structures, is likely to encourage a participative approach towards formulating and implementing changes, in which the people they will affect have an opportunity to exercise their views. For reasons that will be discussed in Chapter 10, this approach has much to recommend on both practical and ethical grounds, not least because conflicts of interests are involved. There is much more chance that a systematic evaluation will bring assumptions out into the open than will a less widely informed judgement made behind doors or in a 'smoke-filled room'. Once assumptions and arguments are made public, wider discussion of their validity and relevance is possible.

The claim to be taking a systematic approach, through using something like the Lockheed method, means that it has to be seen to be thorough. This in turn encourages those guiding the exercise to seek out reasonably precise information from the members of the organization who are most immediately concerned with the focus of possible changes and who therefore have detailed relevant knowledge. Participation is again encouraged. I think that the potential connection here between the development of techniques which facilitate a systematic evaluation of organizational design choices, and the encouragement of participation in that evaluation, is of general relevance. If realized, it should help to clear away some of the mystique from the design process.

Summary

Managers face the problem of maintaining a balance between the number of hierarchical levels in an organization and the spans of control of managerial and supervisory staffs. This trade-off between tallness and flatness in the shape of the formal authority structure becomes a particularly acute problem for the large organization in which both hierarchies and spans of control may become extended beyond the optimum. Growing organizations often find themselves multiplying hierarchical levels in an attempt to avoid increasing the burden of supervision faced by individual managers.

An extended hierarchy brings considerable disadvantages of administrative overheads, communication failure and low motivation among those removed from sources of major decisions. Long hierarchies based on very narrow spans of control may offer people little opportunity for personal discretion and initiative in their jobs. The question therefore arises as to whether spans of control can be widened.

In examining this, some way has to be found of taking relevant circumstances into account, which together contribute to the burden of supervision borne by a manager. Judgements are constantly being made on this matter, and a method used in the Lockheed Corporation is of interest since it demonstrates the possibility of making a systematic evaluation of supervisory burdens, which can then point up any potential for widening spans of control, reducing management levels and economizing on managerial overheads.

Suggested further reading

The issues covered in this chapter have received attention from comparatively few writers, despite their central relevance to the design of organization. Elliot Jaques, *A General Theory of Bureaucracy* (Heinemann 1976) examines hierarchy and spans of control as part of a more general analysis of bureaucratic organization in both private industry and the public sector. His colleagues at Brunel University, Ralph Rowbottom and David Billis, have analysed hierarchy in terms of the stratification of levels of work and drawn out design implications in 'The Stratification of Work and Organizational Design', *Human Relations*, vol. 30, 1977. James Worthy's seminal papers on flattening the shape of organization and other design improvements are (a) 'Organizational Structure and Employee Morale' in the April 1950 *American Sociological Review*, and (b) 'Factors Influencing Employee Morale' in the *Harvard Business Review*, January–February 1950. A study that illustrates how a larger number of specialized departments within an organization tends to decrease spans of control at lower and middle levels but to increase them at upper levels is Robert D. Dewar and Donald P. Simet, 'A Level-Specific Prediction of Spans of Control Examining the Effects of Size, Technology and Specialization', *Academy of Management Journal*, March 1981. A review of more recent relevant discussion and research is provided by Alan C. Filley, Robert J. House and Steven Kerr, *Managerial Process and Organizational Behavior* (Scott, Foresman; 2nd edition 1976), Chapter 18. Two papers on the Lockheed approach are C. W. Barkdull, 'Span of Control: A Method of Evaluation', *Michigan Business Review*, vol. 15, 1963 and H. Stieglitz, 'Optimizing Span of Control', *Management Record*, September 1962.

Other sources mentioned in this chapter were: John Child 'The "Non-Productive" Component within the Productive Sector: a Problem of Management Control' in Michael Fores and Ian Glover (editors), *Manufacturing and Management* (Her Majesty's Stationery Office 1978); R. C. Davis, *The Fundamentals of Top Management* (Harper 1951); V. A. Graicunas, 'Relationship in Organization' in L. Gulick and L. Urwick (editors), *Papers in the Science of Administration* (Columbia University Press 1937); R. T. Lenz, 'Environment, Strategy, Organization Structure and Performance: Patterns in One Industry', *Strategic Management Journal*, July–September 1980; Henry Mintzberg, *The Nature of Managerial Work* (Harper & Row 1973); C. Northcote Parkinson, *Parkinson's Law or the Pursuit of Progress* (John Murray 1958); W. W. Suojanen, 'The Span of Control – Fact or Fable?', *Advanced Management*, vol. 20, 1955; Jon Udell, 'An Empirical Test of Hypotheses Relating to Span of Control', *Administrative Science Quarterly*, December 1967; L. Urwick, 'The Span of Control—Some Facts about the Fables', *Advanced Management*, vol. 21, 1956; Joan Woodward, *Industrial Organization: Theory and Practice* Oxford University Press 1965).

Appendix to Chapter 3 The Lockheed approach to evaluating span of control

From:
1 C. W. Barkdull, 'Span of Control: A Method of Evaluation', *Michigan Business Review*, 15, 1963, pp. 25–32.
2 H. Stieglitz, 'Optimizing Span of Control', *Management Record*, 24, 1962, pp. 25–29.

Definitions of factors

The definitions of the seven factors were established as follows:

Similarity of functions. This refers to the degree to which functions performed by the various components of personnel reporting to a supervisor are alike or different—whether they are the same functions (perhaps organized on a geographic basis) or whether they differ in nature (perhaps grouped because of their relation to one another). Its importance is that as the functions increase in their degree of variability, the more interrelations have to be kept in mind and the fewer number of persons the supervisor can effectively handle.

Geographic contiguity. This factor refers to the physical locations of the components and personnel reporting to a supervisor. Geographic separation of functions makes for greater difficulty in supervision because of the necessity for more formal means of communication, time to get together for necessary discussions, and time to visit personally the separated activities.

Complexity of functions. This factor refers to the nature of the duties being performed by the majority of non-supervisory personnel, and involves a determination of the degree of difficulty in performing satisfactorily. It is generally considered that salary and hourly ratings are a reasonably fair reflection of complexity. Hence this factor was related to the job classifications of the more important of the non-supervisory positions in the component. Generally, the greater the complexity of the function supervised the smaller the number of persons a supervisor should be expected to handle.

Direction and control. This factor refers to the nature of the personnel reporting directly to the supervisor and reflects the degree of attention which they require for proper supervision of their actions. High level competent managers with years of background and experience, or highly qualified scientists with Ph.D.s, will require minimum attention except for general administrative and planning matters; while other personnel might require closer supervision, direction, guidance, and training. This also reflects the extent to which responsibility can be delegated to subordinates; the extent to which problems and decisions can be resolved at subordinate levels; the amount of training they require; and the degree to which objective standards can be applied. The greater the degree to which subordinates require direction and control the smaller the span should be of the subject supervisor. (This factor may appear to measure the same thing as complexity, and to some extent they are counteracting. However, while complexity measures the *work* of the non-supervisory personnel, direction and control measures the degree to which subordinates *require supervision*.)

Co-ordination.   As opposed to the previous factors, which mainly relate to the duties and personnel supervised, the factor of co-ordination (and the next one—planning) reflect the nature of the supervisory position itself. It measures the extent to which the supervisor must exert time and effort (a) in keeping the functions, actions and output of his components properly balanced, correlated and going in the same direction to accomplish the goals of the activity, and (b) in keeping his components keyed in with other activities of the division to accomplish divisional plans and programs. Again, the greater the complexity of the co-ordination functions and the greater the amount of time required to perform them, the fewer number of people who should report to him.

Planning.   This factor refers to the importance, complexity, and time requirements of one of the primary functions of a manager or supervisor— that of reviewing the objectives and the output requirements in the future, and programming the actions, organization, staff, and budgets necessary to accomplish them. Some distinction must be made in the evaluation of a given position as to how much of these functions is actually performed by others for him, and where planning must be done on a continuing basis or might essentially be accomplished once a year when budgets and programmes are proposed and approved. As the importance, complexity, and time required of the supervisor increase, the more prudent it will be to reduce the number of persons reporting to him.

Organizational assistance.   This factor considers the assistance received within the organizational component from direct line assistants, assistants to, staff activities or personnel having administrative, planning and control responsibilities, and (at the first-line supervisory level) leading hands or their equivalent.

Points values assigned to factors

Similarity of functions

One point—identical. Employees would be of the same occupation doing the same type of work. In a typical situation, a particular function (such as assembly) would be organized by teams or groups working on identical units or giving identical service.

   Two points—essentially alike but having distinguishing characteristics in the nature of the functions. This rating would be applied to those components which perform similar work or work of the same nature at different geographic locations.

Three points—similar but with distinct differences in approach or skills required. Typically, each employee or component would be doing work in a general classification (e.g. general accounting, physics, manufacturing engineering) but in different segments of that field (nuclear physics vs ionic physics, or payroll accounting vs property accounting, etc).

Four points—inherently different but with common purpose. This rating, would apply, for example, to those components (such as development manufacturing) which are closely tied to a single end product or result but where each component performs different phases of the total process (such as development assembly, electronic assembly, final assembly and pro-duction control within a development manufacturing activity).

Five points—fundamentally distinct, with different areas of responsibility and requiring entirely different types of personnel skills. The scope of re-sponsibility is fairly broad and the components are organized on a functional basis, each function requiring specialized skills and knowledge.

Geographic contiguity

Location of personnel or subsidiary components are: one point—in one con-tiguous area in one building; two points—in separate locations within one building; three points—in separate buildings within a plant location; four points—in separate buildings in a geographic area (in different parts of one city); five points—in widely dispersed geographic areas (in several separate parts of the state or country).

Complexity of functions

Two points—simple, repetitive duties which require little training (less than six months) and which follow simple and well-defined rules and procedures. Examples would include typing, stock handling, mail handling, simple assembly.

Four points—routine duties of little complexity requiring individuals to exercise some but not a great amount of skill and/or judgement in following rules and procedures. Examples would include production machine oper-ations, reproduction operations, receiving and shipping.

Six points—duties of some complexity requiring two to three years' experience and training and which require the application of reasonable judgement and/or skills. Examples would include production planning and scheduling, equipment maintenance, accounts payable, etc.

Eight points—complex duties involving a variety of differing tasks, requir-ing four to six years' experience and training and which require the appli-cation of considerable creativity, judgement and skills. Examples would include personnel administration, management planning, industrial en-gineering, buying, financial planning, test mechanics, special tool builders.

Ten points—extremely complex duties which might involve a wide variety of tasks which require long training and experience (eight to ten years). Abstract or creative thinking and/or the necessity for consideration of many factors in arriving at courses of action. Examples: research scien-tists, engineering development.

Direction and control

One to three points—minimum supervision, direction and control. Subordinate positions would be filled by highly qualified, trained and experienced individuals who perform within general assignments and with limited direction by the supervisor. Subordinates would not be expected to secure detailed approvals from their supervisors. Subordinates would be top-level professional, technical and scientific personnel.

Four to six points—limited supervision, direction and control. Subordinate positions need only occasional contact with the supervisor. Such contact would be necessary, for example, to obtain overall counselling on a project, to assure that actions are in keeping with company directives and the objectives of the supervisor. Relations with other activities in most cases would be resolved by the subordinates. Internal problems would generally be worked out by the subordinate. Typical subordinate positions would include senior engineers or supervisory personnel in technical and professional areas.

Seven to nine points—moderate periodic supervision, direction and control. Subordinates would be working to a set of fairly well-defined rules of conduct either by professional practices or by company policy and procedure. Exceptions requiring supervisor action and unusual circumstances could be expected to occur with moderate frequency.

Ten to twelve points—frequent supervision, training, and control. Subordinates require continuous regular checking and instruction. The supervisor would be expected to check frequently to assure that subordinates do not make errors in their work.

Thirteen to fifteen points—constant and close supervision, instruction and control. The closeness of supervision could result from the type of work (very important and costly experiments) or from the type of employees (knowledge and skills are such that continual, careful instruction and discretion are required). Unusual occurrences would be referred to the principal for decision. Regular rules, guides or procedures would be very difficult or impossible to prepare.

Co-ordination

Two points—a minimum amount of co-ordination. The functions of the components are such that their work or output does not have a significant effect on other activities. This situation might occur in a pure research activity, the output of which is not required to meet any precise objectives.

Four points—a limited amount of co-ordination. The principal should meet occasionally with his subordinates and/or other components to make sure that their functions and/or output are properly conforming to quantity, timing, or procedure requirements. The resolution of problems would be readily determined from well-defined courses of conduct. Co-ordination might be substantially performed by other departments, such as a scheduling department.

Six points—a moderate amount of co-ordination. Supervisors would be required to integrate output, timing and procedures. Functions of subordinates might be so closely related as to require the principal to keep them co-ordinated.

Eight points—a considerable amount of co-ordination. A significant amount of the principal's efforts would be required in discussing and resolving mutual problems of timing and quality of output and matters of procedure. The functions of his component would be rather closely tied in with other activities so that mutual and complementary action would be desirable. Some of these relationships could be defined, but others could not.

Ten points—extensive co-ordination. A great amount of the principal's time would be spent with subordinates and with others in keeping activities in balance. This would apply to certain staff who work closely with others in developing programmes or resolving mutual problems of a non-recurring nature. This might also occur with a responsibility cutting across several organizational lines. In applying the point values to the supervisory job, a distinction must be made between those situations which require the principal to perform these duties and those where subordinates can accomplish the desired co-ordination without the principal's assistance.

Planning

Two points—of minor importance and complexity, requiring a minimum of time and effort. Functions which are routine in nature where the plans are simple and easily determined based on very precise criteria or where plans are prepared by some external organization.

Four points—of limited importance and complexity requiring some measurable time and effort. Activities which do not require a great amount of planning. The criteria for plans and the boundaries within which plans are to be prepared are broadly defined.

Six points—of moderate importance and complexity requiring a moderate amount of time. Planning would be necessary to accomplish objectives and programmes, and there would be some criteria to follow.

Eight points—of considerable importance and complexity requiring a large amount of time. Some guidance on planning is available but there would be a number of variables without clear guideposts.

Ten points—of great importance and complexity requiring a considerable amount of time and effort. Planning is largely uncharted and deals with many variables, requiring abstract thinking.

Organization

Direct line assistance and staff activities or personnel which have administrative, planning and control responsibilities; multiplier factor: .60.

Direct line assistant only; multiplier factor: .70.

Staff activities or personnel which have administrative, planning *and* control responsibilities; multiplier factor: .75.

Staff activities or personnel which have administrative planning *or* control responsibilities; multiplier factor: .85.

An assistant to, performing limited planning and control functions; multiplier factor: .95.

Leading hands or equivalent (applicable to first-line supervisors only). The number of leading hands (and the accompanying multiplier factors) in the organization are: one leading hand .85; two leading hands .70; three leading hands .55; four leading hands .40; five leading hands .25. (This assumes that a leading hand will give guidance to eight-twelve employees and spend some 20–30 per cent of his time in duties of guidance, job assignment and training.)

CHAPTER 4

The Shape of Organization – grouping activities

'Put a miller, a weaver and a tailor in a bag, and shake them.' Part of an old proverb.

The preceding chapter was concerned with the vertical configuration of people and jobs—how much vertical differentiation there should be within an organization. The present chapter considers the problem of selecting a pattern of horizontal differentiation between groups or sections, departments and divisions. The two issues are linked through spans of control. For example, if people who are performing similar activities are grouped together under the so-called 'functional' principle (discussed shortly), then it may be possible to have quite a large number of them reporting to a single manager or supervisor. Other things being equal, this should encourage a flatter and smaller management structure. However, if the organization comprises a large number of highly specialized sections or departments, perhaps because it operates in a high technology field and/or produces a wide range of different outputs, then the dissimilarity of functions performed and the high co-ordination needs that are likely to arise will tend to encourage small spans of control in middle management and a longer vertical hierarchy.

Given the range of activities to be undertaken in an organization, the question arises as to how they should be grouped together in the most suitable manner. This question applies at different levels of organization—to the grouping of jobs to make groups, sections or teams, to the grouping of these to make departments, to the grouping of departments to make functions or divisions, and to the grouping of functions or divisions within the organization as a whole. In principle, similar criteria such as effective information processing, potential for mutual learning, economy of staffing, and ease of control can be used to evaluate alternative ways of grouping activities and people at each of these levels. Another way of phrasing the question is to ask on what basis an organization should be specialized. There are several models from which to choose, including mixed types. Each model has its own logic which has to be assessed in terms of its appropriateness to the situation at hand.

These models and their logic are now described. Particular attention is then given to the choice between the two most common models, the functional and the product. The product logic has been widely adopted by large diversified corporations through a type of company structure which has come to be known as the 'divisional' form. This can be applied to geographical groupings as well, and it is discussed together with mixed structures such as the matrix form. The chapter closes with a method that can assist in reaching decisions on the most appropriate grouping of activities.

The logic of task systems

When designing an organization it is clearly a fundamental requirement that people be allocated responsibilities which accord with identifiable tasks, together making up the total undertaking as a 'task system'. The nature of the undertaking, whether it be to cure illness or to produce motor cars, determines the operational decisions that have to be taken and the relationships in which members of the organization must engage when doing their work. Typical operating decisions are about the methods and resources used in carrying out the work, the sequence of activities to be performed and how to deal with exceptional contingencies (such as faulty material or a power failure) when these arise. Effective relationships have to be maintained between people who need to exchange information about the planning and progress of the organization's work, and between people who contribute directly to linked stages of the basic process itself.

The system of tasks within an organization as a whole is therefore the point of reference when considering how to group people together in a formal structure. The practical difficulty here lies in the fact that tasks can be seen to fall together on several quite different logical grounds. They may be linked by virtue of shared expertise or function, process, product, time horizon or geographical location. The choice of how to group people and their activities depends on which of these task system logics are felt to be most significant.

Members of an organization may share a common expertise and draw upon the same set of resources in their activities, even though they are applying their efforts to different products or services. Such people belong to the same *functional* area, of which the training function provides an example. The training of operatives within a company could be serving a number of different production lines, and the training of salesmen may similarly be directed towards strengthening several different sales teams. Many of the methods of instruction and some of the same instructional equipment will, however, be used across all these areas of training, as might the same training staff. In other words, there is within the training field a body of shared expertise, experience and resources that can be applied to more than one operational area. This degree of commonality provides a logical link between training activities, and the same logic can be found connecting tasks in other functional areas such as accounting, research or production.

Closely related to the logic which links together tasks falling within the same functional area is the relationship between tasks that share a common *process*. For example, a range of different products can often be processed through the same plant, as is the case with some chemicals such as acids. Different engineering goods can be manufactured by passing through the same configuration of machine tools. In these examples, the same plant is used for similar manufacturing processes. A company can often achieve considerable economies by employing a common production facility for a range of products if this is technically feasible. A common plant facility would normally be administered by one production function, grouping all the production activities involved into a single unit.

The activities of people located in various functional areas will collectively contribute to the tasks of developing, making and distributing a given product or service. Within an engineering company such tasks would include market research, design, development, production engineering, production planning, costing, training of operatives, and sales promotion. A company may be producing several products which are sufficiently similar in terms of markets and technical know-how to draw largely upon the same configuration of specialist contributions. The interconnecting logic here is that different specialist tasks contribute to the same *product* or family of products. An example of this logic applied to the public field can be seen in hospitals where medical, nursing, clerical and technical staff are grouped into different sections dealing with maternity, paediatric, accident and other particular services.

The product-based logic of tasks recognizes how the contributions of different specialists need to be integrated within one complete cycle of work. In contrast, functional and process tasks systems recognize the intrinsically different nature of the specialized resources that are applied to all of an organization's product or service technologies. The product logic is primarily technological, envisaging a flow of work laterally across functional areas. The functional logic is primarily hierarchical, drawing attention to the vertical grouping of people in depth within the boundaries of separate specialized sections of the company.

A further logic linking different tasks is present when they share approximately the same *time horizon*. The fact that some decisions are long term, in the sense of committing resources for some years ahead usually with a correspondingly long period before the pay-off can be assessed, while others are short term, has been advanced as the main justification for a hierarchical division of tasks and of the people responsible for them. This is the argument for, as it were, a vertical specialization of jobs, with time horizon and discretion being progressively restricted as one passes down through the levels of the hierarchy. (Chapter 3 raised the question of whether an extended hierarchy is desirable.) Another aspect of the time horizon logic can be seen in tasks concerned with forecasting future conditions facing the organization. Such forecasts of trends in future demand, technical developments, social changes and the like are brought together as a common foundation for forward planning. For this reason, and because conclusions about the future may have to rely upon shared assumptions about trends in the various sectors, there will be a powerful logic for recognizing the interconnections between forecasting tasks when deciding on where organizationally to locate the people who have responsibility for undertaking those tasks. As a result many larger organizations, who can afford to specialize to this extent, have established 'forecasting' or 'systems' units concerned with preparing integrated long-term forecasts and projections. Some of the contrast between the work of different functions derives from their time horizons. Those for a research and development function, for example, normally reach much further ahead than those of a production operations function.

Finally, different tasks may be carried out in the same *geographical location*. This geographical connection could coincide with the other task system logics, if for example one plant specializes in the production of a single family of products or if a particular function such as research and development is located completely on one site. Whether or not tasks are located together on one site or in the same region can be extremely significant. For, as Robert Townsend (1970) has put it graphically, the potential for disastrous internal breakdown in a company is equal to the square of the distance—measured in hours—between the home base and outlying sites. The other side to this coin is that tasks carried out in the same physical area share some managerial requirements, at least in respect of common services and relations with the local community.

These distinctions between different task system logics are important since they provide the principles by which the activities of an institution can be grouped. Such principles constitute important guidelines for organizational design. In practice they can be combined in various forms, and it is also possible to follow one principle for grouping some activities and another for grouping other activities. It is even possible to overlay one principle on another as in the matrix form. Some of the structures for grouping activities that follow from these task system logics are very familiar, such as the functional structure, the product structure, the divisional structure based on products or geographical areas, or the forward planning group within an organization. One basic choice, to start with, is that between the functional and product models.

Alternative models for grouping activities: functional and product

When an organization is extremely small, consisting of perhaps ten to twenty people, any formal arrangement for defining and grouping their activities is unnecessary. If the members of the organization are contributing specialized skills and knowledge, the allocation of tasks to them can be quite adequately managed within the confines of face-to-face relationships in what is essentially a primary group. Problems of designing formal organizational structures arise with growing size and complexity.

The functional form of structure is normally adopted once an organization grows beyond the primary group stage. It is particularly appropriate if the organization is basing its growth upon a single range of products or services which is sold or dispensed almost exclusively within the one domestic market. The functional form groups activities into separate departments which provide specialist contributions to the common product and its market. The co-ordination of these departments is achieved formally by the chief executive perhaps backed by an executive committee or board. In practice, however, a great deal of co-ordination is often achieved informally via everyday meetings over lunch, and so forth. Figure 4.1 depicts a simple

Figure 4.1 A functional structure

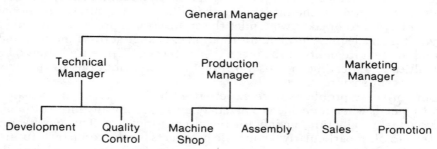

functional structure in a small engineering firm. Within the production area activities are shown to be grouped by process into machining and assembly. The arguments that can be advanced for and against the functional model apply to the process model as well.

The grouping of activities by function offers a number of advantages, which are particularly relevant for the smaller organization confined to one field of activity. It is economical on managerial manpower because it is a simple structure, co-ordination being left to top management rather than to several divisional general managers or to integrating personnel such as product managers. When specialist technical expertise, in say research or marketing, is critical, costly and scarce—and that is especially so for the smaller unit—then it is appropriate to pool available experts together within a single relevant functional department. This helps to maximize their potential level of utilization on a time-sharing basis across the whole organization. It also makes it easier to co-ordinate the specialists concerned. Similarly, when there are economies of scale or of concentrating resources in production (plant); in engineering (e.g. test or laboratory facilities); in distribution (e.g. warehousing) and so forth, it is beneficial to group such facilities and the people operating them together into single functional departments. Finally, a functional structure provides clearly marked career paths for specialists, and so makes it easier to hire and retain their services. They also have the satisfaction of working with colleagues who share similar interests.

Where all the activities of an organization are focused on a single product or service area, and where change is gradual and therefore not necessitating a sharp distinction between current operations and new developments, then a functional structure is likely to satisfy the criteria mentioned earlier. It should provide for adequate information processing; it promotes mutual learning within specialisms; it is economic on staffing and it allows for control on the basis of cost centres, which is sufficient since there is only one integrated revenue source for the organization as a whole to which all cost charges are related.

Difficulties start to arise with the functional model once an organization diversifies its products, markets or services. Diversification is very often a necessary condition for its continued growth. If an institution is becoming larger, more diversified and subject to tight time constraints in adopting new products and services, then it is more than likely that a purely functional form will begin to break down under the strain. It will probably no longer provide for an adequate level of information exchange across functions and around the requirements of the diversified activities. There are liable to be difficulties in allocating the costs of functional contributions to the now several revenue sources.

Some of these problems were experienced by a producer of speciality ferrous metals when it decided to diversify into a technically more difficult type of steel production, mainly for the aircraft industry. This new sector was seen to offer particularly favourable prospects for the company's future growth. Products for the aircraft industry required different research skills and a more refined manufacturing process than did the firm's traditional products. They were also marketed differently, not to a large number of manufacturers (some very small) but to a few aircraft subcontractors producing to strict government-controlled specifications. Some aircraft sales were also to customers overseas, another new departure for the firm.

The company began by setting up a separate section to handle sales of the new steels. It proposed, however, that established functional departments retain responsibility for their production, specification and quality. Very soon, troubles began to emerge. Deliveries of the aircraft steels began to fall behind the fairly demanding schedules normal for that market, and it was extremely difficult to get reliable information from either the technical or the production departments on the status of work in progress. Existing rules on economical batch sizes had not been amended to take account of the new products with their greater value-added and shorter delivery times, and work was thus being held up in the factory. Unexpected technical problems also emerged because the new steels required more delicate handling in process. It was not long before competitors brought out technical modifications superior to the company's own specialized steels, modifications which its technical staff had not anticipated. It was said that the aircraft sales staff should have alerted the company to these developments, but the sales personnel in turn complained that there was little real interest among other departments in the company's new products. The company managing director and the general manager found themselves increasingly drawn into having to sort out operational crises of this kind, which they felt should be resolved at a much lower level.

It was decided after a while to set up a separate technical department and a physically separate production facility for the new steels. These were grouped together with the sales team into a separate division under a product manager solely concerned with aircraft steels. This step was felt to be justified for a sector which was growing at twice the rate of the firm's traditional markets, and where it looked as though an opportunity was being lost because of internal problems. Responsibility for the other products was given to a second product manager. Despite the initially higher costs involved in duplicating certain facilities and offices, much of the uncertainty, poor co-ordination and misuse of top management time disappeared with the new arrangements. The company in fact continued to develop its com-

Figure 4.2 A product structure

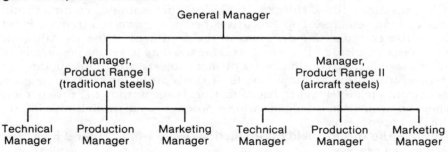

petitive strength in aircraft work and to take advantage of the growth opportunities it offered.

This company had moved from a grouping of activities by function to a grouping by product. The core of its new structure is presented by Figure 4.2.

A product structure becomes a more appropriate way to group activities when an organization produces two or more ranges of products, or types of service, which are different in their technical make-up, production requirements or types of outlet. An extreme case is to be found in the conglomerate corporation, engaged in a range of totally different areas of business, where its subsidiary divisions are sensibly left to operate in effect as separate product units. So far as any particular product is concerned, the more rapid the change in its competitive conditions, the higher the rate of new technical developments, and in general the greater the pressures for rapid response to external changes, then the more advantage the product structure will enjoy over the functional form. For it has the virtue of directing specialized contributions to a common product focus. This is particularly appropriate when there are many urgent joint decisions to be taken between specialists, and when it is necessary to utilize positions such as the product manager in order to co-ordinate and establish deadlines for product developments. Mutual learning and adaptation to change are now focused around the needs of the product as a whole rather than around individual functional specialisms. In addition to encouraging more effective information processing, the product structure permits each product or service unit to be treated as a profit centre in cases where revenues can be accounted for or services valued. Although practical difficulties can arise, which are discussed later (page 96), this decentralized profit centre approach allows control to be based on an evaluation of overall performance and to take on a more arms-length character. This should economize on senior management time, even though the actual staffing of product units is likely to be more costly than in an equivalent functional structure. A complete move to a product structure will mean forgoing the advantages of functional forms that I mentioned earlier. The economy of staffing offered by functional structures may be especially significant in a smaller organization.

In practice, the exact balance between adopting functional and product groupings of activities must be assessed in the light of symptoms which signal the need for a shift in emphasis. For example, communication overload may emerge. Top executives become drawn too frequently into day-to-day co-ordinating decisions to the detriment of the attention they give to strategic issues. Perhaps it is taking too long to get the go-ahead from top management to continue work on new projects, and this is building up a sense of frustration and low morale. If these problems arise, some movement from a relatively centralized functional organization to a product form where co-ordination is lodged within a product group or division will probably be appropriate.

Within the specific field of production, we saw in Chapter 2 how group technology represents a move towards a product logic of organization, in which machines are grouped according to product families or in which groups of people assemble complete units rather than specialize on short cycle operations. The problem that initially stimulated experiments in group technology was the growing complexity of workflow routeing with consequent planning, co-ordinating and lead-time difficulties. The opposite case is illustrated by a situation in which a company's products are losing their competitive appeal because of poor design and quality. The solution to this problem could require some strengthening of functional organization, at least in the technical area, and a greater resistance to pressures for short design-to-production lead times.

Some contrasting effects of organizing on a functional as opposed to a product basis are illustrated by Walker and Lorsch (1968). They studied two manufacturing plants making the same product for the same markets and using the same materials and technology. Their parent companies were also similar. The plants had very similar management styles and objectives, and employed the same range of functional specialists. But in the functionally organized plant only the manufacturing departments and the planning and scheduling function reported to the plant manager, while the other plant had a partly product basis of organization in that all its specialists with the exception of plant engineering reported to the plant manager. (This plant did not, however, have a fully fledged product structure incorporating functions such as marketing.)

Walker and Lorsch found that in the functional structure specialists focused sharply on their specialized functional goals and objectives. They identified closely with their counterparts in other plants and at divisional headquarters rather than with the members of other functions in the plant, or with common plant objectives. Their outlook was generally a short-term one, and the plant had a high degree of formality (job definitions, clear distinctions between jobs) across all functions. In the other plant, with more of a product structure linking functions together, the functional specialists seemed more aware of common product goals. There was more variation in the time horizons adopted; for example, production managers concentrated on routine matters while quality control specialists were more concerned with longer-term problems. This differentiation in time horizon was encouraged by the way the product form of structure brought specialists together in problem-solving and this led to a sensible specialization of effort. In the functional plant, each department tended to worry more about its own daily progress. In the product organized plant, similarly, there were greater differences between functions in the extent to which organization was formalized.

The net effect of these contrasts was that communications were more effective in the product structure plant, and conflicts appeared to be resolved more openly. Managers there were more involved in their work but also experienced more stress in consequence. The functionally organized plant was actually more efficient and less costly to operate, but it was also improving its productivity at a much lower rate than the product organized plant. The product organization appeared to enhance the plant's adaptive capability largely by improving the integration between functions. In stable conditions, when there is time enough to achieve co-ordination through written communications and other formalized methods, the functional structure may be advantageous. In conditions demanding some change and active problem-solving a product form may prove superior because it encourages more intensive communication, confrontation of issues and integration of effort. If the direction of this change is, however, towards a contraction of activities and/or towards cost reduction, a move back to a functional structure would have to be considered (an example is given on page 97 below).

Divisionalization

Larger and diversified organizations today usually draw the boundaries around their main subdivisions in terms of a product or geographical logic, depending on whether they have diversified primarily by increasing their range of product types or by increasing the range of geographical regions in which their operations are located. Some organizations that have diversified in a major way along both these axes have adopted a grid structure, which incorporates both logics for grouping activities with corresponding multiple reporting lines—these are discussed in the next section. Major product or geographical area-based units within an organization are normally designated as divisions.

The divisional form of structure, as it developed in the United States, had three prime characteristics. First, profit responsibility was assigned to general managers of divisions which became essentially self-contained business units. Second, the corporate headquarters had a general office that was mainly concerned with strategic planning, appraisal of policies and projects and overall financial control, including the allocation of resources between the divisions. Third, corporate managers were committed to the performance of the organization as a whole rather than to that of any individual division. During the past two decades large European organizations have increasingly been adopting the essentials of this type of overall structure, though many have not gone so far as their American counterparts in creating a central HQ office in its own right as opposed simply to building up certain central staff groups. As Franko (1976) describes, European multinationals have tended to retain a 'mother-daughter' relationship between the centre and divisions or subsidiaries. In contrast to the more formalized and arms-length American model, in the 'mother-daughter' arrangement the heads of major functions continue to report to (or serve on the same managing board as) the corporate president, and this may be the case for divisional heads as well. Personal contact and shared values are the basis for control rather than formal rules and job descriptions—in terms of the alternatives discussed later in Chapter 6 control is of a personal and cultural rather than a bureaucratic type.

It would be misleading to assume from this identification of prime characteristics that only one form of divisionalization is followed in practice. There are in fact many forms. If a divisional structure is adopted for an organization the problem of how best to group activities still arises within each division. This could be done according to a functional model, there could be a grouping around specific products within the division's general product area, the division could be broken down into area units, or there could be mixtures of these groupings. We are again reminded that decisions are required on how to group activities at several levels in a larger and more complex organization, within as well as between divisions. This leads to a variety of divisional structures.

Stephen Allen (1978) concluded from a study of large divisionalized companies with headquarters in North America that what we typically refer to as divisionalized (or 'decentralized' profit-centre) organizations are in reality a diverse family of institutions consisting of several types. There is a choice of divisional type. Although Allen was able to identify as many as thirteen combinations that managers use when establishing a divisionalized organization, three basic choices were apparent: (1) how self-contained divisions should be in the sense of containing all the key personnel and facilities required, where low self-containment would mean that significant aspects of key functions such as research and development, purchasing or marketing are provided only by central units or shared among several divisions; (2) how complex a set of control and co-ordinative devices such as information systems, planning and control systems, bonus systems and co-ordinative roles there should be linking the corporate head offices with the divisions; and (3) how small and specialized with respect to coverage of an industry or service area each division should be. Allen's very important conclusion is that 'the options available in establishing or reorganizing a divisionalized corporation are far wider than generally believed' (p.363).

The discussion so far has focused on product divisionalization. The divisional form first developed among large business corporations, which are today normally multinational in scope. The product division is the predominant type among multinationals, though area divisions are also found, for example in many airlines and banking corporations. An area approach has also been adopted by many public sector organizations offering a nationwide service.

The sequence of structural changes typically found in multinational corporations is instructive because it shifts from one dominant pattern of grouping activities to another. In many cases the first major change came when a diversification of products within the domestic market encouraged corporations to move from a functional to a product division structure. Sometimes regional expansion gave rise to an area division structure. The entry into overseas activities was often through the purchase of a foreign subsidiary. This might be left to operate largely on its own for a while. Then, as overseas business expanded, it became worth while to group activities concerned with foreign operations into a separate international division, typically managing both foreign subsidiaries and exports from domestic production. If home activities became diversified into different product groups, and if this range of products were then shipped abroad as well, the point would be reached where economies of co-ordination could be achieved through amalgamating home and overseas activities into global product divisions. Even if this product diversification did not take place, as more parts of the world were covered, and possibly local manufacturing sites set up, so again it became increasingly logical to group the whole organization's activities into global area divisions. Finally, the diversity both of products offered throughout the world and geographical regions covered has today led some multinationals (Unilever for example) to experiment with mixed forms of structure in which several principles of grouping activities are found together. The sequence of structural development that has been most commonly followed is shown diagrammatically in Figure 4.3.

The divisionalized structure is the form of grouping activities that most larger and diversified companies now follow, usually with divisions based on different product ranges and sometimes based on geographical location of customers. Compared to the traditional functional form, divisionalization offers several advantages. Major decisions are taken nearer the point of action so relieving top management time for more strategic matters. Profit responsibility is delegated to divisions, which permits the organization's main activities to be evaluated separately. This ability to assess the return achieved by different sectors of activity is an important aid to making decisions on how to allocate investment within the organization. Decentralization of decisions and responsibility is likely to motivate middle-level general managers and provide them with an earlier training in general management.

Figure 4.3 The most common path of structural evolution among multinational corporations

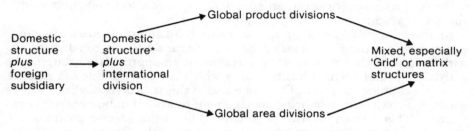

* Among American-owned multinationals it has been more common for the domestic structure to be divisionalized before adding an international division.

Yet problems have emerged with divisional forms. One problem is that there may not always be a clearly superior basis on which to create divisions in the first place. Divisionalization by product may, for instance, lead to poor co-ordination and even open competition between separate divisions dealing with the same customer or client. This is the difficulty faced by one large British food company, which has several divisions supplying the same retailing organizations with consequent diseconomies of distribution, of selling effort and problems of inconsistencies between the trading arrangements offered. A geographical area divisionalization, which might help to avoid these kinds of problems, can, on the other hand, lead to a duplication of production facilities, technical effort and so forth because the logic of common product technologies is not recognized.

The very act of creating divisions, which become the main points of identity for their members, is of course literally divisive. There are quite likely to be conflicts between divisions over the allocation of new investment, and over matters such as the use and funding of shared central services. The interest of a particular division might conflict with those of the organization as a whole if the role of that division is seen to be only a short-term cash generator, while other divisions are seen to have greater potential as areas for development. As a result the high profit earning division would perceive corporate investment to be going elsewhere to lower profit earners.

The delegation of profit responsibility to divisions, which then become profit centres, is organizationally much more feasible if a number of relatively self-contained areas of business can be identified. For the profit centre concept rests on the assumption that it is possible not only to separate out the operations of a previously integrated organization, and to regroup these into divisions, but also to measure separately the profitability of each. The greater the interdependence of each division in the supply of materials, in production operations and in the distribution of materials, products or services, the more difficult it will be to make divisionalization work and the more sophisticated will need to be the accompanying procedures and control systems. This naturally places an additional burden on management and is likely to increase staff overheads. While a divisional structure may generate larger revenues as the result of speedier and more sensitive decisions taken by better-motivated middle level general managers, the additional costs of overheads, sophisticated control and information systems, and conflicts which will probably arise in an organization whose activities retain significant interdependencies, have also to be entered into the profit account.

Another difficulty, which some of our largest organizations are now facing, is that divisions themselves may grow too large and become too diversified, with the result that they no longer represent an appropriate grouping of activities around a single business area which is clearly defined in market and/or technological terms. One response to this is to divisionalize the divisions, which threatens to bring management to a point of horrendous complexity. This is part of the problem of managing ever-growing giant organizations. A number of adaptations are possible. Divisions can themselves be grouped, with the resultant groups reporting to the corporate head office. This three-tier structure reduces span of control problems at the corporate centre. There could also be a move towards a holding-company structure, in which subsidiaries of a manageable size organize homogeneous business units that are linked to a small central unit only on the basis of performance accountability.

Should divisionalization based on products or areas run into difficulties, the functional form is not normally an appropriate structure for a diversified organization to return to. There are exceptions to this, and Lex Donaldson (1979) has documented the case of Japan's largest manufacturer of synthetic textiles, which reverted from a product division to a functional form. Donaldson concludes that the two main reasons for this were increased cost pressure leading to a unification of production and a strategy of developing radically new product areas, which was felt to require increased central control over finance and management personnel for its implementation. However, because so many organizations in all kinds of fields are diversified in their activities and wish to recognize that diversification within their structures without becoming purely divisionalized, there is a growing interest in various types of mixed structure, which may offer some of the advantages associated with more than one logic of grouping activities.

Mixed structures

One form of mixed structure incorporates different logics of grouping activities side by side, as it were. There are several examples of mixed functional and divisional structures. The first is where divisions are retained as operational profit centres, but advisory services, planning functions and the control of shared resources such as mobile plant and stock are centralized on a functional basis. The divisions here have 'low self-containment' in Stephen Allen's terms. This structure has sometimes been called a 'system' model, and it has been used in the airline, construction, petroleum and pharmaceutical industries. It has the virtue of economizing on investment in shared resources as well as helping to maintain consistency in corporate policies. A second example arises when the need for economies in, say, production or research dictates the grouping of all these activities into one function, but where diversity in markets served argues for splitting marketing into area or product divisions.

Rather similar is the 'critical function' structure identified by Channon (1978). Here the organizational structure is normally divided into several product or geographically based operating units with partial profit accountability. One or more critical functions, such as the finance and investment function in an insurance company, are centralized and fall outside the responsibility of the operating units or divisions making full profit accountability impossible. A fourth example is the 'functional-with-subsidiaries' organization identified by Rumelt (1974). This is a basically functional organization, which has also created one or more separate divisions reporting to top management or sometimes to a functional head. The heads of the divisions are organizationally on the same level or below the functional managers. Rumelt found that this type of mixed structure was often used by vertically integrated firms having some side or venture activities, and by firms moving from functional to product-divisional structures.

A different type of mixed structure is the 'matrix', in which one logic of grouping activities is superimposed totally on another. This may just take a temporary form as is the case with what is usually called a project team. Here, a project team or task force is superimposed on a permanent structure, usually of a functional or departmental kind, in order to draw together resources from different functions, or even divisions, for a special purpose. The time period of the project is limited, and it will usually be strategically important to the organization in order to warrant such a radical departure from the normal disposition of responsibilities. The establishment of special project teams can be quite effective in accomplishing major changes or new developments, but if team members remain responsible for their normal work as well they can become seriously overloaded and also experience divided loyalties.

The project team illustrates the principle of the matrix structure, which is characterized by formalized lines of lateral communication superimposed upon the separate vertical hierarchies of departments. Matrix structures in this respect formalize the informal lateral communication that would normally exist between departments and upon which many organizations rely heavily to keep themselves running smoothly. In its more permanent form, this structure is often known as a 'grid' structure when it applies to a whole organization and as a 'matrix' when it is used within a sub-unit of the organization. In a generic sense we are talking of 'multidimensional' structures, but in practice the term matrix is most commonly employed. Within a fairly small and self-contained engineering company, the matrix would mean that an individual like a quality inspector is a member of several activity groupings. He would belong to a functional quality control department, but is at the same time called upon to respond to the requirements set out by two or more product managers in terms of operational priorities. Figure 4.4 illustrates in simple form how such a structure might appear. A grid structure in a large multinational food corporation could mean that a local manager in charge of selling breakfast cereals in Australia will report simultaneously to a world-wide breakfast cereal division and to an area division co-ordinating all of the corporation's activities in Australia.

The first main phase of matrix structure development came when the US Government made it a condition for research and development projects in the 1960s that contractors should have a project management system. This had the advantage of allowing the representatives of government agencies to deal with one individual—the project manager—who had full responsibility for meeting costs and deadlines, rather than having to negotiate with a number of functional heads each only having partial responsibility. The government was in effect insisting that contracting firms made provision for their own effective co-ordination. In these circumstances the firms could either adopt a fully fledged product-cum-project organization, or they could adopt the matrix by superimposing project management on top of the existing functional structure. Those which chose the matrix structure did so believing that it was essential for the technical quality of their work and for the longer-

Figure 4.4 A matrix structure combining functional and product forms. Example of an engineering company.

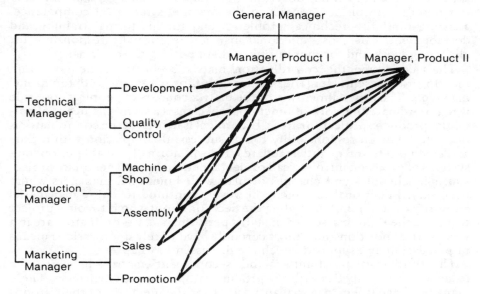

term development of their resources not to break up established functional departments such as research and development.

Today, matrix structures are widely found in institutions as diverse as ITT, Monsanto Chemical, National Cash Register, TRW Systems, and Texas Instruments, financial institutions such as Skandia Insurance in Sweden and Citibank, and management schools such as my own University of Aston Management Centre. In some organizations the matrix structure has been extended to the whole company, as in Dow-Corning and the British Aircraft Corporation, or to major divisions as in ICI. A particularly good description of how a matrix structure evolved in the Lockheed-Georgia Company is provided by Corey and Star (1971).

Although there is considerable agreement on the principle of matrix structure, practical applications vary quite widely. Knight (1977), drawing on British and American experience, has identified three main possibilities regarding the balance of authority within cross-functional matrix structures. In a 'true' matrix, which Knight calls an 'overlay',* the balance of authority between functional management and cross-functional management (product, project or area managers) is approximately equal. The staff concerned explicitly and officially become members of two organizational groupings and report to two managers. The functional manager has to agree to his staff member's allocation to the cross-functional activity with the

---

*There is an inconsistency of terminology in the literature on matrix organization. Knight (1977) uses the term 'overlay' for the 'true' matrix, but another major source (Davis and Lawrence 1977) calls this the 'mature' matrix and reserves the term 'overlay' for Knight's 'co-ordination' and 'secondment' matrix structures.

product, project or area manager concerned. As well as continuing to have a say in the member's time allocation, the functional manager also normally remains responsible for appraising the member's technical competence, assisting him with technical problems, and for his formal training and development. The cross-functional manager is normally responsible for allocating work and for monitoring and appraising its performance.

The second type, the 'co-ordination' matrix, seems to be the most common form at present. Here the balance of authority remains with functional managers. The other dimension of the matrix consists of people whose role is to co-ordinate the work of functional specialists around the needs of particular products, projects or areas. If a project is involved, the co-ordinator is likely to be given responsibility for its successful completion within time and cost targets and quality standards. He will normally be able to operate systems of project control, to call project meetings, and to negotiate project staffing, schedules and changes of plan with functional managers where necessary. Functional managers, however, continue to enjoy managerial authority over the staff, including the decision about who is to join a project team and the right to assess their staff's performance. Co-ordinators are in a weak formal position and almost certainly have to rely upon various means of persuasion and support, which are discussed in Chapter 5.

The third main possibility is the 'secondment' matrix, in which the balance of authority lies with the product, project or area managers. These managers have full managerial authority over the members of their groups or teams who are staff seconded full-time for the duration of an assignment out of their functional departments. If they are moved from one assignment to another, and/or from one team to another, their secondment takes on a semi-permanent nature. In the secondment matrix, functional managers are only likely to retain authority over seconded staff regarding the official appraisal of their technical competence, their formal training and career development.

The secondment matrix attempts to retain the commitment of specialist staff by providing them with a functional colleague group and career ladder within what is otherwise basically a product, project or area-centred structure. The co-ordination matrix attempts to provide more adequately for product, project or area needs while leaving the basic functional structure essentially undisturbed. Neither the secondment nor the co-ordination forms of matrix represents such a break from more conventional structures and the unity of command principle ('one person-one boss') as does the 'true' overlay matrix, where a delicate balance has to be maintained between the two lines of managerial authority.

Experience of using matrix structures has now begun to build up, and the very real difficulties of making them work have become evident. Indeed, Stanley Davis and Paul Lawrence who have reviewed American experience with the matrix form advise: 'If you do not really need it, leave it alone. There are easier ways to manage organizations' (1977: 7–8). It appears, for example, that there is often a three- to five-year period of settling down while people adjust to what is a complex system with dual (or even more) reporting relationships. During this period, the performance of an organization may show little improvement and there can even be set-backs.

The case for matrix structures lies in the argument that they are trying to optimize two potentially conflicting benefits. First, they attempt to retain the economic operation and development of technical capability associated with the functional grouping of common human resources. Second, they attempt to co-ordinate those resources in a way that applies them effectively to different organizational outputs—products or programmes. In the smaller organization particularly, only a limited number of specialized personnel can be employed, and the duplication called for by a product structure could be quite uneconomic. The matrix structure offers a means of balancing the different pulls of resource and demand criteria in conditions where neither a purely functional nor a purely product structure is suitable.

One of the most important reasons for considering a matrix structure is that it may help preserve flexibility in the increasingly more structured setting of the growing organization. Matrix organizations are said to enjoy similar advantages to those of the 'organic' systems described by Burns and Stalker (1961), particularly the capacity to respond quickly and creatively to changes in a dynamic environment. Because people are not wholly members either of a functional department or a product group, it should be easier for them to accept movement between teams and even departments as the need arises. The presence of formally designated multiple reporting relationships and groupings of people is likely to encourage open lines of communication within the organization as a whole. So if an organization is operating in several different areas and experiencing rapid change in some of them, the adoption of a matrix structure may help to match its degree of internal flexibility to that required by the complexity, change and consequent uncertainty of its operating context.

Davis and Lawrence sum up these reasons for adopting a matrix structure by setting out three conditions which they claim should be present simultaneously in *very large measure* before a matrix form is attempted. These conditions are: (1) two or more sectors critical for the organization's success (functions, products, services, markets, areas); (2) the need to carry out uncertain, complex and interdependent tasks; and (3) the need to secure economies in the use of scarce human resources such that their use is shared and flexible. Davis and Lawrence warn that 'until these three conditions are overwhelmingly present, in a literal sense, the matrix will almost certainly be an unnecessary complexity' (1977: 21). They are, it should be added, writing with the 'true' or 'overlay' matrix in mind, which I have indicated does pose the peculiar difficulty of maintaining a balanced dual authority structure and is in this respect the most radical departure from more conventional forms of organizational grouping.

Some of the other advantages claimed for matrix structure are not unique to that particular organizational model. For example, it is claimed that matrix structures release a great deal of top management time from problems of operational co-ordination. While this may be true, so long as the conflicts that can arise in a matrix structure do not absorb top management energies instead, it is a benefit also potentially offered by the divisional type of structure.

Divisional and matrix structures share other advantages. Both in principle involve some delegation of authority, which can motivate and help develop managers below the senior level. The matrix structure may in fact offer the additional motivation that stems from working participatively in teams, and this may be especially important for more junior personnel who now find they have a say in significant decisions. Matrix structures expose specialists to situations where they have to take account of a wider range of considerations than those arising within their specialist area. This should broaden their outlook and involve them in challenges of a more general management nature without the anxiety of being cut loose entirely from their functional mooring, as can happen in a purely product-based structure. Finally, a matrix structure like a divisional one should encourage competition within the organization. This can be a valuable spur to innovation and achievement, so long as its potentially destructive aspects are kept under restraint.

Against these claims for the matrix structure, which still need to be examined closely by carefully designed research, there are known problems. These tend to centre on the conflict that often arises, which can lead to individual stress, defensive behaviour and heavy time commitment to meetings. Administrative costs may also be quite heavy in a matrix. An unpublished survey, which Ken Knight conducted, found that the major problems reported by managers working in matrix structures were 'red tape' (too much time spent in meetings, too much paperwork, and too many people involved in decisions), conflict between managers, a blurring of accountability so that no one is responsible when things go wrong, and stress arising from uncertainties about accountability and from conflict.

The matrix structure attempts to formalize an already existing conflict between functional and product programme criteria. A third dimension of conflict may be formalized as in Dow-Corning where an area-reporting relationship is added to functional and product ones. This formalized conflict tends to generate conflicting objectives and accountabilities at a personal level, creating a highly charged political atmosphere with disputes about credit and blame and attempts to manipulate the balance of power. Galbraith (1973) qualified the difficulties imposed by this radical departure from the classical management principle of preserving a unity of command by saying that most of us were quite used to coping with this type of situation, as we had done in childhood with dual parental authority. It should be recalled, however, just how devastating for the individual this situation can be when the two authority figures are in conflict, and when loyalties are torn apart.

Some degree of conflict between functional managers and product managers is endemic to matrix structure. They will not always agree over priorities of resource allocation or over the time and cost allowed to functional activities. The balance of power between the multiple authority structures is critical but delicate. It must be maintained if the full benefits of the matrix are to be gained. In the move from functional to a matrix structure, functional executives will experience a dilution of their power and of the initiatives open to them, particularly in regard to making innovations and dealing directly with professional contacts outside the organization. Their role may appear to have become purely supportive and reactive. Professional and expert staff working together within functional areas as well-established groups may find these disrupted with the change in structure. They are likely to express considerable anxiety at the weakening of what they see as their specialist identity and clear line of career progression. They may also feel that the quality of their work will be sacrificed to pressures for speed and cost-cutting coming from product or programme managers.

The threat to occupational identity is one source of stress which employees can experience in matrix structure. Other sources of anxiety derive from the conflict that reporting to more than one superior can engender, and from the ambiguity about what is expected, which the fluidity of the matrix form tends to promote. It has been suggested, with these problems in mind, that roles and project objectives should be precisely defined in a matrix structure. While objectives and performance parameters can be defined, it is not clear how roles can be further specified without threatening the flexibility that is one of the advantages of the system. To a large extent conflict and stress is the price that has to be paid for adaptability and change.

A further problem which arises with matrix structures is that they generally incur greater administrative costs than a more conventional structure. The multiplication of hierarchies means an increase in managerial overhead. The presence of conflict means that managerial time has to be devoted to its resolution. Taking of positions can engender excessive paperwork to justify a case, as well as rigid behaviour more usually associated with bureaucracies. Indeed, senior management may find itself becoming excessively engaged in resolving these operational difficulties if the threshold of trust and understanding among functional and product managers is not reached.

These problems are worth facing up to if a move to a matrix structure is felt to reflect the cross-pressures and complexity of information processing that an organization has to face. If an organization is diversified in its activities and is in a field where technical complexity requires that it utilize the services of multiple specialities, and if it is facing competitive time and cost pressures, then a matrix structure with all its cross-cutting strains and stresses is simply reflecting a situation which objectively exists in any case. Many organizations are not in this position, but an increasing number are coming to be.

The matrix structure is the most far-reaching of a number of mechanisms that management can employ in an attempt to improve the co-ordination of different functions or organizational sub-units. The behavioural problems which can arise in a matrix structure serve as a reminder that a purely structural design will not of itself guarantee any desired pattern of behaviour. The structural and behavioural approaches that may be adopted in an attempt to enhance organizational integration are considered further in the following chapter.

A method to assist decisions on the grouping of activities

This chapter has so far discussed the advantages and disadvantages of alternative models for grouping activities at the various levels within an organization. It has also drawn attention to the problems that may arise with any particular model, and to the circumstances that are relevant to choosing between different models. This choice cannot, of course, be avoided in practice, and so this section ends the chapter by outlining a method which can assist in reaching decisions on the grouping of activities. As was the case with the suggested approach to deciding on spans of control, the present method can be used to draw on the detailed operational knowledge which members of an organization will possess. Although it is useful to keep in mind the broad choices I have mentioned as well as the factors that may suggest one of these as the most likely candidate to suit a given situation, it will still be necessary at some stage to work out a solution in detail.

The method I shall describe is intended to assist managers and others to arrive at this detailed solution. It draws upon my own industrial experience and has also been informed by other cases where a similar approach has been employed successfully. The method helps to bring relevant criteria into decisions on grouping activities, particularly effective information processing, economy of staffing and resource use, and control. Underlying the discussion in this chapter has been the theme that people should be grouped together in ways that accord with particularly intense information-sharing needs, while at the same time avoiding undue duplication of effort and creating units that are appropriate for purposes of control. The notion of intensity of information sharing contains several dimensions. Communications between different positions or sections may have to be frequent; they may involve the discussion of complex information requiring shared judgements on how to proceed; they may require the use of common equipment or facilities; or they may be necessary in order to maintain control over standards of work. It is quite feasible to approach the analysis of these requirements, and then to apply the results, in a systematic manner.

A judgement has first of all to be made about how well an existing structure is working. Some of the symptoms of malfunctioning listed in Chapter 1, as well as indications mentioned earlier in this chapter, may be present. Another sign that a regrouping of activities and people might be called for is when the actual informal pattern of interactions between members of an organization diverges sharply from what is formally implied or intended. Various techniques have been developed to plot informal relationships in an organization, such as Weinshall's 'informalagram' (1977), and network analysis can be applied to diagram clusters of such relationships. While the data involved are detailed, there are computer programs which can readily handle these and their use is likely to spread.

If a thorough re-analysis of an existing grouping of activities is thought to be required, then a first and basic step consists of collecting similar information to that suggested for work structuring analysis in Chapter 2. Work structuring is of course precisely concerned with the grouping of activities at the micro level of individual employees and their activities. The level of grouping considered here is broader, and its units of analysis are areas of activity that consist of whole tasks and the groups of staff carrying those out. With this level of analysis in mind, and the attention that is to be given to information processing requirements, it will be appropriate to begin by systematically plotting the various workflows in the organization, their constituent tasks, and the staff involved. The relationship of each activity area (task and staff) to the workflows can then be established giving attention to interdependencies, frequency of communication in the light of those interdependencies, common sources of information (files) to be accessed and updated, and decisions to be made. Most of these data can readily be summarized in flow charts, of the kind frequently used for purposes of systems analysis.

These data provide the basic information for forming judgements about the intensity of relationships required in the organization. The next stage consists of evaluating the links between the tasks which have been identified. One way of doing this is to draw up a list of the activity areas in which the tasks fall. These are then related to each other in the form of a matrix. Each pair of activity areas can now be assessed by reference to various criteria that govern their relationship. These include, first, the basic reasons why the activity areas should be linked. Broadly speaking, activities may have to be linked because they are interdependent in terms of stages in the workflow, in terms of depending on the same data source, equipment or personal skills, in terms of common physical location, and other reasons which correspond to the logic of task systems discussed earlier (see page 86). A second criterion is how close the relationship between activity areas needs to be, and a third criterion is what kind of communication is required. These criteria are themselves interdependent. The reasons for linking activity areas will determine their appropriate mode of communication and closeness. The closeness of relationship will depend on how frequently decisions need to be taken, which depends on the processing and passing of information between the functions, on complexity of the information and so forth.

Part of such a matrix is shown in Figure 4.5, which is based on a hypothetical small batch engineering company. This particular matrix is concerned with the links between certain marketing areas and engineering specifications, factory programming and stock control. The data incorporated are a categorization of the main reasons for a linkage between the areas, a simple scale of how close the relationship needs to be (including the possibility that no formal link at all is desirable), and a classification of what mode of communication should be the norm. On the whole, one would expect two closely related activity areas to communicate on a direct basis, face-to-face or by telephone, but there will be cases where documents are necessarily the mode of communication even in a frequently activated relationship. It is important to stress that the way the matrix is drawn, and the categories of information incorporated into it, depend on what best suits a particular organization.

Following this stage, a diagram can be drawn of the different activity areas, starting with those which it has been concluded should be most intensively

Figure 4.5 Part of a matrix of relationships between activities

ACTIVITY →	1 Market Research	2 Order Handling	3 Marketing Programming	4 Sales Installation	5 Engineering Specification	Etc.
2 Order Handling	3 / 3 / C					
3 Marketing Programming	4 / 3 / C & D	5 / 1 / B or C				
4 Sales Installation	3 / 3 / C	3 / 1, 2 & 3 / B or C	2 / 3 / C			
5 Engineering Specifications	1 / 3 / –	1 / 3 / –	1 / 3 / –	6 / 1 & 3 / A or B		
6 Factory Programming						
7 Stock Control						
Etc.						

(Within each box the three values are given as: Required Closeness / Reasons for Linkage / Type of communication)

Within each box:

Reasons for Linkage	
Required Closeness	Reasons for Linkage
Type of communication	

Required closeness key:
6. Absolutely necessary
5. Especially important
4. Important
3. Ordinary closeness
2. Unimportant
1. Not desirable

Reasons for linkage key:
1. Co-ordination required
2. Sharing of data
3. Transfer of data
4. Economy of effort
5. Use of same equipment
6. Effective control etc.

Type of communication key:
A Face-to-face
B Telephone
C Written
D Formal meetings etc.

related to each other. It may be appropriate to modify scores on closeness of relationship by including notes to identify instances where a close relationship should not be translated into a common grouping, perhaps for professional reasons or because an electronic data processing system can provide the link instead. The closely related activities which it is felt should work together can be linked together on the diagram. Other areas can then be progressively incorporated into the diagram. The gradation in desired intensity of relations between areas may be represented by colour coding or by drawing different thicknesses or sets of lines connecting the activities. Once this diagram is completed, it becomes feasible to delineate clusters of activities that fit together logically. These clusters can then form the basis for a grouping of activities. Part of such diagram, following on from the matrix in Figure 4.5, is shown in Figure 4.6. In a complex exercise involving a large number of relationships, it may be advantageous to use one of the cluster analysis computer programs now available.

An exercise of this kind can provide a useful aid for making decisions on the grouping of activities. It is based purely on the logic of task systems and as such is neutral to considerations that derive from traditional boundaries drawn between functions and the politics which attach to these. In the hypothetical example, a task analysis actually implies that certain 'marketing' activities should operationally be grouped together with 'production' programming and that a technical 'sales' function should go together with 'engineering' ones. Politics and professional differentiations are, however, part of the real organizational world. A purely task-based analysis of the kind described would have to be subject to thorough discussion, not only to test its apparent logic against the criterion of political acceptability, but also to provide an opportunity for identifying any relationships that have been wrongly evaluated.

It is important at every stage to take account of the personal element. The people who occupy jobs and who are in charge of activities can do a great

Figure 4.6 Clustering of related activities previously identified by means of the matrix of relationships

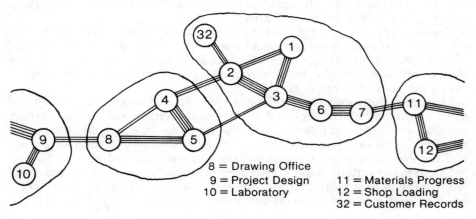

8 = Drawing Office
9 = Project Design
10 = Laboratory
11 = Materials Progress
12 = Shop Loading
32 = Customer Records

deal to condition the effectiveness of communication and working relationships. This factor is relevant to assessments of the potential for making structural changes. Opinion on the personal aspect of relationships as well as on task aspects can be secured through a process of extensive discussions among managers and staff. Indeed, in the absence of such consultation, people are unlikely to appreciate the arguments for structural changes, or feel committed to them. Personal and political considerations are always involved in the design of organization structure.

Some years ago, when a member of the Rolls-Royce Oil Engine Division, I helped carry out an organization design survey similar to that described. This identified a set of relationships between personnel who were concerned with different aspects of customer contact. Their effective co-ordination was being seriously reduced by their membership of separate sales, financial and engineering functions. Following many discussions with all the staff in these areas, they were subsequently regrouped for operational purposes into one marketing function concerned with the major product—diesel engines. This made for a significant improvement in information sharing, relations with customers and general effectiveness. The most important lesson to be drawn from this experience was not so much that the technique of task analysis was useful for assessing the appropriate grouping of activities (which it was) but that participation in the process by the people affected was vital for its successful implementation. For other changes in systems and structure were also planned at the same time by people who were technically more expert, but whose very expertise led them to dismiss the need for much prior discussion. In the event, their proposals generally met with serious resistance from departmental managers and most were not implemented.

The method put forward in this section can be summarized in terms of the following stages:

1 Plot out the workflows (main and supporting; flows of materials and information) in that part of the organization under consideration.

2 Identify the activities (i.e. 'tasks') that are contained in the workflows and note the staff involved. (The combination of an activity and the staff carrying it out will be called an 'activity area'.)

3 Establish the relation of each activity to the workflows, giving particular attention to the interdependencies between activities by way of sequential operations, sharing of information sources and files, common destination of their outputs and the like. Information on frequency of communication between the staff involved is noted.

4 List the activity areas on a relationship chart and relate each activity to every other activity by 'required closeness of relationship' rating. Stage 3 should have furnished information relevant to making judgements on the required closeness of relationships. Other relevant points such as reasons and the desirable form of communication can also be coded.

5 Diagram the activity areas, starting with those which stage 4 has indicated require the closest relationships (indicated by colour code or the thickest joining lines), and then progressively relating the others. When a long list of

activity areas is involved, it may be desirable to diagram out only those relationships requiring high to medium degrees of closeness.
6 From the diagram, develop clusters of activities that logically fit together. (If many relationships are involved, stages 5 and 6 might with benefit be handled by a computer.)
7 Review the clusters that have emerged and refine any apparently misrated relationships or those which are likely to be unacceptable for personal, political or social reasons. While I have stressed the value of involving the persons concerned at every point in the exercise, it will be particularly necessary at this stage to develop agreement on those activities and staff which should be grouped together.

Summary

The activities of people within an organization can be grouped together according to a number of different principles. A functional grouping comprises people employing a similar expertise. A grouping by process recognizes commonalities in plant and technology employed. A product grouping brings together people who are contributing to a common product or service. Other bases for organizationally grouping activities together are their sharing of a similar time horizon or their location on the same physical site.

These principles of specialization are useful in delineating the choices available to organizational designers. Considerations that enter into the choice between, say, a functional or a product structure, or a matrix form, centre very much upon contingencies such as the size of the organization, the diversity of its activities and the speed at which it must adapt to its environment. The two most common models for grouping activities are the functional and product division types. The virtues of low overhead and simplicity characterizing the functional model are balanced by the co-ordinative, motivational and adaptive advantages of the product model.

Mixed and multidimensional structural forms have been developed in an attempt to secure the advantages of both functional and product models. Matrix organization incorporates more than one dimension of authority and influence, with the range of specific arrangements providing different configurations of influence between functional, product or regional managers. The abandonment of unity of command, which is a feature of the matrix, can however heighten conflict and ambiguity of role, especially while the system is settling down.

When examining in detail ways in which activities are, or might be, grouped together, a systematic evaluation of required relationships is called for. The outline of a method for carrying out this evaluation was described in the chapter.

Suggested further reading

A good discussion of the issues covered in this chapter is provided by Jay R. Galbraith, *Organization Design* (Addison-Wesley 1977). Henry Mintzberg,

The Structuring of Organizations (Prentice-Hall 1979) has an interesting Chapter 7 on grouping of activities. Part I of John M. Stopford and Louis T. Wells, Jr. *Managing the Multinational Enterprise* (Longman 1972) analyses the development of organizational forms among multinational corporations with special reference to diversification. Lawrence G. Franko analyses European multinationals from a similar perspective in *The European Multinationals* (Harper and Row 1976). Other sources on groupings employed by major companies include Derek F. Channon, *The Strategy and Structure of British Enterprise* (Macmillan 1973); Derek F. Channon, *The Service Industries* (Macmillan 1978); Gareth P. Dyas and Heinz T. Thanheiser, *The Emerging European Enterprise* (Macmillan 1976); Richard P. Rumelt, *Strategy, Structure and Economic Performance* (Harvard Business School 1974).

Two good treatments of matrix organization are provided by Stanley M. Davis and Paul R. Lawrence, *Matrix* (Addison-Wesley 1977) and Kenneth Knight) (editor), *Matrix Management* (Gower Press 1977). Harvey F. Kolodny discusses the development of matrix organization through earlier functional, project and product/matrix stages in 'Evolution to a Matrix Organization', *Academy of Management Review*, vol. 4, 1979. E. Raymond Corey and Steven H. Star *Organization Strategy* (Harvard Business School 1971) contains a good description and analysis of how matrix organization was developed in the Lockheed-Georgia Company.

Other sources referred to in this chapter were Stephen A. Allen, 'Organizational Choices and General Management Influence Networks in Divisionalized Companies', *Academy of Management Journal*, September 1978; Tom Burns and G. M. Stalker, *The Management of Innovation* (Tavistock 1961); Lex Donaldson, 'Regaining Control at Nipont', *Journal of General Management*, Summer 1979; Jay Galbraith, *Designing Complex Organizations* (Addison-Wesley 1973); William C. Goggin, 'How the Multinational Structure Works at Dow Corning', *Harvard Business Review,* January–February 1974; Robert Townsend, *Up the Organization* (Michael Joseph 1970); Arthur H. Walker and Jay W. Lorsch, 'Organizational Choice: Product vs Function', *Harvard Business Review*, November–December 1968; Theodore D. Weinshall, 'Multinational Corporations' in Weinshall (editor), *Culture and Management* (Penguin 1977), Chapter 15.

CHAPTER 5

Integration

'If a house be divided against itself, that house cannot stand.'
Mark iii, 25.

Lack of co-ordination is one of the charges most frequently levelled against large organizations. 'The right hand doesn't know what the left hand is doing' is an often-heard reaction among clients and customers. There are indeed cases where the system virtually breaks down when subjected to any pressure or urgency. The result is delay, frustration and waste. One example, which was brought to light by a special report of the Carnegie Endowment, concerns the maladministration by two of the world's largest famine relief organizations of aid for 22 million people affected by the West African drought after 1968.

The American Agency for International Development (AID) and the United Nations Food and Agriculture Organization (FAO) are the two agencies in question. The aid donated by countries was generous in itself—up to October 1973 over twenty countries had provided £60 million. Yet sickness and malnutrition continued at an alarming level, considerably worse than that recorded at the time in Bangladesh, which was suffering a similar crisis. The Carnegie Endowment report identifies inadequate bureaucratic organization as the culprit, with several instances of poor integration. Warning telegrams from the drought-stricken area were not adequately collated or acted upon—instead they were tucked away in filing cabinets scattered around the world. Even when the rescue operation got under way, plans proved to be unco-ordinated. Grain piled up in Dakar, Senegal, because there was insufficient transport to move it inland. An observer said that the only plump animals he saw in the area were the rats of Dakar port. The report alleges that these failures were due in part to a lack of co-operation between different groups. It states that over the entire programme, in spite of the dedication of many officials at all levels, there was the shadow of bureaucratic factors in the US or UN which bore hardly any relation to the human suffering in Africa—programmes continued or initiatives neglected out of institutional inertia, rivalries between offices and agencies, and unwillingness to acknowledge failures to the public.

This may be an extreme case, but shades of the same problem affect most organizations. For example, in the mid-1970s an organization with different divisions operating on the same site discovered that one division had been making employees redundant while another had been recruiting similar

111

categories of labour from the market. This expensive and image-damaging process carried on despite the presence of a central personnel department! Why should managers experience such difficulty in co-ordinating and integrating the efforts of the groups and departments in their organizations?

This chapter considers why integration is a general problem in organizations. Some specific examples of integration problems are then provided. The following section considers integration in relation to performance and is in two parts. The first part lists some warning signs that integration is inadequate, while the second looks at evidence that effective integration can contribute to superior performance. The choice of different structural devices to promote integration is then discussed, together with the contribution which teambuilding may make.

Why is integration a problem?

Any organization has centrifugal tendencies, with individuals and departments straining to pursue their own paths. It is in fact something of a wonder that organizations hold together at all. Within a small primary group of up to about twelve persons, there can be considerable pressure from other members of that group for an individual to fit in with group norms or else run the risk of complete rejection. With larger organizational units this system of informal integration and control tends to break down, and rival groups can form. There is a natural tendency for a collectivity of some size to break down into smaller, often competing units. In an organization, this differentiation is usually formalized. People are grouped into separate departments and those departments are allocated different tasks. One department is charged with producing the goods and services, another with selling and distributing them, and so on. This process of internal specialization develops hand in hand with growth in the overall size of the total organization— various research studies have found a high and remarkably consistent correlation between the size of organizations and their degree of internal specialization.

When an organization becomes larger and more differentiated, communication links become more tenuous. The natural tendency is to communicate with others within the same department who share common problems and experiences. These common problems and experiences reinforce people's identity with their own specialized department, at the expense of integrating with other departments in pursuit of an overriding objective. A paradox in grouping activities at different levels of aggregation in organizations is that the more homogeneity and sense of common identity grouping creates *within* departments, the more difficult it may consequently be to achieve integration *between* departments.

The difficulty of preserving awareness of an overriding organizational objective is increased because departments undertake work of quite different kinds requiring different methods; they operate to different time horizons and at a different pace. They have their own objectives to follow, which can conflict with those of other departments when it comes to the practical level of everyday operations. The vigorous pursuit of sectional objectives is likely to be encouraged if staff are rewarded and their career prospects enhanced for achieving these. This sectional behaviour can readily develop because it is often easier to assess individual performance in terms of limited local objectives. Industrial managers are familiar with conflicting requirements such as maintaining high quality and maximizing production at a low cost: mixing orders for different models so as to maximize incoming sales revenue and minimizing costs through preserving economic batch sizes, or the need to avoid stockouts while keeping capital tied up in inventory to the lowest possible level. In organizations where it is necessary to develop a steady stream of new services or products, it can be difficult to maintain agreement between research departments and other departments over the money to be invested in development, the control of its expenditure and deadlines to be met.

Problems of integration generated by the allocation of different objectives and targets to departments are reinforced by differences in outlook and semantics among personnel themselves. Specialist personnel, qualified in different areas of expertise, are recruited to run the various departments. These people will usually have developed an identification with the norms and criteria of their occupational specialism and they may well have pursued a career in that specialism by moving between several organizations. So a personnel officer may regard himself as much a 'personnel man' as a member of Organization X; so might an accountant, a scientist or other specialist. This identification with a particular occupational role will often be sustained by the fact that specialists have to have contact with others in the same special field outside the organization, and indeed many will belong to their own professional associations. A strong identity with their particular field makes it more difficult to integrate one type of specialist with other types. Integration between specialists and line managers is also likely to be a problem. Here the different bases of authority (predominantly hierarchical position among line managers and expertise among specialists), time scales, values, and ways of working can generate mutual incomprehension, which readily leads to animosity and conflict. I found in my own studies of over 80 British business companies that the attitudes of even quite senior managers differed sharply according to the functional area in which they were working. It also became apparent from this research that the more departments an organization consisted of, the more difficult it was for those managers to reach agreement on how to handle problems that came up for decision.

These contrasts between the various parts of an organization, deriving from differences in their targets, ways of working, contacts outside the organization, training and so on, can easily become crystallized in the form of stereotypes. How often the sales department of an industrial firm is caustically referred to as the 'gin and tonic brigade', a comment deriving to a degree from the life-style salesmen have to pursue as part of their job. Equally, production personnel have been called unhelpful reactionaries more than once, perhaps when opposing a marketing request which threatens their schedules and would raise production costs. Other departments (not least the accountants) come in for their share of abuse too. These apparently harmless labels can signify a quite deep-seated antipathy between different parts of an organization based upon considerable misunderstanding of other groups' objectives, methods of work, and problems. Where such stereotypes are entrenched they have to be dispelled before an adequate level of integration can be achieved. The requirement, then, in the words of one thoughtful supervisor is that 'activities should be divided, not people.'

Centrifugal 'strains toward functional autonomy', as one writer has called them can be regulated without very much difficulty if an organization is carrying out its work under fairly stable conditions without too many unplanned developments forcing it to come to rapid decisions and make frequent adaptations. In such circumstances, different departments can be integrated by following certain standard procedures or plans laid down by top management or by mutual agreement. The necessary exchange of information and views between departments can be effected through the programming of regular meetings. Any differences of opinion can be resolved by referring them up the hierarchy to the point where both parties share a superior in common—right up to the chief executive if necessary.

The resolution of conflict and integration of specialist contributions through this kind of system is economical of staff but it clearly takes time. Time becomes a particularly scarce resource when there are pressures on the organization to act quickly. A firm may be under severe pressure from its competitors; a local authority may face a public impatient to hear the results of its planning decisions; a relief agency will be placed under strain by a natural disaster. If the problem in question is a complex one, perhaps involving many technical, legal or environmental issues, then the difficulties of bringing together all the necessary specialist evaluations in a limited period of time become even more acute.

Increases in the complexity of problems and in the rate of change faced by most organizations have been placing more of a premium upon their achieving integration across departments and other constituent units. Increasingly complex environments, plus the growing technical sophistication of products and services, and of the ways in which they are produced, have made it more and more difficult to assign to a single department all the activities requiring co-ordination. Ways must be found to integrate the contributions of several departments. The greater rate of change and the pressures from external competition in business, and the demands for a faster response to social need in the case of public service organizations, also means that information has to be processed more rapidly. In addition, business profits and the budgets of public sector organizations have come under pressure, so reducing the margin which is available to delay a decision or to risk making the wrong decision because of inadequate information. The more that complexity means an organization's work must pass through several departments, the more that information processing demands increase. The less tolerance there is for sub-optimal performance, the greater will be the necessity for managements to secure an intense degree of integration between different parts of the organization.

Some common integration problems

One of the most common problems of integration appears in the relationship between functions such as sales (or client contact) and purchasing, which have to accommodate themselves to the world outside the organization, and functions such as production or engineering, which are responsible for producing goods or services according to factors (such as plant facilities or available product designs) that are in some degree established. This is the problem of integrating the 'peripheries' of an organization with its 'core', and without this integration an organization will not remain viable.

One example of a problem concerning integration between sales and production has been related by A. J. M. Sykes and J. Bates (1962). They studied a British company with six sales departments and 18 different plants. There was constant conflict between the production side, which wanted to limit the range of products in order to increase the volume of output for each one and reduce unit costs, and the sales departments, which attempted to force production to comply with the customer's exact specifications regardless of the case for standardization. Conflict also arose between the different departments on the sales side, because each department tried to secure the earliest possible delivery date for its customers disregarding the system of priorities that the company had laid down. These priorities were intended to give preference to certain types of order, e.g. export, and to certain large and important customers. The sales clerks had been recruited from production and they were able to organize preferential treatment for their 'own' customers through informal deals with the production clerks.

The company overcame these difficulties by setting up a Sales Organization Liaison Department (SOLD) between sales and production. This is shown in Figure 5.1. SOLD's main functions were to secure information on production capacity and sales requirements, to co-ordinate these in terms of delivery schedules for customers, to act as a liaison between sales and production by keeping each informed of the others' requirements, to formulate a comprehensive pricing policy, and to maintain statistics, producing reports for the Chairman and Board. Detailed instructions were drawn up for how SOLD was to operate. It was, for example, required to allocate orders to plants having the capacity to deal with them and which were convenient for customer delivery; it was to give delivery dates to sales departments in accordance with the company's system of priorities, and to progress orders.

In this example, integration was significantly improved by the establishment of a new co-ordinating department and by setting up new procedures. George Strauss (1962) relates another case, from the United States. It concerns problems of integration between purchasing staff and other departments inside the organization, including engineering and production. The buyers' basic responsibilities were:

1 To negotiate and place orders for materials with outside suppliers on the

Figure 5.1 An example of integration between sales and promotion departments (*From:* Sykes, A. J. M. and Bates, J. (1962) 'Study of conflict between formal company policy and the interests of informal groups'. *Sociological Review*, November, pp. 313–327)

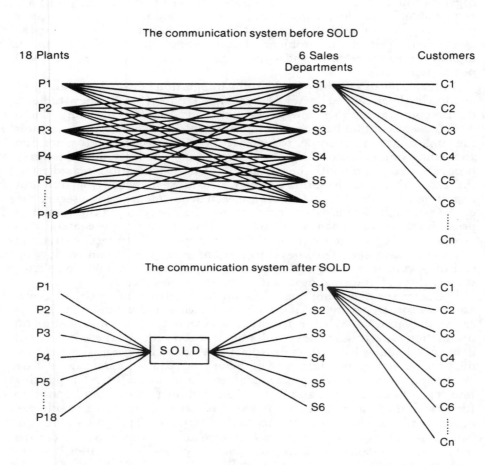

The communication system before SOLD

18 Plants   6 Sales   Customers
                   Departments

The communication system after SOLD

best possible terms but only in accordance with specifications set by others; and

2 To expedite orders; that is, to check with suppliers to make sure that deliveries are made on time.

Conflicts with engineering arose because engineers preferred to specify exactly what they wanted without leaving any discretion to the buyer; also because by training and functional responsibility they looked first for quality and reliability, while buyers were required to take low cost and quick delivery into account as well. Conflicts with production scheduling arose because schedulers, themselves under pressure from sales, would often seek extremely short delivery times or require materials in uneconomic order sizes.

In an attempt to ease these problems in dealing with other departments, the buyers had adopted various devices; some mainly to protect themselves, others in a more constructive attempt to improve integration. Among the latter were the use of direct contact to persuade other departments to take purchasing criteria into account, and an attempt to modify the workflow pattern in order to stabilize the situation. For example, some buyers got the production schedulers to check with the purchasing department about the possibilities of getting quick delivery, before they made out a requisition.

Other areas in which problems of integration commonly occur are: (1) the securing and evaluation of information from outside the organization for planning purposes, especially in a divisional organization; (2) the promotion of innovation and the integration of the specialists concerned into the mainstream of the organization; (3) the creation of effective production management teams; and (4) the co-ordination of complementary services offered by members of different professions. These four areas will be considered briefly, because they help to illustrate the dimensions of the problem as well as some of the solutions which have been tried.

1 Scanning and planning

Aguilar (1967), in his studies of how companies scanned their environments, found one multidivisional firm where integration was seriously deficient. In this firm there was a headquarters group planning function, which saw its role as gathering information that would assist the company in finding completely new areas of business into which to diversify. Each division also had a planning department, securing and evaluating information from outside that could indicate desirable modifications to existing products. These two levels of scanning and planning activity were unco-ordinated with the result that no effort was being put into possibly the most fruitful area for expansion, namely the development of new products within the company's present area of business. Planners at each level, group and division, assumed that the other was covering this gap.

Many organizations are in fact feeling their way towards more effective means of integrating the various activities that feed into the planning of corporate strategy. There is some debate about whether the formulation of strategies should remain a purely general or line management function, or whether it should use the expertise of specialist staff such as corporate planners and marketing specialists. The arguments for involving specialists are several: (a) unless a good part of the groundwork in strategy planning is given over to specialists it may end up by not being done at all, due to the operation of a variant of Gresham's Law ('everyday routine drives out forward planning'); (b) through establishing a specialized planning group, relevant expertise can be utilized and this may lend a certain objectivity to an area of decision-making where line managers tend to argue from their limited departmental or divisional viewpoints; and (c) a specialist corporate planning group can be a means of providing synergy (constructive integration) between the forward plans of the sub-units in a complex diversified organization.

However, one of the biggest problems in using specialists is that it is not easy to ensure that a specialist planning group remains effectively integrated with line management. One difficulty is that when an activity such as planning is delegated, top management may regard it as less valuable. It is easy to question the legitimacy of a staff group for its supposed 'lack of realism' and 'academic' attitudes. This is particularly likely when the group submits proposals for change that are seen to threaten established ways of working or the political balance within the organization.

2 Innovation and change

In the field of developing new products and services, a great deal of attention has been given to the problem of integrating scientists and other research specialists. There are two aspects to this problem: first, the integration of the specialists themselves into effective work teams, and second, their integration with the main-line activities of the organization.

A solution favoured by many managements is to draw together all the staff contributing to a new project into a project team. This is set up for the life of the project to see it through. In order to meet both the integration problems just mentioned, it is important to include as members of the project team not only appropriate technical staff but also representatives of the marketing or customer contact function, people from costing, and from production engineering or its equivalent. Studies of innovation indicate that one of the reasons for commercial failure in new products is a lack of understanding of customer needs, pointing to a serious absence of integration between research and marketing personnel.

A paradox in the organization of innovation derives from the need for the innovators to form a self-contained group of their own with considerable autonomy, and the requirement that this very same group must not be cut off politically and in terms of shared understanding from the main sections of the organization upon which the refinement, production and launching of the innovation depends. The autonomy helps provide the group with an identity and freedom from interference that should motivate creative processes; yet at the same time a bridge must be maintained to the rest of the organization.

When a project team organization is used to try and achieve these requirements, it is commonly managed on the following lines. The team accepts targets agreed with management for accomplishing the various stages of the new development and it is normally subject to budgetary constraints. It is usually left to decide on its own pattern of working. If the project team is acting solely as a co-ordinating mechanism, then it is allowed to decide how to integrate the work going on within the specialized functions it represents. Membership of the team may vary according to the stage of development that has been reached, although it is generally considered important for certain key personnel to remain team members for the total development process. In an industrial development, for instance, one would expect to find research and marketing personnel, at least, involved from start to finish.

This method of integration comes close to the 'organic' system of management (Burns and Stalker 1961). A similar approach is often employed in creative service activities such as advertising, university teaching and the social services. The use of project teams may be a stage on the road to the matrix structure discussed in the previous chapter, and indeed a matrix would represent the permanent application of the project principle if one may loosely describe activity focused on the special needs of products or geographical areas as being of a 'project' nature.

Other specialist groups can be involved in the attempt to foster innovations and changes, as well as research scientists. Examples are operational researchers and systems analysts, organizational development specialists, and internal consultancy groups. These specialists often experience considerable insecurity because, far more than is usually true of research scientists, the employing organization is capable of continuing to operate without them. They may well face criticism from line management that they simply represent an additional overhead cost. As a result, members of these specialist groups often experience self-doubt and behave in a manner that makes co-operation with central established departments all the more difficult. Maladaptive responses to their uncertainty on the part of specialist groups include turning inward and withdrawing from the pressures experienced as coming from other parts of the organization; and an inflexibility in the plans presented to line management, including a refusal to accept criticism. Given that established departments will be predisposed to regard any proposed changes that affect them with reserve if not hostility, this kind of behaviour by specialists can readily lead to a complete rupture in their integration with the organization as a whole.

An adaptive approach to managing this kind of situation breaks down into two aspects: (a) the internal management of the specialist team so that its portfolio of projects, its staffing and its awareness of present and future client needs are adequate; and (b) the management of the team's external links with its client departments in the organization, so that the language it uses and the relationships it develops are those that will enable it to make an effective contribution. The two planks upon which the integration of specialist groups to client departments can be built are mechanisms to link them into decision-making and the securing of senior management backing for their activities, which gives them organizational legitimation. Linking mechanisms are discussed later in this chapter. The value of political sponsorship for specialist innovative activities is indicated by the research of the Science Policy Research Unit at the University of Sussex into successful industrial product innovation, which found that support from a powerful senior manager was one of the main predictors of a project's completion and successful commercialization (Freeman et al. 1972).

3 Production management teams

The backbone of the traditional line and staff relationship is to be found in the area of an organization's core operations—the production area in a manufacturing firm. Here the integration problem is not that of bringing together specialist and other departments to deal with a specific issue or project. It is, rather, a problem of making available to production a range of services on a reliable basis. These services are in nature technological (such as industrial engineering, production engineering and quality control); financial (budgetary control, cost reduction and management control information); personnel (such as recruitment and training) and planning (production control). In a large and complex multi-product, multi-line facility, the integration of these services to production management is a formidable task. In Britain, a common criticism of manufacturing industry is that it has failed to achieve this task adequately both at senior and junior levels of production management.

One attempt to achieve more adequate integration in this area was made by a British confectionery manufacturer. The concept employed was that of a factory director's team, which was progressively extended to lower levels in the production hierarchy. Previously, production, quality control, industrial engineering, maintenance, management accounting, industrial relations, employment and other activities had been organized in a strictly functional manner. This was not conducive to an effective working relationship between production and the service-providing functions. For example, departmental production managers found that the information on costs and variances being provided by management accountants was not presented in a format suited to their needs but in a manner dictated by conventions emanating from the Financial Director's office.

This structure has now been replaced by the creation of a 'Factory Director's Team' consisting of the factory director and his immediate production subordinates, the senior management accountant, the manager in charge of production services (primarily factory and employment services), the industrial relations and quality control managers. At the next level down in the production hierarchy, senior production managers are in turn supported by their own teams consisting of management accountants, production services and quality control specialists. The management accounting function has been broadened into a 'financial performance' function oriented to assisting in performance improvement as well as financial control.

This method of integrating production and ancillary services improved the quality of information available to production and raised standards of production performance. Over a period of years it has greatly facilitated the planning and introduction of new plant in which, through the use of microelectronic technology, production scheduling, quality, cost and maintenance aspects are combined into an integrated information and control system. This development also meant a considerable reduction in numbers employed and, in handling this, personnel staff have been able to proceed in close step with the planning of production developments. There is always room for debate about which functions should be integrated with production in the formal reporting sense. In the example described, quality control and personnel have not been placed under direct production authority. In the case of quality control this is to preserve an independent view on quality standards, which are particularly critical in a food company;

in the case of personnel it is to preserve what are seen to be economies of scale and functional rationalization, given that the personnel function also services all the office areas on the site including several divisional and head office departments. Another feature worth noting in this case is that in addition to lateral integration through the creation of production management teams, vertical integration has been fostered by the overlapping hierarchical membership of those teams. Following the principle of 'linking-pins' first advocated by Rensis Likert (1961), production managers are members of their hierarchical superior's team.

At the junior level of production, first-line supervision often faces problems of integration. One frequently finds in industry that the members of several specialist departments contribute to the organization or manning of production on the shop floor. Departments such as production planning, stock control and quality control impinge directly on the organization of production, while others such as work study, industrial relations and the employment office have an indirect effect.

In studies of first-line supervision that we have conducted at Aston University (Child and Partridge 1982) there were many instances where production foremen experienced conflicting requirements from different departments within management and where they were uncertain of their authority in relation to such departments. Given this uncertainty, the supervisor is not in a sufficiently authoritative position to act as an effective integrator of specialist activities. One approach to this problem could be the creation of supervisory 'teams' to reflect the more senior production teams which have been described. These teams would perhaps only meet periodically, and they would have to be led by supervisors of sufficient calibre. Such an arrangement might help to create conditions in which specialists are co-ordinated by the supervisor, rather than bypassing him and failing to integrate with each other. This kind of problem seems to be less severe in most areas of office supervision, but where it arises a similar approach could be worth considering.

4 Integration of professional services

One field where poor integration has had tragic consequences is the social services in Britain. There have been several cases in recent years of children's deaths that might have been avoided had there been closer working relationships between specialist groups into whose areas of responsibility the cases fell. The Seebohm Report on the development of the social services in England and Wales published in 1968 in fact specifically called for the improved integration of specialist contributions through a move away from existing divisions between health, children, welfare, psychiatric and other fields and towards the creation of a 'generic' approach. Too often it had been the case that, say, a problem of family breakdown had been treated separately by different professional specialists, at the expense of co-ordination between them and to the bewilderment of the clients. Following the Seebohm Report, social services departments tackled this problem in several ways—normally either by creating generic social work teams in which specialists work together, or by giving individual social workers sole responsibility for cases.

Health care is another area of service provision where the integration of different professional contributions is a continuing challenge. In most countries, health care is provided by various professions and disciplines that are organized in discrete specialist hierarchies along functional lines. In the British National Health Service, laterally-related teams and working groups have been used for many years in an attempt to co-ordinate across these specialist boundaries. For example, the use of teams has been considered necessary to integrate contributions stemming from the expertise and distinctive perspectives of medicine, nursing, administration and finance at the local district level of health service administration. There are also numerous teams of actual providers of health care and closely related services, such as doctors, nurses, social workers and psychologists. One difficulty for the working of such grass-roots teams which has had to be faced is the individual responsibility that doctors carry for the patients under their care, which contrasts with the expectations of collective responsibility that other team members will tend to develop.

Many of the integration problems that have been discussed in this chapter arose from deficiencies in lateral relationships across the organization between groups or departments located at about the same hierarchical level. Sometimes the problem also reflected poor vertical integration, as in the example of a gap between HQ and divisions in scanning and planning. In describing these problems, I mentioned some possible improvements including direct contact between the members of different departments, the establishment of liaison units and the formation of cross-functional teams. I shall return to integration mechanisms shortly, particularly those intended to improve horizontal co-ordination, though the vertical aspect is also involved since one option is to co-ordinate through a higher level of management to which the departments report jointly. (This option is, of course, not available in a field such as health care where the main professional hierarchies remain separated right up to the very top.)

However, before proceeding further, it is appropriate to consider how the need for integration relates to the performance of organizations. First, there are ways in which inefficiencies in the functioning of an organization may warn of inadequate integration and, second, there is some evidence from research to indicate that adequate integration is associated with superior performance of the organization as a whole.

Integration and performance

1 Warnings of inadequate integration

Derek Pugh has usefully summarized some of these warning signs in a short article on 'Effective Coordination in Organizations' (1979). Common warning signs are as follows.

1. Persistent conflict between departments   The important point here is to recognize when the same matters of dispute keep on recurring. In that situation conflict has become embedded and amounts to much more than the occasional friction which is to be expected on a variety of issues as these arise. Pugh suggests that persistent embedded conflict indicates a basic failure in integration, and that it can best be recognized when other departments which are involved start accepting it as normal. This is the point of danger at which a threat to performance arising from a persistent integration problem has come to be taken for granted.

2. Fudging integration issues through a proliferation of committees   Committees are themselves important integrative mechanisms that have the advantage of representing various interests and hence of preserving a balance of view and power between departments. However, committees and working parties can end up by fudging inter-departmental disputes and may delay their resolution. They are easy to set up and can readily proliferate into a hierarchy of committees. They only meet periodically and their very balance of interests, coupled with established committee procedure, can give rise to procrastination and inadequate compromises. The spread of committees is therefore paradoxically a sign that adequate integration is probably not being achieved through more appropriate means.

3. Overloading of top management   One mode of integration is to refer matters requiring co-ordination between departments up to the chief executive. This clearly places an additional burden upon him that will conflict with the time requirements of matters that also have to be attended to and that only he can adequately deal with—in particular major policy issues and relationships with important parties outside the organization. Top management overload may therefore be another sign of inadequate integration. In its extreme form it may lead to chief executives and senior managers deliberately avoiding contact with departmental heads seeking to see them with co-ordination problems.

4. The ritual of 'red tape'   The use of procedures set out on paper, and perhaps monitored by reports on paper, is another way in which management may attempt to ensure that integration takes place. The procedures can, for example, specify that consultation should take place between two departments on certain matters. A warning sign is when managers and other members of an organization cease to follow the procedures or cease to take paper reporting seriously, and these simply become rituals. This does not mean that the red tape should then be enforced; probably the contrary since it may well signal that the procedures are inappropriate and that this is perhaps an unsuitable way to secure integration in the situation concerned.

5. Empire-building by co-ordinators   Later on in this chapter (page 131), I mention the need to support the co-ordinator's position so that he can exercise sufficient influence over the departments he is supposed to co-ordinate.

This may mean providing him with support staff. Pugh suggests that this development of co-ordination roles may go too far, so that co-ordinators start to oppose attempts at simpler forms of direct integration which appear to bypass them. If co-ordinators attempt to monopolize co-ordination and block more innovative solutions to integration problems, then the writing is clearly on the wall.

6. Complaints by clients, customers and other external parties   A sure sign of inadequate integration is when people who have dealings with the organization from outside complain that they are told one thing by one department and are then given conflicting information by another department; or when they have to contact a succession of people from different departments over a single issue; or when staff in one department profess ignorance and even indifference as to who elsewhere in the organization may be of assistance. These are actually very common failings that clearly detract from the quality of service an organization is providing and that may, in a commercial context, lead to the loss of valuable business.

In the light of warning signs such as these it may be suspected that there are integration problems within an organization. A simple exercise which can usefully help to pinpoint the areas of difficulty is then to request the managers and/or members of the various units to complete a form of the kind shown in Figure 5.2. This particular design was originally developed for use in an investigation of airlines, and the Figure gives an example of a completed form in which a respondent has scored the relationships shown. In his perception, integration between Flight Operations and In-Flight Services is posing serious problems. The form, however, can be adapted to suit any type of organization. Replies on the form help to indicate where poor co-operation is perceived to exist, whether the perceptions are shared by the units in question, and whether there is a large measure of agreement across the organization on the location of problematic horizontal working relations. As with other systematic ways of seeking opinion from within the organization, this method should provide a basis for discussion of possible improvements. Respondents can also be asked to provide examples of the performance failings they see arising from the lack of effective integration. For all the warning signs that have been mentioned signal a deterioration in performance.

2 Integration and performance

This section describes an important research study that has produced systematic evidence on the link between effective integration and performance.

In a study of ten American companies Lawrence and Lorsch (1967) found that the most successful firms had adapted their internal structures to suit the demands for information processing imposed by the kinds of environments in which they were operating. Six of the companies were in plastics manufacturing, an industry characterized by considerable market and

Figure 5.2 Example of a method to assess perceptions of integration within an organization

We would like to know about relationships between different parts of the organization. Listed below are 8 descriptive statements; each of these might be thought of as describing the general state of the relationship between various units.

Would you please select the statement which you feel is most descriptive of relationships between each of the units, even if you are not directly involved in them.

Scoring of relationships

Relations between these two units are:

1. Sound – full unity of effort is achieved
2. Almost full unity
3. Somewhat better than average relations
4. Average – sound enough to get by even though there are many problems of achieving joint efforts
5. Somewhat of a breakdown in relations
6. Almost complete breakdown in relations
7. Couldn't be worse – bad relations – serious problems exist which are not being solved
8. Relations are not required.

*In-flight Services Scheduling is part of Marketing while pilot scheduling is part of Flight Operations thus creating frequent conflicts between two groups.

Matrix of relations between operating units

	SALES	AIRPORT SERVICES	IN-FLIGHT SERVICES	SCHEDULING ADJUSTMENTS	OPERATIONAL CONTROL	FLIGHT OPERATIONS	MAINTENANCE	RELATIONS BETWEEN REGIONAL DIVISIONS
SALES								
AIRPORT SERVICES	3							
IN-FLIGHT SERVICES	4	3						
SCHEDULING ADJUSTMENTS	3	4	2					
OPERATIONAL CONTROL	3	2	2	1				
FLIGHT OPERATIONS	3	3	6*	1	1			
MAINTENANCE	8	2	4	2	1	2		
REGIONAL DIVISIONS/OFFICES	2	2	3	2	1	3	2	1

technological change, and by much uncertainty about future developments. In this kind of environment it was necessary for research departments to work to long time horizons and to operate in a way that allowed adaptation to new developments. Marketing departments had to work against shorter time horizons than did research, but still faced somewhat more uncertainty than the production function. In the more stable industries studied, containers and food manufacturing, the required degree of difference between functional departments in their patterns of operation was less.

The more that the outlook and behaviour of managers in separate departments had to differ, the more difficult it was for them to achieve integrated effort. A condition for good performance was found to lie in the achievement of an adequate level of integration, and it was more difficult to reach this in a highly differentiated organization. In the successful companies, this tension between a requisite degree of differentiation and a requisite degree of integration was managed through effective mechanisms and procedures for resolving conflicts between departments. While in all the successful companies these procedures tended to involve the open confrontation and working through of differences, the type of mechanisms used and the location of points of integration within the organization varied according to the contingencies faced by the firms in different industries.

In the high performing plastics organizations, with a large degree of internal differentiation, the combination of integrative mechanisms included a special co-ordinating department, plus permanent integrating teams each made up of members from the various functional units and from the co-ordinating department. Direct contact between managers at all levels was heavily relied on. In a high performing food organization that was less internally differentiated, simpler formal integrative devices were employed. Managers within functional departments were given co-ordinative or liaison roles. If a special issue arose that presented a more urgent need for collaboration, temporary teams would be set up, comprised of specialists from the various units involved. Direct contact between managers was also heavily relied on. Finally, in a high performing standardized container manufacturer with a relatively low level of internal differentiation, integration was achieved primarily through the managerial hierarchy. There was some reliance on direct contact between functional managers and also on paperwork systems, which helped to resolve more routine scheduling requirements.

The conclusion that an achievement of effective integration can contribute substantially to high organizational performance is supported by the work of some other researchers, though I should add that much of this work is very preliminary in nature. For instance, a study of British building and printing firms carried out by Philip Sadler and colleagues (1974) concluded that the level of integration secured by management is at least as important a factor in designing organizations as is the maintenance of control. Historically, managements appear to have concentrated more effort on attempts to achieve tight control, and relatively little attention has been given to integration. This is reflected in the conventional organization chart, which normally just illustrates the authority channels through which control is achieved. In the research mentioned, integration appeared particularly important in the printing firms where a low degree of integration between departments was associated both with poor profitability and low job satisfaction among managers.

The choice of integrative mechanism

In deciding on methods to achieve better integration between parts of an organization a choice has to be made with regard to (a) the degree of integration required, (b) the difficulties of achieving this that are inherent in the situation, and (c) the costs of alternative integrating mechanisms. There is, on the whole, an inverse relationship between the sophistication of an integrative device and its overhead cost to the organization. Some of the alternatives are now examined.

James Thompson in his seminal book *Organizations in Action* (1967) identified three main categories of integrative mechanisms, into which fall the examples mentioned so far. The first category is integration through standardization. This involves establishing rules or procedures that channel the actions of each job-holder or department into a direction consistent with the actions of others. Secondly, plans and schedules can be established to integrate the actions of separate units. Integration through planning is somewhat more flexible than standardization in that plans can usually be modified fairly quickly. Thirdly, there is what Thompson called integration through 'mutual adjustment'. This refers to integration through the transmission of information directly between people and the mutual adjustment of their actions in the light of that information. A wide range of integrative mechanisms would fall into this category, including those aimed at increasing direct co-ordination laterally across the vertical divisions of an organization structure.

The traditional bureaucratic approach, which is still normal in most of our large organizations, generally relies heavily on integration through standardization and through planning. An elaborate system of rules and procedures is worked out, improved and gradually extended. These procedures can be designed to formalize what experience has shown to be the best practice in handling a set of recurrent problems. By formulating a body of procedure and operating plans the contributions of separate departments can be clearly specified and so integrated into the task as a whole. If exceptions occur, and these are really seen to be aberrations from a routine, then they can be referred up the hierarchy to a point where the various departments concerned share a common boss. Integration, in other words, is also maintained by hierarchical referral when something out of the ordinary crops up. If matters of procedure and operating policy require some discussion from time to time, a third bureaucratic mechanism for integration can be activated, namely the committee meeting. Although committee meetings fall into the category of mutual adjustment, they are usually highly formal and pre-arranged. In stable conditions, a programme of such meetings is often arranged for twelve months ahead.

There are several merits to this system of integration, which can operate quite adequately when conditions are stable and predictable. Many people like to know where they stand, and bureaucratic integration is based on a system of clearly defined roles and procedures that are there for all to see. It is also a relatively cheap approach to integration, once its procedures and systems have been well tried and tested. It does not call for any overhead of special coordinating staff, nor does it necessarily require a great deal of manpower to be locked up in 'endless meetings'. Nevertheless, once an organization moves into less stable conditions and the burden of processing information increases, the traditional bureaucratic approach to integration begins to creak at its joints.

This has been the experience of a major company. During the last ten years or so, it had experienced a decline in the market share of its main products, generally keener competition, a falling rate of profit, more volatile commodity markets and a distinct worsening in its climate of employee relations. Its British operations had in the late 1970s been subject to government-imposed price restraint. The company had therefore been subject to increasing external change and competitive pressure. In order to cope it adopted policies of expanding product lines and contracting inventory levels, which require much more processing and exchange of information between departments, to improve scheduling, avoid stockouts and so forth.

In adjusting to this greater information processing load, the company worked on a number of fronts. It reorganized many of its production facilities around product groups and established teams of specialists to work closely within new 'divisions' with the division manager. While this means a duplication of certain resources, at the same time it integrates staff more effectively around the production of particular classes of products. In addition various investigations have been under way with a view to improving systems of information handling. These involve using more planning and clerical staff and also extending computerization.

The improving of information processing systems, often through a better definition of required inputs and the use of electronic information technology, can assist in solving the problem of inadequate integration between the different levels of an organization. As well as providing improved feedback of information to operating units, it can provide managers at a higher level with a better picture of what is going on over a range of units. This may help them to balance and integrate these units as a whole.

Other devices are available for improving the quality of lateral integration between groups and departments at approximately the same level. In the absence of any formal provision for lateral integration, informal contact will often arise. People often say that 'If we had to go through the official channels, we would never get anything done on time'. The problem is that one cannot necessarily rely on effective informal arrangements emerging, and those that do, as in the case of the SOLD company with its sales-production liaison problems (see page 115), may not reflect the policy priorities set down for the organization as a whole. In any case, formal integrative arrangements can be designed in a way that facilitates rather than prevents the development of informal relations.

Jay Galbraith (1977) discusses each of these integrative mechanisms in detail. He identifies four alternatives to the bureaucratic approach. First, the organization can increase its resources of manpower or accept lower standards of decision-making efficiency—this is clearly a path leading to low performance. Second, the organization can be divided up so as to group people around the clusters of most intensive communication need—this is the divisionalization approach and will tend to incur additional costs of resource duplication. Third, the organization can improve its vertical information systems to relieve the load on the hierarchy. Improvement of vertical information systems in the past normally required additional investment in clerical staff and computer time. However, the advent of microelectronic-based systems has considerably enhanced the cost-effectiveness of this option through the combination of speed, accuracy, ease of operation and falling real cost of hardware. Chapter 9 discusses these systems. Finally, the organization can attempt another way of increasing its capacity to process information. This is by developing lateral relationships at appropriate points down the hierarchy, along with a complementary delegation of discretion to the people concerned. As we see shortly, although the creation of lateral relationships can also involve overhead costs Galbraith believes that they offer the greatest potential for improving integration.

The following passage, taken from an internal consultative document issued in 1973 by a British company, illustrates the way in which managements have come to appreciate the value in moving beyond traditional formal hierarchical structures by incorporating lateral integrative mechanisms:

> In organization terms we appear to have learned a healthy disrespect for formal structures and relationships and functional boundaries. In a number of areas task-oriented arrangements have been developed which transcend the traditional structures in the interests of overall effectiveness. In an organization of our size and complexity we need a formal structure and clear definition of accountability, but it is a promising sign that we appear to be capable of adapting and evolving appropriate structures to meet changing requirements. Examples of developments in this area include the increasing use of the project team approach (notably in the new product development and engineering areas) and the evolution of our whole long range planning process. Elsewhere there has been an acceptance of the viability of matrix structure (working for more than one boss), and the need for more emphasis on team building, with an acceptance of team objectives.

The various forms of integration through lateral relationships are listed below in order of increasing sophistication, difficulty in design and overhead cost. By and large, the heavier the information processing load, deriving from pressures and complexity in the tasks to be done, the further down the list will be a management have to go to secure an adequate level of integration. In practice, as managements move down the list they generally adopt the more sophisticated integration mechanisms as additions to rather than simply substitutes for those higher up the list:

1 Bring about direct contact between managers or employees who share a problem.
2 If departments are required to have a substantial amount of contact, one

or more of their staff can be given special responsibility to act as a liaison officer with counterparts in other departments.

3 If a development or problem arises that calls for the contribution of several departments until its completion or solution, then it would probably be appropriate to set up a temporary task force to deal with it, with members drawn from those departments.

4 If such inter-departmental problems constantly recur, then permanently established groups or teams provide a method of integration.

5 If the management of lateral relationships becomes a problem, perhaps because of their complexity, then a special integrating role can be set up— that of a 'co-ordinator' or similar title. It may be necessary to endow the co-ordinator with a department of staff as was done in the case of SOLD.

6 A further development of the separate integrating role is to decide that it should have a definite claim upon the resources of functional departments. Indeed these may disappear as separate departments. In industry such integrator-managers are often product managers in charge of the total operations required to market, develop, produce and service a product.

7 The most elaborate and sophisticated method of ensuring lateral integration is to establish a matrix system. Here, an attempt is made to combine integration of personnel within functionally specialized departments with their integration around a common contribution to products or programmes.

The research conducted by Lawrence and Lorsch, referred to in the previous section, concluded that organizations operating in more dynamic environments with greater differentiation between their major functions needed to invest in more powerful integrating mechanisms. The thrust of this conclusion is supported by Van de Ven and his colleagues (1976) who examined 'co-ordination modes' used in 197 units of a large American State government employment security agency. They distinguished between three such modes: (a) co-ordination through setting programmes of work and establishing procedures—an 'impersonal mode'; (b) co-ordination through feedback in a 'personal mode', whereby individuals such as managers, co-ordinators and liaison officers are the means for two or more groups to make mutual adjustments; and (c) a 'group mode', whereby planned or unscheduled meetings serve as the mechanism for mutual adjustment.

It was found that three conditions were associated with the different usage of integrating mechanisms. These were how difficult and variable was the work to be done (conditions which create uncertainty), how dependent employees had to be upon each other in order to get work done, and how large each work unit was in terms of people employed. As uncertainty in the work increased, so lateral communications and group meetings tended to be used instead of integration through programming. As interdependence between employees increased there was a greater use of all integrating mechanisms except for programmes and procedures. As size of work unit increased, so there was more use of impersonal modes of integration based on formalized planning and programming. This last relationship appears to be one more facet of the general association between increasing scale of organization and the formalization of structure.

The research by Lawrence and Lorsch, and by Van de Ven and his colleagues, indicates that combinations of integrating mechanisms are often used by organizations facing high levels of uncertainty and in which the tension between inter-departmental differentiation and interdependency is high. The managements of such organizations, particularly the more successful ones, appear to secure integration through a portfolio of mechanisms rather than through simply adopting one approach and not others. This recognizes the fact that, even in an organization experiencing change and operating with complex interdependencies between departments or work groups, some communications and decision processes can still be handled adequately by means of simpler arrangements which are less costly in time and administrative overhead. For the costs of managing integration have to be weighed against the value and necessity of the benefits attained when assessing whether a particular set of arrangements is inadequate, over-elaborate, or about right. The costs that can arise include (1) the costs of time and manpower involved in more intensive and extensive communication, (2) the associated costs of training, including teambuilding which is discussed shortly, and (3) possible side-effects such that arrangements to improve communications between departments (including perhaps the re-siting of offices) may be at the expense of communications within these departments.

There is a further reason why alternatives to integration through lateral relationships will be retained and even preferred. This is that senior management does not wish to weaken (as it sees it) the element of control. As a result it prefers to rely upon the referral of matters requiring co-ordination up the hierarchy, or to deal with co-ordination as far as possible through formal procedures, or to rely on co-ordination by committees on which senior managers sit and can exercise considerable influence. This may be partly a matter of culture and style in which managers seek to preserve the approach with which they have become familiar. It serves, however, to illustrate further the point that a portfolio of integrative mechanisms is likely to be employed even where integration needs are greatest, and also the observation that some integrative mechanisms will suit a prevailing culture of management better than others.

The understanding and determination of top management are likely to play an important part in the success of integration even when emphasis is placed on achieving this via direct lateral relationships. The general manager may be called upon to resolve conflicts arising in a matrix structure, and if he fails to do this a serious measure of dis-integration could ensue between the two equally powerful sides of an 'overlay' matrix. Secondly, the ability of co-ordinators to exercise any real influence over departmental heads may depend heavily on their ability to appeal to the general manager's authority when necessary. Other ways of enhancing the influence and potential for success of co-ordinators include: (1) filling such positions with persons who are already influential in the organization and are known to have earned the respect of the departments or groups they are called upon to co-ordinate (an important requirement here is that co-ordinators should have some understanding of the work of the departments to be co-ordinated); (2) selecting as co-ordinators people who can cope with the ambiguity inherent in their position; and (3) clarifying the rights that formally attach to the position (such as the right to call meetings and to set schedules for project work), and if necessary providing the co-ordinator with back-up resources and staff.

In considering the ability of co-ordinators to carry out their role, we have touched upon the way in which attitudinal and behavioural factors can support the operation of an element in organizational design. This serves to remind us that although the design of organization structures can influence the patterns of behaviour and relationships in an institution it is always difficult to predict just what its effect will be, because so much depends on the predispositions of the people concerned, how they perceive the structure in question and how they react to it. This is as true of structural mechanisms designed to improve integration as it is of any others. Structural mechanisms may be established in a way that is quite appropriate for achieving integration, but these can have a limited impact if there is interpersonal conflict or animosity between different groups. A certain threshold of trust and willingness to work together is required, and managements may have to devote considerable efforts towards building this up – towards 'teambuilding' as it is often called. The reverse is also true: teambuilding is less likely to produce integration if the structural design is deficient. What can be done, then, to complement improvements in structural integrative mechanisms with improvements in personal relationships between groups?

Teambuilding, an aid to integration

Many problems of integration are caused by the hostile feelings that one group or department may have for another. We have seen that departments will have different goals and criteria of performance, and that it is very easy for them to form unfavourable stereotypes of one another. It is natural for individuals to identify with their own department rather than with other departments or with the organization as a whole. It is also quite understandable that people tend to vent their feelings of frustration or aggression on 'outsiders'. The heads of some departments may feel personal antipathy towards each other, and this in turn is likely to be reflected in the attitudes of their respective staffs.

For such reasons it is quite likely that certain feelings of hostility will manifest themselves between different departments which have to work together, and this will make it more difficult to achieve an adequate degree of integration. Once conflict arises, then its effects will often become cumulative. Within a department, these effects typically include more conformity, 'pulling together' and defensiveness. As groups, the departments 'close-up', seeing only the best in themselves and the worst in others. Communication between the departments tends to decrease, their members do not listen to the 'adversary', personal relations deteriorate, and scoring political points becomes more important than solving common problems on their merits. In fact, the more that relations between departments are defined in terms of 'if they win, we lose', the more likely is a breakdown in integration. The more that relations are linked in people's mind to joint problem-solving, the less likely is such breakdown.

Lawrence and Lorsch (1967) found that successful integration in the companies they studied was characterized by a great deal of open confrontation of issues by the members of different departments. This openness can only be based on a genuine understanding of other departments' outlooks, ways of working and problems. Stereotypes are destructive of this understanding, and much of the task of teambuilding amounts to dispelling them.

There are various methods of achieving this, though it is not easy to break into a situation of deteriorating relationships and start a reversal of the trend. Very often the intervention of a third party, a superior in the hierarchy or even a consultant, is required to start off a frank mutual discussion of the stereotypes that each department has of the other. Understanding and integration can subsequently be built between the departments by reformulating their objectives or targets in terms of an overriding goal that both accept as essential and also attainable. If joint projects are called for, then task forces drawing on members of two or more departments can often provide a positive experience of working together. This can create mutual trust and confidence, as can other ways of bringing members of different departments to work together, such as nominating joint representatives to committees. It has also been found that an effective way of broadening the particular view of the world held by specialists and breaking down the stereotypes they have of another department, is to arrange for them to work in that department. Even short-term interchanges of staff for three to six months can bring considerable benefits for relatively minor costs in additional learning and supervision. These staff not only gain knowledge about another specialism's aims and problems from such interchanges, but they also broaden their attitudes and possibly those of the host department. Such people then become potentially valuable communication links and means of liaison. If, however, a lack of co-operation between departments stems from personal antipathy between their heads or other key personnel, then redeploying one or both may be required before teambuilding can succeed.

In the past, much work on so-called 'organizational development' has concentrated almost exclusively on developing teamwork. This effort has not always been successful, because teamwork cannot be expected to thrive when the structural and environmental conditions are wrong. If departments are put under pressure to pursue mutually conflicting objectives and if the formal structure makes no allowance for their need to work together then the methods I have described for developing teamwork are less likely to bear fruit. Equally, the appropriate structural arrangements have to be operated on a basis of goodwill between people and they cannot guarantee effective integration on their own account. The right integrative mechanisms and interpersonal climate are both required for conflicts of opinion to be handled in a constructive manner.

Summary

Inadequate co-ordination between the different departments and specialist staff of an organization is often a source of frustration to its clientele and a cause of poor performance. Integration is a problem that develops with the growth of organizations and their subdivision into separate sub-units. It is made worse by the varying outlooks of people trained in different functional disciplines and by the conflict between specific criteria of performance that are attached to separate departments. Points at which poor co-ordination is commonly found in an industrial organization include the relations between sales and production, between research and other functions, and between personnel and technical officers over shopfloor priorities. In the social services there has been a problem over the co-ordination of different specialists dealing with the same problem case, and in other multi-specialist services such as health care securing integration is always a challenge.

A range of structural devices can be employed to promote better integration in an organization—from arranging face-to-face meetings right up to the use of a full-blown matrix system. Which provision or combination of provisions is appropriate depends on the degree of integration required, the difficulties of achieving this that are inherent in the situation and the cost of investing time and staff in co-ordinative activities. Structural adjustments can, however, only go part of the way towards enhancing integration. If conflicts between units derive from hostility or entrenched stereotypes then a teambuilding approach aimed at confronting these issues directly will also be appropriate.

Suggested further reading

James D. Thompson provided an important early analysis of integration requirements and mechanisms in his *Organizations in Action* (McGraw-Hill 1967). A comprehensive review of contributions on the subject is Joseph McCann and Jay R. Galbraith, 'Interdepartmental Relations' in Paul C. Nystrom and William H. Starbuck (editors), *Handbook of Organizational Design* (Oxford University Press 1981), vol. 2. Jay R. Galbraith, *Organization Design* (Addison-Wesley 1977) examines in detail the ways in which integration can be improved across the departments of an organization. Paul R. Lawrence and J. W. Lorsch, *Organization and Environment* (Harvard Business School 1967), describe research into American firms which indicates how inadequate integration is associated with poor performance. The same writers in *Developing Organizations: Diagnosis and Action* (Addison-Wesley 1969) describe a practical approach to making decisions on how much specialization and co-ordination between organizational units is required in the light of environmental and other contingencies. A quick-to-read short general discussion is provided by Derek Pugh in 'Effective Coordination in Organizations', *Advanced Management Journal*, Winter 1979.

Two studies that describe how integration problems were resolved through the application of new structural forms are A. J. M. Sykes and J. Bates, 'Study of Conflict Between Formal Company Policy and the

Interests of Informal Groups', *Sociological Review*, November 1962, and Tom Burns and G. M. Stalker, *The Management of Innovation* (Tavistock 1961). John Child and Bruce Partridge, *Lost Managers: Supervisors in Industry and Society* (Cambridge University Press 1982) consider how a lack of integration in management creates problems of role conflict for first-line supervisors. John Child, 'Professionals in the Corporate World: Values, Interests and Control' in David Dunkerley and Graeme Salaman (editors) *The International Yearbook of Organization Studies 1981* (Routledge and Kegan Paul 1982) discusses integration between management and professional specialists. A perceptive analysis of the problems that can arise in the integration of specialist groups with the departments they are intended to service is given by Andrew M. Pettigrew in 'Strategic Aspects of the Management of Specialist Activity', *Personnel Review*, vol. 4, 1975. Kenneth Knight (editor) *Matrix Management* (Gower Press 1977) contains articles by Maureen Dixon and Anthea Hay on problems and methods of integration in the British health services and social services respectively. Alan C. Filley, *Interpersonal Conflict Resolution* (Scott, Foresman 1975), provides a review of methods to resolve the human problems that stand in the way of effective integration. William G. Dyer, *Team Building: Issues and Alternatives* (Addison-Wesley 1977) is a useful practical guide.

In this chapter reference was also made to F. J. Aguilar, *Scanning the Business Environment* (Macmillan 1967); Rensis Likert, *New Patterns of Management* (McGraw-Hill 1961); and to Philip Sadler, Terry Webb and Peter Lansley, *Management Style and Organization Structure in the Smaller Enterprise* (Ashridge College, Management Research Unit 1974). Three other studies cited were Andrew H. Van de Ven, Andre L. Delbecq and Richard Koenig, Jr., 'Determinants of Coordination Modes within Organizations', *American Sociological Review*, April 1976; C. Freeman, A. Robertson and colleagues in the University of Sussex Science Policy Research Unit, *Success and Failure in Industrial Innovation* (February 1972); and George Strauss, 'Tactics of Lateral Relationship: The Purchasing Agent', *Administrative Science Quarterly*, September 1962.

Chapter 6

Control

'Order is Heaven's first law.' *Alexander Pope.* Essay on Man, *Epistle iv.*

'Everything is under control.' Managers say this with thinly disguised desperation as often as they say it with conviction. Control was only one of the basic managerial activities that Henri Fayol identified back in 1916. Yet it has generally received the lion's share of attention. Control has been singled out as a major practical problem by managers themselves and also as the greatest problem about management practice by critics of the system. In fact, many writers regard the main contribution of organizational design to be the means it provides for controlling the behaviour of employees.

Control admits to several paradoxes, one of them being that while the term is in common everyday use it is nevertheless surrounded by ambiguity. This is partly a reflection of its different facets and of its close relationship to those equally fuzzy phenomena, 'power' and 'influence'. There is also frequently some confusion between control as a general process and control systems as specific mechanisms used within that process. Control within organizations is a process whereby management and other groups are able to initiate and regulate the conduct of activities so that their results accord with the goals and expectations held by those groups. A control system is a mechanism which is designed to convey information to assist the initiation and regulation of the activities, but it is not the ability to have them carried out as such. Control, in other words, is aimed at ensuring that a predictable level and type of performance is attained and maintained. Management is not the only group which will attempt to exercise control: workers, technical staff, professional employees and other organizational groups will also do so. Recognition of this immediately introduces the further paradox that control in an organization is not simply a process in which everyone shares with the same goal in mind; it is also a process in which there is resistance and counter-control in pursuit of conflicting objectives.

While the scope of this chapter is limited to the part that organizational design plays, this cannot be adequately understood without some reference to the general nature of control. The first section therefore makes some general observations about control in organizations. This is followed by a closer consideration of the management control process, our understanding of which has shown increasing sophistication in recent years. The third section focuses on certain basic dimensions of choice in designing managerial strategies of control. The next section takes this analysis further by distinguishing the main strategies and their constituent elements. Reference is also made to the types of accounting controls which are compatible with organizational strategies. One of the interesting aspects of recent enquiry into accounting controls lies in the way it has pointed both to the need for consistency between accounting and organizational controls and to the relevance of situational contingencies for the choice of approach. This is the subject of the final section.

Control in organizations

There are two levels of control relevant to organizations. Consideration of these levels points to the connections between control and power, which are still not well understood. It is, however, widely appreciated today that organizations in which people are employed are fundamentally structures of control and power.

The first level is control over the means and methods on which the whole conduct of an organization depends. These include its capital, the form of assets in which capital is embodied, and also its strategic dispositions such as the markets or areas of need to be served, the communities and labour markets in which the organization is located, its relations with competing organizations, with suppliers and with government. This is the level of control which those engaged in debate over the so-called 'divorce of ownership from control' among business corporations had in mind.

The ability that management in particular has to exercise power within organizations derives primarily from control at this strategic level. For this control allows management to redeploy capital, which may involve closing sites and entertaining bids from communities to open new sites. This has provided a basis for securing co-operation from local community authorities to secure 'captured' local labour markets in which the one company becomes a dominant employer, and also for securing guarantees of assistance from workers' leaders in removing restrictive working practices, reducing manning levels and promoting 'industrial discipline'. The ability of management to recruit selectively from an ample supply of job applicants enables it to take on employees who appear more likely to accept managerial authority and indeed to replace them readily should they not perform as management expects. The provision of company housing, of mortgages tied to employment in the company, and of non-transferable benefits such as pensions, are further examples of how control over strategic resources can be used to encourage, even coerce, employees into accepting management control within the organization—control which the mere provisions of an employment contract itself do not guarantee. A similar analysis could be made with respect to control in other strategic areas, such as dominance in a product market or monopoly over providing a public utility service. The general point is that the ability to exercise control within an organization (at what I shall call the second level) is largely dependent on, and certainly facilitated by, control at the first strategic level.

The second level of control comes closer to the main focus of this chapter.

This is control over the production process within an organization, in the sense of determining how the employees of an organization perform their work. The possibility of exercising this control depends on the possession of power. This power may be used in an overtly coercive way, as when employees, particularly in conditions of high unemployment, are threatened with dismissal, which would deny them a substantial part of their livelihood. Power may be used through the ability to offer rewards, such as incentives for attaining certain targets. Thirdly, power may be used through the command of the means of ideological persuasion. Examples are the ability to establish symbolic events such as periodic ceremonies, or to finance a company magazine, both of which are intended to promote a sense of togetherness and an identification with management.

Control, then, at this second level is a realization of the potential offered by the possession of power within organizations. While top management is likely to hold the largest share of such power because it is likely to have most control at the first, strategic, level, other groups will also possess some power. Workers who have special skills required to carry out certain tasks, and who cannot readily be replaced, provide an example of a potentially powerful group. This is particularly the case when, as with certain maintenance workers, management cannot easily predict when their services are required and so substitute for those services in the event of non co-operation.

The strategic level of management is correctly regarded as that level at which objectives are established and translated into policies and then specific plans of action. This recognizes that whoever controls strategic resources and the means to recruit them (such as raising finance) also determines objectives and policies for the organization. This statement is not meant to imply that the strategic process is particularly rational or free from conflict, but rather to make the point that it does not commonly admit of a formulation of objectives in which there is participation by other lower-level members of the organization. If as a result these other members do not fully share top management's objectives (and indeed if they cannot readily do so because in strategic terms they are resources, the costs of which are to be minimized) then the potential is present for resistance to management control.

In fact, there is a conflict of interests inherent in the employment contract which, if it remains at the forefront of employees' minds, will tend to sustain an active and probably collectively organized resistance to managerial control. Such resistance will appear to those engaged in it to offer the best hope of protecting their interests in terms of, for example, the balance between effort required and payment offered or the preservation of labour market power through restrictions on management's ability to erode employees' skills. Competitive pressures, which have steadily increased in the world economy and which oblige managers to exercise more stringent control in an attempt to reduce costs, increase productivity and respond more swiftly to market changes, may heighten employee resistance even to the point where the continued viability of the whole productive unit is at risk. For the reduction of costs in order to preserve some economic surplus is often (though not always) achieved at the expense of the short-term interests of employees at many levels in the organization, and short-term threats tend to take precedence in the minds of people, some of whom will find themselves no longer invited to share in the long-term rewards that are promised.

The consideration of control in organizations provides a perspective for the more specific notion of control in the sense of a control system. This refers to a system which guides the progress of collaborative effort towards certain standards and targets. Control in this respect may appear to be a neutral phenomenon which would be required in any co-operative activity. In circumstances where objectives are shared and there are no conflicts of interests, control becomes in principle only a matter of co-ordinating different people's contributions and adjusting these in the light of progress achieved and/or of changing circumstances. Under these conditions control can be regarded as a technical matter, in which an exercise of power is not necessarily involved as long as every person engaged in the co-operative undertaking pulls his or her weight equitably.

This is how many managers regard control, or at least would like to, and it is the perspective adopted in many writings for managers. It is not, however, an adequate perspective and is likely to be seriously misleading. For control is more than merely a technical matter. It is inherent in the social relationships of employing organizations. In so far as these relationships contain elements of conflict, then the standards which management sets for a control system are liable to be disputed.

A further paradox about control therefore is that it is directed at some issues on which there may be consensus between management and employees, but also at other issues on which there may be conflict. As Littler and Salaman have put it, 'control must be seen in relation to conflict and sources of conflict *and* in relation to the potential terrain of compromise and consensus' (1982: 253). An increase in control achieved by workers over an issue that is in dispute will be at the expense of the amount of control available to management; and vice versa. Control then takes on a 'win-lose' zero-sum character. An example might be control over the level of manning in a department. Where there are issues on which the different parties agree, perhaps such as safety, this win-lose character disappears. It is then possible to share control and for an increase in the devolution of control to employees not to mean a loss in control by management.

In practical terms, this conjunction of conflict and consensus indicates the appropriateness of adopting a portfolio of control strategies rather than just one. Each strategy would be directed towards different issues according to the degree of conflict or consensus involved and, similarly, different approaches might be followed towards different groups within the organization. For example, where there is conflict over employees' work rates, one might expect to find management relying primarily on control through direct supervision or, where performance can be measured, through tying payment directly to work rate. Where there is consensus, such as over safety and perhaps over the quality of products or services, one might expect management to maintain control on the basis of an appeal to an identity of aims, such as campaigns urging workers not to take personal risks. On matters of consensus, discretion is more likely to be delegated to the employee. Moreover, groups of employees whose acceptance of managerial aims can generally be taken for granted and who are usually highly trained as well—groups such as development engineers and operations research specialists—will tend to be subject to a far less direct mode of control than will groups of employees who are likely to resist managerial objectives and who may also require more technical guidance.

Another reason why managements will find it appropriate to pursue a portfolio of control strategies is that control is not likely to be aligned to a single objective. Management has to have regard to efficiency, which tends to be a short-term 'here and now' objective, but it will also have to ensure that the organization can adapt in the future to new circumstances, and this requires preserving some flexibility in working arrangements. It may also be concerned to develop the capabilities of employees and the whole organization's capacity to innovate and learn. These objectives will tend to require some balance between control strategies. For instance, an all-out emphasis on controlling for efficiency may jeopardize attainment of the other objectives if it destroys the goodwill among employees required to adapt working arrangements, or if it removes the time given to training as part of staff development.

It should be apparent from this discussion of the nature of control in organizations that we are dealing here with a complex process which organizational design can affect only to a certain degree. The paradoxes and contradictions inherent in organizational relationships mean that there is likely to be resistance to management control by other groups seeking to enforce some measure of control of their own. This in turn means that it may be misleading to account for resistance to managerial controls, and attempts to subvert them, purely in terms of the control strategy being inappropriate. There is a considerable literature on the way certain control strategies, such as close supervision and heavy reliance on rules, are incongruent with the personal psychological needs of adults. If applied without regard to the wider context just surveyed, this approach could be taken to imply that resistance to control would disappear once an appropriate strategy of control were adopted. While the psychology of control is certainly relevant, it is not the whole story, except perhaps for those members of an organization who are entirely committed to management's goals and policies. In their case, the problem would simply be one of finding a *style* of management control which was acceptable—there would be no conflict with its content and rationale. In the case of other employees who did perceive a measure of conflict with management, no control strategy however sensitive to psychological considerations is likely to be received entirely without resistance.

Management control

Management control involves the definition of what people and units are expected to do, the establishment of criteria against which the performance of their activities is to be assessed, and feedback of information about what has actually taken place. Expressed in this way, a management's choice of control strategy should be compatible with the requirements of the operating situation and with what will best motivate people to carry out their tasks in the manner desired. If, for example, a firm has to innovate and adapt its methods of working in order to compete in a rapidly changing environment, its management should not seek to impose controls that are exclusively oriented towards efficiency. Running a tight ship is no good if it is heading for the rocks and none of the crew dares, or is motivated, to do anything about it.

Figure 6.1 sets out the process of management control in its basic terms, which apply to any authority or power-based relationship across one or more levels of formal (or informal) hierarchy. Since it is the more usual situation, I shall take the authority figure to be a manager and the person subjected to control to be a subordinate employee. It would, of course, be possible to envisage a worker-management situation in which the authority figure is an elected worker director and the subordinate is a line manager.

The manager is assumed to have certain goals, in the sense of work that he wishes others to accomplish in a manner which will satisfy or surpass certain levels of performance. If such goals are not present, at least at an implicit level, it is difficult to see how any kind of management could begin to get under way. Goals can be refined down into more specific and precise standards. These standards may take the form of output targets or instructions and guidelines as to how to carry out the work that is required. The work that managers expect to be carried out is therefore expressed by such instructions. The next logical step in the process is that work is done accordingly by subordinates, resulting in certain outputs.

This part of the control process is one of executive instruction. It corresponds most closely to the traditional view of control being imposed essentially from above. In the historically longest-established approach to control involving personal command and supervision of work, often backed up literally by a whip hand, this might have appeared to give those in the driving

Figure 6.1 The process of management control

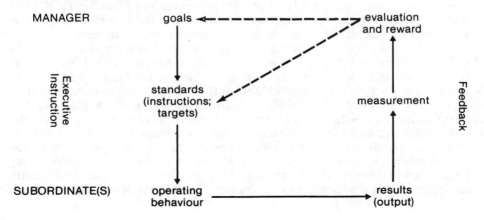

seat a satisfactory translation of goals into results. Nowadays, and this is written with absolutely no regret, circumstances are very different in many societies and there are plenty of opportunities for results to deviate considerably from managers' intentions. The goals themselves may be unrealistic and in conditions of complex organization, competition and change, it is a major planning headache to try to settle upon goals that match capabilities to perceived opportunities. Second, the standards which are set may not be adequate and/or may be overtaken by changed conditions. Third, what is expected of subordinates, and/or the terms of rewards for what is expected, may not be acceptable to them and they may therefore decide not to work according to managerially set standards. Their collective organization, through informal work groups and perhaps also through formal union membership, is likely to provide some degree of protection for their action.

Managers therefore face the need to secure motivation and feedback from those at whom control is directed. While the level of motivation that subordinates have for following management's wishes may be limited in varying degrees according to how they perceive their best interests to be affected, this does not mean that managers should not at least try to clarify what they expect and perhaps attempt some persuasion as well. In this connection, John Machin (1979) describes a methodology he has developed within managerial hierarchies which assists in the clarification of what is expected of subordinates largely through several stages of discussion. There is some evidence from research studies to suggest that many subordinates gain reassurance and greater satisfaction from having a clear appreciation of what managers expect of them. It has to be said again that discussion and participation in the setting of standards and targets do not guarantee agreement between manager and subordinate, but in a non-punitive context they may usefully expose areas of disagreement, reaffirm areas of agreement and reduce misunderstanding.

Feedback involves an attempt to measure the results of subordinates' work, either directly or indirectly, and the evaluation of these measured results against both goals and standards. A motivational element can also be incorporated into this part of the process in so far as it is possible to link the level of reward to the quality of results achieved (see Chapter 7). Results which fall short of expectations may be judged to indicate a need to revise the level of standards or perhaps to improve their presentation. The shortfall, especially if it is persistent, may indicate that the goals themselves are not realizable in their present form. Chris Argyris (1976) has characterized a situation in which managers are willing to encourage and listen to feedback in a way that places goals set for the organization under continuing review as one in which 'double-loop learning' is taking place. He considers that this level of feedback and learning will increase the effectiveness of decision making, and policy making, though he admits that it is not easy to attain the openness required. This depends upon a high quality of undistorted feedback, which subordinates may not be willing to provide if they believe it will threaten their interests or if they are otherwise in conflict with management. It also requires a willingness on the part of managers to learn from the feedback and not to discard any negative content because they too see it as personally threatening.

The multidimensional nature of management control

Three further points now need to be made about management control: (1) that there are several dimensions along which management control can vary: (2) that management control has to satisfy a range of criteria; and (3) that other policies can provide significant support for management control strategies and these policies should be regarded as part of the general process of control.

Management control is not homogeneous. The matters to be controlled may range from tangible items such as units produced to relatively intangible factors such as the quality of co-ordination. It is usually possible to measure tangible items relatively objectively and numerically; with less tangible items reliance has to be placed on subjective measures often expressed in linguistic terms. The system of management control may be operated to emphasize the provision of feedback on past events, or it may be intended to promote feedforward as well. Feedforward takes place when predictive information is used as a basis for assessing whether it is necessary to adjust plans; it can enter the management control process through reports submitted by subordinates and via advice transmitted by managers who have been alerted to changing conditions perhaps by specialist forecasting staff. A third dimension of variation is in the philosophy of management control, which may range from one of directly commanding subordinates over specific tasks to one in which there is an attempt to agree general objectives with subordinates who are then left to consult the manager on the conduct of specific tasks as they see fit. We shall see how variations along these dimensions, particularly measurability of outputs and directness of supervision, are reflected in alternative control strategies.

It was mentioned earlier that management control is unlikely to be directed towards a single objective. A second point of elaboration therefore is that control has to satisfy a range of criteria. It amounts to more than a manager just maintaining operational efficiency within his or her area of responsibility. There are also requirements for integration, development and flexibility to be met. Chapter 5 indicated that integration between different areas of responsibility was becoming more critical. Although the maintenance of control within an organization as a whole implies that integration is achieved between its parts, the bulk of attention in the past has been on achieving control vertically within departmental hierarchies. Devices such as departmental budgets have emphasized this. The attention managers pay to keeping control in their own departments may, however, be at the expense of the attention they give to lateral integration with other departments. If managers believe they are expected to demonstrate that they are maintaining control over their own subordinates as a basic criterion of their competence, rather than that they have encouraged liaison or collaborative working between their staff and those in other departments, then integration is likely to suffer despite its importance for the success of the organization's activities as a whole.

There is also today a greater awareness of the need to encourage development and to promote the conditions for flexibility within organizations. Development encompasses a whole range of organizational learning opportunities including a greater strategic understanding and improvements in techniques. It benefits from both good feedback and feedforward processes. In this respect, development enhances management's capacity to *take the risks* associated with seizing new opportunities. This contrasts with flexibility, which concerns the organization's ability to adapt to change. Flexibility is therefore a major element in the organization's capacity to *absorb risks*, when these arise in the form of new and perhaps unexpected events (such as a competitor introducing an innovative rival product or an epidemic in the area served by a hospital) which require the organization to change its activities and way of working. The levels of development and flexibility which management can achieve for an organization are both likely to depend on securing accurate feedback from and maintaining goodwill among employees. These are benefits which a strategy of control unacceptable to employees is likely to undermine.

I suggested earlier that the element of conflict between management and employees will tend to set limits to goodwill and to the willingness to provide full and accurate feedback. If this area of conflict can be reduced through policies which reward the members of an organization for improvements and high performance, and which enhance employees' normative acceptance of managerial objectives, then barriers to development and flexibility may be reduced. Managements have too often responded to high levels of employees' achievement by cutting the rate of reward through reducing bonus rates and/or raising subsequent work norms, and have even allowed the eventual reward for increased productivity to be the loss of jobs. These responses may be understandable in view of the pressures inherent in a competitive business system and which are also very evident in the public sector today. They will, however, almost certainly inflict considerable damage to employees' motivation towards improving future performance, to the quality of feedback they are willing to provide, and to their acquiescence in changed working practices when the need for flexibility arises.

Policies on rewards are a particularly important example among a collection of policies that can provide significant support for management control strategies. This is the third point of elaboration I wish to make before returning to the control strategies themselves. The design of reward systems has a close bearing on the operation of management control for the following reason. The employment relationship is based on a contract in which the employee's capacity to work is purchased in return for certain rewards, the normal contractual one being remuneration. The actual achievement of productive work from the employee requires that management finds ways of directing his or her capacity to work towards activity which fulfills the objectives it has set for the organization. In other words, it requires control. The process of managing productive employment is therefore one of dynamic tension in which the control process can be facilitated by the design of reward systems that match the type of tasks required to be done and the behaviour which is desired of employees. Rewards can extend beyond the design of payment systems to include positive policies on other features which employees value, such as the degree of variety and autonomy built into job design or the opportunities provided for participation. Chapter 7 discusses the design of reward systems further.

Other policies in support of management control strategies are less formal and direct than the reward system, but they contribute none the less to the general process of controlling personal behaviour within organizations. Mention was made earlier of the selective recruitment of employees who are thought to possess norms and values acceptable to management and compatible with the emphasis of its control and reward systems. Some managements, for example, have favoured employing different generations from the same family, not only because a 'suitable' family background has been identified but also because senior members of the family with long service can be expected to assist in controlling younger members. Other ways were also mentioned of how managements can influence employees' attitudes and behaviour through the dependence of communities on the employing organization. The exercise of control through developing a cultural identity with the organization and its management, though discussed later as a major control strategy, is comparable with the policies discussed here in that it does not directly programme employees' actions. These policies are, rather, intended to inculcate predispositions among employees to act in ways that are in line with managerial requirements.

Design choices in control

In working out a policy on control, choices have to be made in terms of several organizational design dimensions. These are:

1 the degree of centralization and delegation;
2 the relative emphasis between formalization and informality;
3 the degree of personal supervision.

Decisions on each of these choices, and on the overall mix between them, are matters of judgement. This judgement can, however, be informed by theory and practice on the appropriateness of alternatives approaches for particular situations. I shall begin to develop this contingency perspective in this section and then pull its strands together at the close of the chapter. It will also become apparent how different combinations of design alternatives characterize the major control strategies that are found in practice.

Centralization or delegation?

I have expressed the choice in these terms because a great deal of confusion has surrounded the term 'decentralization'. For some people decentralization implies participation or devolution; that is an extension of control from the top of a hierarchical system to lower levels. For others, the term suggests divisionalization, which in fact normally involves a shift in the means of control towards a combination of delegation and formal procedures, but does not necessarily entail any significant *transfer* of control. The definitions I shall follow are, first, that centralization is a condition where the upper levels of an organization's hierarchy retain the authority to take most decisions. Second, delegation is a particular meaning of the term 'decentralization' and describes a condition when the authority to make specified decisions is passed down to units and people at lower levels in the organization's hierarchy. Centralization also implies that control information is passed to the top of an organization, while delegation implies that some passes to lower levels.

Centralization and delegation are not simple dichotomies. There is a considerable choice of possibilities and variations in between. For example, it will probably be sensible to delegate routine operational decisions, while it is unlikely that non-routine and strategic decisions will be delegated to any marked degree. Also a divisionalized organization which has operational decisions delegated to divisional heads may at the same time have highly centralized divisions—this has sometimes been a source of considerable complaint among divisional departmental managers. Another point is that centralization and delegation as discussed here refer to the taking of decisions rather than to the involvement of people either in general initial discussions or the implementation of decisions already made. These other aspects involve questions of participation and integration which have been discussed in previous chapters.

Both centralization and delegation are strategies for maintaining control, and each has certain advantages which have to be traded-off in the light of the conditions an organization must cope with in its particular circumstances. Centralization is an approach where control is exercised by confining decision-making to a small group of senior people or even one person. In other words, no-one else has the right to act on his own account and discretion. Delegation is an approach where decision-making is passed downwards and outwards within the formal structure, but where there are strict limits imposed on the scope and the type of decisions that can be made without referral upwards; for example, a formal rule which states that 'You, as manager of X department can spend up to £1000 on consumable items without having to obtain the signature of the manager above you so long as that expenditure falls within the limits of your monthly budget.' Alternatively, decisions on how to perform tasks may be delegated but subordinates are required to work towards certain measurable results. One can see from these examples that, although the decision has been passed down the hierarchy, an attempt to maintain overall control is very clearly incorporated into the arrangement.

What are the main trade-offs between centralization and delegation? These have been reviewed in a very useful article by Howard Carlisle (1974) and I shall draw upon his work. The arguments for centralization are:

1 If decisions are made at one point or among a small group of managers it is easier to co-ordinate the activities of the sub-units or individuals who report up to senior management. If, for example, a company is promoting several different product lines to the same consumer market, centralization will make it easier to establish a co-ordinated programme.

2 From their position in the organization, senior managers have a broad organization-wide perspective on what is going on and how far this conforms to policies that have been agreed and established. They are therefore in a better position to make decisions that will accord with these policies and be consistent with the interests of the entire organization. This will avoid a loss of control due to people at lower levels making decisions which are optimal for their department or sub-unit but sub-optimal for the organization as a whole.

3 Closely related to the previous argument is the fact that centralized control provides a way of keeping the various functional areas of an organization—marketing, production, research and development, finance—in an appropriate balance one with another. This can be done by centralizing decisions on resource allocation, on functional policies, targets, and so forth.

4 Centralization can economize on managerial overheads. It can avoid the duplication of activities or resources if similar activities are carried on independently by, say, different divisions within the same organization. Also, the centralization of management may allow for certain staff or specialist support personnel to be justified in desirable areas, whereas if management were more dispersed among segments of the organization it might be difficult for any one segment to justify employing its own staff or specialist personnel. This is one reason why functions such as planning, purchasing, legal and personnel are often centralized, feeding in to a senior management level where the major decisions on such matters are taken. This argument is, of course, part of the case for a functional grouping of activities discussed in Chapter 4.

5 Top managers are generally proven by the time they reach senior positions, and they normally have more experience than other employees. It is to be expected, therefore, that they should be particularly capable of making good decisions and exercising appropriate judgement—this speaks for centralized control.

6 Finally, when strong leadership is required as in times of crisis and keen external pressures, centralization encourages this by focusing power, authority and prestige onto a central key position or senior group. It affords an opportunity for speedy decision-making in reaction to unexpected crises because of the advantages of centralized communication and co-ordination already mentioned.

To set against these factors in favour of centralization, there are considerations in support of the opposite policy, one of delegation. These may be summarized as follows:

1 One of the complaints of senior managers is that they become over-burdened and cannot cope with all the matters that require their attention. In a comparison of average working hours among British and American managers (Child and Macmillan 1972) this problem appeared to be most acute for top American executives some of whom were clocking up 80 or 90 hours per week in the office plus undertaking businss-related social engagements. The problem was less marked among British managers, but in both countries it was senior people who worked longer hours on the job. If top executives are overloaded then the effective control they can exercise will be diminished and they will tend to sit on decisions which may require speedy attention. This is one of the most powerful arguments in favour of a delegated system and it obviously carries most weight in conditions of large-scale operation, complexity, rapid change and other features which add to the decision-making load of executives. Delegation can relieve some of this burden and make an organization function more effectively by leaving senior managers with more time for policy matters of long-term consequence.

2 There are motivational considerations which speak in favour of delegation. Behavioural scientists have long argued that most people (in Western societies at least) are willing to give more to their jobs when they have a high degree of individual freedom, discretion and control over their work. This assumes that their own personal goals are broadly compatible with those contained in corporate policies, though many psychologists would argue that commitment to corporate goals is most likely to be generated when the individual feels he is obtaining something personally worthwhile from his job. The opportunity to make decisions and be involved can help to provide such personal satisfaction and commitment. This case for delegation is put to a particularly severe test in situations where people's tasks are closely interdependent with those of others. The question then arises whether all concerned will be sufficiently motivated and committed to integrate their activities without centralized direction.

3 Management involves judgement, the ability to cope with uncertainty and other attributes, which are developed through having appropriate experience. Delegation of responsibility, as in the divisional structure where profit responsibility is attached to divisional managers, has proved valuable to many organizations in helping them to develop their stock of managers capable of assuming 'general management' positions. Delegation, then, can be a powerful aid to management development.

4 Delegation generally permits greater flexibility—more rapid response to change—at operating levels in organizations because decisions do not have to be referred up the hierarchy unless they are exceptional in nature. This advantage becomes particularly marked in the larger organization where hierarchies are likely to be more extended (and communication up and down will be slower) and where a greater number of matters are likely to crop up for decision over a given period.

5 There is a further consideration, related to point 4. The person immediately involved with the problem will usually be more aware of local

conditions or other relevant circumstances than will a senior manager, sometimes several levels removed, who is more remote. So long as he is aware of, understands and accepts corporate policies, the person on the spot is likely to make better decisions. A problem sometimes arising here is that the matter requiring attention has longer-term policy implications. In this case, delegated decision-making could lead to inconsistencies in actions taken on behalf of the organization, and these might clearly have serious consequences. This is an instance where attention to developing a strong identification with top management objectives would permit delegated decisions to be made with some assurance that local personnel were aware of and accepted the corporate philosophy and strategy of the organization.

6 Finally, by establishing relatively independent sub-units within an organization where middle managers and even supervisors are responsible for their own operations, delegation can result in more effective controls and performance measurement. This is because separate spheres of responsibility can be identified and control systems applied to these units in order to provide more adequate feedback to higher management. For example, costs can be identified with, and allocated to, particular operations and responsibility is then rendered more specific. Much the same control advantage was seen to accompany job enrichment schemes which gave employees the responsibility for producing distinguishable units of work rather than for minute partial tasks only. In the divisionalized form of organization discussed in Chapter 4, semi-autonomous units are normally established with profit responsibility, and local management is given a high degree of operational independence so long as its division meets profit targets. Sometimes divisions will be set up in parallel on a competitive basis as a stimulus to performance, and corporate management then in effect acts as a capital market in terms of allocating finance and controlling its use through assessment of rates of return. This may serve to restore some characteristics of the free competitive market where these have otherwise been severely weakened by oligopoly.

It is apparent, even from this brief review, that much of the choice between centralization and delegation has to be made in the light of specific conditions and situations. In military situations, where surprise and speed of reaction are usually vital, the flexibility offered by delegated control is in most cases more effective. While a small army can sometimes operate effectively under the centralized control of a dynamic and tireless leader (and here one is thinking of ancient rather than modern times), large modern armies cannot proceed in this matter without serious liability. A good example emerges from the Middle East War of 1973, in the comparison between the remarkable adaptiveness of the small collection of a few brigades which under General Arik Sharon crossed over to the west bank of the Suez Canal, working out their own tactics as they advanced day by day, and the paralysis which affected the centralized Egyptian Army. A considerable time elapsed before the Egyptian Commander-in-Chief knew what was happening and by then it was too late. The following remarks by the *Sunday Times* Insight Team provide an interesting commentry on the relative virtues of centralized and decentralized control under conditions of the extremely variable environment of open war about which Rommel said 'Speed of reaction in command decides the battle':

> There was no Egyptian equivalent to the incessant Israeli patrol and reconnaissance activity. Junior commanders simply fought the Israelis as and when they presented themselves, and gave no priority at all to making combat reports [feedback]. And even divisional commanders—men on the equivalent level to Arik Sharon—had little independence of action. The effect was that there were no real command centres closer to the fighting than Ismail's war room. An Egyptian officer, when asked, after the war, who had been the overall *field* commander, replied that it was [General] Ismail, sitting in front of his multi-coloured maps.
>
> (*Sunday Times*, 30 December 1973, p.30).

The choice between centralized and delegated control must be made, first, in respect of different types of decisions, which will vary in their strategic importance, and second, for the whole range of organizational decisions in the light of the contingencies and capabilities that apply to the organization and its context *in toto*.

In studies I have carried out within British companies, and in similar investigations conducted by Professor Alfred Kieser in West Germany (Child and Kieser 1979), the degree of centralization or delegation was assessed comparatively for a range of separate decisions. Strategic decisions, such as determining a new product or service, spending unallocated sums on capital items, and creating new sub-units within the organization, tended to be taken at board and/or chief executive levels. In contrast, operational decisions to do with matters such as the methods of work to be used or when overtime was to be worked were considerably more delegated, usually to a supervisory or superintendent level in British firms, and to a superintendent or production manager level in German firms. These differences in degree of centralization between different types of decisions are clearly sensible and reflect the intrinsic weight and long-term effects of the decision. However, this need to differentiate between decisions is a point that not all writers on the subject have taken into account. It is once again part of management's need to strike a balance.

Professor Carlisle, in the article cited, distinguishes 13 variables that are of primary importance in 'determining the need for a centralized or decentralized structure'—that is, whether the approach to control should veer towards centralization or delegation over the whole range of decisions to be taken. Some of these 13 variables are more pervasive contingencies than others and I shall single these out for discussion—size of organization, geographical dispersion of operations, technology and nature of the environment. Labour and product market conditions are also of considerable relevance among the environmental factors which Carlisle does not consider. The full list presented and discussed by Carlisle is:

1 The basic purpose and goals of the organization.
2 The knowledge and experience of top-level managers.

3 The skill, knowledge, and attitudes of subordinates.
4 The scale or size of the organization.
5 The geographical dispersion of the organization.
6 The scientific content or the technology of the tasks being performed.
7 The time frame of the decisions to be made.
8 The significance of the decisions to be made.
9 The degree to which subordinates will accept and are motivated by decisions to be made.
10 The status of the organization's planning and control systems.
11 The status of the organization's information systems.
12 The degree of conformity and co-ordination required in the tasks and operations of the organization.
13 The status of external environmental factors such as governments and trade unions (Carlisle 1974, p.15).

Centralization, delegation and contingencies

The larger an organization, the more likely it is that a centralized approach to control will generate top management overload. One of the most difficult transitions for the young firm that is growing up comes when the chief executive, who may be the founder, has to hand over some of the reins to subordinates. Many are reluctant to do so, out of a fear of losing control, insufficient confidence in the ability of others or just sheer stubborn pride. But unless some adjustment in the system of control is made it is almost certain that the continued growth and development of the organization will be held back. As an organization grows it becomes more difficult for any one executive or top management team to have the time or knowledge to make all major decisions. These decisions will become more frequent and demanding, since not only will the scale of operations be so much greater but they are quite likely to be more diversified and complex as well (more products, more geographical markets, and so on). So, large organizations are forced to move towards delegation in order to keep their wheels turning and it is quite clear from the results of comparative research studies that this connection between size and delegation is generally found to operate in practice.

Geographical dispersion is another contingent factor which sets up pressures for delegation. The more scattered an organization's operating sites the more difficult it is for any one individual to keep an eye on the details of what is going on elsewhere. The costs of communicating such details and referring decisions to the centre rise as the number of locations increases, and the delays which would ensue become intolerable. A further consideration is that junior managers in scattered or more remote locations are in a better position to make decisions relating to their activities, because they know local conditions well and are therefore able to assess the circumstances of any issue that arises.

Larger size and geographical dispersion, which in practice generally go together as organizations develop, can be seen in these ways to generate greater structural complexity that sets up pressures for delegation. Complexity in its various forms is quite significant for the decision on how far to delegate. In regard to technical complexity, it has been found that companies in science-based industries such as electronics and pharmaceuticals tend to have a greater overall degree of delegation than is found in other companies not handling advanced product technologies and not employing such a high proportion of experts capable of making operational decisions.

The technology employed and type of environment being served are relevant to decisions on control because of the requirements for information processing they impose. Where an organization is providing products or services under relatively stable conditions, it may (other factors being equal) be in a favourable position to operate a centralized system of control since its information processing requirements are fairly routine and probably not too intensive. In that case, decisions can be referred up the hierarchy and any delay this entails may be tolerable. For this reason, I have found that organizations operating a more integrated type of production technology producing standardized products tend to be more centralized (allowing for their size and other factors), while organizations using a more flexible, less integrated technology suitable for variable work (such as one-off production) tend to delegate decision-making to a greater extent (Child 1973).

Other investigators have found a similar connection in practice between the degree of delegation and information processing requirements, whether such requirements are assessed by reference to their source in the environment (stable or dynamic market, technical and social conditions) or by reference to the way they affect how the work is done (technology). Although the size of the organization we are talking about makes a significant difference here, generally speaking it seems that stable conditions permit a higher degree of centralization and the delegation of less authority down the hierarchy than do rapidly changing and less predictable environments. It is only in the quite small organization that a concentration of decision-making in one person's hands makes for superior adaptation to external changes. As an example of the disasters it can perpetrate in a large organization witness the incapable German military response to pressures towards the end of the Second World War.

The information processing capabilities available in organizations are generally enhanced by the application of cheap and reliable microelectronic equipment. As Chapter 9 will indicate, this new technology in principle permits a considerable extension of access to information to many levels of the organization, and its low cost permits investment in facilities for the more rapid inputting, processing and dissemination of information to anyone plugged in to the data lines. The possibilities for delegation are thereby enhanced, though it must be said the studies conducted so far in Britain do not suggest that management is very often using new technology to this end. Indeed, quite the reverse has been observed in research which colleagues and I have undertaken on the introduction of electronic point-of-sale (EPOS) systems in retailing, where the consequently more precise data on sales has tended to be used so far to extend centralized control over ordering decisions, stocking level decisions, size of labour establishment and in-store performance.

The preceding analysis of environment as a relevant contingency for the choice between centralization and delegation has concentrated on the requirements it imposes for information processing. This is a point that primarily concerns efficiency and technology. Andrew Friedman (1977), however, has pointed out through his studies of the British silk ribbon-weaving, hosiery and motor-car industries, that another aspect of environment, market power, has been systematically related to the choice of managerial control strategies including the centralization–delegation dimension. In conditions where a company's competitive market position is strong and where the ability to capitalize on this might be threatened by collective action on the part of employees enjoying high demand for their labour, Friedman's analysis suggests that managements will wish to maximize workers' commitment to the firm and their willingness to respond flexibly to opportunities. As a result, workers are likely to be accorded relatively high delegation (autonomy) and light supervision combined with attempts to increase their identification with management. In contrasting conditions, in a declining product market with redundancies weakening the power of workers in the labour market, Friedman's analysis points to a shift towards more direct control over workers including a reduction in delegation to them and closer supervision over their work. Friedman suggests that labour market conditions in particular are likely to influence the type of control adopted, at least towards operative level employees.

2 Formalization or informality?

Another means of controlling the behaviour of an organization's employees—that is, rendering their activities more predictable in a desired direction—is to establish written policies, procedures, rules, job definitions, and standing orders which prescribe correct or expected action, and then to back these up with systems for the documented recording of what has taken place in the way of communication and performance. These devices are all marks of formalization, known less affectionately as 'red-tape'. Formalization is central to a bureaucratic strategy of control.

Formalization can be a complement to moves along the centralization dimension in conditions where it becomes desirable to delegate. Given the investment in time required to establish a highly formalized system of administration and the fact that rules and procedures once established tend to take on a life of their own, formalization is clearly an approach best suited to conditions of relative stability. While all organizations require both some stability and some change, the question is in what proportion? The relative advantage of formalization depends on what balance between change and stability needs to be struck. Although conformity to the demands of the job and predictability are essential in any organization, such conformity should not be blind since the consequent loss of initiative is a serious cost to the organization.

One of the facts of life for organizations is that as they grow they become more formalized. Research studies which have measured the degree of formalization have shown that a knowledge of an organization's total employment alone permits their level of formalization to be predicted with a reasonable degree of accuracy (over 50 per cent of the variation in formaliz-ation is usually predicted by size in manufacturing concerns—see Child 1973). Just as growth sets up pressures for delegation, so it is also accom-panied by formalization. Ross Webber (1969: 47–48), writing on 'Red Tape Versus Chaos', described how this process took place in the Xerox Company:

> From 1958 to the present, the old family-dominated Haloid Company, manufacturing specialized photographic products, was transformed into the modern Xerox Company, which jumped from $27 million to over $700 million a year in revenue.
> In the late 1950s, the company was in a chaotic state . . . Job descriptions were few, policies broad, procedures ignored, and controls weak. Yet the com-pany was successful . . . because of top management's ability to define direc-tion. Joseph Wilson, the president, spent much of his time selling the Xerox Company to his own managers, describing the revolutionary and beneficial impact of its information technology on society, and also pointing out how each manager's own interest would be served if the company advanced.

At this stage in the company's development, a lack of formalization encouraged its management to take initiatives—a premature introduction of procedures would have interfered with the spontaneous, innovative, organic type of approach that was being followed successfully. The company began to grow rapidly and formalization began to develop accordingly. Once the market for its new technology had been opened up and expansion got under way, Xerox management's main concern turned to internal costs and efficiency. Decisions became more complex and more people had to be involved; procedures were set up to make sure that information reached everyone concerned, that contributions were co-ordinated and that the best methods (once established) were recorded. Webber (op. cit.: 48–49) gives an example of this rationale and what it entails:

> A Xerox research and development engineer has indicated how elaboration of procedures has affected him. In 1959 when he had an idea that required funds, he would walk into the office of the vice-president with scratch pad and pencil, sit down, and sketch out the idea. A decision would be made quickly, and the researcher would begin working. Today, the same researcher must complete in multiple copies a regulation project form indicating potential equipment cost, material requirements, potential return, cash flow, and on and on. This is not simple red tape; multiple forms are not prescribed just to complicate the lives of people in the organization. Decisions about fund allocation are much more complex than in an earlier and simpler day. More and different projects are involved—they must be compared with one another on some consistent basis; and priority decisions must be reached with regard to organization objectives. Standard procedures for capital fund applications facilitate comparison, pre-diction, and control, essential functions of management in any organization.

Formalization assists control, and co-ordination, in the ways just de-scribed, in circumstances where there can be a substantial area of stability in an organization's activities. When an organization grows and centralized control becomes less and less effective, formalization serves to establish a framework of rules and systems within which decision-making can be delegated with reasonably predictable results. In fact, it has been found that large business organizations which combine delegation and formalization as their strategy of control tend to perform better on financial criteria than do equally large companies which are more centralized and less formalized (Child 1975). Environment and the nature of the business are, of course, relevant too, and a large firm operating in a dynamic environment can find itself in special difficulties since its size speaks for high formalization while its need to remain innovative and adaptive speaks for low formalization. Many have commented on the lack of innovativeness among large firms, and this structural dilemma has a lot to do with it.

When formalization is newly introduced into an organization, or is increased, it is apt to be met with resistance. Not only are people's established informal ways of doing things threatened but also they are likely to view the intervention of formal systems as an attempt to reduce their discretion, even if the intention is only to improve co-ordination or information retrieval. If formalized controls are resented for this reason, or because they are overtight and misdirected, then the people affected will probably respond by rejecting the controls and their avowed purpose in ways that could range from paying lip-service, to active sabotage, supplying false data and so forth. There are plenty of examples in industry and public life of how procedures when followed to the letter become self-defeating— 'working to rule'. 'Making out with the pencil' is also familiar enough, where achievement of expected standards is recorded on paper but the reality falls far short. An interesting case study of problems that can arise with the introduction of formalization has been written by John Berridge (1980) on the basis of his experience in the hospital service.

In the case study, which is based upon a real-life situation, a Medical Records Filing Department in an urban hospital is faced with a substantially increased load of work when the hospital takes over additional out-patient duties. The department functioned in an informal and relatively autonomous manner, with considerable flexibility in manning. It enjoyed high morale and gave good performance. The department was in effect operating as a semi-autonomous work group. Nevertheless, the view adopted by the hospital authorities was that because of the increasing scale of work the department would benefit from the introduction of more formalization, in terms of formal procedures, working instructions and systems. The intention was also to increase managerial control—to 'get a grip' on matters, as the man introducing formalization put it. The consequences of increasing formalization, and of the way this was done, were far from those anticipated. The members of the department resented the attempt to break up their close-knit group and informal working practices, which they had every reason to believe were efficient. The change was initiated and implemented without any discussion and when inefficiencies and lapses began to appear the response of management was to institute periodic spot checks, insist on new procedures and generally turn on the pressure. This did not help at all in a situation where the staff already felt under pressure to make the new system work somehow, and they began to take short-cuts. About six months after the change to more formalization, matters came to a head when a patient's records could not be found when required by a consultant. This case also serves to illustrate some of the problems of introducing change, which are discussed in Chapter 10.

Formalization may become necessary, but it carries with it dangers such as the type of non-acceptance by staff that I have just described. There are other points to guard against as well. If formal procedures, routines and plans are followed blindly, then an organization will lose direction. This is the much-discussed 'displacement of goals by means', which critics hold out to be the hallmark of a bureaucracy (itself the epitome of the formalized organization). For example, the German general staff in 1914 felt committed to follow the Schlieffen Plan, which had been meticulously drawn up years before, even when it became clear that the price of this rigidity was Britain's involvement in the war. The staff of some social welfare agencies investigated by American researchers have been found to adhere to procedures and formal performance criteria, even when this was clearly contrary to the best interests of individual clients (Blau 1955).

The problem is that once they become established and accepted, standing orders and procedures work to close out alternative perspectives and options—'the matter is settled; it cannot be re-opened'. The advantages of control which are gained when plans and procedures are newly formulated, and hence particularly relevant to the situation, may be lost if the appropriateness of these provisions in changed circumstances is not reviewed at frequent intervals. The more change the organization is experiencing the more frequent this review should be.

3 The degree of supervisory emphasis

Another method of control is to supervise subordinates' activities closely. This will require relatively narrow spans of control and will lead to a high proportion of managers and supervisors within an organization's total employment of staff. Close personal supervision is not the same as centralization since it does not necessarily mean that decisions are taken only at the upper levels of the hierarchy, though it will tend to transfer some decision-making from subordinates to supervisor. The purpose of close supervision, from a control point of view, is akin to that of formalization in that it imposes checks or limits on the discretion subordinates can use. Yet, again, the two are not the same and may even be substitutes. The setting out of rules and procedures may be an attempt to programme subordinates' actions in a way that spares the need for close supervision as a means of passing on or explaining instructions and ensuring that certain methods are followed. Personal supervision can also be used as a complement to formalization in situations where it is felt necessary to check that employees are keeping to formally laid down rules or job specifications.

Chapter 3 discussed the contingencies which were likely to be of relevance to supervisory emphasis. As noted, a high supervisory involvement ('burden of supervision') might be required for reasons other than that of maintaining control in a narrow sense—if, for example, a manager has to co-ordinate widely disparate types of activity or to be on hand to discuss complex or novel technical problems that his department deals with. A high degree of supervisory presence does not therefore necessarily simply mean close direct personal control, though it is liable to. As a means of control, supervisory emphasis is probably best suited to situations in which subordinates are lacking in skill and commitment to their work, the very type of employees that management may well have hired because of their low wage levels and low propensity to organize effective collective opposition. It may also be appropriate to periods of rapid development in which formalization has lagged behind, though it will normally cope very poorly with the integration across departments which rapid change may also require.

On the whole, supervisory emphasis incurs the significant disadvantages of overhead cost, reduction in employee motivation and attenuation of the hierarchy. Most modern thinking on organization therefore favours moves towards a reduction of supervisory emphasis and the encouragement where possible of 'self-control' by those doing the work. Some developments in practice have followed this path, though with the greatly enhanced capabilities which microelectronic technology offers for monitoring, there is also a trend towards substituting technological supervision for human supervision.

Strategies of control compared

Centralization–delegation, formalization–informality and the degree of supervisory emphasis are three major structural dimensions of control. The appropriate position for an organization to adopt on each dimension will vary according to its circumstances. These dimensions are not, however, independent of each other, but in fact serve complementary functions for management. In particular, the use of formalization as a means to 'structure' the activities of people within an organization may facilitate both an increase in delegation and a reduction in close supervision.

In an interesting study of five Canadian post-secondary community colleges, Heron and Friesen (1976) examined the relative use of these three control dimensions over the period of college growth and development. This is practically the only study so far to have recorded such data over time on a comparative basis. What it showed was that as the colleges grew larger:

1 their degree of formalization increased fairly steadily;
2 their degree of delegation increased overall, but was reduced for a while during growth;
3 their 'supervisory emphasis' (low first-line supervisory span of control and high percentage of managers to total employees) at first rose in step with delegation and subsequently tended to fall.

These relationships point to a number of tentative conclusions. First, the difference between small, young and larger, older organizations was marked. The small, young organization tended to be highly centralized, to have little formalization and not a great amount of close supervision. As growth proceeded, delegation increased, but this was accompanied by a rise in close supervision and, after a while, by a rise in formalization. Then a crisis of control appears to have been reached in which formalization was increased sharply, delegation decreased, but supervisory emphasis declined. At this point, it seems that formalization was rapidly being instituted as a control strategy in place of reliance on direct supervision and that, while formal procedures and job definition were being implemented, some degree of re-centralized decision-taking had to compensate for the relative reduction in direct supervision. In later stages of development, formalization tended to increase fairly steadily, delegation was re-instituted and extended, and the degree of supervisory emphasis grew once more before stabilizing.

These interpretations are extremely tentative and go beyond those which Heron and Friesen have felt it appropriate to offer. They serve to make the point, however, that management is faced with some choice in its structural approach to control, in that different configurations are possible along the three dimensions identified. This choice will probably be constrained by the prevailing situation, but may still allow for some expression of what is felt to be desirable managerial philosophy. Today, in view of the need to secure sufficient flexibility to cope with present rates of change and also inspired by Japanese levels of employee commitment, there is a growing interest in finding ways of promoting committed self-control and relaxing all three structural control mechanisms.

There are four particularly significant strategies of control in organizations. Each one contains several control features. Although more than one strategy can be adopted within a single organization, these will tend to be applied to different types of unit undertaking different types of work. The attempt to apply more than one strategy to a particular group of people engaged on similar work could be counter-productive. It runs the risk of exposing employees to inconsistencies and of destroying initiative if not actually provoking active resistance due to resentment at what is perceived as control over-kill. To some extent what I shall call 'cultural control' can be used to support the other three types but employees who accept cultural control in its fully developed form are likely to resist a heavy application of other strategies as well. This last reaction is particularly likely in Anglo-Saxon cultures with their emphasis on individualism and personal independence. There is some evidence to suggest that the heavy imposition of control through the use of more than one strategy simultaneously may be more attuned to cultures where passive acceptance of authority is the norm and is combined with low trust and low skills.

Table 6.1 lists the four strategies of control and their more common constituents. The first type, *personal centralized control*, is an approach which is often found in the small owner-managed enterprise. It is also a form of control which used to be associated very much with the internal subcontractor in building and civil engineering, the 'butty' in coalmining, and comparable arrangements in engineering and iron and steel making. From the perspective of top management, however, internal subcontracting is a form of output control. The centralization of decision-making and initiative around a

Table 6.1 Four strategies of control in organization

Each strategy will utilize one or more of the features listed[1]

1 *Personal centralized control*
  1.1 centralized decision-taking
  1.2 direct supervision
  1.3 personal leadership: founded upon ownership or charisma, or technical expertise
  1.4 reward and punishment reinforce conformity to personal authority

2 *Bureaucratic control*
  2.1 breaking down of tasks into easily definable elements
  2.2 formally specified methods, procedures and rules applied to the conduct of tasks
  2.3 budgetary and standard cost-variance accounting controls
  2.4 technology designed to limit variation in conduct of tasks, with respect to pace, sequence and possibly physical methods[2]
  2.5 routine decision-taking delegated within prescribed limits
  2.6 reward and punishment systems reinforce conformity to procedures and rules

3 *Output control*
  3.1 jobs and units designed to be responsible for complete outputs
  3.2 specification of output standards and targets
  3.3 use of 'responsibility accounting' systems
  3.4 delegation of decisions on operational matters: semi-autonomy
  3.5 reward and punishment linked to attainment of output targets

4 *Cultural control*
  4.1 development of strong identification with management goals
  4.2 semi-autonomous working: few formal controls
  4.3 strong emphasis on selection, training and development of personnel
  4.4 rewards oriented towards security of tenure and career progression

Notes: 1 The type of employees who are recruited can be varied to suit employment under each of these control strategies, within the constraints of cost and supply imposed by labour market conditions.
  2 Some authorities, such as Richard Edwards (1979), distinguish this as a separate control strategy.

leadership figure is the fundamental characteristic of this approach. Decisions are passed to the person at the top of the organization or in charge of the unit concerned. Control consists very largely of making sure through personal inspection that such decisions are carried out. Indeed, the leader may well spend a significant proportion of his time personally supervising the work. Once the organization is large enough to employ someone to supervise the details of everyday operations, the locus of centralized decision-making will tend to become separated from that of close supervision. The authority of the leader will generally rest upon his rights of ownership, or upon very special personal qualities (charisma), or technical expertise. A major criterion in allocating rewards and punishment is likely to be obedience to the leader's authority. Indeed, under these circumstances it is easy for favouritism to develop and to distort feedback.

The other strategies of control normally involve less centralization and less personal supervision by the senior manager. While, of course, centralization of feedback and decision-making is a matter of degree and can be varied according to the intrinsic importance of the issues at hand, a heavily centralized approach to control becomes increasingly difficult to sustain as organizations grow and as their operational complexity develops with diversification and technological advance. The sheer size and diversity of many large organizations today, and their consequently attenuated lines of communication, enforce a degree of decentralization in which control parameters are established with some reference to objectives and/or operating standards generated in sub-units such as divisions. A great deal of information relevant to the control process is generated by such sub-units, some of it technically complex, specific to the special nature of their activities and therefore not readily evaluated by top management. In a large, complex organization, top managers will not have the time to be immersed in details since as the leaders of prominent organizations they will find many external demands on their time. In short, a number of factors in the development of organization move their managements away from personal centralized control.

Bureaucratic control and output control both make use of formal structural mechanisms in an attempt to preserve managerial control without having to rely on centralization or close personal supervision.

The *bureaucratic control strategy* is a very familiar one, not only in the public service where it may be said to have originated, but also in larger organizations of all types. Its rationale is an attempt to ensure predictability through the specification of how people in the organization shall behave and carry out their work. Formalization in the sense of written definitions of jobs and procedures is the most characteristic feature of the bureaucratic control strategy. In industry, the breaking down of tasks into constituent elements is a common practice which, through the simplification involved, makes possible the specification of standard methods for the performance of each element. We have here, of course, the three Ss of scientific management— specialization leading to simplification and enabling standardization. Scientific management is a classic example of this control strategy. In some situations a combination of technological design with rules laid down by management can define and constrain employees' work behaviour within quite precise, and soul-destroying, limits. An extreme example of this combination was the automobile assembly line in the early days of companies such as Ford, where the adherence of employees to rules of conduct binding them to management's definition of how their job design should lock into technology was reinforced by close shopfloor supervision plus rewards for compliance and severe punishments for non-compliance.

Reward and punishment systems can therefore be designed with the intention of reinforcing this control strategy. Compliance and 'keeping your nose clean' can be rewarded by upgrading, admission to staff status, the award of more favourable employment benefits and (not least) job security. These prospects of incorporation into the more privileged sector of employment—which labour economists designate as the primary segment of the internal labour market within organizations—have close affinities with the offer of job security and a progression of benefits according to length of tenure that is made available to the compliant official in a public service 'bureaucracy'. Non-compliance, in contrast, may well invoke in increasing order of sanction, a bar to further progression, downgrading, and ultimately dismissal.

The accounting control systems that are most compatible with the bureaucratic strategy of control are budgetary control and control of variance from standard costs. Budgetary control involves a regularly repeated process of formulating a budget, often on an annual basis, followed by a set of budget reports usually submitted on a much more frequent basis (often monthly). Since budgets are typically broken down into expenditure norms for specific tasks or operations, they are in effect structured controls over the behaviour of units, groups or individuals. Similarly, a standard cost-variance control system involves a process of determining what costs should be under specified operating systems, using these costs as standards of performance, measuring actual performance and then evaluating this against the standard costs. The determination of standard costs is, in effect, establishing a major parameter for the ways in which subordinates can go about doing their work. The whole bureaucratic strategy is aimed at the control of how things are done and how people in organizations behave—it is a 'behaviour control' approach that William Ouchi (1978) has contrasted to the 'output control' approach discussed below.

A characteristic of bureaucratic control, and indeed of all the strategies apart from personal control, is that it permits managers to delegate without necessarily losing control over what is going on. The bureaucratic strategy permits a delegation of routine decision-making within formalized limits to discretion. Output control, to anticipate, permits delegation since subordinates are explicitly monitored for results achieved. Cultural control, the fourth type, permits delegation in so far as subordinates have a strong identification with goals set for the organization and trained competence to carry out their work and exercise discretion to predictable and adequate standards.

Output control depends upon having the ability to identify tasks which are complete in themselves in the sense of having a measurable output or criterion of overall achievement. An output in this sense does not have to be an end-product—it could be a piece-part manufactured to agreed standards, a batch of microchips or a sub-assembly. Common criteria of achievement, applied to individuals or groups, product lines and whole units respectively, are quantity of items processed, value added and profitability. Once outputs or criteria for overall achievement have been identified, it is possible for management to specify output standards and targets. Rewards and sanctions can be linked to the attainment of performance expressed in output terms, and in this way a direct incentive is created for subordinates to meet and surpass output standards. The efficiency of this incentive will depend greatly on the degree of trust in management's intentions to honour the equation between rewards and performance. If this trust is lacking both the incentive value of the system and the accuracy of information released to management is likely to suffer. Assessments of performance are liable to create tension and resentment if any suspicion of inequity is present.

The kind of financial accounting system most suited to output control is what Flamholtz (1979) has called 'responsibility accounting'. This assigns financial responsibility to specified organizational sub-units, measures the performance of those units, and provides feedback on performance both to the persons assigned responsibility and to those who supervise them. The assignment of responsibility for a rounded activity may be in terms of investment centres in which those responsible have authority over revenues, costs and capital investment; profit centres where control is delegated over revenues and costs but not investment; or cost centres where control is delegated over costs but not over revenue-generating decisions or over capital investment.

The output control strategy is clearly aimed at facilitating the delegation of operational decision-making without incurring the costly and potentially demotivating paraphernalia of bureaucratic controls or of relying on close personal supervision. Once output standards have been agreed with subordinates, it is often possible to leave them to work free from detailed control over how they do things, in what has come to be called a 'semi-autonomous' relationship to management. It also has the merit of directing the process of control towards the issue that really counts for the long-term survival of the organization, its performance; though the problem is likely to arise of conflicts between the criteria assigned to different sub-units competing for resources or custom.

From the historical standpoint, it is interesting to note that a forerunner of the output control approach was widespread in the nineteenth century. This was the system of inside contracting under which the factory and site owner supplied raw materials, usually provided the machinery, and took responsibility for the use or sale of the output. The workers were in the employment of a subcontractor who carried out his own recruitment and labour management. The owner agreed a contract price with the subcontractor for a given level of output, or a price per unit of output. This arrangement relieved the owner of the problems of managing workers directly, and enabled him to adjust the labour force readily in the event of changes in demand. The risk of uncertainty in demand for production was thus passed on to the inside contractor (Littler 1982).

If output control is in principle such an attractive strategy for management, what stands in the way of its general adoption? One problem is that the autonomy of individual workgroups or teams, which output control encourages, can stand in the way of introducing technological advances that require a more integrated system of production (for example, mechanized or automated transfer equipment). However, in this situation it may be feasible to shift the focus of output control up a level to plant rather than group output. Work groups will also resist management suggestions for improved methods of working, if these threaten their internal structure or are seen as preludes to re-negotiating the rate of payment per unit of output downwards. There is again a parallel here with internal contractors who sought to restrict management's knowledge of the true costs of the work done by their teams in order to keep their price high at the expense of the profit available to the owner.

Another practical problem with output control may be the difficulty of establishing suitable and agreed measures of output—how for example do you measure the output of the foreign service or of the legal department in a business company? On the other hand, if the processes whereby results are achieved are not well understood and therefore not codifiable by management, as in some professional activities and industrial research, output controls may be called for because it is not feasible to apply a bureaucratic strategy.

Organizations offering professional services and heavily staffed by professional people and trained specialists tend to exemplify the fourth strategy of control: *cultural control*. The rationale of this strategy is very much one of maintaining control by ensuring that members of an organization accept as legitimate, and willingly comply with, managerial requirements. A strong professional identification is one example. What Ouchi and Price (1978) have called the 'industrial clan' is another. Perhaps the most striking example of industrial clans can be found in the larger Japanese corporations, where extremely high levels of productivity and employee loyalty to the corporations are usual. An important foundation for this commitment appears to be a common socialization into corporate culture and the ready acceptance of its values and beliefs.

As with output control, subordinates who are subject to an effective cultural control can be given considerable freedom to decide on how to go about their work, assuming that they possess the necessary skills and abilities. The difference is that there is not necessarily any reliable or valid way of assessing the quality of their output, at least in the short term. The full worth of a personnel department's engagement in management development work may not, for instance, become apparent for some years. Management can contemplate semi-autonomous modes of working with few formal controls if there is a high degree of consensus within the organization. In order to increase the chances of such consensus, or cultural homogeneity, there is likely to be an emphasis on careful selection of new recruits, on their training and general socialization into the culture. Rewards are likely to be oriented towards security of tenure and progression up a career ladder. There is, in short, a development of a strong 'internal labour market' within the employing organization. To the extent that employees and subordinates in any organization accept management's right to give executive instructions then one could argue that a degree of cultural control had thereby been achieved—what has been called a 'pragmatic acceptance' of a social system in which there will be inequalities of power and authority. Cultural control goes further in that it is a consciously designed strategy for developing pragmatic acceptance into a much more enthusiastic support for management's purposes and is thereby a means for fashioning employees' behaviour along desired lines.

Cultural control combined with personal autonomy to follow strongly internalized norms of competence and conduct has long been the mark of the professional. Professional people, more than most, resent having administrative controls imposed on them when they become employees of large institutions. The proportion of professional and trained manpower in the working population of most societies is steadily increasing, and this in itself is establishing the requirement for a new approach to control. The question arises whether or not to extend this approach to other employees, developing a comparable mode of self-control within agreed cultural parameters worked out through discussion and negotiation. Experiments in 'autonomous group working' are a move in this direction.

If the momentum of the 1970s towards industrial democracy and participation returns, it is likely that we shall see further moves away from centralization and formalization in favour of a framework of mutually agreed methods of working. As John Dickson (1981) has pointed out, participation can be used as a means of organizational control through establishing a framework of rules which, among other things, limits the issues that can be raised. The new approach would combine elements of cultural and output control. It could lead to self-managing units or teams having responsibility for meeting agreed targets and completing projects. The teams' self-management would be assisted by a more frequent feedback to them of information on their progress against targets, budgets and so forth. Advances in information processing technology will facilitate this considerably. At longer intervals, the teams would evaluate their progress with higher management. The principle here is rather similar to the relations between head office and divisions in a large decentralized multidivisional enterprise. It is also beginning to emerge in a form of home-working, where data lines link people working in their own homes with a central office. This is in effect a new type of subcontracting arrangement with payment being made for a given amount of work or work time, usually to senior staff who can be relied on to accept the cultural norms of the organization.

This approach to control can only work with agreement on operating objectives. It depends upon the presence of some shared culture among the members of an organization. It is interesting to note the great effort which many large divisionalized companies are investing in building a common culture among their managers, as a means to ensuring some predictability of behaviour and commitment to central corporate goals. Some multinational corporations, for example, use frequent job rotation among key executives in order to speed up their socialization into the corporate culture, build them into the corporate verbal information network and, in developing a close self-conscious elite, generally ensure their loyalty to and understanding of top management objectives when decisions of considerable consequence are delegated to them (Edstrom and Galbraith 1977).

If this newer approach is successful it may sustain a common outlook among people in organizations far more effectively than more traditional strategies of control. For it offers what is probably the only way of reconciling the underlying need for the management process with employees' desire for more participation and self-fulfilment. It is also the type of control that seems best suited to handle the increasing rate of industrial change and uncertainty, where new markets, projects, processes, techniques and other developments become a way of life. In such conditions, specialist employees, rather than higher management, become the font of required knowledge and information, and traditional bureaucratic formalization with its built-in delayed action cannot cope with the speed of information processing and response that is required.

While cultural control may of itself foster identification with the objectives of corporate management, it should be noted that it is usually supported by substantial material inducements. This is certainly true of salaries paid to the managers of multinational corporations. In the large Japanese corporations, which are often cited as examples of cultural control, initial entry to employment is competitive and there is a considerable loss in security and material benefits should an employee have to leave, since the large companies offering generous fringe benefits are reluctant to recruit from each other. In these circumstances, there is a significant material inducement to show identification with the company.

Accounting controls, organizational controls and relevant contingencies

I have suggested that certain types of accounting control are consistent with particular organizational control strategies. Recent discussion and research on management accounting have developed our understanding of how the design of accounting controls relates to organizational control as a whole and how the selection of the overall organizational control package can be made more usefully if contingent factors are taken into account. Considerations of consistency and contingency are therefore raised. A good introduction to the work which has been under way on this topic is provided by David Otley (1980).

An accounting control and information system will only comprise one element in the control structure of an organization. It should therefore be designed to be consistent with other systems of control and information which are in use (the reverse is also true, of course). Otley points out that in practice managers often regard one of the purposes of their accounting system as being to cope with known weaknesses in organizational design. This suggests that several different combinations of accounting and organizational control may give the desired results under given circumstances, and that consistency between the different control features is a relevant consideration in addition to matching situational contingencies. As Otley states, 'the folly of attempting to construct a contingency theory of the AIS (accounting information system) outside of the context of an overall organization control package is thus apparent' (p.421).

The grouping of activities has implications for the design of accounting controls. In a functionally structured organization where one general manager is responsible for the entire range of its activities, for their performance and for investment, a fairly high degree of centralization may be his chosen approach. An accounting system consistent with this approach would designate responsibility for investment to the general manager (as the investment centre). This leaves the possibility of designating functions such as manufacturing as a standard cost or a profit centre, and marketing as a revenue or a profit centre, depending upon the degree of influence which the functional managers can have (or are intended to have) over relevant parameters. When a product divisional form of structure is adopted, the divisions are almost always treated as profit or investment centres, very much in keeping with the strategy of output control. The intentions of a matrix structure to achieve on both efficiency *and* effectiveness can be frustrated if primarily cost or productivity oriented functional unit controls are not complemented by accounting systems oriented towards overall project or product costs and revenues irrespective of the functional units in which these may have been incurred or generated. A way of summarizing this point in more general terms is to follow Richard Vancil (1973) in saying that the choice of a design for assigning financial responsibility should be made in the light of the type of delegation and grouping (specialization) built into the overall organization structure and of the strategic vision the structure is meant to support.

In a comparison of 27 manufacturing and service companies in North America, conducted by Bruns and Waterhouse (1975), it was found that where decision-making was generally centralized, less complex accounting controls were used, such as standard cost-variances. Where, on the other hand, a bureaucratic control strategy was followed, accounting controls were not necessarily more complex, but managers at different hierarchical levels perceived that greater control was exercised throughout the organization and that they participated more in the budgeting process. It has also been suggested in a review conducted by Kerr and Slocum (1981) that the cultural strategy of control, which normally involves a high level of participation in the operation of accounting systems and other controls, is more appropriately adopted along with organic forms of organization in which the nature of variability and complexity in the activities undertaken may render ineffective an attempt to control centrally or formalistically. On the other hand, they suggest that where mechanistic structures are used 'formal leadership functions' will provide an adequate control framework. These include formalization, setting budgets, use of output standards, reward and punishment systems, and various types of personal leadership appeal and persuasion.

Reference to the conditions under which mechanistic and organic structures are appropriate, and the link to accounting controls, carries us into a contingency perspective which envisages variations in organizational design to suit different circumstances. A range of contingent factors relevant for the choice of accounting and organizational controls has been proposed, but it is still premature to derive firm conclusions from this relatively new area of enquiry. However, Otley in his paper concurs in broad terms with Kerr and Slocum's review, when he concludes that one contingency in particular stands out, 'namely unpredictability (variously referred to as uncertainty, non-routineness, dynamism etc.)' (p.423). The greater the unpredictability inherent in the activities of an organization or one of its units, the less useful will it be to rely upon either a centralized strategy of control (unless the organization is very small and entrepreneurially led) or a bureaucratic strategy of high formalization. This means, for management accounting, that reliance on standard cost-variance and budgets should, in unpredictable conditions, either be serviced by advanced information processing that permits short-term recalculations and adjustments, or make way for decentralized responsibility accounting methods.

Contingency analysis is always made more complicated and more tenuous by the fact that multiple contingencies are normally present. For example, in unpredictable conditions, a small organization which is not highly diversified or scattered geographically and in which the information processing load is thereby kept down, can possibly be controlled in a personal centralized mode without the development of a complex accounting information system. If, in contrast, the organization is larger and more diversified, delegation will probably be more appropriate with accounting controls directed where possible towards outputs. When unpredictability, complexity and the burden of information processing are all very high, then decision-making may have to become diffused throughout the organization, formalization is more of a hindrance than a help, and management's best bet is probably to rely upon cultural control. Accounting may no longer be very helpful as a control mechanism, but is instead largely confined to providing a historical record.

Studies into retailing stores conducted by Ouchi (1977, 1978) in the United States and Piper (1980) in Britain draw attention to the relevance which complexity in an organization's operations has for the design of financial and organizational controls. Although complexity is conceptually distinct from unpredictability due to change, it is comparable in the uncertainty it is liable to create for top management, which finds that it cannot possibly have a close knowledge of what is going on. In multiple retailing companies, indicators of complexity include the range of products offered, diversity of product range, and variability between outlets in terms of size, location and product mix. Piper's case studies suggest that the greater the complexity the lower the level of financial control structuring, where indicators of structuring are complexity of the model used in financial planning, frequency of performance evaluation, extent to which financial standards are used, and extent of feedback to store management on performance against standards and budgets. Moreover, greater complexity was accompanied by a more decentralized pattern of decision-making.

A lower level of financial structure measured in these terms is consistent with an output control strategy rather than bureaucratic or centralized ones. With this in mind, Ouchi's conclusion can be seen to be comparable, namely that when managers have limited knowledge of the 'transformation processes' involved in an organization's work they will find output control to be more appropriate than bureaucratic control so long as outputs (i.e. final results) can be measured. Output control was also found to be the more effective in larger organizations with many hierarchical levels. Clearly, personal centralized control is not possible in such cases without imposing enormous strains on top management, while the impact of bureaucratic control is liable to become diluted across many hierarchical levels. A final observation that emerges from Piper's work and some other studies is the perhaps obvious point that accounting controls are liable to become more elaborate and specific, and have more emphasis placed upon them, when the organization is under competitive or financial pressures.

This section, then, has introduced the practical need to design organizational controls and accounting controls in conjunction with each other. In the attempt to achieve a consistent approach in this way, the choice of control strategy has to be made with reference to the type of activities undertaken by the organization and to other situational contingencies. This is a most complex field of management planning, which is not always addressed adequately in practice and where relevant research is unfortunately still sparse and exploratory. Table 6.2 summarizes contingencies which this chapter has discussed in connection with the choice of control strategy, but a drawback with such a table is that it does not cope with the reality of multiple contingencies. For example, centralized and bureaucratic control strategies tend to be listed together, but size of organization is likely to be a major deciding factor between them. Similarly, output and cultural controls often appear together and indeed I have suggested that they can be mutually supporting. However, the measurability of outputs is likely to be a deciding factor between them.

Table 6.2 Strategies of control and related contingencies

Contingent factors	When	Control strategies likely to be appropriate (/ = and/or)
1. Demand for products or services (market and competitive strength)	strong weak	output/cultural centralized/bureaucratic
2. Position of employees in labour market	strong weak	output/cultural supervisory emphasis/bureaucratic
3. Employee skills and expertise	high low	output/cultural supervisory emphasis/bureaucratic
4. Environmental variability: unpredictability of activities	high low	output/cultural centralized/bureaucratic
5. Technology: range of activities and interdependence	complex simple	output/cultural centralized/bureaucratic
6. Task characteristics: outputs	measurable not measurable	output other types
7. Task characteristics: knowledge of transformation processes	good limited	centralized/bureaucratic output/cultural
8. Size of organization	small large	centralized other types

Summary

Control in organizations is a focus of conflict as well as a basis for achieving co-operative effort. It is necessary to note this paradox in order to appreciate the limitations to the contribution that organizational control strategies can make. The conjunction of conflict and consensus also suggests that different approaches to control will be appropriate depending on whether the issues are ones over which management and employees agree or not.

When working out a policy on control, choices have to be made in terms of several organizational design dimensions. These are, first, how far to delegate decision-making, second, how much to formalize procedures and working practices and, third, how much emphasis to place on direct supervision. Different choices are likely to suit different circumstances, and various configurations of the design dimensions are possible. Four particularly significant strategies of control are identified and each represents a particular configuration of dimensions. These strategies are personal, centralized control; bureaucratic control; output control; and cultural control.

One of the elements entering into each control strategy is the management accounting system. These systems need to be consistent with the organizational control strategy as a whole, while the appropriateness of the different strategies will depend upon contingent factors in the organization's operating situation.

Suggested further reading

Graeme Salaman, *Work Organization: Resistance and Control* (Longman 1979) analyses the design of work and control in organizations drawing attention to areas of conflict. His article with Craig Littler, Craig R. Littler and Graeme Salaman, 'Bravermania and Beyond: Recent Theories of the Labour Process', *Sociology*, May 1982, also provides an insightful, though difficult, analysis. John Storey, *Managerial Prerogative and the Question of Control* (Routledge and Kegan Paul 1983) is another academic treatment, which draws upon a wide range of literature and examples to conclude that managerial control is a more complex, yet more precarious, process than has been appreciated.

Andrew L. Friedman, *Industry and Labour* (Macmillan 1977) traces the relationship between market conditions and modes of controlling the workforce in British industries, and links this to employment policies. Chris Argyris, *Personality and Organization* (Harper and Row 1957) discusses areas of conflict between the more traditional approaches to management control and the psychological bases of motivation. Edward E. Lawler III and John Grant Rhode, *Information and Control in Organizations* (Goodyear 1976) also gives attention to motivational and behavioural considerations and has a good analysis of how control systems can encourage behaviour that is not intended by management. Roger L. M. Dunbar, 'Designs for Organizational Control' in Paul C. Nystrom and William H. Starbuck (editors), *Handbook of Organizational Design*, vol. 2 (Oxford University Press 1981) discusses ways of facilitating the process of control. Chris Argyris again in 'Single-Loop and Double-Loop Models in Research on Decision Making', *Administrative Science Quarterly*, September 1976 draws attention to the need for control processes to contribute to managerial learning.

On control in the Ford Motor Company, see Huw Beynon's *Working for Ford* (Penguin 2nd edition 1983). An informative history of a developing approach towards control in a large corporation, General Electric, is recorded in Ronald G. Greenwood, *Managerial Decentralization* (Lexington Books 1974). Alfred D. Chandler, Jr. and Herman Daems, 'Administrative Co-ordination, Allocation and Monitoring', *Accounting, Organizations and Society* vol. 4, 1979 examine the complementary development of accounting and organizational control techniques in American and European firms.

Other sources mentioned or used in this chapter were John Berridge 'Changing Complex Information Systems: Medical Records at Anersley Hospital', in *Systems Organization: The Management of Complexity*. Block 3 'Organizations', (The Open University Press 1980); Peter M. Blau, *The Dynamics of Bureaucracy* (University of Chicago Press 1955); William J. Bruns, Jr. and John H. Waterhouse, 'Budgetary Control and Organization Structure', *Journal of Accounting Research*, Autumn 1975; Howard M. Carlisle, 'A Contingency Approach to Decentralization', *Advanced Management Journal*, July 1974; John Child, 'Predicting and Understanding Organization Structure', *Administrative Science Quarterly*, June 1973; John Child, 'Managerial and Organizational Factors Associated with Company Performance—Part II A Contingency Analysis', *Journal of Management Studies*, February 1975; John Child and Alfred Kieser, 'Organization and Managerial Roles in British and German Companies', in C. J. Lammers and D. J. Hickson (editors), *Organizations: Like and Unlike* (Routledge and Kegan Paul 1979), Chapter 13; John Child and Brenda Macmillan, 'Managerial Leisure in British and American Contest', *Journal of Management Studies* May 1972; Dan Clawson, *Bureaucracy and the Labor Process* (Monthly Review Press 1980); John W. Dickson, 'Participation as a Means of Organizational Control', *Journal of Management Studies*, April 1981; Anders Edstrom and Jay R. Galbraith, 'Transfer of Managers as a Coordination and Control Strategy in Multinational Organizations', *Administrative Science Quarterly*, June 1977; Richard Edwards, *Contested Terrain: The Transformation of the Workplace in the Twentieth Century* (Basic Books/Heinemann 1979); Henri Fayol, *General and Industrial Management* (Pitman 1949); Eric Flamholtz, 'Behavioral Aspects of Accounting Control Systems' in Steven Kerr (editor), *Organizational Behavior* (Grid 1979), Chapter 12; R. P. Heron and D. Friesen, 'Organizational Growth and Development', *University of Alberta, Edmonton, Working Paper*, March 1976; Steven Kerr and John W. Slocum, Jr., 'Controlling the Performances of People in Organizations', in Paul C. Nystrom and William H. Starbuck (editors), *Handbook of Organizational Design* (Oxford University Press 1981), vol. 2; Craig R. Littler, *The Development of the Labour Process in Capitalist Societies* (Heinemann 1982); John L. J. Machin, 'A Contingent Methodology for Management Control', *Journal of Management Studies* February 1979; David T. Otley, 'The Contingency Theory of Management Accounting: Achievement and Prognosis', *Accounting, Organizations and Society*, vol. 5, no. 4, 1980;

William G. Ouchi, 'The Relationship Between Organizational Structure and Organizational Control', *Administrative Science Quarterly*, March 1977; William G. Ouchi, 'The Transmission of Control through Organizational Hierarchy', *Academy of Management Journal*, June 1978; William G. Ouchi and Raymond L. Price, 'Hierarchies, Clans and Theory Z', *Organizational Dynamics*, Autumn 1978; J. A. Piper, 'Determinants of Financial Control Systems for Multiple Retailers—Some Case Study Evidence', *Managerial Finance*, vol. 6, 1980; Richard F. Vancil, 'What Kind of Management Control do you Need?', *Harvard Business Review,* March–April 1973; Ross A. Webber, 'Red Tape versus Chaos', *Business Horizons*, April 1969.

CHAPTER 7

Reward Policies

'Rewards and punishments are the basis of good government'. **Proverb.**

A whole range of rewards and punishments are in daily use within organizations, and these are quite central to the process of employment. An employment contract specifies the remuneration, and possibly other benefits, offered to an individual in return for making available to the employer his or her capacity for work. That capacity, however, still has to be converted into an active contribution towards the attainment of organizational objectives. Policies on rewards and punishments (reward policies) are intended to elicit this contribution. They are therefore an essential complement to the process of control.

The specific objectives of rewards and punishments are different. Rewards are in principle intended to encourage the type of behaviour which precedes them, while punishments are intended to prevent a repetition of previous behaviours. For management, the criterion of success for reward policies is that they motivate employees to commit high levels of physical or mental effort towards performing required tasks well. A condition for their success is also that the employees concerned regard the rewards offered to them as attractive and fair, and any punishments as legitimate and merited.

The most tangible rewards are extrinsic ones. These are attached to jobs rather than deriving directly from their actual content. The principal extrinsic rewards are pay, fringe benefits, security of employment, promotion, special awards and status symbols. In contrast, intrinsic rewards come from the qualities of work and relationships within the jobs themselves. They are less tangible than extrinsic rewards and more difficult to adjust, but their effects are not necessarily any the less important. The qualities which may generate intrinsic rewards for employees include variety in job content, responsibility, autonomy, social interaction, participation in setting targets and determining methods of work, and feedback of information. The developments in job design and work restructuring which were considered in Chapter 2 are therefore also policies on the kinds of intrinsic rewards to be offered.

Punishment is involved whenever an otherwise expected reward is witheld or any other sanction is applied and linked to a specific behaviour which it is wished to discourage. For instance, management may refuse to make a bonus payment under certain circumstances, as in a British confectionery plant where, under a recent agreement, a monthly bonus of 3 per cent is witheld from any individual or group refusing to be redeployed between jobs according to the terms of a flexibility provision. To quote from the agreement, 'Refusal to carry out the work will be treated as a disciplinary offence'. Delaying a person's promotion would be another example of witholding a reward. A more severe sanction, that of dismissal, actually terminates the employment contract and is normally linked to specific offences such as theft at work. When considering the points this chapter makes about reward policies, the punishment aspect should be kept in mind. Indeed, at a time of high unemployment the threat of punishment in terms of losing their jobs assumes major proportions for many people.

This chapter analyses the main issues and choices concerned in reward policies. A reward policy involves the selection of a portfolio of rewards and the design of the precise form in which they are offered, with the intention of motivating employees to contribute effectively to a set of organizational objectives. The fact that a wide range of rewards is available, that these can be applied in different forms, and that there are multiple objectives to be achieved, makes this an extremely complex subject on which many contrasting opinions and theories are voiced. The intention here is to provide an introduction and a guide to key aspects of the topic, and to point the way to detailed treatments which others have offered.

The design of reward systems is so complementary to that of organization that it is quite appropriate to regard the subject as an aspect of organizational design. Previous chapters have drawn attention to several examples of the interdependence between organization and reward systems. Chapter 2 noted how modifications to work organization may require the abandoning of individually based incentives in order to support a group mode of working. Chapter 3 discussed the problem of aligning a salary structure with the design of hierarchical levels of authority. Chapter 6 indicated that suitably designed rewards should contribute towards the operation of an organization's control system by encouraging subordinates to achieve given standards or targets. To be successful, then, the focus of rewards must be compatible with the tasks and structures laid down for the organization, which gives them a *contingent* aspect. Rewards also have to assume some importance for the people concerned in order to activate a response from them, and this lends them a *motivational* aspect.

The first section below considers the criteria that management and employees apply to rewards. These criteria highlight the contingency and motivational aspects of the subject. The next section looks at analyses which suggest conditions for linking together these two aspects in an effective manner, and the practical implications which follow. The final section reviews specific forms of financial reward, and discusses the contingent and motivational considerations relevant to a choice between them.

Criteria applied to rewards

1 Managerial criteria

Jay Galbraith (1977) identifies a number of employee behaviours which management may expect a system of rewards to encourage. These

behaviours are necessary to achieve the goals established for the organization, though their relative saliency will depend on the type of work the
organization undertakes and the conditions in which it is currently
operating.

First, people have to be attracted to fill job vacancies in the organization
and to feel sufficiently satisfied with the rewards these offer not to leave for
another employment. Labour market conditions are clearly very relevant
for the level of reward that will satisfy this criterion, particularly the ease
with which an employee can attain alternative employment offering
superior rewards (or fewer disadvantages) and accessible from where he or
she is prepared to live. The cost of labour turnover to the organization is,
however, itself contingent. It depends on the investment in skill and
experience that is lost when an employee leaves in relation to the cost of
obtaining a replacement, including any time and expenditure needed to
bring the new recruit up to the required standard. In some circumstances
there may be very little cost, as when labour turnover provides an opportunity to adjust employment levels downwards without incurring severance
payments or creating a climate of fear about job insecurity. There are also
occasions when people decide to leave their jobs because they are not suited
to them, which in effect rectifies an error in their original selection. Another
aspect of this 'join and remain' criterion of reward policy is the avoidance of
absenteeism. The costs incurred by organizations as a result of absenteeism
usually far outweigh those due to industrial disputes. In short, the first
managerial criterion for assessing the quality of its reward policy is that it
should attract and retain employees who have qualities appropriate for the
division of labour contained in the structural and technological design of the
organization.

A second managerial criterion is that rewards should increase the predictability of employees' behaviour so that they can be depended upon to carry
out the duties requested of them consistently and to reasonable standards.
For instance, opportunities for upgrading or even promotion will tend to
increase the predictability of behaviour among employees who have some
ambition if it is apparent that certain types of behaviour enhance the prospects of career advancement. Indeed, some critics have suggested that
reward policies of this kind can generate behaviour which is over-
dependable in the sense of conforming unduly and uncritically to what
higher management expects. This could run counter to the criterion of
innovative behaviour which is discussed shortly.

A third criterion is that management will look to its reward policy to
secure a degree of commitment and a level of effort from employees that
goes beyond mere predictability and dependability. The extent to which
that extra percentage is forthcoming may make a significant difference to
the competitiveness of a business company or, in the case of a public agency,
to the quality and cost of services provided.

The three criteria mentioned so far relate primarily to the goal of
organizational efficiency—the attainment of high employee productivity
and the minimization of costs. Nowadays, with the high rates of change and
competitive pressures experienced by many organizations, two further

criteria, mentioned in Chapter 6 in connection with control, have become prominent, namely flexibility and development. Management has to create the conditions in which any necessary flexibility in the throughput of work and in deployment of labour can be achieved. At the time of writing, flexibility has become a prime requirement in many sectors of manufacturing because of the need to switch production more frequently between batches, which are now smaller in a period of depressed demand. Another consideration is that flexible deployment will economize on manning, and will also suit the possibilities now being offered by computer programming for running more complex and varied configurations of work through given production facilities. Where the need for flexible deployment between tasks or workflows exists, rewards should be such as to encourage a willingness among employees to accept a broadening of their jobs, including (1) an extension of skills learned and applied, and (2) working together with members of other crafts, specialisms or departments when required. For example, upgrading might be offered when relevant new skills are acquired, or a bonus might be paid for accepting flexible deployment provisions.

The continued development of an organization benefits from its longer-serving employees acquiring new skills and experience. It also depends on the capacity of at least some members to suggest, and indeed argue for, change and innovation. Certain employees occupy jobs in which it is particularly important that they recognize and deal with new problems and challenges in an innovative way. Research and development personnel are the most obvious example, but others include site installation engineers, salesmen involved with contract negotiations and workers who may be constructing prototypes or working with methods or equipment that could be improved. A reward policy should encourage innovative behaviour among those employees from whom it is particularly required. A more debatable question is whether it is appropriate to reward suggestions for innovation from any member of the labour force. One difficulty is that employees lacking the necessary training or experience with problems may suggest impractical solutions which cannot justify a reward, despite the positive intentions and work that may have gone into the suggestion. On the other hand, some managements who believe strongly in the innovative potential locked into their workforce do persist with organization-wide suggestion schemes and claim considerable benefits from them.

Five criteria which management is likely to apply to rewards have been identified, and these refer to the kinds of behaviour that it may seek to encourage: (1) attracting and retaining required personnel; (2) encouraging dependable behaviour; (3) securing high commitment and effort; (4) encouraging flexibility; and (5) fostering innovation. These criteria are clearly contingent to the type of personnel required, the nature of the work being undertaken, and the particular pressures for change and innovation being experienced by the organization. In some situations, certain criteria will be more salient than others. Some criteria may apply to certain sections of the workforce. Particular criteria will also be more readily satisfied through one kind of reward than another. For example, incentives which are intended to encourage a high level of individual effort may inhibit the willingness of workers to accept flexible deployment between tasks, if they believe that other tasks do not allow for equally high levels of measured output. The evolution of a policy on rewards will therefore require a decision on the balance of emphasis which management considers appropriate to its priorities and its assessment of contingencies, and from which a design for its reward systems should in principle follow.

The five criteria are each concerned with the kind of behaviour that management is seeking to encourage among employees. A sixth criterion is, in contrast, structural in nature. This is the requirement that differential levels of reward, particularly pay, should accord with the structure laid down for the organization, at least in terms of the relative hierarchical and status position of job categories. The traditional means of meeting this structural requirement has been job evaluation, which is the process of analysing and assessing different jobs on a systematic basis in order to establish their relative worth for purposes of payment. Skill, knowledge required and accountability are typical of the factors taken into account in job evaluation schemes. Job evaluation can be allied to the use of rewards to promote desired behaviour if it is used to establish a base level of reward that specifies a differential between one job category and others, on top of which additional rewards linked to behaviour and performance are then offered. The basic structure of rewards has to be aligned to the general structure of the organization, not only to preserve orderliness but also to reflect the logic of that structure in terms of features such as the hierarchical differences in level of work which it incorporates. This structural criterion is also compatible, in principle, with the importance which employees attach to differential payments and the way that these should 'fairly' reflect differences in the intrinsic nature of jobs and the qualifications required to fill them.

2 Employees' criteria

The criteria which employees apply to rewards give an indication of their motivational potential. Psychologists have tended to regard these reward criteria as deriving from the needs of individuals at work. They have debated whether individuals will differ considerably in their perceived needs, preferences and values, or whether instead a general model can be discerned, which applies in a more or less similar manner to all people at work. Those commenting from a sociological or industrial relations perspective emphasize that the most influential criteria which employees apply to rewards are social in nature. That is, they are collectively held by socially defined groups of employees, such as the members of a given occupation, and they are particularly informed by comparisons with other social groups. This fundamental contrast in approach therefore boils down to whether the value which people at work place on rewards, and the basis on which they assess the adequacy and reasonableness of rewards, derives primarily from their outstanding human needs or from norms shared within the social reference group to which they belong.

There has been a tension for a long time now between those psychologists who recognize that there are a large number of specific needs which human beings seek to satisfy, and others who have striven to reduce this complexity and to establish order by means of grouping, classifying and developing a typology of needs. Clearly, if any such ordered typology could validly be established it would well suit the purposes of people such as managers who are concerned with the practicality of motivating people to act in certain ways, and who cannot apply too complex a model without incurring undue cost and possible confusion. This helps to account for the popularity of Maslow's (1970) grouping of human needs into only five categories which he then suggested formed a hierarchy such that only when the needs in one category were satisfied did those at the next highest level become salient for the individual concerned. This 'need hierarchy' envisaged an upward progression from fundamental 'physiological' or material needs, through 'safety' or security needs, 'social and affiliation' needs, 'esteem' needs, to 'self-actualization' needs at the highest level. Although Maslow's formulation of his need hierarchy lacked an empirical foundation, it achieved wide acceptance and has influenced many managerial and academic views about employees' likely motivational responses to particular rewards. This includes the notion that as people become more affluent, they will attach a diminishing value to further increments of pay (in real terms at least) and an increasing value to other, intrinsic, rewards.

Herzberg (with Mausner and Snyderman 1959) in what was in effect a further simplification, distinguished two categories of rewards relating to Maslow's need hierarchy. First, rewards that satisfied lower order needs such as pay and working conditions were considered as components of a 'hygiene' factor. Any inadequacy in these rewards would create dissatisfaction, but their adequate provision would not generate any motivation to perform the work itself any better. Second, rewards such as achievement, responsibility, recognition and interesting work, which are addressed to Maslow's higher needs, were considered to form part of a 'motivating' factor. Such rewards, Herzberg argued, will encourage commitment to high performance in the conduct of work as well as generate satisfaction. The influence that Herzberg has had on thinking about job enrichment has been considerable (see Chapter 2). However, the methodology of the studies from which he derived his theory has been criticised, and many subsequent investigations have failed to support the admittedly elegant simplicity of his formulation. We return to the problem that it is doubtful whether people really think of their needs or goals in terms of just a few categories, whether any two people share exactly the same hierarchy of preferences, or whether such hierarchies remain consistent over time as circumstances and stimuli change. The static universalistic model implied by the Maslow and Herzberg formulations certainly fails to address the much more realistic discussion of employees' reward criteria advanced by sociologists.

While needs such as subsistence and personal safety might appear to be absolute and universal in nature, further consideration indicates that even these are subject to a social definition which varies from society to society as well as between classes within society. This is clearly apparent with definitions of what constitutes a 'poverty' level, and it is also apparent in the varied definitions of what is a 'safe' environment. In other words, norms of what is acceptable and expected are socially defined and do not arise in an unmediated way directly from individual needs. The role played by norms is particularly important in the case of pay.

Norms of fairness are extremely significant for employees when they evaluate the rewards they are offered. Research suggests that people make two comparisons when assessing fairness. First, a comparison of what their balance of reward to inputs (such as time and effort) is, relative to what they expected it to be. Second, how this balance compares with the rewards others are receiving for their inputs. People attach greatest significance here to the comparison with others who are in the same socially defined group, such as the same job. This gives rise to the so-called 'comparability principle', that people doing the same work should be given the same pay regardless of whether they are employed in the public or the private sector, in flourishing or in ailing organizations. In theory, a perfect labour market would ensure comparability. While the evidence of what people who perceive themselves to be over-rewarded will do in consequence is rather mixed, the effects of perceived under-rewarding are much clearer. Under-rewarded people will typically reduce the level of their inputs, making less effort or fewer personal sacrifices, or they will leave their employment if that can readily be done.

Norms of fairness in the context of comparison with others also help account for the fact that differentials in rewards between people occupying job levels that are adjacent in terms of skill, qualification required or authority generate more frustration and conflict than do absolute levels of reward. If employees only applied criteria relating to their levels of personal need, one would expect absolute levels of reward to be salient. In practice, differentials are more of a problem. Elliott Jaques (1976) has argued that an acceptable policy for the allocation of incomes will not be found until the problem of equity in differential payments is understood and resolved. He concludes from his studies that people share deeply felt norms about fair differentials, which are based upon differences in the intrinsic level of responsibility in particular jobs. Others have pointed out how the comparisons that enter into notions of fair rewards rest upon long-established customary traditions which are institutionalized within particular sectors of work. For example, skilled craftsmen expect to secure a higher level of pay than non-skilled workers, even when the two groups are performing identical tasks equally well.

Comparability is a basic principle which employees apply to rewards. Several dimensions of identity may enter into the comparisons which are made. For example, in a recent study of Cadbury-Schweppes' cocoa bean processing factory at Chirk in Wales, Alan Whitaker (1982) identified three points of reference which entered into employees' evaluations of their levels of pay. The first dimension of comparison was with rates of pay offered by other jobs in the local community, and the comparison here was favourable. This favourable local point of reference had a more marked effect on employees' motivations and willingness to accept managerial requirements in the early days of the plant, which when it first opened had provided jobs for unemployed local coal-miners. A second dimension of comparability was that of skill, which meant that workers with skill qualifications brought into the plant expectations that they should enjoy a differentially higher level of payment even for doing the same work. A third dimension involved reference to the balance between rewards and inputs that prevailed in other plants within the same division of the company and located elsewhere. This comparison became easier to make as the new workforce at Chirk developed its system of union representation and as those representatives came into contact with their equivalents in the other plants, a contact encouraged by the initiation of company-wide participation and communication structures in the mid-1970s. The comparison with other plants in the company gave rise to a less favourable evaluation of the rewards which management offered at Chirk.

The evaluations that employees give to rewards will also tend to vary according to their circumstances in the labour market. The level of reward that they will find acceptable for the job they are asked to do, and the conditions under which they are expected to perform it, varies with the strength of the workers' position in the labour market. The importance attached to different rewards may also be subject to labour market considerations. There is evidence that at a time of widespread unemployment, employees give less prominence to job enrichment or participation, which according to Maslow and Herzberg meet higher order needs, than they give to retaining a job itself and the income it provides. (It should be said, however, that evidence on the effects of unemployment demonstrates how most jobs also provide people with significant social and status rewards which are sorely missed.) In other words, the criteria applied by employees to the rewards offered them are not only based on norms of comparability and fairness, but also refer to their relative power in the labour market.

It is not possible to generalize about the expectations that people have of rewards from employment. Particular categories of employee, such as professional staff, may tend to share certain priorities, but these are liable to become re-ordered as labour market conditions change. In any case, the members of any category or group are individuals who determine their own personal priorities and views over what are acceptable rewards in the light of factors such as their previous experience and their domestic circumstances. The people working in an organization will therefore defy any confident generalization both as individuals and as members of distinct groups whose expectations about the quality of intrinsic rewards as well as a fair level of pay and benefits are likely to differ: skilled and non-skilled manual workers, office staff, technical staff, various professional groups such as accountants, engineers, lawyers and scientists, and the different levels and segments of management. The degree of diversity among employees and their likely expectations about rewards pose the practical dilemma of how far to institute complex differentiated reward policies to match this diversity and how far to preserve simplicity, economy and control through a standardized approach.

Debate and enquiry also continue over the relative importance people are likely to attach to intrinsic and extrinsic rewards. This is a complex question. For example, it is commonly believed that employees who have gone through a long course of professional training, and taken on board traditional professional values, will attach greater importance to intrinsic rewards. Yet there is also reason to believe that this has been because, on the whole, professionals can take generous levels of pay and certain 'perks' for granted. When their favourable extrinsic rewards have been threatened, professional staff such as doctors in the British National Health Service have given a very high priority to them. Further evidence of the shifting importance attached to intrinsic and extrinsic rewards comes from the finding that employees tend to give pay a higher rating around the time of pay negotiations (Daniel 1973). The problem, then, is that the answers people will give to questions on the relative importance they attach to intrinsic and extrinsic rewards can be influenced by whether or not a particular reward is at issue with management.

We may conclude with greater certainty that pay is important for almost everyone. The people for whom it is not a particularly significant reward are fairly readily identifiable through their association with an exceptional vocation, such as priests and charity workers. While many people would probably welcome an improvement in intrinsic rewards such as variety, interest, autonomy and knowledge of results, not all of them necessarily expect to receive such benefits. Those who do will often have undergone higher levels of education and training, or advanced up their organization's hierarchy, and will have had their expectation of good intrinsic rewards encouraged by the occupational and industrial cultures in which they have developed themselves.

The expectations people have about rewards, and the value they place on different rewards, constitute important components in 'expectancy theory', which is discussed shortly. Rewards intrinsic to jobs were discussed in Chapter 2 in connection with job design and work structuring. Autonomy and the feedback of information on performance, two other commonly cited intrinsic factors, were discussed in Chapter 6 on control. The last section of this chapter, on the choice of rewards, concentrates on payment systems, partly because of the coverage already given to intrinsic rewards, and partly because of the continuing prominence of pay as an issue.

Matching motivation with contingent requirements

The effectiveness of a reward policy can be judged by how far it directs the motivation of employees towards criteria which represent the conditions for organizational success. To state the matter in these terms is not to deny the importance for employees of maintaining a high level of reward, or indeed to imply that they should not themselves take part in laying down what constitutes success for their organization. It is simply to reaffirm that organized effort is a collective effort and that a policy over rewards must therefore be aimed at reinforcing that collective enterprise.

The inherent conflict between management and employees over the level of rewards offered is well recognized, and it usually centres on the question of pay. This conflict puts at risk any attempt to find a policy that reconciles employee and managerial reward criteria, and which therefore aligns motivation with contingent requirements. The problem is made worse by the different points of reference that managers and workers may apply to the issue of reward levels. For example, management will probably seek to establish rates of pay that reflect the going rate within the local labour market. If it suits the contingencies of its demand, technological and cost structures, it may offer additional payments for shift working or for the flexible deployment of labour. Employees, in contrast, may well expect to receive a level of reward for the job, in terms of pay and status, which corresponds to what they perceive to be the national norm. This is especially likely if they consider themselves to be members of a nationally recognized craft or profession. They may also regard as illegitimate the linking of rewards to a flexible mode of working which erodes the specialized distinctiveness of their occupation. Strong occupational identities of this kind, backed up by organized occupational associations or unions, are a particular feature of the so-called 'Anglo-Saxon' nations.

It is useful at this point to distinguish between the *level* of rewards and the *process* of rewarding. Although the example just given illustrates the possibility that conflict will arise in the process of rewarding (such as offering additional payment in return for flexibility), most of the conflict in employment is focused on the level of rewards, and on the rate of pay in particular. This is bound to become an issue from time to time, and employees are always likely to apply norms of comparability, which management may not readily accept. Perhaps all that can be said about this in the present context is that it demonstrates the validity of the maxim that success breeds success. The management of a successful organization, so long as its hands are not tied by a higher authority, is in a position to offer its employees a favourable level of reward thus deflecting employee and union concerns over the maintenance of comparability towards other less successful managements.

The process of administering rewards does not contain the same inherent conflict, though it may generate friction and complaint. The question is now whether rewards can be used to align employees' behaviour with contingent requirements, which management expresses as performance objectives. Here some useful guidelines can be drawn from social science research. Two lines of research are particularly relevant. The first is associated with what has come to be known as 'Expectancy Theory' and it draws attention to the conditions which are necessary if rewards are to direct people's behaviour at work towards performance in the terms that this is defined for the organization. The second line of research is associated with what is known as 'Conditioning' and draws attention to the behavioural consequences of how the scheduling of rewards is actually related to the occurrence of the actions that it is intended either to encourage or discourage.

Expectancy theory in essence states that people will decide how much effort they are going to put into their work according to what they perceive they are going to get out of it, and according to how much they value the outcome (or dislike it in the case of sanctions or punishments). As with many ideas in social science, this sounds like common sense. Yet paradoxically it draws attention to a number of requirements for directing motivation along required channels which are frequently neglected in practice. Expectancy theory has arisen from a realization that two factors are of significance for reward policies: the extent to which employees' goals match the requirements of the job and, secondly, the presence of feedback to employees so that effort can actually be seen to be rewarded.

There are several links in the chain that expectancy theory regards as vital for an effective reward system. These have been integrated by Porter and Lawler (1968) into the model which is set out in Figure 7.1. The first link gives its name to the theory—'expectancy'. This concerns the relationship which employees perceive to exist between the amount of effort they put into their work and the level of performance they are recognized as having achieved. In other words, do they expect greater effort or application to lead to better performance? Employees must believe that they can control the quality of their job performance; if they do not they will see no point in trying harder. Note that what management recognizes as performance is important here, because this will provide the basis for any feedback and rewards which are received. The model also suggests that the relationship between employees' efforts and their performance will be mediated by (1) their abilities and competences, and (2) by their perceptions as to what their job entails and the best way to carry it out ('role perceptions'). These mediating factors point to the potential contribution of training and the setting of understood and accepted goals towards the translation of effort and goodwill into effective performance.

The next main link in the chain has been called 'instrumentality'. This refers to the relationship that employees perceive between their performance and the outcomes of that performance in terms of rewards and punishments. At issue here is the extent to which what management calls 'good' performance is actually rewarded, and whether the rewards offered adequately offset the costs and risks borne by the employee. The probability of increased effort leading to increased reward is very likely to affect the amount of effort people will think it worth while to expend in the first place, and therefore constitutes an important feedback loop. In other words, even if they do conclude that greater effort on their part leads to better performance, this effort is hardly going to be encouraged if it is not seen to lead to any additional reward. As noted earlier on page 172, rewards may be of an extrinsic or an intrinsic kind.

The third main link in the expectancy theory model concerns the satisfaction that employees can draw from the rewards they are offered for the performance they have achieved. The notion of fairness will enter employees' minds to the extent that they have a view of the level and kind of rewards which 'ought' to be available to the type of person performing the type of work required in a particular job. The issue of equity also enters into the way rewards are seen to be distributed in relation to performance and to any deprivations which people have to suffer in carrying out their work, such as working on a night shift. The important point here is that employees are unlikely to be satisfied with the rewards they receive if these are not perceived to be equitable. Dissatisfaction will weaken the motivating power of these rewards.

Finally, the potential for rewards to motivate employees to increase or at

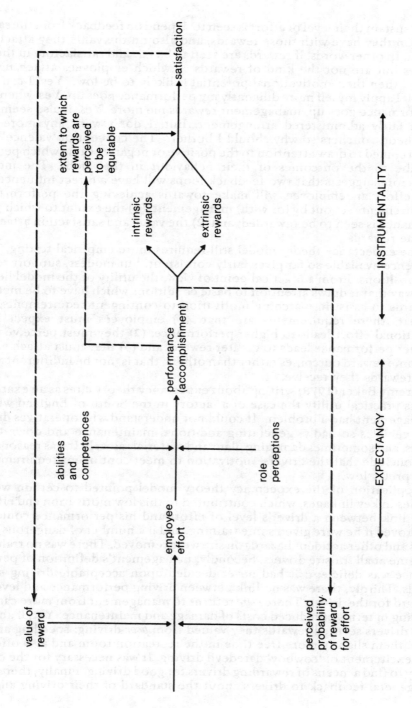

Figure 7.1 Relationships between reward, effort and individual performance

Adapted from: Lyman W. Porter and Edward E. Lawler III, *Managerial Attitudes and Performance* (Richard D. Irwin 1968, p.165).

least sustain their level of effort is seen to depend on feedback from the satis-faction they have with those rewards, and also on the value they attach to them. In other words, if rewards are seen to be fair and satisfactory in them-selves but are not the kind of rewards to which employees attach much value, then their motivational potential is likely to be low. 'Yes, I can see that if I apply myself more diligently my performance goes up. Yes, when my performance goes up, management rewards me more. Yes, it also seems to be a fairly administered arrangement. But, I don't want any more ∗∗∗ luncheon vouchers so why should I bother?' The concept of 'valence' has been coined to draw attention to the positive or negative value which people ascribe to the outcomes of their behaviour in their jobs. The model therefore suggests that two feedback loops will have a direct influence on the effort an employee will make towards achieving the performance requirements set out by (or with) management: (1) the extent to which per-formance is seen to be rewarded; and (2) the value and satisfaction attached to the rewards.

The expectancy theory model still requires more empirical testing. The evidence available so far gives fairly consistent, but modest, support to its propositions. From a practical point of view, the utility of the model lies in the way that it draws attention to basic conditions which have to be met for rewards to assist in matching motivation to contingent requirements. To repeat, these requirements are that: (1) employees must expect that additional effort leads to higher performance; (2) they must perceive that higher performance leads to greater reward; and (3) they must attach value to some reward outcomes rather than others; that is, not be indifferent as to the rewards they receive.

Jeremy Baker (1978) writing about expectancy theory cites as an example of its practical utility the case of a factory in the South of England where management had a problem. It could not understand why operatives drove site vehicles so badly, generating additional maintenance and down-time costs, and sometimes damaging plant and materials as well. It was reasonable to conclude that the drivers' motivation to meet contingent requirements was pretty low.

Application of the expectancy theory model pointed to certain weak-nesses in key linkages, which contributed to this low motivation and effort. The link between a driver's level of effort and his performance could be improved if he were given some training, and if a number of dangerous cor-ners and other accident hazards on site were removed. There was no training scheme at all for site drivers. Secondly, management's definition of perfor-mance was deficient; it had never decided upon acceptable driving stan-dards. Thirdly, there was no link between driving performance and level of reward for the driver. There *were* returns to management from more careful driving in terms of reduced costs of damage and maintenance. Yet, if anyth-ing, drivers secured rewards they valued from *poor* driving: speeding about gave them slightly more free time in the recreation room and also offered the excitement of 'cowboy' daredevil driving. It was necessary for the com-pany to find a means of rewarding drivers for good driving. Finally, there was no general feedback to drivers about the standard of their driving and its consequences. However well or badly the man drove, no one told him. A policy to link rewards to quality of driving would also have to bring this informational feedback loop into being. As Jeremy Baker comments, 'None of the points in this analysis are revolutionary, and half of them were mentioned at various meetings called to deal with the problem' (1978: 9). Nevertheless, setting out the problem systematically in terms of the expectancy theory model did greatly help management to obtain new insight.

Expectancy theory clearly places the onus on management to reward what it wants to happen and not something else or nothing at all. As Steven Kerr (1975) has pointed out, writing on 'the folly of rewarding A, while hoping for B', it is surprising just how often this misdirection of reward can be found in practice. The problem often arises when the quantification of some objectives is more difficult than the quantification of others. For instance, in most management-by-objectives (MBO) systems, objectives or targets go unspecified in areas such as creativity or teamwork where it is difficult to measure them. This leads to management formally rewarding the attainment of certain objectives only at the expense of not motivating employees to achieve the others however important they are to the long-term success of the organization. Incentive payments linked solely to output produced may, for example, lead to a serious neglect of quality by the workers concerned. A comparable problem arises in non-business organizations where it poses an equal challenge to the designers of reward systems. For example, in universities it is hoped that teachers will not neglect their teaching responsibilities, but they are rewarded primarily for their research and publications. Doctors are liable to a great deal more punishment if they err in declaring a sick person well than if they prescribe treatment that is not necessary. Both are errors that can have serious consequences for the patient, yet the balance of punishment and reward is far from symmetrical between the two.

The importance of knowing what employees value for rewards is also brought out by expectancy theory. Do they place a higher value on an increment of certain intrinsic rewards or of particular extrinsic rewards? How are employees' evaluations likely to shift over time and can this be predicted in relation to changing conditions in the economy as well as by reference to the changing domestic and personal circumstances of individual employees? A precise application of expectancy theory would lead one to consider the individual employee. While this is often not practical from the point of view of administering a reward system, none the less it does suggest the usefulness of distinguishing different categories of employee who tend to place somewhat different values on rewards, and for whom different reward policies would therefore be appropriate.

Expectancy theory is a cognitive theory which assumes that employees will adopt a stance towards work and its reward that is thoughtful and rational in terms of their objectives and preferences. It almost certainly overstates the extent to which people really go through a process of deliberate and precise calculation when deciding how to respond to the rewards they are offered. Nevertheless, this cognitive emphasis is a valuable corrective to earlier psychological theories which tended to look upon people at work as responding to relatively inarticulate needs in a manner not too far removed from animal behaviour. While expectancy theory does not explicitly take account of social influences such as custom and practice or cultural norms, it is consistent with the need to locate the issue of how people respond to rewards within the context of perceptions of equity and trust, which are so important an element in industrial relations. If employees do not regard the rewards they are offered as fair, and if they do not trust management's intentions, then according to expectancy theory they will not be motivated to work towards management's contingent requirements. Scepticism over management's long-term intentions to continue to honour the scale of rewards attached to performance helps to explain why on many occasions workers fail to respond to such incentives. It would be rational for them to do so if they could trust management's intentions to honour the scheme or not to withdraw other benefits such as job security once productivity rises. Failing this trust, it may be more rational for workers to continue to control and restrict output levels.

Conditioning theory contrasts with expectancy theory in that it is not cognitive; instead it regards people as organisms who respond to stimuli. Conditioning is concerned with methods that induce learning in animals or people, where learning may be defined as a relatively lasting change in the frequency of occurrence of a specific behaviour. There is more than one kind of conditioning, though all involve stimuli which carry a positive or negative effect for the individual concerned. 'Instrumental conditioning' is the kind most relevant to a discussion of reward policies. Here a person is placed in a situation where he or she learns that certain behaviours are instrumental in producing a reward or a punishment. A reward is commonly called a 'positive reinforcer' and a punishment a 'negative reinforcer'. A basic law of instrumental conditioning is that a behaviour which is rewarded is likely to be repeated, while a behaviour that is not rewarded, or indeed punished, is less likely to be repeated. Rewards and punishments are not always reinforcers, when, for example, they do not modify a person's behaviour. They will, of course, normally be offered on the assumption that they do reinforce employee behaviour.

This again appears to be expressing common sense. Studies of conditioning do, however, point to some more subtle considerations. First, there seems to be a wide measure of agreement that reinforcement should be positive rather than negative, constructive rather than destructive. This is partly because negative reinforcement can generate a great deal of emotional upset, and also because it is directed at training people what not to do rather than in the desired behaviour. The ratio between positive and negative reinforcement also has to be considered. A high incidence of negative feedback is likely to produce negative demotivating side-effects: 'All you get around this place is kicks'. On the other hand, the frequent use of positive reinforcement combined with the occasional deserved reprimand or punishment is likely to be quite effective and to be regarded as fair: 'Old Jim doesn't usually complain about my work; it must have been really bad for him to have done so on this occasion.'

Another consideration is that reinforcement has more effect if it is immediately contingent on the behaviour. Reinforcement serves two functions, to sustain motivation and to provide feedback, and the value of the feedback function in particular is lost if delay occurs. On the other hand, it will tend to be costly to administer rewards or punishments without delay. If this is to be done by an employee's manager, it implies that the manager must continually be diverted from other matters in order to review the employee's performance. A balance has obviously got to be struck, but the point about immediacy and contingency of feedback helps, for example, to account for the very limited conditioning value of rewards such as annual profit-sharing bonuses. They are nice to receive, but employees cannot readily link variations in bonuses to any particular behaviours for which they were responsible, partly because of the long time delay, and partly because an individual lower down in the organization is not likely to perceive that his or her behaviour has much effect on a company's profitability.

There are a number of alternative possibilities in the way that reinforcement is linked to behaviour. The basis on which reinforcement is designed to follow on behaviour is known as a schedule of reinforcement. Reinforcement can be 'continuous': each time a behaviour occurs there is positive or negative feedback. This may take an intrinsic form such as a supervisor's comment, or it may take the form of an extrinsic reward or punishment. In contrast to continuous reinforcement, there is the possibility of intermittent reinforcement by which the reward or punishment is given after some, but not each, occasion of the behaviour. Intermittent reinforcers can be given at set time intervals, such as a weekly bonus. This is an 'interval' schedule. Ratio schedules entail the delivery of reinforcement after a certain number of actions have been performed, such as a scheme which allows employees to go home early once a given quota of work has been completed. A further distinction lies between fixed intermittent schedules where the frequency of reinforcement does not change, and variable intermittent schedules where it does. A monthly pay cheque is a fixed intermittent schedule, while a personal tour of the factory by the managing director at varying intervals constitutes a variable schedule. Based on the results of laboratory experiments, it appears that while continuous reinforcement may be the fastest way either to establish or to stop a particular behaviour, ratio schedules are conducive to the highest incidence of a desired behaviour. Up to a point, it may be possible to 'stretch' a ratio schedule so that reinforcement is given at progressively less frequent intervals with the same effect; from a managerial perspective this has the advantage of economizing on the expenditure of resources. However, there is the obvious risk that stretching may destroy the credibility of a reward policy, and one also has to question its morality.

The whole subject of conditioning raises ethical problems because it amounts to a refined form of manipulation. It can be argued, of course, that this is what sophisticated management is all about, and that it is in any case better to discuss the matter openly rather than to pretend it does not exist. Conditioning does not take a cognitive view of mankind; its originators thought in terms of stimulus–response rather than in terms of a calculating reaction to rewards and punishments. Most of the research into conditioning has been conducted in laboratories rather than in the real world of work.

The approach therefore has its limitations, yet it is nevertheless addressed (like expectancy theory) to the very practical question of how to design rewards which will encourage the behaviours that management judges to be required. The considerations raised by conditioning research are primarily concerned with the balance between rewards and punishments, and with their timing. These complement the considerations raised by expectancy theory which concerns the fundamental linkages required to get a reward system operating in the first place.

The choice of financial reward systems

1 The importance of pay

Although it is rightly said that happiness cannot be bought with money, as the universal medium of exchange money is obviously the key to a great many things that matter to people. Edward Lawler (1971) quotes tellingly from Ecclesiastes: 'Wine maketh merry; but money answereth all things'. Even Frederick Herzberg, major proponent of the theory that money does not motivate, is reported as admitting that 'it sure as hell helps me sort out my priorities!' Observation of the way people behave suggests that for most of them making money is a prime goal. This seems to apply no less to those who are fortunate enough to have jobs which offer considerable intrinsic rewards than it does to those for whom pay is one of the few rewarding features of their jobs. Many hospital consultants in Britain, for example, are keen to add lucrative private work on top of the salaries they receive from public funds, just as many senior executives attach considerable importance to their salaries, bonuses and marginal rates of income tax.

Money is valued for a number of reasons. It is an instrument that enables people to purchase what they want, so to some extent the value of money to individuals is determined by the value for them of what it can buy. The possession and spending of money is also a symbol of personal success and status; a basis on which one person's standing and worth may be compared with another's. This helps to account for the importance that employees attach to the differential between their level of pay and others'. Psychologists have also suggested that money can come to be sought for its own sake. Individuals may acquire a drive to make money because a lack of money is associated in their minds with not being able to meet basic material needs and is a possibility which provokes anxiety. Additionally, because money is associated with other desired rewards, it assumes the incentive power of those rewards and this may result in people being conditioned to seek money just as Pavlov's dogs salivated at the ringing of a bell rather than at the sight of food itself.

It is not surprising then that the payment of money is a reward which evokes considerable interest among virtually all employees at all levels within organizations. This interest is not confined to the needy or to those for whom money may be in part a compensation for a low quality of working life, although the underlying reasons for an interest in pay may vary between different employees. It is instructive to note three points in the light of the downgrading of pay as a motivating factor by many advocates of job enrichment and an improved quality of working life. First, in Herzberg's original study of accountants and engineers (employees who already enjoyed good pay and intrinsic rewards), pay was the one reward that was quite frequently reported as generating *both* satisfaction and dissatisfaction (Herzberg et al. 1959). Second, as Chapter 2 noted, many schemes ostensibly aimed at enhancing intrinsic rewards via job enrichment or work restructuring have offered higher pay at the same time. There is reason to believe that this has been an important inducement for employees to accept the changes, particularly when manning was also reduced. Dramatic reductions in manning have indeed been achieved in cases such as the British steel industry through the offer of substantial cash payments. Third, there is evidence that greater increases in employee performance are achieved through monetary incentives than through job enrichment programmes (Locke et al. 1980). Pay and material fringe benefits remain central features in contracts of employment and are prominent issues in collective and individual bargaining.

The value that people place on pay compared with other potential rewards from employment may vary according to external contingencies over which management has little control. Domestic circumstances can dictate what leeway an employee has to trade pay off against other benefits. An international perspective identifies some societies in which materialism is less of a central cultural factor than in others. Nevertheless, these are matters of degree. There is very little evidence to challenge the conclusion that pay constitutes a reward with a high positive and negative motivating potential. Pay is expressed in terms of a perfect scale of measurement which makes it easy to compute and to adjust when it is linked to a measure of performance. Bearing in mind the message of expectancy theory, this means that in principle pay lends itself particularly well to two necessary conditions for linking motivation and the fulfilment of operational contingencies; namely it constitutes a valued reward and one which can be attached to performance in a highly visible manner. Pay is also wholly compatible with the accounting basis of modern organizations operating within a money economy; as a charge upon the organization it can be readily computed whereas the cost of some intrinsic rewards such as the time spent in 'satisfying' social relationships at work can not.

There are a number of methods through which pay can be offered as a reward, and certain pros and cons are claimed for each. Alternative methods are now considered, together with their suitability to a particular organization's policies and circumstances.

2 Methods of payment

Methods of payment can be classified in terms of several underlying dimensions, of which the following are particularly significant:

1. The feature to which payment is tied: this may be intrinsic to the job (as with an assessment of job requirements and conditions in job evaluation

schemes) or it may relate to performance in a job or collection of jobs. Among the criteria applied are (a) *time*: the number of hours an employee gives to the job; (b) *effort*: the amount of work achieved or some other measure of energy expended; (c) possession of/requirement for *skill or competence*; (d) *status*: which may be an attribute of the individual such as age or length of tenure, or of the job such as hierarchical position.

2. Whether or not an incentive element is built into the method of payment. This dimension concerns the extent to which management reciprocates variations in performance with variations in level of payment.

3. Frequency of payment, and in particular whether payment follows immediately upon satisfaction of the criterion to which it is attached or is deferred until later.

4. The unit to which the basis for payment relates: while it is the individual who is paid, the level of payment may also be determined on a workgroup, department, plant, or whole organization basis.

Table 7.1 sets out six commonly used methods of payment, and summarizes their broad characteristics in terms of the above four dimensions. Job evaluation has been omitted from this table on the grounds that it is intended to provide the foundation for a payment structure rather than constituting a method of payment *per se*. A survey conducted during 1979–80 in 401 manufacturing plants within five British manufacturing industries found a widespread use of job evaluation, not just as a basis for determining the level of flat time rate payments but also in quite a few cases combined with output incentives and other bonus payment methods (White 1981).

A summary such as Table 7.1 cannot include the detailed variations that are to be found in the practical application of each payment method. Its purpose is, rather, to facilitate the process of comparing different methods and to begin to bring to bear on such comparison a consideration of the requirements and conditions to which one method of payment may be better suited than another. It should also be noted that Table 7.1 and its subsequent discussion do not explicitly deal with special provisions for managerial remuneration. The same general considerations apply to managerial schemes with regard to items such as incentive payments, but details vary according to contextual circumstances such as local tax policies. In the case of incentives for managers, there is also the special problem of what criteria to select as a basis for bonus payments. The section on 'Suggested Further Reading' mentions two sources on managerial remuneration.

A *flat time rate* system involves payment of a wage or salary at intervals specified in a contract of employment or similar agreement. Wage payment is normally weekly and salary payment monthly. The payment of a wage or salary is dependent upon fulfilment by the employee of an agreed number of hours of work, or more accurately attendance at the workplace. It is 'fixed' in the sense that adjustments are made infrequently, normally on the basis of periodic increments or through individual or collective bargaining. If management and employees agree that the latter should work above the hours of work which have been established as normal, then overtime may be paid for the extra (usually at a higher time rate) or time off may be given later

Table 7.1 A classification of methods of payment and their key characteristics

Underlying Dimension	Method of Payment					
	I Flat time rate	II Output incentive	III Merit rating	IV Measured day work	V Negotiated productivity improvement or flexibility scheme	VI Profit-sharing
(1) the feature to which payment is tied	fulfilment of agreed hours of work. Basis of rate is often job evaluation. May also be status, going rate in labour market	a set formula relating to: level of output achieved (production incentive); level of sales achieved (commission), and similar	performance assessed subjectively by supervisor and his immediate superior	meeting production norm	(1) increase in productivity/saving in costs due to negotiated changes in work rules and methods; (2) negotiated improvement in flexibility of manning	increase in organization's profit
(2) presence or not of incentive element	additional payment may be made for additional hours worked if these are required by management	yes – payment may be entirely or primarily dependent on work achieved (eg. piecework) or may consist of bonus additional to base rate	yes; but weak if criteria for merit are not stated clearly	yes; failure to meet production norm may lead to withdrawal of agreed bonus and/or to disciplinary action. But often weak in practice	yes; may be one-off payment, or payment of agreed % of savings, or bonus guaranteed while improvement is maintained, or payment for additional skills used in flexible working	weak and indirect
(3) usual frequency of payment	weekly (wage);* monthly (salary). Reward for additional hours may be deferred (eg. time off given in lieu at later date)	weekly*	usually a deferred bonus or increase in wage rate/salary level*	weekly*	once-and-for-all; or deferred periodic bonus/payment of % of saving	long deferred; usually yearly
(4) unit to which basis for payment is normally related	individual (once allocated to a specified job or job category)	individual, work group or department	individual	individual or group	often plant-wide; may be limited to specific groups with which agreement is negotiated (e.g. maintenance tradesmen)	whole company or could be profit-centre such as division, subsidiary.

*wages: normally paid weekly but often calculated on basis of hourly units 'in lieu'. The unit for determining payment is to the individual, though the rate of payment is likely to be fixed for a particular job or job category. This method of payment does not reward the performance of work itself—it does not vary pay level according to quantity or quality of output or even according to flexibility and co-operativeness in the manner of working. In principle, it rewards dependability of attendance, though this incentive is in practice often weakened by the ease with which employees can take time off for short-term 'sickness' and the reluctance of many employers to monitor the time-keeping of staff closely (especially of salaried staff over matters such as lunch-breaks) and to adjust their payment levels according to time-keeping performance.

The major considerations leading to the widespread use of fixed time rate wage and salary payments are: (1) that in many jobs performance cannot be accurately measured; (2) that with the advance of more highly mechanized and automated technologies the need for effort is being replaced by a need for reliable monitoring using cognitive and judgemental skills; and (3) that fixed time-rated payment confines conflict and resentment over payment levels to relatively infrequent periodic intervals and so provides a more favourable basis for those managements seeking to develop a 'cultural' philosophy of control based on high normative commitment among employees. A basically fixed wage or salary system may be supplemented by negotiated productivity and flexibility agreements or by profit-sharing (both discussed below). While these modifications or extensions do bring in a link with performance, this is sometimes just on a once-for-all basis or, in the case of profit-sharing, involves a long-deferred payment.

Output incentive schemes, on the other hand, tie payment (normally a portion of total remuneration) to the output achieved either by an *individual* or a *group*. When the topic of 'incentives' for non-managerial employees is discussed it is usually with reference to these schemes, although they are not the only methods of payment to contain an incentive element. Examples of output incentives schemes are piecework (payment per unit produced), premium schemes (where part of take-home pay is fixed; but a percentage—usually between 10 and 30 per cent—is a bonus linked to output achieved, and commission schemes such as paying an additional amount of money to salesmen for each extra sale (or incremental sales value) secured. The motivational power of such payment schemes may be substantial if the conditions highlighted by expectancy theory are fulfilled. In the first place, an opportunity to earn extra payment has to appeal to employees—if they face a high marginal rate of taxation, for example, this appeal may be weakened. Secondly, the extra reward must be worth the additional costs in effort or personal inconvenience which are involved. Third, employees must trust management's good faith in offering incentives in at least two respects: (1) they must perceive that they can realistically achieve the bonus which management is offering and (2) they must have reason to believe that on attaining higher levels of output management will not attempt to renegotiate a lower rate of incentive payment simply because employees have benefited. This last requirement points to the need for management to avoid gross errors in fixing rates because of poor quality of work measurement, and subsequently attempting to rectify such errors by renegotiating the agreed rate.

There has been a long-running controversy over the relative merits of fixed wages and salaries on the one hand, and output incentive schemes on the other. These merits have usually been considered from a managerial standpoint only, despite the fact that the choice has major implications for workers and their shopfloor representatives. To a surprising extent, the debate has also been conducted in black-and-white terms without reference to the circumstances of particular organizations and their labour forces, including the custom and practice which has become established in them over the course of time. The debate has extended to a comparison between output incentives and all schemes in which level of payment is not directly modified or necessarily adjusted according to performance achieved. Less strict forms of measured daywork would, for example, be included in the second category.

The following is a summary of the main arguments raised in this controversy:

1 Arguments for output incentives and against fixed time rate or similar schemes

1.1 Higher output per manhour   Chapter 2 noted that research by the Swedish Employers Confederation had found consistent evidence that output incentive payment schemes tended to enhance labour productivity. Among 36 Swedish plants which changed from piecework to fixed wages there was an average fall in productivity of between 10 and 20 per cent. This fall-off usually occurred within three to four months after the change-over to fixed payment. Thirty-seven other companies had changed to a premium system: 21 started with a piecework system and on average increased their productivity between 5 and 10 per cent; 16 started with fixed wages and increased their productivity by between 25 and 35 per cent. A conventional wisdom among those with experience in British manufacturing industry appears to be that a productivity loss of the order of 20 per cent can be expected when changing from output incentives to time-related payment. The problems that can arise when a change is made from a variable output incentive to a fixed level of bonus are discussed further in connection with measured daywork.

1.2 Less supervision and greater freedom for employees   An important factor behind the arguments to abandon piecework schemes was the conclusion that these had led to a loss of managerial control over the production process. Incentive schemes incorporate an output control philosophy, which delegates control over methods and, by implication, over output levels to the workers concerned. They can legitimately ask management to leave them alone to get on with their work as they see fit on the grounds that they will be the first to suffer if a high level of output is not attained. The attractiveness of such arrangements to any workers who value autonomy is clear, as it is to those among their representatives who seek to enhance the significance of their role in workplace relations through an active involvement in negotiations and the handling of grievances about incentive rates and conditions (such as production breakdown) under which incentives have to be suspended. For management, there may be a considerable saving in supervision if workers are motivated by incentive payments to undertake some normal supervisory duties themselves such as ensuring an adequate supply of materials, requesting maintenance of equipment when required, and generally preserving the conditions for efficient production. Under a fixed time-related payment system, the burden falls upon the supervisor to motivate workers to perform at a high pitch since the level of their pay is not at stake.

1.3 Opportunities to achieve high earnings   An output incentive scheme that successfully links performance to pay is not only likely to provide a high level of production for management but also to afford employees the opportunity to take home a high level of earnings. In principle, such a scheme allows them to choose their own trade-off between effort and earnings, though clearly the more this choice is actually exercised on a fragmented individual basis within an integrated workflow the more likely it is that imbalance and unacceptably high levels of buffer stock and work-in-progress will arise.

2 Arguments against output incentives and in favour of fixed time rate or similar schemes

2.1 Loss of management control   There are several ways in which management control may be weakened by the use of output incentives. In principle, when work measurement is applied to output incentive schemes both for establishing bonus rates and for measuring output, it should provide managers with useful control information on individual or group performance, on the effectiveness of present manpower deployment, on departmental organization and generally on components of labour cost. The reality is often rather different because employees will perceive it to be rational for their interests to beat the system and increase earnings through informal incentives. Work measurement is far from being an exact 'science' and workers can often push their earnings in an upward 'drift' on the basis of poorly measured tasks or subsequent modifications in working methods. Workers will tend to assign as much output as they can to those periods of the day which management recognizes as 'productive time' and to exaggerate 'waiting time' as much as possible. If the incentive rates set for different items of work do not provide a reasonably steady income, because some are 'loose' and others 'tight', then it is rational for workers to bank and cross-book work to even-out the variations. These practices will provide management with misleading production information, which may create particularly serious problems for scheduling complex batch or multi-part production systems.

Wage drift can also disturb the parities and differentials in the organization's payment structure: those between production workers on incentive and any who are not; between production and indirect workers; and between production workers and supervisors. If these are to be maintained, non-production earnings also have to be raised which obviously adds to overall employment costs. Output incentives applied to only one section of the workforce therefore create difficulties in preserving the integration of the workforce.

Management control also tends to be weakened in other respects. Workers are far more reluctant to be redeployed from jobs to which they have become accustomed and on which high bonuses can be earned, so that flexibility is difficult to achieve. Quality of work may decline because workers cut corners in search of higher output, unless a stringent and costly system of inspection is introduced. Safety may also suffer with the pressure for output. Disputes over piece-rates or bonuses are liable to lose production time through industrial action and, more seriously still, may lead to so much disruption that the predictable programming of production becomes impossible.

While the likely loss of management control in these ways would appear to bring a corresponding benefit in autonomy for the workers concerned, this may be somewhat illusory. Miklos Haraszti (1977), describing his experience as a worker on piecework in a Hungarian engineering factory, wrote of 'a semblance of independence with piece-rates'. The incentive system still imposes an output requirement upon workers if they are to achieve their target level of earnings, and they have to cope with the uncertainties of variable materials, variability in machine performance and breakdowns, other delays, and their own possible ill-health as potential obstacles to this achievement. Haraszti sees 'insecurity' as the main driving force in all forms of payment by results: 'It chases us remorselessly every minute of the day' (1977: 56).

2.2 Strains on labour relations It follows from the way in which output incentive schemes tend to highlight the struggle over workplace control that they place additional strains on labour relations. Conflicts arise over piece-rates or bonus rates: some are loose and some are tight because their setting is an imprecise process involving an economic and political game between both parties. Subsequent attempts to renegotiate frequently give rise to industrial disputes. The pressures which workers may experience with tight rates, and supervisors with loose rates or when their workers restrict output, tend to exacerbate conflict. So also do disturbances to payment differentials. The fluctuations in weekly earnings which can arise with output incentive schemes through no fault of the workers concerned, due to shortages, poor planning or changing levels of demand, are another source of grievance and conflict. If workers are able to institute their own informal practices designed to reduce fluctuations in earnings, this represents a loss of control on management's part and a deterioration in the quality of production information available to it.

2.3 Discouragement of innovation   Under many output incentive schemes there is a lack of reward for any worker (or group of workers) who finds an improvement in methods. For unless there is some arrangement for sharing the gains from the improvement, the result of declaring it to management is likely to be a downward revision of the output incentive rate. From a short-term perspective at least, it is far more rational for the worker to keep the improvement to himself as a means of easing the pressure upon him. Incentives proposed by management, including those accompanying the introduction of new products, are likely to generate a period of heightened conflict, grievance and negotiation because of the changes in job content, new work measurement and setting of bonus or piece-rates that are involved. Together with the problem of redeployment already mentioned, it can be appreciated that output incentive schemes may well inhibit the flexibility required to adjust to changing circumstances when such schemes are focused on the individual worker or small group.

2.4 Cost of administration   While output incentive schemes may save on the amount of direct supervision required, they are inherently costly to administer. Specialists in work measurement are normally required, though they may also be expected to provide benefits of a more general industrial engineering nature. Staff have to be allocated to the calculation of incentive payments, while additional supervisory time may well be taken up handling the larger number of workers' queries about their pay which generally arise under these more complex payment methods.

Merit rating is an attempt to reward performance of a kind which is not particularly tangible and measurable by 'objective' indicators. Criteria such as 'willingness to bear responsibility' or 'co-operativeness' are examples. The basis for determining merit payment is a necessarily subjective assessment, usually by the person's supervisor and the supervisor's immediate superior. Combined with systems of regular appraisal, a form of what is essentially merit rating is frequently applied to the adjustment of white collar, supervisory and managerial salary levels. Merit rating schemes can cause considerable contention because their subjective basis lends itself to charges of favouritism and inequity. They can also degenerate from being a method of allocating rewards for individual merit to becoming annual collective across-the-board departmental awards. This was the case in the UK Ford Motor Company before 1968, where merit awards reflected the bargaining power of strategically placed groups such as toolmakers rather than considerations of performance itself (Beynon 1983).
Research into subjective ratings of performance has pointed to the generally weak level of agreement between ratings given by the superior and those perceived to be appropriate by the person being rated. Studies which I conducted with Bruce Partridge (1982) into the ratings of supervisors' performance came to the same conclusion and indicated how characteristics of the rater substantially influenced the ratings given. Although merit rating has the virtue of applying the incentive principle to indirect work, it is often disliked by managers and held in suspicion by workers because of its largely

subjective foundation. It was used for production workers in only 15 per cent of the British manufacturing plants surveyed by the Policy Studies Institute, and for maintenance workers in only 12 per cent of the plants (White 1981).

Measured daywork was actually used for production workers in even fewer of these plants (8 per cent), with the best known examples being located in the motor industry (British Leyland, Ford, Vauxhall). A strict form of measured daywork actually operated in only 2 per cent of the plants. In this form, workers contract to produce to certain production levels for which they are paid their basic time rate plus a bonus for acceptable performance. If the agreed performance level is not achieved through some fault on the workers' part, the bonus element is withdrawn. A variant on this builds in a series of steps whereby several performance levels are identified and incremental bonus payments tied to attainment of each one. Other, less strict, so-called measured daywork schemes simply agree production targets with the workers concerned, but achievement or otherwise of the targets is not directly linked to changes in payment levels.

Interest in measured daywork was at its height in Britain towards the end of the 1960s. This method of payment appeared to offer attractions for both parties to the pay bargain. It offered workpeople the opportunity of stable earnings, which were guaranteed so long as they maintained a certain level of output, and it was regarded by some as a natural step towards salaried status. It offered management the prospect of controlled, predictable output levels, avoidance of localized disruption within integrated production systems, and in general an opportunity to gain the initiative over the production process. Measured daywork formally acknowledged the measurement of work, using techniques such as work study and job evaluation which could increase management's control over the method and pace of work. It also promised a reduction of the opposition to redeployment and mobility which exists under output incentive schemes, and of opposition to new methods of production. It was a relatively inexpensive system to administer and avoided other problems associated with output incentives, such as wage drift and conflicts over rates and differentials.

Measured daywork has, however, clearly not caught on as extensively as once expected. From a managerial perspective, the biggest single problem with measured daywork lies in its dilution of the incentive effect, especially when levels of payment are in practice not adjusted according to the achievement or otherwise of output norms. Measured daywork relies on the substitution of managerial control, through work measurement by industrial engineers and direct supervision, for the significant degree of worker control over the work process that often characterizes output incentive schemes. The resources and sophistication required to establish this managerial control were not always available when measured daywork was introduced into British plants. British Leyland exemplified the problem in the early 1970s in its principal car body press shop and in several assembly plants, where the levels of worker effort dropped substantially. If disciplinary action is taken in response to poor production levels, this is likely to dissipate the stability in labour relations which is one of the benefits sought from measured daywork. A further problem lies in the inflexibility which can arise from the burden of the measurement exercise required if production norms are to be changed. This can inhibit the upward adjustment of these norms.

Negotiated productivity improvement or *flexibility* schemes are a broad category covering a range of agreements which provide additional payment for productivity and cost improvements. Productivity bargaining had become established in several oil refineries by the 1960s and has continued to develop in various forms. Productivity bargaining involves an acceptance by the workforce of a change in work rules or work organization that is expected to improve productivity. This change may be once-and-for-all, as is sometimes the payment for it. Otherwise payment is generally made as an addition to existing rates. In Britain, more recently, self-financing or productivity-pool type schemes have become more common, influenced firstly by government pay restraint policy guidelines in the late 1970s, and currently by competitive pressures towards increasing productivity. These more recent schemes tend to introduce a collective bonus of some kind payable to a section or to the whole of the workforce in an establishment, in return for an identifiable improvement in productivity. Sometimes a collective bonus is paid for an agreement on flexible manning, which is calculated to reduce overall labour costs. The principle of these schemes is not very different from older cost reduction schemes such as the Scanlon Plan, which involved management-worker co-operation to find ways of reducing costs and the payment of an agreed percentage of cost savings achieved.

The benefits of productivity, flexibility and cost-reduction schemes can be significant so long as real and not pseudo improvements are rewarded. They direct the attention of both managers and workers towards change and productivitiy enhancement in a manner which draws attention to the common interest and should improve the climate of industrial relations. When such schemes cover a whole plant or establishment, they can help to break down the barriers and demarcations which are otherwise the product of multi-unionism. Flexibility provisions will increase managerial control over the deployment of labour—as was once said to the writer, 'without flexible manning, you have a situation that when equipment is operating normally the operator is busy and the fitter is idly looking out of the window. When the equipment requires attention, the exact opposite applies.' Not least, these payment schemes can offer substantial gains for the employees concerned so long as they do not lose their jobs as part of the productivity improvement.

There is no doubt that flexible manning has become a particularly significant managerial objective in many organizations, and that this has stimulated interest in payment schemes designed to assist its introduction. For example, the much-publicized agreement which Toshiba signed at its Plymouth plant with the British electrical trade union includes a provision under which the employer has the right to full flexibility of deployment within a worker's capability. In return, pay is graded according to skill level, and any worker can demand to be trained in additional skills and to be upgraded when competent in them. At the time of writing, the Ford Motor

Company is thinking of renegotiating its 13-year-old wage structure, which is based on an inflexible complex job evaluation structure incorporating 506 job descriptions in five pay grades. The management's intention would be to obtain substantial increases in productivity by removing outdated job demarcations. A major food company has already taken this road, buying out demarcations between maintenance trades and between production and service workers.

The attractiveness of rewarding flexibility lies partly in the potential for reducing manpower. It is appropriate for the successful utilization of new technology, some applications of which require a substantial realignment of skills from the physical to the cognitive and conceptual. Where new technology such as the employment of robots displaces low-skilled labour performing routine tasks, the concept of a smaller, elite, multi-skilled workforce becomes an attractive one particularly because its commitment to the organization can be cemented through up-grading as further skills are required and because it would be highly flexible in its deployment. In competitive conditions, where the ability to adjust operations to meet changing or special demands is a successful strategy, flexibility becomes an obvious requirement. Indeed, flexibility achieved at relatively low cost is likely to be the saving factor for many small and medium-sized companies.

Profit-sharing is a long-established feature of payment policies in some companies. Its origins lie in the attempt to eliminate profit as fundamental source of conflict between employer and employees in the capitalistic firm. Under profit-sharing a certain percentage of annual profit is distributed among the employees. As well as having the objective of increasing the general level of co-operation and commitment to the organization as a whole, some see in profit-sharing an encouragement to improve the performance of the organization through increased effort or acceptance of change. Moreover, the annual reward is only paid when the company can afford it, when a profit is made. Profit-sharing may not do much harm unless it means that certain investments are forgone or that external financing through equity issue is available on less favourable terms, but it is unlikely to have a dramatically favourable effect either. The long period of deferment makes the reward seem remote and uncertain in relation to any particular actions by an employee. Profits are also determined by many other factors unrelated to employees' efforts, and the fact that it is a company-wide indicator also makes it difficult for an individual to relate to his or her performance.

3 Considerations in the choice of a payment system

Michael White in his book on the Policy Studies Institute survey (1981) points to 'powerful tides and cross-currents of fashion in payment systems' (p.26), a shifting back and forth which has been encouraged by the need to accommodate to the impositions of changing government pay policies. Payment systems, in British industry at least, are introduced and discarded quite frequently, which in White's view 'confirms that in very many firms, management is still groping for the right systems' (p.131).

Our brief review of six main methods of payment indicated that each is liable to have certain advantages and disadvantages. It is impossible to assess which method might be most suitable without reference to the specific context in which it is to be established. Some schemes such as output incentives clearly have a powerful motivational potential, but would be inappropriate for employees whose output cannot be measured or who do not make a direct service contribution to facilitating the measurable output of others. Other schemes such as flat time rate payment are conducive to a calmer industrial relations climate, but of themselves generate no momentum towards change, development or productivity improvement. Flat time rate payment may, nevertheless, suit jobs to which the contingent requirements of reliability, dependability and commitment are attached (such as a personal secretary).

Some authorities have in the past taken rather dogmatic positions for or against particular methods of payment, Lord Wilfred Brown's (1962) case for abandoning piecework in favour of straight time payments being a well-known example. Other writers, most notably Tom Lupton and Don Gowler (1969), view different payment systems as suiting different situations. Lupton and Gowler in fact set out a detailed method which is intended to enable managers to assess how well a particular payment method is likely to suit an organization's 'situational profile'. This profile is built up from 23 variables which together describe four sets of influences that are believed to affect how well a given method of payment operates. The four sets concern (1) technology, (2) labour markets, (3) the effectiveness of disputes procedures, and (4) structural aspects such as labour costs as a percentage of total costs, and the number of job grades, work units and shifts. Lupton and Gowler argue that it is possible to profile 'the circumstances of a firm, or a department, or workshop of a firm, or even the job of any individual' (p.13).

The Lupton–Gowler analysis is a normative one—that is, it is intended to point to those payment systems which should be used in organizations, or with sections of organizations, possessing certain characteristics. For example, the type of technology used is relevant to whether a worker controls the pace and quality of production or not. Output incentives are better suited to situations where workers can control the levels of their output. Type of technology is also associated with the probability of breakdown and particular forms of technology are likely to be used according to how frequently management plans to change throughputs. For these reasons technology may also be a guide to the appropriateness of payment methods which facilitate redeployment of manpower within the workplace.

Michael White (1981) has complemented this normative approach with a descriptive analysis, from the Policy Studies Institute survey, of those organizational characteristics which were associated in practice with a tendency to choose one type of payment system rather than another. The most important conclusions were:

1 The major factor associated with the use of job evaluation is size of establishment; larger establishments are more likely to use this method.
2 Flat time rate payments and merit rating were found more frequently in

smaller establishments. Merit rating also tended to be found in non-union establishments—unions are often opposed to this method because of its subjective basis.

3 Individual output incentive systems were more likely to be found in plants where the proportion of maintenance workers was small and where there was no separate union for craft workers. Both individual and group output schemes were somewhat more likely to be found in companies where management was taking active steps to improve labour utilization.

4 Productivity schemes tended to overlap with the payment of plant bonuses. Both were associated with policies to improve labour utilization and payment of plant bonuses was more common in factories with two or more unions.

5 Surprisingly, no consistent association was found between technology and type of payment system utilized, though this may be because detailed measures of technology were not employed.

While normative and contingency analyses of the type presented by Lupton–Gowler and White respectively greatly inform a rational approach to choosing a payment system, certain practical considerations stand in the way of following their logic to its fullest extent. One is the fact that in any already-established work situation, custom and practice and tradition will have institutionalized existing payment systems. It may take a major effort of negotiation to shift this historical legacy and it could be expensive to buy it out. This may not, however, be an insuperable obstacle. A more important problem is likely to be the difficulty of administering the highly complex and differential payment systems structure which could result if the fine-tuning to contingencies that follows from the Lupton–Gowler method, is adopted. For their approach would imply not only that different levels of staff should have their own pay systems (which while quite common is tending to disappear with harmonization), but so also should different categories of employee working in different sections each with its own contingent characteristics.

Having warned against over-complexity, there is, nevertheless, a case for considering the combination of different payment methods in order to utilize their respective advantages. White's survey indicates that this has in fact been happening in British industry, where there is a trend towards the use of somewhat more complex and multi-faceted payment systems. For example, self-financing productivity schemes have often been added onto previous arrangements such as plant-wide bonus schemes. Collective (group, departmental or plant) incentive schemes have frequently been combined with a basic structure founded on job evaluation. The recent thrust towards flexibility has added further components to existing productivity schemes.

Donaldson and Lynn (1976) report on an interesting combination of incentives within the pay system in a Northern Ireland plant which bottled gas in cylinders. The site management informally negotiated a piece-rate agreement which gave workers more pay when the demand for output was high (the winter period), and allowed early finishing when the level of production required was low (the summer). This combination of two incentive elements suited management's need for flexible production and the workers' life-style—afternoon leisure is less attractive in the dark winter months. The scheme led to greater co-operation from the workers, so that supervision could be relaxed and aspects of work group autonomy increased. There were resultant increases in productivity and a decline in voluntary absenteeism.

The issue of complexity in payment system design is one of several trade-offs which have to be made when constructing a reward policy. It concerns the choice between a simple and a complex system. Other choices are between a standardized system or one that is sensitive to individual differences; between a relatively fixed or rigid system and a relatively flexible and adaptive one; and between systems which attempt to influence motivation and those which are more conducive to the development of co-operative relationships. Table 7.2 sets out these broad 'choices of emphasis', as White has called them, in summary form. While the table illustrates these choices by reference to payment systems, they apply to the design of policies for rewards as a whole.

Summary

Policies on rewards and punishments are intended to secure a high level of performance from employees. They are therefore complementary to the process of control. Punishments are negative rewards and include the withholding of an otherwise expected reward.

To be successful, the focus of rewards must be compatible with the tasks and structures laid down for the organization, which gives them a contingent aspect. Rewards also have to be sufficiently important for people to secure their motivation. The contingent aspect is expressed in managerial criteria for rewards, while the criteria which employees apply to rewards give an indication of their motivational potential. Social scientists have advanced a number of theories to account for employee reactions to rewards, some referring to individual needs and some to social influences. Two bodies of research which point to some of the practical considerations in matching the motivational potential of rewards with contingent requirements are expectancy theory and the study of conditioning.

Money is a particularly valued, versatile and effective reward. Six common methods of payment can be distinguished in terms of: (1) the feature to which payment is tied; (2) the presence or not of an incentive element; (3) the normal frequency of payment; and (4) the unit (individual, group, etc.) to which the basis for payment is normally related. The six types of payment systems are flat time rates, output incentives, merit rating, measured daywork, productivity or flexibility schemes, and profit-sharing. Each system has advantages and disadvantages. This suggests that there may be advantages in combining features from more than one system, despite the greater complexity which results. Simplicity versus complexity is one of the choices which have to be made when designing a payments system, and indeed a reward policy as a whole. Other choices are between standardization for all employees versus a varied application, fixed versus adaptable

Table 7.2 Broad choices in the design of payment systems[1]

1 Simplicity *or*	**complexity**
Example: flat time rates or traditional piecework without additional features	*Example:* job evaluation in conjunction with various types of incentives, bonus or profit-sharing schemes
In a period of change and pressure makes it easier for managers to exercise control and keep track of costs	Provides management with more options to respond to various requirements; but difficult to get the balance right or predict cost implications
2 Standardization *or*	**differentiation**
Example: all employees on flat time rates and grouped into few job categories	*Example:* extensive use of merit-rating; or executives allowed to choose between percentage of their pay made up by profit-related bonus
Ease and low cost of administration. Avoids risk of charges of favouritism	Recognizes individual differences and adapts payment system to these, thus enhancing motivational potential
3 Relatively fixed or rigid *or*	**flexible and adaptable**
Example: measured daywork	*Example:* corporate profit-sharing or added-value bonus system
Attractive in terms of maintaining discipline and control in face of change and pressures	Attractive in terms of avoiding confrontation with workforce
4 Attempt to influence motivation *or* **emphasis on building harmonious** or increase individual performance	**collective relationships**
Example: output incentive schemes	*Example:* plant-wide bonuses, profit-sharing
Maximizes motivational potential and helps to control direct costs in face of intensifying competition	Conducive to co-operative, harmonious industrial relations, and to achieving flexible manning

1. Based largely on the discussion in Michael White, *Payment Systems in Britain*, Gower Press 1981, pp. 37–38.

systems, and emphasis on promoting individual performance versus emphasis on promoting harmonious collective relationships.

Suggested further reading

Jay R. Galbraith in his book *Organization Design* (Addison-Wesley 1977) devotes several chapters to the design of reward systems and examines the issue both from a motivational and a contingency standpoint. His treatment does not, however, betray much awareness of the significant conflicts which can focus around rewards. Lyman W. Porter and Edward E. Lawler III, *Managerial Attitudes and Performance* (Irwin 1968) develop an integrated expectancy theory model. Edward E. Lawler III provides a clear and insightful discussion in his chapter on 'Reward Systems' in J. Richard Hackman and J. Lloyd Suttle (editors), *Improving Life at Work* (Goodyear Publishing Co. 1977). While this compares a range of rewards, it concentrates on pay and builds on Lawler's earlier book, *Pay and Organizational Effectiveness* (McGraw-Hill 1971). Very little has been written on the use of punishment and a useful review is Richard D. Arvey and John M. Ivancevich, 'Punishment in Organizations: A Review, Propositions and Research Suggestions', *Academy of Management Review*, January 1980. On professional employees see John Child, 'Professionals in the Corporate World: Values, Interests and Control' in David Dunkerley and Graeme Salaman (editors), *The International Yearbook of Organization Studies 1981* (Routledge and Kegan Paul 1982).

In addition to Lawler's writings there are a number of useful contributions on payment systems. A handy comparison of wage payment systems remains Peter H. Grinyer and Sidney Kessler, 'The Systematic Evaluation of Methods of Wage Payment', *Journal of Management Studies*, October 1967. Angela M. Bowey has edited the *Handbook of Salary and Wage Systems* (Gower Press, 2nd edition 1982), which is very comprehensive and contains contributions by different specialists. Michael White, *Payment Systems in Britain* (Gower Press 1981), reports a large-scale survey carried out by the Policy Studies Institute and also highlights major issues and possibilities in payment system policy. Tom Lupton and Don Gowler's *Selecting a Wage Payment System* (Kogan Page 1969) develops an ambitious and complex contingency-based approach. Guides on specific provisions for managerial payments and benefits are published in many countries; a British source is Tony Vernon-Harcourt, *Rewarding Management* (Gower Press 1982, revised annually). Paul Miller's, The Rewards of Executive Incentives', *Management Today*, May 1982 makes some interesting suggestions.

Other sources mentioned in this chapter were Jeremy Baker, 'Keeping Wheels Turning', *Accounting Age*, 24 February 1978; Huw Beynon, *Working for Ford* (Penguin, 2nd edition 1983); (Lord) Wilfred Brown, *Piecework Abandoned: The Effect of Wage Incentive Systems on Managerial Authority* (Heinemann 1962); John Child and Bruce Partridge, *Lost Managers: Supervisors in Industry and Society* (Cambridge University Press 1982); W. W. Daniel, 'Understanding Employee Behaviour in its Context' in John Child (editor), *Man and Organization* (Allen and Unwin 1973), Chapter 2; Lex Donaldson and Richard Lynn, 'The Conflict Resolution Process', *Personnel Review*, Spring 1976; Miklos Haraszti, *A Worker in a Worker's State* (Penguin 1977); Frederick Herzberg, Bernard Mausner and Barbara B. Snyderman, *The Motivation to Work* (Wiley 1959); Elliott Jaques, *A General Theory of Bureaucracy* (Heinemann/Halsted 1976), Chapter 14; Steven Kerr, 'On the Folly of Rewarding A, While Hoping for B', *Academy of Management Journal*, December 1975; E. A. Locke, D. B. Feren, V. M. McCaleb, K. Shaw and A. T. Denny, 'The Relative Effectiveness of Four Methods of Motivating Employee Performance' in K. D. Duncan, M. M. Gruneberg and D. Wallis (editors), *Changes in Working Life* (Wiley 1980); Abraham H. Maslow, *Motivation and Personality* (Harper and Row, revised edition 1970); Alan Whitaker, *People, Tasks and Technology: a Study in Consensus* (University of Lancaster, Dept. of Behaviour in Organizations 1982).

PART III

ORGANIZATIONAL CHANGE

Chapter 8

Organization, Performance and Change

'Change of fortune is the lot of life.' Traditional proverb.

This book began by noting that when companies and other bodies are successful, some of the credit is usually attributed to good organization. It is widely assumed that the design of organization has an effect on performance. A decline in performance or a change in the conditions affecting performance therefore provide *prima-facie* reasons for considering making changes to organization.

The apparently straightforward relationship between organization, performance and change actually begs some difficult questions. What is 'success' or 'good performance', and how is organization to be judged as a contributory factor? What do available theory and research indicate about the way that organization relates to performance? What do the responses to these questions tell us about the circumstances under which changes to organization may be required?

This chapter addresses these questions. In so doing, it draws together the discussion of organizational choices in Part II of this book with the consideration of organizational change in Part III. Performance is a central part of the linkage. In so far as decision-making on organizational design is a rational process (which is not wholly the case), the process of considering alternative organizational arrangements will have to refer to performance criteria and a view will be taken about the consequences for performance of adopting each alternative. In forming this view, some account must be taken of how readily changes to existing organization can be brought about. Equally, the conclusion that a change is required, probably because of a perceived performance inadequacy now or in the future, will trigger off the process of making an organizational choice. Whichever way round one looks at the link between choice and change in organization, those involved in the decisions will proceed on the basis of a theory about the relationship of organization to performance.

The contribution of organizational design to performance is therefore a central issue in this chapter, which is divided into four sections. The first considers the problem of defining what constitutes 'good performance' or 'effectiveness' for organizations. Performance criteria for the design of organizational structures and systems are then discussed. A third and longer section examines three perspectives on how organizational design can affect performance. The final section considers the implications for organizational change which stem from these perspectives. Throughout this chapter the term 'organizational design' should be taken to include all the aspects covered in previous chapters.

The problem of defining 'good performance'

Paul Goodman and Johannes Pennings (1977) comment that 'effectiveness' is one of the most pervasive yet least well delineated of constructs applied to organizations. It enters into virtually any theory of organizations and there have been many writings on the definition of organizational performance, yet no general agreement has been reached.

The different definitions which have been offered reflect opinions on a number of issues:

1 Whether one should look for a single dimension of organizational performance, such as return on investment for a business firm or proportion of patients cured for a hospital, as opposed to a range of dimensions, which in the case of the hospital might also take account of cost per patient stay, length of waiting time for admission, and alternative treatment uses of the medical resources. If several dimensions or criteria are chosen, the problem arises of how much weight to give to each.

2 Whether or not to regard organizations as a rational set of arrangements which have been established in order to attain certain goals. If they are so regarded, then good or at least satisfactory performance can be defined with reference to attainment of these goals. There are complications, however, since not all members of an organization necessarily come to it with the same purposes or priorities. Secondly, whether goals are appropriate both in content and in the level at which they are set could itself be said to constitute an aspect of performance. For example, the purposes set for an organization may fail to meet a significant need, while target levels of performance might be unrealistically high or unnecessarily low. In these instances poor goal-setting could threaten an organization's survival. Some writers on organization have therefore advanced a systems view of performance as an alternative to the goal model. This takes as its measure of performance the survival of organizations based on their capacity (1) to attract needed resources, (2) to integrate these effectively, and (3) to adapt to change. In directing attention to the fundamental requirements for organizational survival, the systems perspective highlights performance criteria of an economic and financial nature in so far as all organizations consume resources which normally have to be paid for. Financial criteria are most clearly of significance for business organizations, but their relevance for public service and community organizations should not be overlooked.

3 A further issue concerns the definition of constituencies. These are the groups of people who determine the relevant standards by which performance is to be judged. In many countries, the only legal constituents of the private business firm are the owners, but many would argue on both pragmatic and moral grounds that the firm's constituency also includes

employees, customers, suppliers, the local community and government. While all its constituents may have a common stake in the survival of an organization, their specific requirements of it may well conflict. This introduces a political dimension to the definition of good performance.

4 The question of time-span also arises in the definition of performance. Performance criteria can be optimized in the short term at the expense of the long term. For example, short-term profit can often be boosted in companies through cuts in expenditure on new product development, market research and advertising, but the longer-term consequences are likely to be harmful. What time period, then, should be adopted for assessments of organizational performance? This question again has a political dimension since the mobility of capital is on the whole greater than that of labour, particularly at times of job scarcity. A short-term profit maximizing approach may therefore benefit investors at the expense of employees who have a longer-term stake in their organization's prosperity.

Some of the difficulties surrounding the definition of organizational performance are technical in nature concerning, for example, the establishment of comparability in the application of accounting concepts. The more fundamental problems are, however, essentially of a political nature because they concern the value which different parties to the organization place upon alternative objectives. The design of organization is involved in the matter of alternative objectives in two respects. First, the direction of collective units towards different ends, such as growth via diversification or profit-enhancement via consolidation, will tend to call forth different organizational structures. Second, certain ends are incorporated within the design of organization itself. Different designs of organization present alternatives in the provisions they include for employees to share in control, to enjoy autonomy, to exercise skills in their jobs, and generally to achieve a superior quality of working life.

Criteria for organizational design

It is clear that a number of different criteria can be applied to the design of organizational structures and systems. This follows from the alternative ways in which good performance may be defined. It also follows from the possibility that certain organizational arrangements may be valued in themselves, or at least regarded as 'right and proper', even if they do not represent the only or even the best way of securing high performance for the collectivity as a whole.

The debate over the respective roles of efficiency and power in shaping modern organization becomes relevant at this point. In attempting to understand why organization has developed to its present extent, leading to the dominance of very large bureaucratic enterprises and public bodies, some analysts have concluded that this results from the greater efficiency of co-ordinating transactions through formal organization rather than leaving these to the market mechanism. They acknowledge that there are still some circumstances in which market transactions may have the edge in terms of factors such as flexibility and avoiding fixed overhead costs, and writers such as Oliver Williamson (1975) have developed an extensive contingency analysis of these circumstances. The significant point for the present is that this line of argument attaches criteria of *efficiency* to organization as a method of co-ordinating and regulating transactions and tasks.

The critics of this argument maintain, however, that to understand the genesis and purpose of organization simply in terms of efficiency is historically incorrect and misleading. In their view, the nature of past and present designs for organization has to be understood as manifesting at least in part the wish of entrepreneurs, leaders and managers to maintain centralized hierarchical control, and in so doing to preserve an advantageous economic and social position for themselves. Similarly, groups of workers occupying strategic positions in the process of production may be able to maintain a preferred mode of work organization, and to justify this by reference to established 'custom and practice'. This alternative view therefore sees organization as fulfilling criteria of *power*. It looks upon traditional hierarchical organizational structures as embodying relationships of power and control which those in the top positions are reluctant to surrender.

The efficiency rationale for organization treats its design as a *technical* issue. It asks which design leads to the most efficient management of the various contributions and transactions required for carrying out the tasks of the unit in question. This conception of organization fits a systems view of performance, but one where no fundamental conflicts of interest within the system are envisaged. By contrast, the power rationale regards the design of organization as a *political* issue. It expects to find organizations designed in ways that are consistent with existing power relationships. This perspective comes closer to the constituency and goal models of performance in recognizing that different groups have different goals and interests. It anticipates that one group will occupy a dominant position and that others may not necessarily accept this position, or the organization structure which reflects it, as legitimate.

It is realistic to recognize that both technical and political considerations enter into the specific criteria which can be applied to organizational design, even though most of the literature has given prominence to the technical aspects only. These specific criteria have come to light in previous chapters and include control, communication and information processing, adaptability and flexibility, development and innovation. These are all functions that organization is expected to serve or attributes which it is expected to foster. They are clearly requirements for the effective and continuing operation of a collective unit, and this book has discussed ways in which the design of organization could contribute to their achievement. There is, nevertheless, a political dimension to each criterion. Chapter 6 developed this point with regard to control, which is not simply a matter of designing a system to enable work to be monitored but is also an issue of contention between management and workers around the so-called 'frontier of control' in the workplace. Similarly with information processing; widespread dissemination of information within an organization is often helpful to the collective effort but it may be resisted by senior management because it implies a right to comment and could encourage a demand for wider participation in decision-making which management would not find politically welcome. The criterion of flexibility embraces the political issue of whether or not to respect the established demarcations of specialized departments and jobs. The criterion of innovation contains within its ambit the issue of who shall have the right to innovate and make changes within an organization.

There will always be a degree of tension between the various criteria for organizational design. Even among a senior management group where political differences may amount to no more than personal rivalry, there could well be disagreement over the balance to be struck between criteria such as efficiency and flexibility. Efficiency may require long production runs based on standard products with both control and integration being achieved by formalized and/or hierarchical means. Flexibility, on the other hand, may require being prepared to offer new designs or modifications to suit specific customer needs and relying much more on cross-departmental meetings and teamwork focused on specific projects. The intrusion of the political dimension, which means that people will attach value to particular forms of organization in their own right, only adds to the potential tension between such requirements.

The persistence of competing criteria and models for organizational design, even in business companies where ultimately financial considerations are dominant, is encouraged by the difficulty of specifying what effect organization actually has on overall performance. Organization is only one of the influences which bear upon performance. Some of these influences are external and may lie outside management's ability to predict or control. Others stem from the quality of management itself and of its policies. Quality of management is a pervasive factor affecting all aspects of behaviour within an organization. Management policies have a strategic aspect which affords the organization a certain potential to achieve performance, and they have an operational aspect which relates to how well the internal activities of the organization are performed. The role played by the design of structure and systems within this complex of influences on performance is virtually impossible to quantify apart from the aspect of cost. While it is possible to specify processes on which organizational design will have an impact, such as control, integration and information processing, these processes are diffused throughout the organization and they are also affected by the competence and motivation of the people who are involved.

The presence of multiple criteria located within the area of organizational politics, and the ambiguity about the effect of organizational design on performance, would seem to make it rather unlikely that any single design will emerge clearly as the most acceptable or successful, even within a relatively homogeneous sector or area of activity. Nevertheless, the design of organization has been singled out as a significant factor in achieving good performance by senior managers and experienced consultants. Two of the schools of thought which have developed on this issue go so far as to suggest optimum organizational design characteristics—in the first case for all situations and in the second case for given situations.

Organization and performance

This section considers three major perspectives on the relationship between organizational design and performance. The great majority of writings on this subject have been concerned with business organizations, though some work has now been accomplished in public service areas such as hospitals. In order to cover all three perspectives on a comparable basis, the present review will concentrate on the conclusions drawn from business organizations where the overriding performance criteria are profit and growth. The final section of this chapter will then draw out the implications of these three perspectives for organizational change.

There is a long history of searching for principles of 'good' management practice. The design of organization is part and parcel of the practice of management and so in this vein the endeavour to identify universal organizational prescriptions continues. The search for *'universals'* is the first approach to be discussed.

The second approach starts from a recognition that organizations do not all operate under the same circumstances or with the same infrastructures. Every organization is located within a particular configuration of contingencies deriving from its own situation. These contingencies depend on the market and technological environments in which it operates, its scale and diversity of operations, the technology applied to its work, and the type of personnel it employs. According to this perspective, a one-best design of organization cannot be specified, since an appropriate design is the one which best suits the contextual and operational contingencies that apply. This has therefore come to be known as the *contingency* approach, more precisely called the task contingency approach since it refers to the organizational needs that are seen to stem from the objective of carrying out tasks effectively. Additionally, there is a political contingency view, which recognizes that in practice organization reflects the distribution of power between management and other groups (and between sections of management itself). This distribution of power is in turn affected by market conditions and by political action in society, which can, for example, generate legislation to afford workers certain rights of control. Political conditions are therefore also identified as contingencies and as potential sources of change in organizations.

The third approach stresses the importance for performance of *consistency* in organizational design. It recognizes the problem that could arise should different contingencies hold conflicting implications which then generated internal inconsistencies in organizational design. It also recognizes the need for structures and systems to be consistent with the established culture of the organization and the philosophy of its management, but in contrast to the universal approach, it does not consider that any one set of practices is necessarily superior.

The search for universals

Two major studies have recently attempted to identify characteristics which are widely found among successful business companies. Thomas Peters and Robert Waterman (1982) report an investigation of forty-three American companies in their book *In Search of Excellence*. These companies had all remained in the top half of their industries over a twenty-year period in terms of at least four out of six measures of growth and profitability. Peters and Waterman concluded that eight basic practices characterized these successfully managed companies. The second study is by William Abernathy, Kim Clark and Alan Kantrow (1983) in their book *Industrial Renaissance*. They consider the changes that are required if American companies, particularly in manufacturing, are to survive new competitive conditions. They draw heavily on Japanese examples to suggest a number of superior practices. A few earlier studies had also concluded that certain managerial characteristics and practices were consistently associated with higher performance, but cause and effect relationships were often not clear. Even the Peters and Waterman study suffers from the absence of a comparison with poor-performing companies that would indicate whether their practices were markedly different. However, the two recent books are superior to previous investigations because of their closer familiarity with the companies studied, and this provides some evidence on the performance consequences of changes made within them.

There is quite a high degree of consistency among the characteristics of successful companies uncovered by these enquiries, which is interesting in view of the different industries and situations involved. Some of these characteristics are elements of organizational design or are closely related to it. The following is a distillation of the organizational attributes which have been linked to superior economic performance in the available research:

1 An emphasis on methods to communicate key values and objectives and to ensure that action is directed towards these. (Some studies suggest that managements in higher performing companies select a few key objectives and then concentrate resources single-mindedly on fulfilling them.)
2 The delegation of identifiable areas of responsibility to relatively small units, including work groups. These units are encouraged to carry out their responsibilities with considerable autonomy and scope for initiative, but they are subject to performance assessments which manifest a preservation of tight central control.
3 Use of a simple lean structure of management which is intended to avoid the rigidities of bureaucracy, the complexities of the matrix and the overheads of both.

Peters and Waterman conclude that in high-performing companies the commitment to clear, often single, objectives is linked with 'a bias for action'. They emphasize the role of intense informal communications both for infusing this commitment through the organization and for bringing together collective contributions where these are required in planning action. This is integration through direct contact: a visible and accessible management (for example, Hewlett-Packard's 'management by wandering around'), and the use of small, short-lived task forces. In Chapter 5 I noted that it is always difficult to achieve integration, but went on to suggest that the investment of time and effort in integration should be tailored to suit the circumstances. In contrast, the perspective here is a universalistic one, finding virtue in one particular approach to integration because this is seen to generate a greater commitment to key values and objectives and is also geared towards getting appropriate action taken quickly. While this intense and informal style of integration may be more costly in time and personal stress than more formal methods, it encourages flexibility and innovation which have both become more significant as performance requirements under modern conditions of keen competition and rapid technological advance.

The second set of universalistic recommendations looks to economy, flexibility and innovation in the organization of production and other contingency tasks. The economy is in manning and supervision, the flexibility in deployment, and the innovation in a constant direction of attention to ways of improving performance. These are virtues which writers such as Abernathy and his colleagues find in the approach to work organization within larger Japanese companies. In this approach, the work group or team is the basic unit, in contrast to the emphasis on the individual worker or job in the western scientific management tradition. The group performs some of its own supervision, and there is economic manning through flexible deployment. People within the group do whatever needs to be done rather than restricting their contribution to the defined limits of particular jobs. For management, quality circles based on work groups have the attraction of directing the contributions of workers with first-hand knowledge towards possible improvements, while they are also part of a system which maintains individual standards of performance through group pressures. In the Japanese context, the processes of participation and initiative at work group level are closely directed by performance requirements. Awareness of these requirements is fostered by the widespread distribution of information and discussion throughout the hierarchy. Strong reinforcement is usually provided by the prominent display of performance levels attained.

The delegation of initiative and responsibility to work groups combined with the maintenance of central control by means of regular performance assessments is part of the simultaneous loose-tight coupling which Peters and Waterman include among the eight characteristics of 'excellent' American companies. Although so much reference has been made to Japan, this approach does not in fact draw on concepts new to western thinking. There are antecedents, for example, in autonomous work groups and in output control, while the general philosophy has parallels with the principle of divisionalization. There are probably just two significant features about the Japanese example. First, the effective, indeed relentless, way in which the theory is actually put into practice. Second, the way that this application is supported (in the larger dominant companies) by policies on long-term employment and welfare benefits, and also by ideologies, which reinforce personal commitment to the company and its prosperity. This second feature, of course, draws attention to the significance of achieving an overall synergistic consistency in policies on organization.

Peters and Waterman conclude that successful companies generally have simple organizational structures with small numbers of corporate staff. They contrast such structures with matrix organization which, in their view, not only proliferates managerial overhead but also dilutes priorities in the name of balance and in the confusion of multiple reporting relationships. The recommendation of simple lean structures is consistent with the argument in favour of minimizing the levels of management which was set out in Chapter 3, and which is supported also by studies such as that by Lenz (1980). It also implies a criticism of bureaucracy which typically works through formalized procedures and a large component of specialized staffs. In this connection, research which I conducted in 82 British companies, indicated that the more profitable ones tended to employ fewer people in staff functions such as finance and personnel as opposed to the core areas of production and marketing (Child 1974). The faster-growing companies also tended to have less formalized structures. More recently, colleagues and I have contrasted the greater use of staff specialists in British manufacturing companies compared with their counterparts in West Germany, and have suggested ways in which this is likely to contribute to inferior performance in the British case (Child et al. 1983). Although these studies leave questions of cause and effect unresolved, they are consistent with the view that simple lean structure may be a 'universal' of effective organization.

The three main organizational design thrusts that I have distinguished in the 'universals' perspective are of particular interest, since it will be seen in the following chapter that they represent changes which new micro-electronic technology is expected to facilitate. New technology makes available new opportunities for direct fast communication over distances. It can be used to promote the local initiative of small groups or individuals by making relevant knowledge readily available to them and by permitting a more precise and faster recording of performance achieved. New technology is expected to reduce the size and complexity of managerial establishments. If changes in these directions continue to be regarded as generally desirable, following the universalistic argument, then the new technology should make them easier to accomplish.

The search for universals of good organizational design continues the tradition of the early theorists who formulated general principles of management. While some of these principles were criticized for their imprecision, others such as 'unity of command' (people should report to only one superior) were quite specific. However, like these principles, the 'good' practices recommended today do not take into account the nature of each organization's operations and situation. For example, the recommendation to employ simple lean management structures, which is consistent with unity of command, is in contradiction to use of the matrix form. It is useful in so far as it points to problems that can arise in matrix structures, but what it and other general precepts fail to do is to indicate the circumstances under which it may be worth while incurring the additional costs and problems of more complex structures because other benefits or possibilities are thereby realizable. It is also likely that other recommendations, such as delegation of responsibility, may be difficult to apply in certain countries—in this case because of ingrained cultural attitudes about the reservation of initiative to persons of high status and/or formal authority.

It also has to be borne in mind that the nature of any connection between 'good practice' recommendations and organizational performance is not firmly established. For instance, a large part of the Peters and Waterman sample of 'excellent' American companies comprised high technology and project management organizations. It is possible that the recommendations advanced by these writers are well suited to companies of this sort located in high-growth markets and employing significant proportions of highly qualified self-motivated staff. But they may be less suited to companies in stagnating traditional industries and employing relatively few highly qualified staff. This raises the question of how far it is the business opportunities in a particular sector and the nature of its products and services that encourage the development of certain managerial practices and modes of organization through their direct consequences for growth, rate of change and type of employees hired. The problems of teasing out cause and effect in the absence of close knowledge of how specific organizations have developed over time, speak for caution in accepting the general validity of claims about good managerial and organizational practice. It should be noted that Peters and Waterman are not able to tell us the extent to which their good practices were also to be found in less 'excellent' companies.

Yet another consideration suggests that it is necessary to work out a design of organization appropriate to each particular case rather than relying too heavily on universal recommendations. Any organization has to satisfy a number of performance criteria, and to strike a balance between, say, economy, flexibility and innovation that suits its present situation and the assessment of future developments. It was noted in connection with control and reward systems, how each of these performance criteria are most readily served by somewhat different modes of organization. As the weight given to different criteria changes over time, as it may, it follows that the most appropriate design of organization will alter. Indeed, students of the innovation process such as Zaltman, Duncan and Holbek (1973) argue that the initiation and implementation stages within innovation itself are facilitated by different modes of organization. They conclude that initiation is encouraged by employing or accessing a wide range of different specialists and facilitating intense open communication between them via decentralization and a low level of formalization; while implementation is best served by using a more compact range of staff and a greater reliance on formal procedure and central direction for co-ordination, budgetary control and programming. To the extent that different objectives and performance priorities will be pursued both in one organization over the course of time and between organizations at a point in time, then managements may well be advised to consider a variety of organizational forms, changing these when circumstances change, rather than rely upon one recommended approach only. This, of course, is the essence of the contingency argument.

Considerations of contingency

Many authorities take the view that the design of organization most conducive to high levels of performance can only be formulated when account is taken of contingent circumstances. According to this so-called 'contingency' approach, there are no general principles or best practices of organization. Managers and others who are involved in organizational design have to work out and weigh up the situational implications of the contingencies they happen to face.

The contingency perspective developed from a view of organizations as open systems, the survival of which is seen to depend upon maintaining a balance of exchange in transactions with the environment sufficient to provide resources for future activities. It is recognized that the management of organizations is undertaken in conditions of uncertainty and dependence, both of which create risk for management. Uncertainty arises from an imperfect understanding of events and from incomplete control over the actions taken both by employees and parties outside the organization. These sources of uncertainty make prediction a hazardous exercise. The dependence of management upon the goodwill and support of other groups carries with it an element of threat to the success of its policies and possibly to the organization's survival in its present form.

The levels of uncertainty and dependence, and therefore risk, facing management will vary between different cases, but these factors will never be wholly eliminated. This lack of perfect control over the situation means that the context and conditions in which an organization's work is carried out have to be regarded as contingencies. That is, they are relevant and variable parameters for which allowance and adjustment in management practice and organizational design have to be made. The pressures for organizational forms to be adjusted to fit or match changing environmental conditions has been expressed by the so-called 'population ecology' model. This posits a process of natural selection over time such that organizations which survive are those whose features are adapted to suit their habitats, be these the conditions of particular industries, societies or whatever. It is quite clear therefore that the contingency approach regards organizational change as a regular, if not almost continuous, necessity in the light of continually changing conditions.

The contingency view, which has come to be recognized as such within the literature on organization, would be more correctly labelled the 'task contingency' approach. It focuses on the tasks to be performed within an organization and develops the thesis that for these to be carried out effectively the organization of the work and of the people contributing to it must be designed with existing contingencies in mind. Environment, diversity, size, technology and type of personnel are the categories of contingency most often identified. The task contingency approach seeks to identify those organizational designs which will be efficient for given contextual situations.

It was noted earlier in this chapter how, in reality, power as well as efficiency is also a consideration in organizational design. What might be called a *'political contingency'* perspective has emerged, in recognition of this point. While not so widely known in the literature on organizational design, the political perspective is highly relevant. It raises the question of which organizational arrangements are acceptable to management and other groups, and it suggests that unacceptable ones will be resisted and therefore inefficient. The power to influence and/or resist policies on organizational design is of central interest to this perspective. It concerns the relative power of management, workers and specialist groups within business companies, and that of different professional groups, occupations and administrators within public sector institutions such as hospitals. The distribution of this power will shift largely according to conditions in labour and product markets, which determine the supply and demand for employment of the various groups. It can also be modified by legal provisions, which accord specific groups exclusive rights to carry out certain tasks and to control training and recruitment. According to the political contingency perspective, macro phenomena at the level of whole societies, and indeed in the international economy as a whole, are significant for changes in organization. These include the business cycle, levels of government expenditure, the pattern and rate of new entry into labour markets, and the legal and political context of different countries.

Both the task and political contingency perspectives carry strong messages about the conditions under which pressures for organizational change will arise. They are now reviewed in turn.

The task contingency approach: relevance of environment, diversity, size, technology and personnel

This approach relates strategic contingencies to organizational performance both directly and also indirectly through their relevance for the design of organization which should be adopted. The basic argument is as follows. Contingent factors such as the type of environment or the size of organization have some direct influence on levels of success. There may, for example, be economies of scale open to the larger organization. Certain environments, such as particular industries, may provide greater opportunity or are less competitive. Second, it is assumed that a set of structured administrative arrangements consciously adapted to the tasks that are to be done, to the expectations and needs of people performing the tasks, to the scale of the total operation, to its overall complexity, and to the pressures of change being encountered, will itself act to promote a higher level of effectiveness than will a structure ill-suited to these contingencies. Organization structure is seen in this way to modify the effects of contingencies upon performance.

1 Environment   According to task contingency theory, different approaches to organizational design are conducive to high performance, depending on whether or not the environment in which the organization is operating is variable and complex in nature, or stable and simple. Variability in the environment refers to the presence of changes that are difficult to predict, involve important departures from previous conditions, and are likely, therefore, to generate considerable uncertainty.

Complexity of the environment is said to be greater the more extensive and diversified the range of an organization's activities, which correspondingly take it into more diverse sectors of the environment. These diverse sectors are all relevant areas of external information that it should monitor. There is evidence that the degree of environmental variability is a more important contributor to uncertainty among managerial decision-makers than is complexity. I shall discuss variability now and return to complexity in a later section on diversity of operations.

The general conclusion which emerges from available research is that, in conditions of environmental variability, successful organizations will tend to employ the following structural characteristics:

(a) Arrangements to reduce uncertainty. These might include staff support for sophisticated search and information processing activities, and attempts to gain greater control over the conditions under which inputs are acquired and outputs disposed of, even to the extent of vertical integration.
(b) A relatively high level of internal differentiation. The critical nature of a variable environment means that an organization is under pressure to employ specialist staff in boundary or interface roles—in positions where they form a link with the outside world, securing and evaluating relevant information. This may well involve the establishment of more specialist departments, which increases the internal differentiation of the organization's structure. With a great deal of external change, there will be some pressure to delegate organizational decision-making to the 'people on the spot' who are in a position to respond quickly. This in a sense increases the vertical differentiation of an organization through a dispersion of decision-making.
(c) A relatively intense level of integration, achieved through flexible and participative, rather than formalized, processes. If there are many significant external changes to which an organization has to adapt, and if it becomes internally differentiated through setting up specialized roles to cope with such areas of change, then it will also need to give particular attention to the maintenance of integration among its personnel. These personnel are now organizationally more differentiated from one another and require greater co-ordination, while the context of change itself places a greater burden upon integrative mechanisms because it means that the co-ordinated response to new developments has to be made without undue delay. In a variable environment, contingency theorists conclude, flexible rather than highly formalized or hierarchical methods of co-ordination and information-sharing are appropriate. These generally entail a high level of face-to-face

participation in discussion and decision-making, with an emphasis on close lateral relations among members of different departments instead of formal links up and down hierarchies or via periodic formal meetings. The use of new information technology such as teleconferencing permits direct face-to-face interaction between people who are physically separated. This method of working also implies a higher degree of delegation down the hierarchy with operational decisions being left to the people most familiar with relevant information, though information technology now permits rapid checking with more senior managers.

Studies which have examined the performance of organizations in variable environments in relation to their structures have produced sufficiently consistent findings to support the conclusions presented. Each study, of course, examines the structural elements I have mentioned in more detail. In the United States there is the well-known work of Paul Lawrence and Jay Lorsch (1967) as well as studies by Robert Duncan (1973), Pradip Khandwalla (1973), Anant Negandhi and Bernard Reimann (1973), among others. Of British studies, Tom Burns' and G. M. Stalker's (1961) is the best known. All are listed at the end of this chapter.

My own research has indicated that companies in the variable science-based environments characterizing electronics and pharmaceuticals which were achieving above-average levels of growth tended to rely less on formal procedures and documentation than did slow-growing companies. Among firms in more stable environments, high growth companies relied more (but only marginally so) on formalized methods of integration than did less successful firms (Child 1975).

These organizational differences between high and low growth companies located in contrasting environments were most marked in certain areas of management. Within the stable sector, faster growing companies had significantly more formalization in the production area, especially in matters like defining operator tasks, training operators, and recording their performance. The faster growing companies, particularly in variable environments, made less use of formal training procedures and standardized personnel practices, and of formal hierarchical channels for communication.

2 Diversity   It was seen in Chapter 4 that, among large American firms, product diversification on a multinational level was adopted as a means for sustaining a path of continued profitable growth. Studies of these companies suggest that organizations which group their basic operations into divisions once these operations become diversified will tend to achieve higher levels of performance.

This proposition expresses the fundamental argument for divisionalized organizational structure, which has become the dominant form among large business firms today and which can also be seen in some large public undertakings. Organizations having a spread of different products or services, and with outlets in a number of regions, operate in a complex total environment. Such organizations are also likely to be large. Because of their size and diversity, they will almost certainly experience communications difficulties.

To overcome these problems, it is logical to create decentralized, semi-autonomous operating units or divisions, which can group formal relationships in a way that reflects the necessities of exchange and co-ordination around common problems. These commonalities usually centre around product groups favouring a product division type of organization, but they may also centre on geographical regions, favouring an area division structure. If both product and regional co-ordination are equally vital, then a mixed, or 'grid' structure may be logical.

The detailed research of Stopford and Wells supports the argument that these divisionalized arrangements work. They found that American multinational corporations which have divisionalized their structures in response to a diversity of activities, tend to be superior performers. The more successful firms have usually adopted the kind of divisionalization—internal divisions, global area divisions, global product divisions, mixed or grid structure—that considerations such as product diversity and level of involvement in foreign business would logically dictate. Large diversified European firms began to adopt divisionalized structures during the 1960s, partly in emulation of the American example, but mainly because increased competitive pressures forced them to adopt a more effective structural model. However, it should be noted that none of the research so far carried out has demonstrated the presence of a *strong* connection between diversification, structural design *and* performance.

3 Size of organization   The reasons why larger organizations generally employ a greater degree of delegation and formalization than do smaller ones have been examined in previous chapters. This trend towards 'bureaucracy' in larger organizations has been deplored by critics such as E. F. Schumacher who argue that 'small is beautiful'. The problem of the large organization, they say, lies in the dead weight of bureaucratic administration that it takes on. In an attempt to hold together its many divisions and departments, the large organization emphasizes conformity to rules and systems, a trait which has prompted the observation that 'a new idea has never come out of a large corporation'. Many studies of organization have confirmed that large scale does indeed breed bureaucracy in the form of highly compartmentalized jobs and areas of work, detailed procedural and paperwork systems, long hierarchies, and delegation of routine decisions to lower level managers within precise discretionary limits.

Much as critics may decry bureaucracy, I found, in the research mentioned, that the more profitable and faster growing companies, in the larger size category of 2,000 employees and above, were those which had developed this type of organization (Child 1975). The larger the company, the greater the association between more bureaucracy and superior performance. At the other end of the scale, among small firms of only a hundred or so employees, the better performers generally managed with very little formal organization. Figure 8.1 illustrates these findings.

Poorly performing large companies tend to specialize their staff less, to have less-developed systems and procedures, and to delegate decision-

Figure 8.1 Size of organization, bureaucracy and performance (*Source*: Child 1975)

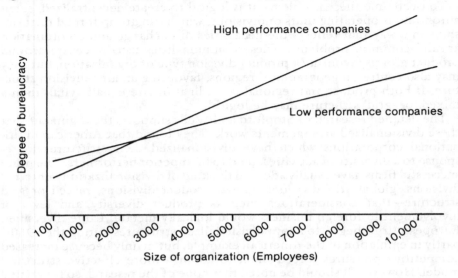

making less extensively. It is also worth noting that among the poorly performing companies the strength of the association between changes in size and changes in structure is noticeably reduced, compared with that among high performers. The high performing companies appeared to have matched their structures better to their size.

In the faster growing and more profitable companies, as total size increases so the development of specialized roles takes place quite rapidly in the areas of finance and accounting, production control, methods and work study, personnel and general administration. The following systems and procedures tend to be among those used more extensively by high performing companies as they grow larger: sophisticated financial controls applied to a wide range of activities; a precise definition of operative tasks by management, the application of work study and methods; the use of labour turnover statistics; the planning of recruitment; and the regular updating of company forms and documents.

Comparisons of larger companies within the same industry clearly illustrate this trend. For example, I studied three of the largest British national daily newspaper groups. One was the superior performer by a substantial margin, in terms of growth, return on assets, and return on combined circulation plus advertising sales. This group operated a highly formalized type of organization—it had developed a more elaborate set of procedures and systems covering a wider range of activities than had the other two companies, and it relied heavily on written communication and records. Indeed, its most distinguishing feature lay in this heavier use of documentation, especially job descriptions, manuals, work records, and the like.

The newspaper industry represents a relatively stable environment. When the nature of each organization's environment is taken into account, as well as its size, the association between organization and performance becomes more complicated. The need for companies operating in a more variable environment to keep a check on the formality in their organization, especially its routine-enforcing elements, probably explains why it is the successful companies in a more stable environment that most rapidly take on a formal bureaucratic type of structure as they grow larger. I found that the rate at which companies tend to develop bureaucratic structures as their size increases varies according to their environment and performance in the following sequence:

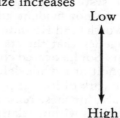

Rate of development in organizational structuring and delegation as size increases

1 Below average performers in stable environments   Low
2 Below average performers in variable environments
3 Above average performers in variable environments
4 Above average performers in stable environments   High

Managers, it appears from this research, have to take note of multiple contingencies, such as environment plus size, when planning the design of their organization. When there is not much variability in the environment, the need to develop organization to suit size becomes relatively more dominant. In this environment the better performing companies tend to develop formalized structures at a faster rate as they grow than do poor performers. When the environment is a variable one, however, these differences in structural development are reduced, because the contingency of coping with uncertainty tends to offset the contingency of coping with large scale. In a variable environment, the *rate* of increase in formalization accompanying growth in scale was found to be higher among good performers, but the absolute level of their formalization only reached that of poor performing companies at a size approaching 10,000 employees. In other words, smaller high performing companies in a variable environment tended to be particularly free of a bureaucratic style of structure: they were highly centralized and without much formalization. The picture is complex indeed, as most practical managers are well aware!

4 Technology   The term 'technology' is employed in almost as many senses as there are writers on the subject. Not very much of the research on links between technology and structure has looked for possible effects upon organizational performance. Joan Woodward's pioneering studies suggested that when organizations make structural arrangements to fit their technologies, they secure a superior level of performance. Woodward's view of technology concentrated on the physical organization of workflows. Does the organization have heavy plant and a rigid sequence of production, as in automobile assembly? Or does it have fairly light plant and flexible production, as in the manufacture of some electronic equipment and, even more so, in service industries? Unfortunately, neither Woodward nor subsequent investigators adopting her approach have employed precise measures of performance.

Khandwalla (1974), in later research conducted among 79 American manufacturing companies, found that the more profitable firms were those which had in definable respects adjusted their structures according to the 'mass output orientation' of their technology. High performing firms producing large quantities of standardized products (mass production and continuous-process companies in particular) tended to employ sophisticated control systems and also to delegate decision-making. These relationships were not evident among the firms achieving a low annual return on net worth, and Khandwalla's findings draw one's attention to a possible contingency that the standardization of production presents for structural design. Sophisticated controls are more readily applicable under standardized conditions, while delegation (as was noted in Chapter 5) itself requires a framework of formal control. The potential benefits of controls and delegation are, for these reasons, probably greatest under standardized operating conditions within relatively stable environments. However, the picture is changing because new information technology offers a greatly enhanced potential for control and adjustment under non-standardized and changing conditions (see Chapter 9).

The research I conducted in Britain indicated that the pattern of specialization in production and ancillary areas such as production control and maintenance was predictable in terms of the technology employed. In addition, the proportion of total employment allocated to some of the ancillary functions varied along with differences in technology. For example, more rigid technologies, such as a process type, tend to have relatively few production control specialists and less internal specialization within production control departments where these exist. Most control is actually built into the technology itself.

These associations between technology and the structure of employment lead one to ask whether, along with environment, size, and diversity, there is some logic of adjustment to contingencies here. If there is, does the extent to which organizations adapt to the logic predict differences in their performance?

The closeness of fit between technology and the pattern in which roles were specialized did not vary significantly between good and poor performing companies. What did distinguish the more successful firms, however, was that they tended to vary their investment in manpower devoted to production support activities according to differences in their technology. For instance, among companies using heavy plant and more rigid production systems, the more profitable and faster growing ones had significantly larger percentages of their total employment given over to maintenance activities. In other words, allocation of manpower in relation to technological requirements appears to improve performance.

5 Type of personnel   It is a cornerstone of the behavioural approach to management that organizations which adopt forms of structure consistent with the expectations and perceived needs of their personnel will tend to attract a greater contribution from them towards high performance. Most readers will be familiar with the views on this subject of influential organizational psychologists such as Chris Argyris, Frederick Herzberg, Rensis Likert and Douglas McGregor. They have argued for structures and styles of management that secure a higher degree of commitment to the organization from employees by more adequately meeting their expectations and their needs as mature adults. Only by working towards these structures can personal needs be harnessed to the requirements for effectiveness placed upon the organization as a whole. In a broader context, moves to enrich jobs and the developments in industrial co-determination also reflect this view since they start from the premise that employees' expectations and perceived needs are not being fulfilled adequately by existing forms of work organization.

The results of many research studies indicate that the general argument is valid (e.g. Lorsch and Morse 1974). Indeed, some would call it a truism. While it is unnecessary to review familiar ground, some qualifications are in order. The argument refers to the expectations and perceived needs of personnel. This reference to the perceptual level is important for, whatever the nature of universal psychological needs, it is clear that different types of people do not have the same requirements of their work at the conscious perceptual level. One has only to compare the professional employee with the manual worker to realize that sociocultural factors are crucial in shaping different expectations of what constitute legitimate conditions of work. The rate of unemployment will also modify job-seekers' views of what is an acceptable organization of work since security or keeping a job as a means of livelihood rather than as a means of fulfilment assumes greater significance when work is scarce. Similarly, comparisons between different countries have indicated that different supervisory styles and strategies of control are effective with employees located in different cultural milieux where different attitudes toward work and authority are evident. Finally, as noted in Chapter 2, there are situations in which technology can set limits on the design of jobs and the restructuring of work. In these situations the costs of investment in a different technology have to be weighed against the likelihood of further motivational contributions to performance.

Managements need to spend time ascertaining the expectations of different groups among their employees if they want to have a reliable idea of which arrangements will secure the willing commitment of those employees. The basic point is that the employees of an organization constitute a major contingency in the design of its structure. Their power to resist organizational arrangements of management's choosing is a possibility raised by the political contingency approach.

Limitations of the task contingency approach

The task contingency approach remains the dominant paradigm in the field of organizational design. It is supported by a large body of research which appears to testify to its validity and practical utility. This picture is, however, somewhat misleading, and there are difficulties and limitations in the contingency approach which the practising manager should bear in mind.

One major limitation of the contemporary task contingency approach lies in the lack of conclusive evidence to demonstrate that matching organizational design to prevailing contingencies contributes *importantly* to performance. There are two problems here. First, the discovery of a simple correlation between match of organization to contingency and level of performance does not demonstrate that organization is the causal factor. Second, non-organizational variables may turn out to have higher levels of association with performance. I shall examine these problems in turn.

The problem of causality was mentioned earlier (page 216). It qualifies the interpretation which can be placed upon several major contingency studies employing cross-sectional data. For in addition to the possible effects organization has on performance, the performance achieved constitutes a vital feedback of information to managers which may stimulate them to make adjustments to structure. Lawrence and Lorsch (1967), for instance, found that poorer performing organizations failed to develop integrative mechanisms adequate to match their degree of internal differentiation. They argued that inadequate integration led to poor performance. However, because more elaborate integrative mechanisms (co-ordinators, frequent meetings, even matrix systems) are more expensive, it is possible that their non-adoption was partly a reflection of an existing condition of poor performance and scarcity of resources. It may also have reflected the tendency to centralize decision-making and to tighten control through insistence on hierarchical referral which is a typical managerial response to poor performance. Both these reactions reduce the intensity of lateral integration.

Another study by Lorsch and Allen (1973) found in a comparison between two high performing and two low performing conglomerates that the latter had a more complex set of rules and systems, laying a heavy emphasis on control and co-ordination but at the same time permitting a relatively low degree of differentiation between headquarters and divisions. The writers interpreted this structural configuration as being dysfunctional for performance in diversified firms, but one could also argue that it is just the kind of recentralizing managerial response to be expected when performance is substandard in the first place.

Present uncertainties about the direction of causation in statistical associations between organization and performance could be reduced if investigators were more often to examine data over time. Most studies have been cross-sectional and few have paid attention to the reasons and processes by which new forms of organization were adopted. It is very difficult therefore to be sure that a close matching of organizational design to task contingencies is a significant determinant of superior performance. In this respect, a re-analysis of Rumelt's data on US corporations by Lex Donaldson (1983) is suggestive but not conclusive. Donaldson is able to show that companies which had structures mismatched to their strategies tended to reorganize to reduce the mismatch, albeit often after a time lag of several years. (In this case, divisionalization with diversity, and functional structure with non-diversity would constitute 'matches'.) While the presumption is that the change was motivated by considerations of sub-optimum performance, the analysis is not conclusive. Donaldson does not present performance data and it is always possible that the fashion for divisionalization propagated by consultants may have played a part.

In the area of environmental, strategic and structural relationships, where the contingency approach is most developed, studies such as those by Channon (1973) and Rumelt (1974) suggest that strategic policies on diversification and growth may themselves make a far more significant contribution to financial performance than does the degree to which structural forms have moved in line with such strategies. Franko (1976), studying large European business enterprises, all of which had remained viable over many decades, concluded that for the most part structural changes had not closely followed changes in product strategies. Pennings (1975) found, in 40 branch offices of a large United States brokerage organization, that the degree of fit between environmental and structural variables appeared to have little bearing on the effectiveness of the offices. The proportion of variance in effectiveness, with reference to both production and personnel criteria, that was explained was primarily due to organization structure *per se* in isolation from environmental contingencies.

It remains, therefore, very much an open question as to just how significant an influence on organizational performance the organizational design-contingency match really is. Another reason for this uncertainty lies in the fact that most research has treated contingencies virtually as God-given constraints. This ignores the possibility that some organizations may be less dependent than others upon their environments, and in a more secure position with respect to maintaining their target levels of performance.

The variable of dependence has come to be recognized as a major explanatory factor both for structural and performance variation. An organization, which, for instance, has achieved some degree of monopoly or has found a protected niche in the environment, might well be in a position to control or ignore environmental contingencies. In so far as it has little to fear from the threat of better performing competing organizations, then it can also afford to accept a level of sub-optimal performance if it chooses not to match its structure to suit prevailing contingencies. In the language of economic theory, whenever there are imperfections in the competitive situation or in the public accountability of organizations, the possible inefficiencies resulting from what contingency theorists would regard as a mismatch between organizational design and contingencies are likely to have limited implications for the survival of that organization.

There are in practice imperfections in the economics of resource allocation and competition, especially for non-business organizations. Even in the business sphere, inefficient organizations often take a long time to die and many survive protected by concentrated ownership, by their location in the interstices or niches which fall between major competitive markets, and so forth. For these reasons, and also because it may be far more significant for performance to achieve certain strategic objectives aimed at manipulating contingencies themselves (such as dominance in markets, economies of scale, and standardized production) than to achieve the optimal structural design, one finds that there is usually some variation in the structures of otherwise comparable organizations. This variation is sometimes sustained over many years without much apparent effect on success or failure.

A further problem has not been recognized sufficiently: that multiple contingencies will be present at the same time. Most researchers have so far failed to adopt a multivariate analysis of contingent or contextual variables in relation to structural design and performance. They have concluded that organizational design should be decided with reference to environment, or with reference to scale, or technology, and so on. But what happens when a configuration of different contingencies is found, each having distinctive implications for organizational design? A large firm may, for example, be operating in a variable environment. Following the guidelines of the contingency approach, should it set a limit on its levels of internal formalization in order to remain adaptable, or should it allow this to rise as a means of coping administratively with the complexity that tends to accompany large scale? This question helps to explain why larger firms frequently experience difficulties in sustaining the rate of innovation required by highly variable environments, and why the quality of their R & D relative to expenditure is often inferior. Another commonly found example of conflicting contingencies concerns job design, in those situations where there is a trade-off between the economics of assembly-line mass production or de-skilling forms of automation and the social (and sometimes economic) benefits which may accrue from technologies that build upon workers' skills and motivations.

All organizations function within a context of multiple contingencies. To the extent that considerations of contingency have force, this poses a significant organizational design dilemma because the structural implications of each contingency are unlikely to be the same. The solution usually adopted is an internal differentiation of the organization into separate or semi-separate units. For example, a large organization entering a dynamic environmental field will often create a separate and relatively small subsidiary unit to deal with the new area of operation—the creation of 'venture management' units fits into this category. The small venture subsidiary will find it easier to adopt the flexible, less formalized type of organizational design that is appropriate for an innovative strategy within a new variable environment. Companies such as Motorola have been known to modify technologies in order to permit enriched jobs or autonomous work groups in part of a plant but to retain a traditional form of engineering in other parts where the demand for new job designs was less keenly expressed. One also quite often finds organizations making a differentiation between units employing a mass-output standardized technology to meet a stable environmental demand, alongside other units employing a more flexible technology to meet more variable demands.

If adaptations of this kind are made in order to meet multiple contingencies, they are likely to promote intra-organizational structural variation.

Several studies have found evidence of such variation between segments of organizations which face different contingencies in regard to routineness of tasks, skills and technologies utilized, and type of personnel employed. Lawrence and Lorsch (1967) found that inter-functional differentiation increased in companies operating in dynamic environments, particularly because 'boundary spanning' roles such as marketing and research had to function in a mode more closely adapted to the conditions of their relevant environmental sectors. If adaptation to multiple contingencies takes the form of divisionalization or the creation of separate subsidiaries, the patterning of structural variation is likely to correspond to these sub-unit boundaries possibly combined with an overlay of inter-functional differences.

A major problem with intra-organizational structural variation of any kind is that it is likely to promote internal conflicts, tensions, and poor communication—in short, problems of integration. The main theme contained in the work of Lawrence and Lorsch and their colleagues at the Harvard Business School has, of course, been that a balance needs to be drawn in organizational design between differentiation and integration, which implies that the higher the degree of intra-organizational structural variation, the greater the burden of maintaining integration that is imposed.

Integrating mechanisms generally become more costly of time and managerial overheads as they become elaborate—involving more frequent meetings, the appointment of co-ordinators, project managers, or even a full matrix structure with two or more overlying managerial hierarchies. In addition, internal differentiation within an organization tends to promote or reinforce sub-unit goals and stereotypes which are always a potential source of conflict and its attendant inefficiencies. The inter-group hostility and rivalry which often accompanies differentiation cannot necessarily be dissipated by the introduction of structural mechanisms for integration. It is interesting in this connection to note Rumelt's (1974) finding that American corporations diversifying into related fields have generally been superior performers. This may well be partly because related diversification does not require radically different forms of structural design in newly established divisions.

Up to this point, two limitations to the task contingency approach have been noted: (1) continuing uncertainty over whether the match between contingencies and structure has much influence over performance; and (2) a recognition of the inconsistencies which could arise if organizational design were matched closely to multiple contingencies which 'required' different structures and systems. Criticism of the task contingency approach in these terms, however, continues to accept its rational view that the sole purpose of organizational design is to achieve efficiency. Another ground of criticism challenges the adequacy of this rationalistic assumption, and maintains instead that the viability of organizational design also depends on how well it reflects political realities. What may be called a political contingency view has developed from this critique and draws attention to factors such as the attachment of managers and other groups to particular modes of organization, the relevance of market conditions for their power to impose or sustain these preferred solutions, and the more general influence of the political and institutional systems found in different countries.

The political contingency approach: relevance of managerial preferences, market conditions and political context

1 Managerial preferences   The great majority of organizations are based upon hierarchy, and in these it is senior managers and administrators who most obviously influence the choice of organizational design. While they undoubtedly do take some account of task contingencies, their judgements are also based on other considerations. Studies of managerial decision-making suggest that familiar solutions and precedents tend to get carried over into new decisions. A managerial culture or 'philosophy' builds up in this way, and will probably be paralleled by the historical growth of 'custom and practice' at lower levels in the organization. Both are likely to have a conservative influence on the extent to which organization is changed in response to task contingencies.

Organizational design is not neutral over the distribution of power and status along the hierarchy. Some arrangements imply a greater concentration of power and status at the top than do others. Managerial policies reflect a view on this essentially political matter, and this means that options such as the delegation of decision-making or arrangements for participation can get ruled out even in circumstances where considerations of task contingency would speak in their favour. For example, a study of Dutch firms conducted by Guy Geeraerts (1983) found that larger size was accompanied by increased delegation—which is consistent with task contingency analysis—only in organizations managed by non-owners. The matching of delegation with size was not apparent in firms managed by their owners. This suggests that owner-managers preferred to follow the political principle of not diluting their power despite the task contingency warning that this reduces effectiveness as organizations grow larger. In cases like this ownership becomes a political contingency because of the strong managerial preference for a particular mode of organization to which it gives rise.

The conditions under which management, or indeed any other powerful group, can sustain the organizational design it prefers constitute a contingent factor in themselves. One aspect to this is the organization's dependence on external groups and their likely reactions. How long and to what extent can a less effective but preferred form of organization be sustained without incurring threats to the survival of the unit or to the incumbency of its leaders? A public bureaucracy such as a foreign affairs ministry in which it is difficult to apply efficiency audits may possibly be able to do this for a very long time. There will be much less scope to maintain a preferred but inefficient form of organization in a company with a high and dispersed equity base, and operating in competitive markets.

2 Market conditions   Another aspect concerns the conditions which affect the relative power of management and employees within a place of work and the implications this has for organization. Andrew Friedman (1977) has made a valuable contribution to our understanding here. In common with other writers in the radical tradition, Friedman is concerned with the conditions under which workers can successfully resist managerial strategies of control. These strategies in the dominant scientific management tradition have sought to subdivide work into simple tasks which can then be standardized, to define jobs narrowly so as to match these tasks, to determine methods in advance in detail, and to exercise close supervision. Friedman describes this approach as the 'direct control strategy' and it involves the deskilling and degradation of work. He contrasts this strategy with the other—'responsible autonomy'—in which workers are given enriched jobs, enlarged responsibility and light supervision. Attempts are made to enlist workers' co-operation through policies that emphasize their identity with management, and fulfilment of output targets tends to be the main criterion of control.

Through his studies in British industries, Friedman concludes that there are identifiable market conditions under which the one strategy or the other is likely to be adopted by management. Direct control has tended to prevail when stagnant or declining product demand and competitive conditions stiffen managerial resistance to workers' demands and encourage the tightening of controls in a search for cost reduction. Management is also in a stronger position to enforce direct control when labour markets are slack and labour is in plentiful supply. Conversely, in periods of growth with buoyant product markets, high profits can be made so long as delivery to the market is not interrupted. In these conditions, management will be more inclined to meet worker demands which are likely to press in the direction of responsible autonomy—that is, towards greater worker control over the immediate production process. The prospect of continued security of employment provides a foundation for gaining workers' commitment to stay with their present employer and to accept managerial objectives. This prospect is clearly enhanced if the organization enjoys competitive strengths and long-term growth in its product markets. If and when such growth gives rise to labour shortages, it will reinforce the choice of a responsible autonomy strategy since this is more likely to retain labour and because tight labour markets give workers greater power to enforce their preferred mode of organization.

While changes between direct control and responsible autonomy strategies cannot be made very rapidly (since they involve a major shift in management philosophy and infrastructure), this type of analysis can be very helpful in accounting for changes in work organization design that have occurred over the longer term in particular countries and industries. It can in fact usefully be extended to take account of other features which contribute to the labour market power enjoyed by particular groups of employees and which in turn affects their ability to press for a preferred organization of work. For example, some professional groups such as doctors and crafts such as printers have been in a position to control the rate of new recruitment into their occupational labour markets through their regulation of vocational training and certification. If successful, this maintains a scarcity value for their members and, coupled with professional or craft mystique, forms the basis for sufficient autonomy from management to permit the self-regulation and organization of their work. This degree of autonomy and control is in many cases now threatened by a growing supply of qualified manpower, a displacement of expertise by new technology and economic pressures for improved productivity.

In English-speaking countries professional bodies and craft trade unions have controlled vocational training to an extent not found in most other countries where such training is often regulated by the State. Vocational training tends to stamp a particular pattern of specialization upon organizations as well as imparting norms about the control and supervision of work. It provides an example of how the institutional arrangements found in different countries are themselves a contingency which is necessarily reflected in organizational design. Another example is the influence on control and interpersonal relations which can derive from the views on human nature expounded by the world's religions, particularly those which retain a strong influence over education.

3 Political context   Similarly, the political system in a particular country will have a bearing on the structuring of the organizations located there. This is apparent if we compare business organizations in western capitalist societies with their counterparts in socialist societies. The centralization of planning and control in most socialist countries contrasts with the decentralization inherent in the use of market mechanisms, and is in turn reflected in the greater centralization of decision-making within organizations in socialist systems. The formalization of socialist organizations also tends to be higher than that of western equivalents, which reflects the high formalization of their superordinate planning systems and regulative bureaucracies. Legislation to give employees rights of formal participation in organizational decision-making provides another instance of how national politics can help to mould organizational design.

The political contingency approach reminds the designers of organization and agents of change that they always have to take into account the realities of power within the institution where they are working. The viability of any organizational arrangements depends on their political acceptability as well as on their contribution to formal tasks and official objectives. When planning changes in organizations, recognition has to be given to deeply held managerial preferences, even though these may sometimes appear to be rather more in the nature of prejudices. Groups of employees, who may be in a strong position to resist or subvert organizational or job designs unacceptable to them, will have their own ideologies and established customs and practices that they wish to preserve.

The culture of a company or other body will be built on foundations such as these, often over a long period. Whether a management which believes in the need to break with that tradition is likely to succeed in carrying through change will depend not only upon the skill and preparation with which it is introduced (and this is considered more fully in Chapter 10), but also upon the political contingency of how much power management and employee groups have, respectively, to impose and to resist. Finally, the influence of national political systems and institutions is of particular relevance to companies that are expanding into international operations. They are likely to have to modify their standard job definitions and possibly supervisory and other control policies if they recruit local workers and staff who are products of education and training peculiar to each country. Cultural differences may reinforce this need for variety in organizational practices. Change will also be called for to suit the economic and political structures in different countries.

Considerations of consistency

Khandwalla (1973), in an examination of the organizational structures of 79 American manufacturing firms, was led to conclude that the internal consistency of structural design is significantly associated with levels of organizational performance. The structural features assessed in this study were arrangements to reduce uncertainty with respect to the environment, the degree of differentiation within the organization and the extent to which integrating mechanisms were employed.

Khandwalla found that firms which adopted these three structural features in proportion to each other tended to be more profitable. In less profitable firms there was far less consistency between the elements of their structural design. Khandwalla adopted a contingency interpretation of his findings to the extent that he believed that for organizational effectiveness, 'the particular design would depend on, among other factors, whether it is a large firm or not, and how uncertain its external environment is' (p.492). At the same time, however, 'what the findings suggest is that the gestalt or configuration of an organization is likely to be a more potent determinant of its effectiveness than any of the individual components of this configuration' (p.493). If that configuration matches up to the organization's contingencies, then performance should be further enhanced.

For reasons already discussed it is likely, taking an organization's structural design as a whole, that there will be some conflict between the principle of matching structural arrangements to every contingency and the principle of retaining a high degree of internal consistency. The importance of the consistency factor is still to be researched, but given the limitations of the contingency argument it may prove to be quite significant. This much is suggested by a study I conducted in 1974 on four North American airlines and one European carrier. The more successful airlines employed different forms of organization despite operating with many of the same contingencies. What distinguished them was not so much a matching of organization to contingencies but rather a high degree of internal consistency in the approach to management and organization they had adopted.

Two of the airlines, which for reason of confidentiality I shall call A and B, were superior performers on most criteria to the other two airlines, C and D. The European airline E was a moderately good performer. Table 8.1 illustrates the contrast with reference to a calculation of profitability and growth.

Table 8.1 Performance of five airlines

Airline	Net profit as % of equity and long-term debt			Change in net profit levels $ million
	1972	1973	1974	1972–1974
A	5.62	12.40	11.50	+62
B	0.12	3.03	5.81	+81
C	2.68	1.89	−3.45	−81
D	1.26	0.82	−0.98	−18
E	2.11	4.94	3.79	+9

What distinguished airlines A and B from C and D was not that they adopted similar organization structures but that the structures utilized were internally highly consistent. This characteristic is particularly interesting because the four airlines shared many contingencies. They operated in similar environments and were direct competitors on some routes. They employed similar technologies and had comparable fleet compositions. They were faced with almost identical operating decisions. All were large airlines, with employment ranging from approximately 22,000 to 50,000 personnel. The main contextual difference lay between airline A and the others, in that its route structure was geographically somewhat more compact.

Airline A was not divisionalized and had no profit or cost centres. Its planning and managerial time horizons were relatively short. It allowed very little autonomy to its main line management units. It employed centralized but very frequently activated decision-making processes, concentrating these onto a top executive group which met daily. This permitted a rapid response to variance from plans. Overall, this approach enabled the airline to have an economic and flexible managerial structure. It is, none the less, a remarkable structure to find in a large corporation. It was probably made viable by the airline's policy of concentration on the domestic airline business, geographical contiguity, a very long service management who had built up considerable trust and understanding of one another and, finally, a consciously fostered 'open-door' policy to facilitate communications. Conflict was low in this airline and was on the whole settled on an informal interpersonal basis.

The other high performing airline B was a complete contrast, except for the fact that it also operated through a highly consistent structure. This airline had divisionalized by region and by major resource area. It had attached full profit responsibility to its cost centres. It delegated authority on expenditure, staffing and other decisions to its divisions. It employed a highly formalized approach to financial and resource management using sophisticated controls. It planned ahead to a relatively long time horizon, using a powerful corporate planning group to provide co-ordination and review. Conflict resolution was largely by means of direct and open confrontation of issues and was part of the formal decision process. In short, this company was consistent in employing all the main elements of a structure which most authorities would say is appropriate to a large organization having a geographic spread of operations and a range of resource areas.

The two poorly performing airlines C and D each had a structural framework for decentralized operations, but neither was using this to the full. In particular, both the airlines placed severe restrictions upon delegated decision-making while at the same time retaining the costly paraphernalia of formalization and the staff functions to support it. Airline D, for example, had some elements of regional divisionalization including cost centres, a corporate planning function and a long time horizon, but other elements were missing. It had no profit centres and there was limited delegation whereby, for instance, approval for capital projects was not considered to be authorization for expenditure and several further decision hurdles had to be cleared. Information gathered from branches involved the use of elaborate and highly formalized procedures and was very time-consuming especially as conflicts tended to be resolved not at middle management level but were referred up the hierarchy instead. This airline had a large managerial and staff overhead for the scale of its business (see Table 8.2), yet it remained relatively centralized. By operating an inconsistent structure in this manner it was not deriving the full benefits of any structural model. Staff in both airlines C and D were aware of the problem and advanced reasons for retaining centralization. In airline C it was ascribed to poor quality divisional level management and in airline D to public accountability, but one cannot be certain that either was an overriding consideration.

Contrasts between the airlines begin to provide some clues as to why organizational design consistency had an effect on performance. Consistency is likely to make for a lower level of conflict and personal frustration. In airline D, where it was possible to explore issues in greater depth, it was clear that many managers were frustrated and demotivated because there was an inconsistency between those aspects of the system spelling out a decision-making role for them and the hurdles which were placed in the way of activating that role. In the opposite case, an organization in which there is decentralization without a framework of procedures for maintaining control and integration is likely to incur penalties of communication break-

Table 8.2 Managers and staff-support personnel as a percentage of total employees*

Airline	%
A	15.1
B	18.5
C	18.9
D	23.6
E	9.1

*Staff-support personnel include finance, computer and system services, personnel, corporate planning.

down and strains towards sub-unit rather than whole-unit goal optimization.

If the structural inconsistency is of the kind found in airline D, then it may generate two other costs. Managerial overhead will become inflated because additional roles, even whole departments, have been created in order to service a comprehensive set of decision-making procedures. At the same time, however, the overload on top management is not reduced through effective delegation, and is actually increased to the extent that an inflated managerial component has the result of widening spans of control. In airline D the chief executive's span of control was eight subordinates, while in the other three airlines it was five or six. In situations like this one in effect finds a 'mock bureaucracy', which fails to gain acceptance or to operate meaningfully, but which none the less absorbs time and resources.

The European airline E operated at a similar level of business to airline D, but was financially more successful. It generated approximately the same revenue as D, but with some 6,000 fewer personnel. Its organizational structure reflected some of the economy of airline A, but it had even lower managerial and staff overheads, employing a very flat structure. Its managerial philosophy was consistent with such a structure. Delegation was emphasized, and status based solely on formal job titles and hierarchical position was to a large degree avoided. There was an informal approach to interpersonal relations, with co-ordination and consultation emphasized rather than command. The significant point in the present context is that this philosophy was compatible with the form of organizational structure employed, and no serious inconsistencies were apparent. The fact that the organization of this profitable airline was also distinctive but consistent suggests that different approaches to organization are viable within a single industry, and that possibly the most critical criterion for their viability is a reasonable degree of internal consistency.

The proposition that several different models of organization can be viable within a single industry or sector like airline transportation so long as these are internally consistent is at variance with both the universals and contingency approaches. The universals school accepts the need for consistency but only within the assumption that there are general best practices. The recommendations of the contingency approach can encourage organizational inconsistencies, as we have seen. However, if some kind of satisfactory weighting can be worked out within management's strategic assessment as to the relative significance of different contingencies, then the contingency approach would point to the virtue of achieving consistency between organization, strategic and environmental variables. This 'gestalt', as Danny Miller (1981) has called it, still implies a single optimum solution for a given environment and is therefore at variance with the consistency argument as I have formulated it.

When one looks at cases of the highly successful companies that continue to pursue their own distinctive but consistent policies on organization, it is striking how well embedded these policies often are in the history and culture of the firm. The Marks and Spencer retail store in Britain provides a good example, pursuing 'the gospel according to Saint Michael' as one newspaper put it, part of which is to avoid taking on the rigidity and remoteness of bureaucracy as the company continues to grow. Tradition provides a base for consistency and may well supply much of its psychological force in encouraging commitment, a sense of purpose and a general motivation to perform well. The strength of people's identity with particular organizations is a factor which both universalistic and contingency approaches tend to overlook because their focus is upon general relationships rather than specific cases. That identity adds both consistency and uniqueness to each organization.

Implications for organizational change

The three perspectives on the relationship between organization and performance have different implications for policy on organizational change. Taken together, however, they suggest a number of considerations which practitioners should find useful when arriving at judgements on the subject.

The universals approach implies that successful organizations should be regarded as examplars of good managerial practice, including good organizational design. This does not, of course, make any allowance for the different market, social or other contexts in which organizations are located, let alone for any features that are unique to an individual organization such as its culture. With this in mind, it would seem more realistic to draw from the universals perspective the recommendation to be aware of how successful firms are organized but then to assess whether their practices suggest any improvements that are relevant to the particular needs and situation of one's own organization. If they do, change may be called for.

The recommendations for organizational design that are found in recent universalistic writings derive to a large extent from studies of larger firms which have managed to maintain high growth and vitality. Their practices represent a possible antidote to the problems which can beset the larger organization as it ages. These are the problems of poor communication and narrow departmental vision; blurred responsibility; creeping inertia; and the growth of a costly, unproductive, time-consuming staff overhead. Writers like Peters and Waterman warn against the very real possibilities of decay in vitality and singleness of purpose, which can occur in organizations as they take on a middle-age spread, a decay of which Parkinson was well aware when formulating his famous 'Law'. If decay has set in with deleterious consequences for the organization's capacity to innovate and adapt in a changing world, then the practices identified in 'excellent' American companies or pursued in dynamic Japanese firms may provide a useful pointer towards the kinds of change that would restore vitality. Again this is a recommendation to look to other organizations which have a superior edge in performance in order to identify potential lessons for the way to organize. Nevertheless, this is no short cut to the subsequent process of judging whether these or any other possibilities represent the type of organizational change that will suit a specific case.

The contingency approach is highly aware of the specific case, though in terms of how it fits into a number of more general categories (environment, diversity and so on). Contingency analysis has two major implications for policy on organizational change. The first is that organization must develop in line with strategic variables, so that forward organizational planning should accompany strategic planning. Strategies are intended to change contingencies such as markets served, diversity, scale, technology and sources of recruitment. According to the contingency view this will require corresponding changes in organization. In addition, a whole array of long-term forecasts are available that aim to provide advance warning of changes in strategic variables. These forecasts are not only relevant for task contingencies such as the changing structure of competition in product markets; they also point to developments in labour markets, skill availabilities and technology, which are political contingencies relevant to future policies on workplace, job design and reward systems.

The so-called 'strategy, structure and performance' approach within business policy has attempted to systematize the implications for organizational change of developments in strategy. The basis is that structure must fit strategy in order for high performance to be attained. Writings in this vein have generally concentrated on just two strategic characteristics, growth and diversification, and they have devoted much more attention to the grouping of activities than other aspects of organization. Chapter 4 discussed the ways in which patterns of grouping activities have tended to change along with the strategic development of huge corporations (see page 95). Authorities such as Alfred D. Chandler (1962) and Bruce Scott (1970) attempted to pull the strands of this approach together through advancing the concept that organizational structure develops through a number of distinct stages according to growth and diversification. The implication is that organizations in which structures are not developed to suit these new strategic contingencies will suffer in performance. Figure 8.2 is a simplified representation of the strategy, structure and performance argument showing the changes to organization structure that are 'required' as product lines multiply and markets diversify.

The second issue raised by the contingency approach concerns the frequency of organizational change. Most organizations operate within continually changing conditions, which has led some to draw from contingency analysis the recommendation to fine-tune organization on a continuing basis. This favours an adaptive approach to organizational change as opposed to occasional root-and-branch reorganizations. There is considerable controversy around the question of whether to carry out frequent changes on an adaptive or incremental basis or whether to favour major changes conducted at intervals measured in terms of at least several years. Sir Michael Edwardes, for example, used the phrase 'rolling reorganization' by way of a critical comment on the frequent changes in the British Leyland motor company's management structure which he regarded as disruptive.

Several points can be made in favour of adaptive change. It ensures that the suitability of organizational structures and systems for current and anticipated conditions is kept under constant review. It encourages an awareness among members of a collective body that organization is a significant issue. If these members become used to having regular reviews of

Figure 8.2 Four stages of development in organization structure

	Stage 1	Stage 2	Stage 3	Stage 4
Number of product lines or services	single	single	multiple product lines or multiple geographical markets	multiple product lines and geographical markets
Differentiation of production and market transactions	no significant differentiation in production or transactions	differentiated stages of production but integrated transactions	differentiated product lines or market transactions	non-integrated product and market transactions
Organization structure	little or no formal structure; 'one-man show'	specialization based on function or process	specialization based on product or on geographical area (divisions)	grid or matrix structure based on product and geographical area

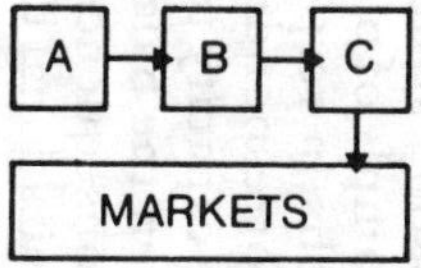

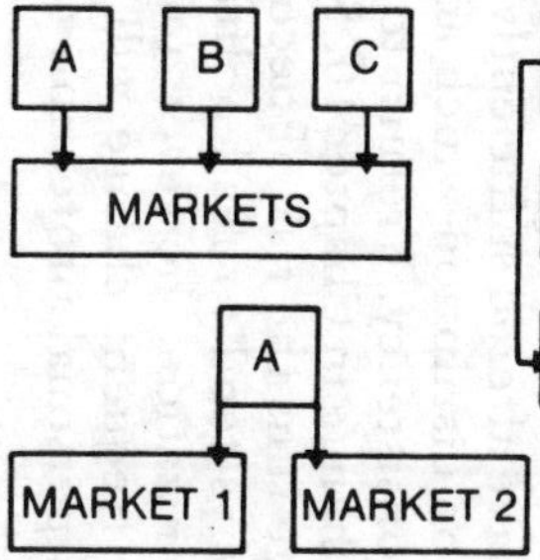

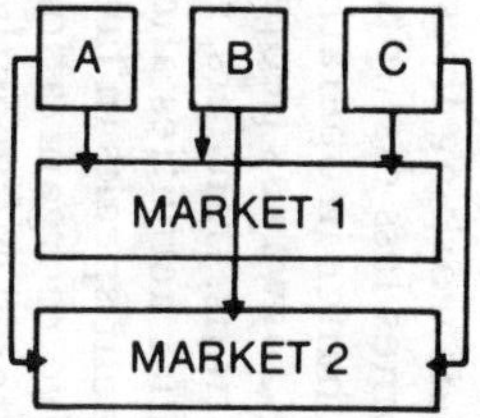

organization followed by changes, they are likely to come to accept these as normal features of their working lives with the result that the implementation of change becomes less disruptive and problematic. A further argument is that adaptive change in operating procedures and working practices is bound to take place anyway as people attempt to cope with new circumstances, and as promotions, transfers, recruitment and re-training alter who is undertaking particular activities and how.

The contrary argument speaks in favour of confining change to carefully planned comprehensive reorganizations which are undertaken only when circumstances have altered sufficiently to warrant them. This point of view refers both to the disruption which accompanies change and also to considerations of consistency. I return to the disruption and general costs of organizational change in Chapter 10. Suffice it here to make the point that continual change runs the risk of becoming continual disruption. The fact that people always tend to read political and status significance into any change of organization, however minor and incremental, adds to the possibility that frequent change will generate a higher level of activity associated with personal protection or opportunism than with the work at hand.

The consistency perspective points to a danger in making piecemeal changes to a whole organization structure in response to changes in particular contingencies. An example of piecemeal change would be the further specialization of units or jobs in response to a diversification of product range without making any corresponding adjustment to maintain necessary levels of integration and the capacity to resolve conflict. If adaptive change means piecemeal change then the balance of the organization can become impaired with deleterious consequences for performance. The argument is that the elements in an organizational design should be mutually reinforcing, and this point has emerged in the preceding chapters. Control strategies, for instance, represent mutually reinforcing configurations of points along dimensions such as centralization, formalization, direct supervision and reward system. If the organization were to be changed along only one of these dimensions, the degree of mutual reinforcement would be threatened. Therefore, organizational change has to be planned with a view to the set of structures and systems as a whole so that it takes the form of a shift between one consistent configuration and another. This speaks for planned periodic change rather than more continuous adaptation.

Danny Miller (1982) has provided a formal analysis for the choice between adaptive incremental changes to organization structure as opposed to having stable intervals punctuated by periods of comprehensive change. He recognizes the force of both contingency and consistency arguments and expresses these in terms of a trade-off between two costs: (1) the cost of organization structure being inappropriate to the contingencies imposed by environment and strategy; and (2) the cost of destroying complementarities among structural elements. Miller concludes that when long-run estimates of (1) are less than those of (2), the structure should not be changed. Performance will benefit if, instead, there is a delay until the appropriateness of an organization's structure for its context declines to a level where it becomes warranted to plan a wholesale change-over to a new and consistent structural configuration. Miller suggests that whether it is functional to undertake adaptive ('evolutionary') or wholesale ('revolutionary') change will depend on how predictable the environment is, and on whether changes in the environment are of the kind that require substantial alterations to organization structure ('exclusive environments') or whether they can accommodate several structures including minor modifications of present ones ('inclusive environments'). In predictable inclusive environments, for example, any environmental change is clear at an early stage and is expected to endure, while the difficulties in modifying structure are small; so that organizational change should be undertaken without delay. By contrast, in unpredictable environments there is reason to delay undertaking organizational change until the nature of the changed context becomes clear. How major a reorganization is then called for depends on how 'exclusive' of structural variation the new environmental conditions are.

One aspect of consistency as a requirement in organizational design concerns its compatibility with the values and practices embedded in the history of the company or institution. This directs attention to the extent to which organizational change is taking place in a context that breaks with the past. The greater the discontinuity, the more readily can a new organization be designed *de novo* without its own internal consistency being jeopardized by the continuing influence of previous practice. This is undoubtedly one reason why take-overs are often necessary for a wholesale change to be accomplished, involving as they often do a clean sweep of senior management and a major shock to the established expectations of other employees.

The same general point also accounts for the attractiveness of greenfield sites for reforming managements. This is not just a question of being able to design new physical facilities. The fully greenfield site also permits management to establish a framework of working practices and administration before hiring new personnel, and moreover to select those categories of new recruits that are most compatible with the desired approach. In Chapter 2, I noted the significance of carefully controlled new recruitment for the success of new work structures in greenfield sites. Some greenfield sites are staffed with employees transferred from established facilities, and in such cases one would expect a corresponding import of their established working practices and attitudes, which may generate resistance to any new model of organization with attempts to change it back to traditional practices. A third case is where a greenfield site is used as an opportunity to establish a new, consistent approach to organization, which is then promoted as a desirable point of reference for reform in older established units. Lessons from an exemplar of this kind located within the boundaries of an organization can be disseminated by the rotation of staff into the greenfield site so as to experience the new approach first-hand and who are then transferred back to other units convinced of the desirability of change. One problem with the reference to other organizations as exemplars, as in the universals writing I have noted, is that this overlooks the need for a mechanism to transfer and disseminate the good example within one's own organization.

Summary

When organizational change is undertaken, this is generally justified in terms of seeking improvements in performance. The ways in which the design of organization contributes to performance are clearly relevant to the type and extent of change recommended.

Difficulties surround the definition of 'good' organizational performance. Different parties to an organization may not attach the same value to alternative objectives. Particular groups, including management, may value a certain structure of organization even though it gives rise to inefficiencies. In practice, therefore, organization serves political as well as technical ends. These are reflected in criteria for organizational design and change.

Several different perspectives on the relationship between organization and performance inform the question of organizational change. These perspectives point respectively to (i) generally recommended best organizational policies, (ii) organizational designs which suit specific contingent characteristics relevant to the organization's tasks, (iii) designs which are appropriate to, and acceptable in, the political situation of the organization, and (iv) designs which are consistent internally and with the style and culture of the organization. In our present state of knowledge the relative merit of each perspective is not clearly established. Each one, however, has practical implications for the consideration of organizational change.

Suggested further reading

The papers edited by Paul S. Goodman, Johannes M. Pennings and associates in *New Perspectives on Organizational Effectiveness* (Jossey-Bass 1977) consider the major theoretical and methodological problems surrounding the assessment of organizational performance. Different perspectives are also compared in Kim S. Cameron and David A. Whetten (editors), *Organizational Effectiveness* (Academic Press 1983).

Thomas J. Peters and Robert H. Waterman Jr., *In Search of Excellence* (Harper and Row 1982) claim to have identified management and organizational practices which characterize high performing American corporations (and are supposedly commonplace in major Japanese corporations). Reforming American industry through learning from Japan is also an underlying theme in William J. Abernathy, Kim B. Clark and Alan M. Kantrow, *Industrial Renaissance: Producing a Competitive Future for America* (Basic Books 1983). While these two books have their eye mainly on larger corporations, an older study by Jonathan Boswell analysed *The Rise and Decline of Small Firms in Britain* (Allen and Unwin 1972) and identified a number of managerial features that were general correlates of success.

There are now quite a few studies within the task contingency school, which accord with the view that the form of organization conducive to high performance will depend on the context within which operations take place. Studies which have found that the match of organizational design to performance varies with the type of environment include the following: Tom

Burns and G. M. Stalker, *The Management of Innovation* (Tavistock 1961); Paul R. Lawrence and Jay W. Lorsch, *Organization and Environment* (Harvard Business School 1967); Robert B. Duncan, 'Multiple Decision-Making Structures in Adapting to Environmental Uncertainty: The Impact on Organizational Effectiveness', *Human Relations*, vol. 26, 1973; Pradip N. Khandwalla, 'Viable and Effective Organizational Design of Firms', *Academy of Management Journal*, September 1973; Anant Negandhi and Bernard C. Reimann, 'Task Environment, Decentralization and Organizational Effectiveness', *Human Relations*, vol. 26, 1973. Peter H. Grinyer, Masoud Yasai-Ardekani and Shawki Al-Bazzaz, 'Strategy, Structure, the Environment, and Financial Performance in 48 United Kingdom Companies', *Academy of Management Journal*, June 1980 is a major study taking strategic as well as environmental variables in account, but which found little relationship between the match of organization to contingencies, and performance. This finding contrasts with two earlier studies which found that a match between strategy and structure among business corporations was associated with superior performance: John M. Stopford and Louis T. Wells, Jr., *Managing the Multinational Enterprise* (Longman 1972); and Richard P. Rumelt, *Strategy, Structure and Economic Performance* (Harvard Business School 1974). Lex Donaldson's re-analysis of Rumelt's data is contained in 'Explaining Structural Change in Organizations', unpublished paper, Australian Graduate School of Management, Kensington, N.S.W., May 1983. The aspect of strategy given particular attention in these studies was diversification.

Research into technology as a contingency for organizational design starts with Joan Woodward's classic *Industrial Organization: Theory and Practice* (Oxford University Press 1965). A useful review of studies is contained in Bernard Reimann and Giorgio Inzerilli, 'A Comparative Analysis of Empirical Research on Technology and Structure', *Journal of Management*, vol. 5, 1979. The author's own research included an examination of size as a contingency and is reported in John Child, 'Managerial and Organizational Factors Associated with Company Performance', *Journal of Management Studies*, October 1974 and February 1975. A less academic report is John Child 'What Determines Organization Performance? The Universals vs. the It-All-Depends', *Organizational Dynamics*, Summer 1974. Jay W. Lorsch and John J. Morse, *Organizations and their Members* (Harper and Row 1974) develop the view that members are a contingency for organizational design on the basis of research showing that where there was congruence between members' personality dimensions, the immediate working context and the type of wider environment, organizations were more successful.

The germ of a political contingency view is contained in the analysis presented by Tom Lupton in *On the Shop Floor* (Pergamon 1963) where differences in workplace behaviour and organization are partly accounted for in terms of external market characteristics. Andrew L. Friedman, *Industry and Labour* (Macmillan 1977) has considerably developed this approach in comparative and historical research which indicates how the mode of workplace control within firms varies according to product and labour market conditions. John Child and Monir Tayeb 'Theoretical Perspectives in Cross-National Organizational Research', *International Studies of Management and Organization*, Winter

1982–83 discuss the 'political economy' perspective in comparisons of organizations located in different countries.

Danny Miller's discussion of the choice between incremental and periodic comprehensive change is contained in 'Evolution and Revolution: A Quantum View of Structural Change in Organizations', *Journal of Management Studies*, April 1982. Alan Sheldon, 'Organizational Paradigms: A Theory of Organizational Change', *Organizational Dynamics*, Winter 1980, discusses the problem of how senior staff in organizations can learn to face up to the need for comprehensive change, with illustrations from American health care organizations.

Sources referred to in this chapter but not yet mentioned were: Alfred D. Chandler, Jr., *Strategy and Structure* (M.I.T. Press 1962); John Child, Michael Fores, Ian Glover and Peter Lawrence, 'A Price to Pay? Professionalism and Work Organization in Britain and West Germany', *Sociology*, February 1983; Guy Geeraerts 'The Effect of Ownership on Organization Structure in Small Firms', unpublished paper, University of Tilburg, 1983; R. T. Lenz, 'Environment, Strategy, Organization Structure and Performance: Patterns in One Industry', *Strategic Management Journal*, July–September 1980; Jay W. Lorsch and Stephen A. Allen III, *Managing Diversity and Interdependence* (Harvard Business School 1973); Danny Miller, 'Towards a New Contingency Approach: The Search for Organizational Gestalts', *Journal of Management Studies*, January 1981; Johannes M. Pennings, 'The Relevance of the Structural-Contingency Model for Organizational Effectiveness', *Administrative Science Quarterly*, September 1975; Bruce R. Scott, *Strategies of Corporate Development* (Harvard Business School 1971); Oliver E. Williamson, *Markets and Hierarchies* (Free Press 1975) and Gerald Zaltman, Robert Duncan and Jonny Holbek, *Innovations and Organizations* (Wiley 1973).

Chapter 9

New Technology and Organization

'In case you haven't noticed, we are in the midst of a revolution'. Richard P. Rumelt, 'The Electronic Reorganization of Industry', *paper given to Conference of the Strategic Management Society, London, October 1981, p.1.*

Richard Rumelt is expressing here a widely-held view that the 'new technology' of microelectronics has revolutionary implications for the nature of work and organization. The scale of the changes that are foreseen, and indeed are already under way, has led many commentators to draw a parallel with the first industrial revolution. Introducing *The Microelectronics Revolution* (1980), which is one of the most comprehensive collections of writings on the subject, Tom Forester cites the opinion of the former British government Chief Scientist that microelectronics is 'the most remarkable technology ever to confront mankind'. It would appear that, in this new form, technology has emerged as the major contingency which organizational designers have to take into account.

The 'new technology' of today employs miniaturized electronic circuitry to process information. It is an information technology that substitutes for or complements people's mental and clerical capabilities, in contrast to mechanical technology which normally substitutes for people's physical capabilities. 'Automation' combines information and mechanical technologies, thus providing the facility to programme machinery and (in the case of true automation) for the equipment to monitor and adjust on the basis of electronic feedback as in the case of servo-controlled robots and computer-controlled industrial processes. There is at present considerable imprecision in the use of the terms 'new technology' and 'information technology' (IT). Some argue that IT should only be applied to the activities that used to go under the heading of 'data processing' plus integrated filing and communications (e.g. International Data Corporation 1983). However, the British Government's understanding of IT, when designating 1982 as Information Technology Year, covered any application with a computing or electronic content, including production automation. It is certainly more logical to extend the meaning of IT to cover all applications in which some electronic processing of information is involved.

The application of technology to the processing of information is itself not a new phenomenon. It could be argued that it goes back at least as far as semaphore signalling, and certainly the telephone and calculating machines have been with us for many years now. The first electronic digital computer appeared in the United States in the mid-1940s and there were approximately 1,000 computers in use in that country by the mid-1950s. By that time and into the 1960s, computers and automation were already being heralded as the foundations of a second industrial revolution and there was considerable debate about the impact they would have on levels of employment and on the nature of work and organization. Few clear-cut conclusions emerged from this debate, which in any case tended to assume that the use of computers and automation would spread faster than actually happened. Many of the issues now being raised in connection with the application of microelectronics are the same as those in the earlier debate, concerning as they do possible consequences for unemployment, the skill content of jobs, control over the conduct of work, centralization/decentralization, and management structure. The core technology of the so-called microelectronics revolution, integrated circuits etched onto silicon microchips, itself lies in direct line of descent from the early valve-based computers and their transistorized successors. What therefore is new about 'new technology'?

It is not so much the principle of applying electronics to information processing that is new as the radically changed nature of the hardware now available which has increased the range of practical applications enormously. In particular, microelectronic technology is distinguished by its (1) cheapness, (2) reliability, (3) compactness, (4) speed of operation, (5) accuracy, and (6) low energy consumption. The falling real cost and growing versatility of microelectronics have opened up a wide range of new applications in the design of products, in the processes of their manufacturing, in the provision of services, and in office work. Examples of these applications are listed in Table 9.1.

In many applications, specialized items of equipment incorporating microelectronics are used in conjunction with a larger computer as a central information processing unit. For example, in electronic point-of-sale (EPOS) systems electronic cash registers can access information on prices from a central retail company computer and feed back to it information on sales of specific items through a given checkout point. While the design of powerful central processing computers is itself benefiting from microelectronics, the most significant development lies in the very rapid diversification and expansion of specialized and 'peripheral' microelectronic equipment which brings electronic information processing into so many new uses. All the current projections are for this growth to continue. For instance, the market for intelligent data terminals (which contain some local processing and storage capacity of their own) has been forecast to grow during the 1980s by around sevenfold both in the United States and Western Europe. The market for new office equipment is growing at a rate of 34 per cent a year in the USA. The increase in the world market for computer-aided design and computer-aided manufacturing equipment (CAD/CAM) has been forecast to be 230 per cent over the years 1982 to 1986 despite the recession in manufacturing industry. The market for industrial robots in Western Europe is expected to grow at a compound annual rate of 51 per cent between 1981 and 1986. The United Kingdom, however, has exhibited

Table 9.1 Examples of the applications of microelectronics

PRODUCTS

1 *Completely new products:* pocket calculators, electronic games.
2 *Radically improved products:* digital watches, electronic typewriters, computer-numerical-controlled (CNC) machine tools.
3 *Improvements to existing products:* washing machines (programmers), motor vehicles (controls and performance monitors), television sets (remote control, circuitry, teletext facilities).

MANUFACTURING

4 *Computer-controlled manufacture:* CNC machines, robots, flexible manufacturing systems, process plant monitoring and control.
5 *Computer-aided design (CAD):* aerospace, architecture and building, engineering.
6 *Computerized stock control and warehousing:* motor vehicle parts for manufacture and sale of spares. Also examples in service sector: retail store stocks, hospital pharmacies.

PROVISION OF SERVICES

7 *Financial:* automatic cash dispensers/tellers; customer records via visual display units (VDUs), electronic funds transfer.
8 *Medical:* computer diagnosis, automated laboratory testing, intensive care monitoring.
9 *Retailing and distribution:* automated warehousing, stock control, electronic point-of-sale (EPOS).
10 *Libraries:* computerized information systems, lending records based on use of bar-coding.
11 *Information services:* videotex (interactive and one-way systems, via modified TV sets and telephone lines).

OFFICE WORK

12 *Word processing and electronic filing.*
13 *Communications:* electronic mail and facsimile transmission, teleconferencing and networking.

---

a lower rate of new technology adoption, particularly in manufacturing (Bessant 1982).

This chapter examines ways in which the rapidly growing application of new technology is a vehicle for changes to jobs and organization. The term 'vehicle' is an appropriate one because the directions in which the application of new technology is being steered cannot simply be ascribed to a logic inherent in the technology itself. It is particularly important to take into account the economic context in which new technology is purchased, the purposes which management attaches to it, and the influence which other groups party to its design and implementation may exert. Consideration of these factors helps to identify both the significant strategic intentions that lie behind the adoption of new technology and the possibilities of choice in how jobs and organization are designed to accompany it. When automation and computers were first introduced, there was a great deal of misleading talk about the so-called 'effects' of technological advance, as though it established a necessary and set pattern for job and organizational design. There has been some discussion about today's new technology in similar terms. It is misleading because it obscures the essentially political aspect to the introduction of new technology with respect to the process itself and to the design solutions which emerge from the distribution of power within the organization concerned.

Management normally has the initiative in the introduction of new technology, particularly in conditions where the prevailing level of unemployment does not admit of much organized resistance to its intentions. In other words, the dominant influence over which new technology is selected and over how it is applied, will be management's. The strategic purposes which managers attach to new technology are therefore highly relevant, as are the general philosophies they hold. With this in mind, the section immediately following outlines the strategic purposes that can be discerned in the use of new technology. In this section and through the chapter as a whole, I shall concentrate on applications of new technology to the operations and management of organizations as opposed to new technology that is incorporated in the design of final products. Other sections in this chapter then consider the relevance of new technology for (1) employment and job design, (2) integration and control, and (3) the role and structure of management. While attention is given to the design choices which are apparent in these areas and the considerable variety of new technology applications is noted, a final section does suggest that certain trends are emerging in western societies. The degree of consistency in these trends is in large measure due to the kind of priorities which managements are required to pursue in capitalist economies, and this of course returns our attention to the strategic purposes of investment in new technology.

The strategic purposes of new technology

The strategic intentions that managers have in mind when introducing new technology will vary in emphasis according to the priorities and purposes of their organization and the problems and prospects it faces. Nevertheless, the following are usually prominent: (1) reduction in operating costs; (2) increased flexibility; (3) improvement in quality of the product or service; (4) increased control and integration. There is some interdependency among these strategic intentions, and they are all concerned with enhancing the organization's ability to absorb the risks posed by external competition or by other threats to the organization's standing and survival. A consideration of the ways in which application of new technology may assist the achievement of these strategic intentions will begin to account for how it affects jobs and organization.

Reduction in operating costs

Although the claim of a long-term decline in corporate profitability has occasioned some disagreement among economists and accountants, there can be little doubt that businessmen in many countries have perceived profit levels to be under pressure, particularly since the oil crisis of 1973. As public expenditures have been cut back in real terms under the combination of recession and monetarism, so the administrators and managers of public service organizations have also experienced growing pressures to reduce their operating costs.

New technology may offer several possibilities for cost reduction. The first, and the one that has been particular dramatized at a time of high unemployment, is through reductions in manpower. In some applications, microelectronics makes it possible to design machines which can completely take over the tasks previously carried out by people. An example is the automatic spot welding of body frames for Austin Metro cars using robots: each line is now manned with one operator per line instead of an estimated requirement of 80 operators per line with conventional technology. Other new technology permits the introduction of more efficient operating systems which economize significantly on staffing. For example, one study has predicted that office automation (involving word processing, electronic filing and electronic mail) will reduce secretarial and typing jobs by 17 per cent over the period 1980–90 (EOC 1980). Where the volume of work required is rising, new technology may permit throughput to increase without an increase in manning. This is the case, for instance, with clinical chemistry laboratory testing in hospitals where a modern configuration of an automated analyser linked to a computer greatly increases testing productivity and avoids the manual recording of results. New technology may also save on manpower costs through providing a combination of faster operations and the provision of detailed information on work loading, which in turn permits the more economical allocation of manpower as the situation demands. EPOS systems in supermarkets permit a speeding up in the rate of customer checkout and also provide detailed data on patterns of load to which staff deployment can be precisely adjusted during the week.

A second possibility which new technology offers for reductions in operating costs results from the rapid access it provides to precise information on items such as stock levels, patterns of stock usage and availabilities. For example, hospital and area pharmacies have reported considerable savings in drug costs, together with the ability to offer a more certain supply, consequent on the acquisition of minicomputers which store information on drug stocks and movements, and which are used to operate automatic reordering procedures. Another comparable example is found in information systems which now link together some automobile stockists and parts suppliers. In addition to inventory savings and the ability to provide a better service, these applications sometimes permit a modest reduction in staff costs because manual paper processing is eliminated.

A third source of cost reduction is closely allied with both the substitution of electronic systems for human action and the improvement of product or service quality. This lies in the reduction of wasted material and time made possible by the greater precision and lack of fatigue of programmed electronic devices. This advantage can be found with many computer controlled manufacturing operations, particularly those where the system can cope with variability in material or parts (if it cannot cope with such variability, the electronically controlled machine may produce work of inferior quality to that controlled by a skilled worker). Another example is computer medical diagnosis in certain areas of illness such as hypertension where the range of symptoms is limited and their relation to underlying causes reasonably well known. Here, new technology can among other things avoid mistakes due to physician fatigue, such as failing to ask for all the relevant information. For example, one hospital consultant stated to the author that doctors forget to measure the patient's blood pressure in 10 per cent of hypertension diagnoses. Such mistakes can be costly not only in medical terms but in terms of wasted time and expenditure on inappropriate treatment.

Increased flexibility

Increased flexibility is a strategic requirement which has grown in emphasis and is often linked with cost reduction. From a manager's point of view, one of the most attractive features offered by new technology is the prospect of being able to run a range of production items through a single facility with the minimum of cost and upheaval when changing from one type to another. In the past, when an organization was producing a range of products it usually faced a choice between integrating their production into a single facility under the management of a unified production function or duplicating production facilities into separate specialized pieces of equipment, lines or even whole plants. The latter solution would tend to generate a comparable duplication, even divisionalization, within production management. As we saw in Chapter 4, this solution should enhance the organization's ability to adjust to the schedules of demand for each product but quite possibly at a heavy cost in additional capital investment and managerial overhead.

The computer programming of equipment permits its rapid adjustment to suit changes in production, given the generic limits within which it is designed to perform. The development of computer-aided design (CAD) adds to this a far greater speed of product modification and redesign, and research is proceeding apace to link the CAD/CAM (computer-aided manufacture) stages directly together. In this field the availability of relatively inexpensive microelectronics is permitting a synthesis between areas that were previously segregated because each was tied to costly large computers, namely computer graphical design, numerical-control machine tools, production schedules, and industrial robotics (see page 259 below). The new integration between these areas greatly reduces the cost of product change and significantly improves the economics of flexibility.

A somewhat comparable case to the manufacturing one can be seen with the development of the more advanced type of computerized teller in banking. This can readily receive commands from the customer for a whole range of transactions and services such as paying-in, withdrawal, crediting of other accounts, and issuing of a statement. The one piece of equipment offers a service which is more flexible than non-automated banking both with respect to time of day and also to the number of manual clerical operations that are required.

Rumelt (1981), in the paper cited at the beginning of this chapter, suggests that the use of CAD/CAM avoids the need to have large production units, for 'once computers begin to specify parts fabrication needs in a standardized language, and once automated facilities exist that can turn these specifications into a part, the need to have them within the same enterprise diminishes' (p.7). The manpower saving aspects of new technology also points towards smaller organizational units. Thus both the cost reduction and the flexibility intentions which management attaches to new technology may have further implications for organizational design via the contingency of unit size.

Improvement in quality of the product or service

The quality of products and their design tend to be more salient marketing requirements than price with many of the sophisticated manufactured goods of today. A premium is similarly placed on the quality of many services, not least those in the public sector which directly affect personal well-being. In the case of manufactured products, new technology can enhance quality both through its incorporation within their intrinsic design and through ensuring their manufacture and testing to more precise limits. In the case of services, new technology can significantly improve quality through the rapid provision of superior information. For example, electronic monitoring in hospital intensive care has contributed very importantly to the improved prospects of saving desperately ill people—it provides detailed monitoring and immediate notification of a change in condition. A further feature of new technology that can contribute to raising the quality of collective activities is its ability to bring disparate information together into one location where a team of people can work together. Previously they may have had to work in separate locations closer to the source of relevant information.

Increased control and integration

The example just cited concerned the contribution of new technology to increased integration. Control and integration are, of course, fundamental requirements for the successful functioning of an organization and were discussed in Chapters 5 and 6. Managements will therefore look to new technology to assist in meeting these requirements in ways that are more effective and less costly. In both cases it is the ability to transmit information directly across distances and the capacity to apply computational or synthesizing routines when called for which are the key advantages of new technology. Information can be passed directly from the scene of operations to management. It may even be possible to avoid reliance on the honesty or accuracy of an operator by securing data automatically, while the provision of analytical routines to assist management's interpretation is not likely to pose a major difficulty. The feedback loop in the control cycle is therefore significantly strengthened. Integration is enhanced by electronics through the ability (1) to bring together a range of information into one location, and (2) to link physically separated individuals in an interactive mode via teletex, communicating word processors, audio and audio-visual teleconferencing. The relevance for organizational design of these new technological contributions to control and integration is discussed in a later section.

Relevance to employment and job design

The changes in employment, job design and reward policies which have accompanied the introduction of new technology display considerable variation. This can only partly be attributed to differences in the design and application of the new equipment itself, since there are instances where variation in job design and work organization is found alongside the same new technology. The changes which have occurred must also be attributed to non-technological factors such as (1) whether management's philosophy has been to increase productivity through achieving greater throughput with employment levels maintained or through substantial reductions in employment, (2) management's view with respect to the use of employees' skills and their division of labour, and (3) the strength of resistance and counter-influence mustered by employees and their representatives. In view of the considerable differences between industries and sectors of work in the changes which have taken place, the general level of discussion offered here must necessarily be confined to identifying certain more common trends which can be discerned within the overall varied picture.

The relationship new technology may have to changes in the level of employment is of concern to organizational design in so far as it affects the size of units of employment and modifies the attitudes of people at work towards change. However, the issue itself is obscured by the extreme difficulty in distinguishing between reductions in employment attributable to lack of demand and those attributable to the introduction of labour-saving technology. At a national level there is the further complication that while in one organization new technology is purchased in order to save jobs, in another organization which produces it, employment may be thereby enhanced or at least maintained. The issue is so complex that in reality nobody is in a position to make a straightforward statement about the relationship between technological change and the level of employment. What is clear is that the overall trend among users of new technology is towards saving labour and that this is heightened by the stagnation in the world economy. While the threat to employment leads naturally to a defensive attitude among those at work, it also facilitates a managerial intention to introduce new technology on its own terms. These are likely to include changes to the structure of employment and jobs, which in other circumstances might well have been successfully resisted by employees' collective organizations.

One such change stems directly from the policy of economizing on the overhead costs per unit of output or service produced. Investment in new technology is frequently used as an opportunity to push for the introduction of continuous shift working on the grounds that the capital must be fully utilized. Considerable interest has been expressed in the possibilities for staff to work at home, linked by terminals and data lines to a central office— as was noted in Chapter 6, the major attraction here for the employer is again the saving in overheads. On the maintenance side, the possibility that some new technology offers of incorporating self-diagnostic fault-finding together with readily replaced modular components can make it feasible to allocate such routine maintenance to operative employees while contracting out occasional work of a major nature. Again, the overhead of a permanent specialized maintenance itself can be substantially reduced.

Policies such as these, associated with the use of new technology and intended to reduce overheads, have a considerable impact upon the structure of employment and the content of jobs. For example, staff working at home tend to become self-employed contractors and as such they, rather than their erstwhile full-time employer, bear the risk of providing a secure future income flow. The control they have over how the job is actually carried out and over their pattern of working time goes up substantially, however. Policies on maintenance of the kind described demolish the traditional demarcation between operative and maintenance work, and involve the addition of skills to the operative's job. This is a particularly interesting example in the light of the widespread fear that new technology takes over skills previously used by the worker. Loss of skills is clearly apparent in the extreme case where jobs are completely displaced by the introduction of new technology and where employment creation is confined to a few jobs concerned with the design, programming and maintenance of new equipment and systems. (Very often the jobs that are lost were filled by women and the few that are created are filled by men.) In less clear-cut cases, however, a loss of the ability to exercise certain skills may be accompanied by an opportunity to exercise new skills of a qualitatively different kind, such as maintenance skills or monitoring skills. If the displaced skills or competences had a direct bearing on levels of work achieved and were rewarded by output incentive schemes, it will probably be appropriate to acknowledge the exercise of new skills through a different payment system perhaps related to the performance of the organization or plant as a whole.

A policy choice exists between using the introduction of new technology as an opportunity to build upon the skill and experience of existing members of the organization and using new technology as a means of degrading such skills, replacing them with programmes and systems devised by a new body of 'experts'. This choice has been illustrated very clearly by the case studies which Barry Wilkinson (1983) reports. Many of the cases were of plants in which computer numerical-controlled (CNC) machinery had been installed. In the majority of instances management had established a new programming section to write and test programs for the operation of these machines, so degrading the role of the shopfloor worker to that of machine minder. The skills involved in setting up machine tools and in adjusting them to cope with variability in materials or working conditions were now to be transferred to program writers.

In the more exceptional cases, a different approach was adopted. This was to regard the enhanced capabilities of the CNC machine as a means for building upon the already existing skills and experience of the machinist, so that he or she would have the responsibility for programming, or at least for editing and adjusting programs. In actual fact, Wilkinson found that even where management made strenuous efforts to keep all aspects of machine programming away from the shopfloor, workers often reassumed control over the machines through undertaking instruction in programming in their own time and gaining access to control boxes with keys they had made themselves. He observed that the use of skills by those on the spot could avoid considerable wastage of time and material when the need for unforeseen adjustments arose.

The conclusion Wilkinson reached from his research is of considerable significance, and further expresses the thrust of the argument developed in this present book:

> There is *no* inherent logic in microelectronics which demands that tasks become ever more mundane; nor does the technology *demand* that skills be increased and work become more interesting and fulfilling. The way in which work is organized, and thus the quality of working life of the shopfloor worker, is a responsibility which managers cannot shirk by reference to the notion that everybody has simply to adapt to technology's demands
>
> (Wilkinson 1982: 40).

The approach that management adopts towards skills and job content when introducing new technology is part and parcel of its overall policy towards employment. In particular, it is connected with the decision as to how the organization's labour force is to be segmented. Labour market analysts have pointed out that there is an 'internal' labour market within the organization, the structure of which is determined by policies over recruitment, conditions of employment, promotion and careers (Loveridge 1983). The widespread introduction of job evaluation structures is an obvious way in which the hierarchical framework of internal labour markets is set down. An internal labour market is distinguished from the external labour market by, among other characteristics, a definition of skill, job content and grading in terms peculiar to the employing organization, and by a relatively high security and continuity of employment within that organization.

The internal labour market of an organization is itself likely to divide into what some have called 'primary' and 'secondary' segments, and it is this distinction that is particularly significant with respect to the application of new technology. The primary segment of an internal labour market would be manifested by a hard core of employees who enjoy stable employment in jobs that utilize specific skills, require long on-the-job training, have good prospects of promotion or upgrading, enjoy favourable working conditions, autonomy and responsibility, and are relatively well paid. The secondary segment would be identified by jobs which are less stable, lower in skill content and not so well rewarded intrinsically, but which nevertheless are not filled directly from outside the organization and are deemed to require some degree of special training and/or experience within the organization.

Considerable fear has been expressed that new technology will be applied with the intention of transforming the employment position, job content and rewards of people at work so that they are shifted from the primary to the secondary segments of internal labour markets and from the secondary internal segment to outside the internal market altogether. In other words, the technology would be used to substitute for the specialized skill content of jobs and for the need for their incumbents to have had substantial training. Within the internal labour market, such a process would block off opportunities for upward progression and upgrading and indeed would degrade skill. The usually large proportion of employees already in the secondary internal labour market segment would in these circumstances face the threat of being forced towards peripheral positions in the general labour market outside the organization, and of becoming dependent upon casual temporary employment offered and withdrawn according to the level of economic activity. In short, the question is whether or not new technology is to be used to force the majority of people at work into a de-skilled and readily replaced status, and possibly into a loss of employment altogether.

I have suggested that there appears to be some choice in the way employment is structured and jobs are designed around new technology. On the one hand, there may be an intention to use new technology to extend existing skills and responsibilities, and to move in the direction of granting most employees a primary internal labour market status. On the other hand, management's intention may be to confine this status to an elite comprising senior management and professional-cum-technical specialists, with the employment status and job content of the remaining workforce being degraded. This latter policy is one of using technology to replace rather than enhance human capital.

Examples of both approaches can be found, though the second would seem to be the more common. Wilkinson (1983) describes the case of a firm manufacturing lenses and spectacles in which job rotation was introduced as a means of preserving the intrinsic content and interest of jobs concerned with lens preparation where the introduction of new computer-controlled machinery had reduced the skill and judgemental component of individual tasks. This policy of job rotation was accompanied by careful personnel selection and considerable attention to training, which in turn provided possibilities for future promotion to supervisory jobs. The firm was clearly adapting its policies on employment and work organization to the introduction of new technology in a manner that used technology as a support to its workers, and that in fact enhanced their standing and opportunity within the internal labour market. Another instance of a broadly similar approach is provided by a food company which, having reduced its workforce considerably, is using the possibilities offered by microelectronics for integrating production and maintenance monitoring (plus features such as self-diagnosis of faults) to introduce an enhanced shopfloor role which combines operative and maintenance tasks and which offers upgrading once appropriate training has been successfully completed.

Policies such as these are not, of course, simply altruistic. They provide employers with a valuable increase in flexibility of deployment which is likely to permit more economical manning. By creating an economically sounder basis for long-term job tenure in times of poor employment prospects, such policies also foster commitment and enhance possibilities for normative control; in so doing they bear some resemblance to the employment policies practised in larger Japanese organizations. If this approach is adopted, the increase in flexibility sought would require a considerable simplification of many of the job evaluation and payment structures currently in force within organizations if these are not to stand in the way of flexible deployment and a ready adaptation to changes.

The alternative philosophy, which regards new technology as a means for downgrading and even replacing labour, is nevertheless more frequently encountered in practice. The ultimate aim, or ideal point of reference, for this approach is the organization without labour and with few managers or staff either, apart from a small group of top managers, specialist staff, marketing and public relations personnel. Considerable interest is being shown in the almost unmanned prototypes of factories run as 'Flexible Manufacturing Systems' in which transfer as well as actual machining, welding, and so on is automated. The attraction for employers is not confined to flexibility (ease and speed of re-programming between batches), important though that undoubtedly is. It also lies in the avoidance of labour costs, industrial relations problems, and the overheads involved in providing ancillary services for employees such as canteens, employment offices and car parks.

Where new technology has been applied in the service sector, elements of the same philosophy can be found. For example, in some department stores it has been management policy for some years to substitute part-time for full-time employees, as well as reducing total numbers through innovations such as central cash-and-wrap stations and subcontracting the sale of some specialities to concessionaires. The trend towards part-time employment was reinforced when new technology became available in the form of electronic point-of-sale (EPOS) systems fronted by cash registers incorporating devices to scan bar-coded individual sales items. These made readily available much more precise information on customer flows, sales profiles and stock levels. In turn, this meant that sales staff could be deployed more economically and their hours adjusted to suit the pattern of load, and this can be achieved more readily if the staff work on a part-time or temporary basis. It also meant that routine programming could be applied to some store buying decisions with a saving in staff time, while the substitution of electronic for manual information processing permitted reductions in office staffing. The only expansion in the scope and numbers of jobs with these retailing developments has come in systems, computing and senior levels of financial management. A somewhat comparable service sector example is provided by banking. Here the technical feasibility for equipping 'satellite' branch banks, which are automated and un-staffed, reinforces an existing trend towards a dual employment situation in which special services, mortgages and management of securities are provided by teams of experts in centralized district offices while the traditional branch bank manager and counter staff are first relegated respectively to routine supervision and mundane cash-transaction work, and then begin to be superseded altogether.

From an organizational design perspective, the question arises: 'why choose one employment philosophy in connection with new technology rather than the other?' There is, of course, a major social and political issue here concerning the extent to which as a society we should seek to disengage human activity performed in return for an economic livelihood from the particular mode we have come to take for granted, namely employment within organizations. How that issue is resolved is going to have major implications for the employment policy of any particular organization since it will be transmitted through legislation, fiscal and other governmental measures. For the time being, the following contingencies are among those likely to be regarded as relevant to the choice of employment policy in connection with new technology: (1) the amount of non-programmable skill and judgement which is utilized in the performance of tasks; (2) the degree to which the work being done necessarily contains a personal service element; (3) the extent to which the pattern of work required to be done is unpredictable; and (4) the risks involved should electronic systems break down—for example, the risk to life or the risk of theft.

The more that such factors are present, the more rational would be a choice to use new technology to augment rather than to replace the skills and experience which employees can offer. This is because these skills offer a valuable basis for flexible adjustment to unplanned and new conditions which arise with non-routine work. Moreover, by combining technological aids with human skills the opportunity is created for a continuing learning process, which the application of programmed electronics alone does not offer. However, it is not just a question of a rational response to task contingencies. For political reasons too, this philosophy of employment is more likely to be pursued in the type of circumstances mentioned. For where there is uncertainty and indeterminacy regarding the work to be done and how best to do it, the services of employees with relevant skills and experience have to be relied upon. Even if technology is developed which can substitute for some of these qualities, such employees may remain in a strong position to control its introduction and to block any attempt to dislodge them from their existing control over the work process, unless their work can now be performed by less qualified workers or contracted out.

Relevance to integration and control

Information technology is a technology for communication and calculation. As such, it would be difficult to overstate its relevance for the processes of integration and control within organizations. It can facilitate integration by making information readily accessible to different members and sections via joint terminal access to common files; indeed, the practical problem which then arises for managements concerned about 'confidentiality' is how to bar access to information through security codes! Information systems permit instantaneous personal communication between groups of organizational members; this may be audio only or incorporate visual facilities as well (teleconferencing). The same applies to written communication through various types of electronic mail system. Thirdly, modern information technology permits a physical as well as analytical unification of control information. For example, information on the status of a production plant's workflow and stocks can be displayed in the same location as information on the condition of its equipment from a maintenance perspective. If required, data on temperature, humidity and so forth in the production environment can also be added. While the possibilities this creates for organizational design are explored in the following section, one can see that an integration of information such as just described takes away much of the rationale for inherited patterns of job specialization between, say, industrial engineers, maintenance and production workers, and their respective supervisors.

Information technology extends the possibilities for management control in three main respects. First, it provides faster and more precise knowledge of operating conditions and results. Second, it reduces the scope for indeterminacy in the behaviour of employees. Third, it unifies previously segmented control systems and thereby increases the potential for a comprehensive and balanced assessment of performance. Although mention has already been made of the first two aspects, they may usefully be clarified through further discussion.

Faster and more precise knowledge of operating conditions and results stems from the feedback offered via information technology. I have discussed the case of how EPOS systems offer greatly improved feedback to store managers, buyers and accountants in retailing. In engineering, feedback from numerical control machines that are directly linked to a computer can greatly assist the complex process of parts processing. Hospital laboratory automation combined with the computerization of patient and test data provides faster feedback to doctors in hospital wards (if the wards are linked via VDU terminals to the computer), as well as facilitating precise calculations of trends in results and signalling abnormal results. Examples have also been given from food manufacturing and hospital pharmacies.

Fast and precise information provides a basis for flexible response as conditions change and 'emergencies' arise. It makes it feasible to achieve a closer match between the deployment of staff and the demands of any one section of the organization at a particular time. Clearly, flexible deployment may have to be negotiated and recomposed, and the range of appropriate skills and/or experience must be available. Modern technology not only boosts the speed and precision of feedback, it can also deliver it anywhere in the organization, including directly into a senior manager's office. It therefore becomes possible to achieve improvements in control over matters such as progress of work, inventory levels and scrap rates without having to rely on middle and junior managers as intermediaries. In some situations reliance will still have to be placed upon human co-operation, accuracy and honesty for the entering of data into the information system. However, it is now possible in large measure to avoid the necessity for having information interpreted and passed through the management hierarchy, which Chapter 3 indicated could give rise to considerable distortion.

In the previous section on employment it was suggested that the encroachment of new technology on skills is less likely in situations where there is uncertainty and indeterminacy about the work to be done and how to do it. Having said that, it is possible to find examples where the technology is being used to enhance management control by reducing areas of indeterminacy. There is a growing number of electronic applications which, with appropriate software, can capture the special knowledge held by experts and subsequently exercise this repeatedly as a routine. Once this stage is reached, the mystique of special expertise is dissipated as a basis for resisting the imposition of managerial standards for cost, efficiency and output. I have instanced how EPOS systems can generate routine reordering procedures which avoid reliance on a buyer's personal judgement. In computer-aided design (CAD), the skills of the draughtsman are superseded, and to some degree the mystique of design itself is reduced with respect, for example, to the computation of centres of gravity and stresses. In some areas of medicine, the accuracy of computer diagnosis matches that of trained physicians and does not suffer from any human inconsistencies. In cases such as these, where expertise and skill can be captured in the form of software, the potential exists for management to establish behaviour control in the sense that the way tasks are done now becomes a matter of routine. When allied to the output control which can be provided by information technology through its potential for feedback of results, these developments hold out the prospect for a considerable enhancement of managerial control. However, the employees concerned will almost certainly resist this extension of control, while limits are also imposed by the need to retain the element of human creativity.

New technology is also facilitating the unification of hitherto fragmented control systems. In manufacturing, the dream (now being translated into reality with Flexible Manufacturing Systems) is of a unified control system complementary to integrated computer-aided design, manufacture and production systems. Such a system would combine controls in regard to physical movements, condition of plant, stocks, wastage, energy consumption, unit costs and deployment of personnel. Integrated control of this kind can optimize the overall balance of production activities and maximize flexibility of adjustment.

In hospitals which have installed patient information systems, it is possible to integrate information relevant to a particular patient within his or her file: length of stay, treatment given, drugs prescribed, laboratory tests performed and costs incurred, for instance. This information is relevant to the medical and financial control of treatment for a particular patient. It is also possible to use the same systems to control the treatment practices of a particular doctor by integrating information on the length of stay of his or her patients, treatment success rate, laboratory tests requested, drugs prescribed, and other services used. In retailing, the combination of EPOS units and computers permits the unification of control systems, which within the individual store encompass sales transactions, shelf-stocking, display and cash control, and staff deployment, and at the more general management level encompass sales analysis, merchandise control, accounts control, credit sanctioning and labour productivity. Within the field of physical distribution, new technology offers the possibility of more effective overall control through the integration of systems for customer order handling, warehouse stocks, finished goods control, distribution centre operations and transport. Each of these operations will normally be accompanied by systems for accounting and labour costing. Where the information required

to integrate these systems is scattered throughout several different departments, it can really only be brought together into a unified control system by
using a computer.

The unification of control through modern information technology
encourages a corresponding integration and simplification in organization
structures. As the interdependencies between financial activities are made
more visible through integrated control systems and shared data services, so
the logic of team-working and networks emerges as the 'natural' basis of
organization rather than patterns of work and communication defined predominantly by departmental boundaries. Structural barriers of a vertical
kind are also likely to weaken. The integration of control information, its
ready access to top management, and the availability of powerful analytical
models renders redundant the roles of consolidating, interpreting and passing
on information which formed a significant part of many middle managers'
and some staff specialists' jobs. This development therefore works towards a
reduction in the middle ranks of management, a contraction in hierarchical
levels and a slimming of staff and other support roles below the strategic
level.

Relevance to the role and structure of management

Back in the 1950s when computers first began to be introduced as aids to
managerial (as opposed to scientific) information processing, some commentators predicted that the results would be (1) a reversal of the trend
towards delegated decision-making, and (2) a substantial slimming down of
middle management and associated clerical staffs. This forecast did not
prove to be a reliable guide, partly because the application of mainframe
computers to management control and information systems was generally
much slower in coming than had been expected. Instead, lower-level
routines such as payroll and accounts tended to figure prominently among
the early uses of computers.

With the potential of new information technology for making precise data
speedily available to any level of the organization, and for integrating information and offering analytical facilities such as trend analysis, the questions
of centralization and of the role for middle management become highly relevant. Indeed, they present some significant organizational design choices.

As Chapter 6 noted, the argument over centralized versus delegated
decision-making drew attention to a tension between efficiency and flexibility. The case for centralization rested partly on its efficiency: centralized
decision-making involves fewer people, less formalization, and less investment in control and integration systems. The case for delegation rested partly
on its flexibility: when decisions are left to people who are closer to the
action they can respond to changing circumstances without the delay that
ensues from having to make a case for action which is passed up the
hierarchy for authorization. The use of new technology to enhance information systems such as those monitoring production processes, retail sales
or distribution now offers an opportunity to resolve some of this tension between efficiency and flexibility in decision-making. As such it opens up the

option of re-centralizing decision-making discretion, particularly when the problem of swamping senior managers with information is also mitigated by the availability of programs to integrate data and simplify its presentation.

From the evidence that I have seen in Britain, this option of re-centralization is being taken up in a majority of organizations. It is consistent with the employment policy, discussed earlier, which aims at consolidating a small elite of senior managers and associated specialist and technical personnel within a primary sector of the internal labour market while placing other employees into a secondary segment and/or out into the external labour market. However, there is no overwhelming technical reason why information technology cannot be used to facilitate the opposite policy, namely more effective delegation. This can be done in two main respects. First, by plugging each local unit of an organization into a common file system so allowing it to be immediately aware of the situation of other units and of the wider consequences of decisions it might take. In fact, by feeding its proposed courses of action into a common information system and signalling any departure these would entail from rules or precedents, a local decision unit could inform the centre and other units and elicit a swift comment. The balanced view and awareness of the whole, which are advantages claimed for centralization, could thereby be taken into account within a delegated system. Second, the improved analytical facilities of new information technology, such as programs for sensitivity analysis and financial modelling, when combined with greatly improved data could be used to enhance the capacity of local units to make 'sound' judgements in their decision-making. Previously, this capacity may have only been available to senior personnel located in a corporate office.

Centralized decision-making runs counter to many behavioural science recommendations about the motivational potential of permitting people to assume responsibility and of giving them feedback. It also stands in direct contradiction to the principle of enhancing the participation of people in decisions which affect them and to which they can contribute with some knowledge and experience. In the context of the wider debate about participation and individual responsibility, the new information technology makes no less possible the implementation of devolved and democratic decision processes than it does the creation of an Orwellian 1984. It could be used to facilitate either development, both in the management of organizations and in the governance of whole societies.

The application of modern information technology permits substantial changes in the content of managers' work and in the structure of management. It has long been a complaint among managers, and a finding substantiated by the research investigations which have been conducted, that too much of their working day is taken up in dealing with a succession of problems and incidents of a short-term character. Many of these immediate problems arise from inadequate communication, a lack of information and the absence of routines which adequately utilize the information available. Situations where the collation and transmission of information take place through personal contact, or through written reports followed by personal contact, also require a substantial portion of managerial time to be given over to information processing rather than to planning, evaluation and other activities oriented towards a longer-term perspective. Some middle management and clerical jobs may indeed be almost wholly taken up with information processing. New technology has the potential to improve information deficiencies and to relieve the time devoted to communication, especially between physically separated locations. If this potential is realized, it should increase the time top management can devote to strategic issues and also economize on middle managerial and clerical manpower.

The introduction of superior technological facilities for communication has some relevance for the grouping of activities that is adopted (see the discussion in Chapter 4). They may make it possible to place less reliance upon roles, such as liaison officers or convenors of meetings, designed to ensure that the necessary degree of integration takes place within an organization, and instead to substitute a use of new communications technology which distributes information more effectively and permits ready interaction over spatial distances. Structural arrangements intended to improve integration are costly in manpower and can blur the allocation of responsibility. Chapter 4 instanced the problems that can arise with the use of more complex structures such as the matrix model. If, with the application of new technology, the linkage and overlays between different activities can be secured with a reduced investment in co-ordination roles, then a simplification of management structure should be possible.

There are a number of ways in which information technology could assist in the reduction of managerial staff, particularly in the middle ranges, and hence in the compression of management hierarchies. If, as has been mentioned, the technology can be used to establish routines which substitute for behaviour control based on personal supervision, then the manpower component engaged in such supervision can be reduced. Similarly, a substitution of technology for people is possible in roles concerned with the processing and recording of information, and with co-ordination. The potential connection here between new technology and staffing within the management hierarchy is, nevertheless, subject to policy considerations. If middle management and its clerical-cum-secretarial support staff are regarded simply as a now outdated element in pre-electronic information and control systems, then use will be made of the new technology to substitute for them. If, on the other hand, middle management is seen to have other valuable functions to which it was previously difficult to give adequate attention, then its role will not be regarded as redundant. These other functions might concern improvements in the everyday operation of departments, staff development and the creation of a strong shared culture and level of understanding among staff. In the economic circumstances prevailing at the time of writing, the former policy option is tending to prevail over the latter. In fact, since the mid-1970s a desire to reduce middle management and white-collar staff has been evident which pre-dates the impact of new technology but which now gives direction to the way it is tending to be applied.

To summarize, the development of more sophisticated information technology is becoming associated with (1) the relief of senior managers from having to devote time and effort to securing feedback and intervening in short-term problems where routine procedures were inadequate, (2) a tendency towards re-centralization, which is encouraged by this release of top managerial capacity, and (3) a simplification of management structures, which also eases some of the supervisory burden on top management. This link between technology and management is not deterministic. There are policy alternatives to consider just as with employment and job content at operative and routine clerical levels. The outcome of the process of negotiating and deciding on the use of new technology is not always predictable—indeed, the following chapter will indicate that this is the case generally with the introduction of change into organizations.

There is a danger of exaggerating the speed and extent to which management structures and the organization of work are likely to change along the lines indicated in this chapter. Firstly, while there is a rapid growth in worldwide expenditure on new technology, the rate at which it is adopted varies both between industries and countries. In Britain, for example, the textile, clothing and leather industries use new technology far less than do the engineering or food and drink industries (Northcott and Rogers 1982). Surveys also indicate different national rates of new technology adoption (Economist Intelligence Unit 1982; International Data Corporation 1983).

Secondly, there is evidence that new technology, when it is introduced, is not necessarily accompanied by significant changes in organization. For example, Bjorn-Andersen and his colleagues (1979) found that changes to existing work organization and job content were not seriously considered as design issues when European banks introduced computers, and the subsequent changes to organization were minimal. Robey (1977) has argued, from a review of research, that organizations require particular structures according to the contingencies in their situation and that computerization is essentially malleable, providing whatever is needed to realize more fully management's requirements. I have suggested in this chapter that the newer microelectronics technology now being introduced is likely to have a more substantial effect on the nature of jobs and organization. This opinion takes into account the greatly enhanced cost-benefit potential of the new technology, as well as the economic pressures now bearing on organizations, which should encourage their managements eventually to take advantage of that potential.

Technology and the future of organization

Technology is undoubtedly regarded as a major force in the world today, one which excites fear as much as it does hope. It is of considerable importance to consider who and what is controlling the way technology is used. The view that technological advance is a kind of juggernaut which carries the shape of work and organization relentlessly before it needs particularly critical examination. For it suggests that we do not have a real choice in the matter.

The same issue was central to the so-called 'machinery question' at the beginning of the industrial revolution Berg (1980). Did the new power-driven industrial technology cause work to be organized centrally into factories? Modern research suggests that while the then new technology was helpful in various ways to early industrialists, the establishment of factory organization was a prerequisite for the successful introduction of new technology and was already being adopted for other reasons such as the direct supervision over workers' methods of working that it permitted. A basic issue therefore is whether technology has an imperative status for the design of work and organization, and on the whole the answer for today's new technology seems to be negative as well. In many sectors of activity it is doubtful whether an optimum technology can be said to exist, both because there are imperfections of knowledge and because many non-technological factors also affect performance. So in practice some variation of technology is usually found even in the one sector. Secondly, there is evidence to show how a variety of combinations of technology and work organization may be arrived at through the processes of experiment and negotiation. This is a point which has indeed been made repeatedly throughout the present book. The more it is appreciated that the introduction of technology into organizations is a political process around a political issue, the more it will be recognized that existing economic, social and political institutions, together with the dynamic tensions between them, create the conditions governing the way technology is applied.

Having said that, it is clearly hazardous to offer any general predictions on how technology will affect the future of organization. There is also the objection that the offering of predictions, if believed by others, will tend to discourage that very process of experiment and discovery which nurtures a precious recognition that we may have some choice in the matter. Nevertheless, I have also suggested in this chapter that some fairly general trends may be discerned at least within the western capitalist economic systems with which I am more familiar. Others, such as Charles Handy (1982), have ventured to take prophecy even further, and so a few words are offered here by way of a summary on these trends. Any consistency that is apparent in the contemporary use of new technology derives to an important extent from the pressures within capitalist economies to regard profit maximization and cost minimization as priorities, and from the long-standing economic perspective of people at work as costly 'factors of production'.

On the whole, the new microelectronic-based technology is expected to reduce problems of organization for two main reasons. First, because it greatly improves the transmission, storage, accessibility and analysis of information. Second, because it makes possible the reduction in size of organizations through a replacement of operatives, clerical and middle management personnel. So we are likely to see a halt to the earlier trend towards a continued inflation in the numbers of people employed within organizations, though a growth in those organization's capital values and volume of work may well continue. (I have in mind here organic growth rather than growth through acquisition and merger.) The type of organization which is less likely to contract in size is that offering personal services where the continued presence of the service provider is required, and where a minimum threshold of activity must be maintained to justify the cost of high-level specialists and their usually expensive equipment. Hospitals are a case in point, though even here it may be possible to keep the size of units down through rotating specialists between them or confining their range of activities to a few specialisms only.

It may be feasible to run these generally smaller organizations of the future along less bureaucratic lines, both because of their smaller size and because improved information technology should render control and integration less reliant on formalization. It was suggested earlier that we are already seeing a trend towards a sharper division of employment by which, within an organization, a relatively small group would be located within the primary segment of the internal labour market, while other employees (probably the majority) would find their employment within any particular organization less secure and stable than before—in fact, many may lose previously stable jobs and enter a casual or unemployed role. Some commentators, such as Handy, have envisaged that many managers as well as ordinary employees will in future be offered short-term contracts with payment related to work done and renewal dependent upon performance. The core of staff enjoying stable salaried employment within organizations could become very small indeed, confined to senior executives, staff concerned with external relationships (such as marketing), technical staff dealing primarily with non-routinized work such as product development, and a personnel-cum-administration group to service the organization and co-ordinate contract workers. With these compact staffs enjoying relatively high stability of employment, in easy communication through information technology and having common access to the feedback of well-ordered operational information, the ground would be fertile for a high degree of collective identity and an ability to rely on a substantial normative element in the control process. Sir Adrian Cadbury (1983), one of Britain's most thoughtful industrialists, has argued in similar vein for a concentration of organizational staff on core activities, and flexible working arrangements that include individualized contracts for work done or time given. He links these developments to the prospect of achieving greater participation and consensus within the smaller core organization that remains.

This appears to be an attractive scenario, but only for a minority of the population. A social problem of enormous proportions attends the rest of society. Can the majority of people achieve meaningful activity and an adequate livelihood under these conditions? To what extent will their interests really be catered for in a society where the concentration of resources in organizations persists but where these organizations are staffed by relatively small groups who may not identify their interests any longer with the majority? Even if the management problem of organization is eased through the application of new technology, the social and political problems of organization are likely to be exacerbated.

Summary

New technology employs miniaturized electronic circuitry to process information. The advantages of new technology over previous information technology lie in its cheapness, reliability, compactness, speed of operation, accuracy, and low energy consumption. The range of its practical applications is correspondingly greater. The worldwide growth of investment in new technology is rapid.

New technology has become a significant vehicle for changes in employment and organization. The changes which management seeks reflect its strategic intentions in introducing new technology, including reductions in operating costs, increases in flexibility, improvements in the quality of products or services, and enhanced control and integration. A major issue is whether new technology is used to complement and augment skills or to substitute for them, and even to displace labour altogether. In some circumstances employees may be able to resist the use of new technology to degrade their jobs.

Possibilities for management control are extended by new technology; in particular it facilitates the unification of hitherto fragmented control systems. It can also assist integration through its enhancement of communication. These possibilities present opportunities for change within management in regard to the hierarchical location of decision-making, the complexity of co-ordinative arrangements, and the size of middle management. While, in the longer term, new technology is expected to reduce the problems of managing organizations, there is some doubt about the speed with which the opportunities it presents will be taken up.

Suggested further reading

The literature on new technology is growing almost as explosively as the technology itself. It is therefore particularly important to keep up to date, and with this in mind I shall only suggest a few readings available at the time of writing which offer a wide-ranging coverage and/or present significant points to consider.

The collection of papers edited by Tom Forester, *The Microelectronics Revolution* (Blackwell/MIT Press 1980) remains a very useful comprehensive guide. Liam Bannon, Ursula Barry and Olav Holst, *Information Technology: Impact on the Way of Life* (Tycooly Publishing 1982) contains a wide range of papers given to an international conference on the subject. The report by the Council for Science and Society on *New Technology: Society, Employment and Skill* (CSS, London 1981) discusses the issues contained in its title and points to the possibilities of policy choices in the way new technology is applied. Many reports and predictions have appeared on the relevance of new technology for employment, such as that by J. Sleigh and others, *The Manpower Implications of Micro-electronic Technology* (Her Majesty's Stationery Office 1979), and Christopher Freeman and others, *Unemployment and Technical Innovation* (Frances Pinter 1982). Less has appeared on new technology and changes to job content and work organization. An interesting report on case studies of such changes was produced by Income Data Services, *Changing Technology* (IDS, London, Study no. 220, June 1980). David A. Buchanan and David Boddy, *Organizations in the Computer Age* (Gower 1983) analyse findings from case studies of manufacturing plants. Two sources on the service sector are John Marti and Anthony Zeilinger, *Micros and Money* (Policy Studies Institute, London 1982); and Jonathan Gershuny and Ian Miles, *The New Service Economy* (Frances Pinter 1983).

Useful material on the relevance of new technology for management is contained in journals such as *Management Today*, which published a special survey in April 1982 on 'The Automated Office', and another survey in November 1982 on physical distribution ('Delivering the Goods'), which considers the application of new technology in some detail. International Data Corporation prepared a report for the June 1983 *Management Today* on 'The Impact of IT'. Two references mentioned in this chapter also appeared in *Management Today*: Barry Wilkinson's 'Managing with New Technology' in the October 1982 issue and Charles Handy's 'Where Management is Leading' in the December 1982 issue. Barry Wilkinson, *The Shopfloor Politics of New Technology* (Heinemann 1983) was also mentioned.

Other references were Maxine Berg, *The Machinery Question and the Making of Political Economy 1815–1848* (Cambridge University Press 1980); John Bessant, *Microprocessors in Production Processes* (Policy Studies Institute, London 1982); Niels Bjorn-Andersen, Bo Hedberg, Dorothy Mercer, Enid Mumford and Andreu Sole (editors), *The Impact of Systems Change in Organizations* (Sijthoff and Noordhoff 1979); Sir Adrian Cadbury, 'Cadbury Schweppes: More than Chocolate and Tonic', *Harvard Business Review*, January–February 1983; Economist Intelligence Unit, *Chips in Industry* (London 1982); EOC, *The Impact of Telecommunications and Information Technology on Equal Opportunities* (Equal Opportunities Commission, London 1980); Ray Loveridge, 'Labour Market Segmentation and the Firm', in John Edwards et al. (editors), *Manpower Strategy and Techniques in an Organizational Context* (Wiley 1983), Chapter 7; Jim Northcott and Petra Rogers, *Microelectronics in Industry: What's Happening in Britain?* (Policy Studies Institute, London 1982); Daniel Robey, 'Computers and Management Structure: Some Empirical Findings Re-examined', *Human Relations*, vol. 30, 1977; and Richard P. Rumelt 'The Electronic Reorganization of Industry', paper presented to the Conference of the Strategic Management Society, London, October 1981.

Chapter 10

Undertaking Reorganization

'I was to learn later in life that we tend to meet any new situation by re-organizing, and a wonderful method it can be for creating the illusion of progress while producing confusion, inefficiency and demoralization' Gaius Petronius Arbiter (AD 66).

Despite this word of caution from the ancient world against undertaking reorganization, it has become an accepted truth of our times that organizations have to adapt to a fast-moving world in order to survive. The pressures generated by a combination of world recession and rapid technological change reinforce Warren Bennis's warning that 'change is the biggest story in the world today, and we are not coping with it adequately' (1969: 1). This is a message that most people who work in organizations would probably accept if you asked them, yet in practice it remains extremely difficult to bring about organizational change. In large complex organizations, a push towards change can take a long while to show any result even when it is made with all the authority of top management. As one managing director put it: 'You kick the backside and six months later the shoulders twitch'. Those organizational leaders who succeed in getting substantial changes made, like Sir Michael Edwardes in the case of British Leyland, are singled out for their exceptional achievement. Reorganization may be a rational necessity in modern times, but it often appears to be a political near-impossibility.

Previous chapters have indeed pointed to the significance of bringing about changes in the design of organization from a 'rational' standpoint. The rationality here can refer both to managerial effectiveness criteria and to employee criteria, such as increasing the organization's capacity to provide good incomes and satisfying work. The whole notion of designing organization implies a corresponding ability to implement the outcome. In fact, the processes of design and change will tend to merge in situations where design progresses through recurring cycles of proposal, implementation, review, and further proposal, and where at the same time it succeeds in gaining the participation and support of organizational members. Reference to the gaining of support, however, exposes the political character of change. For the design of organization can never be divorced from members' perceptions of personal advantage or disadvantage. Reorganization is therefore likely to generate resistance stemming not simply from personal difficulties in coping with uncertainty but also from the need to defend group interests. These defensive groups can be found just as much within management as outside it. We therefore have the paradox that a rational perspective accepts the need for changes in organization and for planning these, while a political perspective expresses the need to negotiate such changes and if necessary to resist them. This reflects the general duality of consensus and conflict which runs through organizational life.

This chapter is concerned with 'reorganization', which is the bringing about of changes in the design of organization and work structures. The rational perspective will tend to come to the fore in the first three sections which discuss respectively pressures for reorganization, the identification of a need to reorganize, and some specific questions which may aid analysis. The political perspective informs a fourth section which considers problems of implementing reorganization. This is not to say, of course, that the earlier analytical phases are non-political in nature. For, as became apparent with the introduction of new technology, a very significant stage for groups outside top management to influence the outcome of change is when its initial premisses are established.

Pressures and stimuli for reorganization

Previous chapters have identified ways in which it is appropriate to shape the design of jobs and structures so as to suit the circumstances under which organizations carry on their operations. The need to maintain consistency between elements of structure has also been emphasized. As circumstances change, it is therefore incumbent on the manager to examine the implications of the change for organizational design, and to decide whether any reorganization is required. Change has indeed become so ubiquitous in modern industrial societies that many large business companies in North America and Europe have established specialized organization planning departments, giving them the task of constantly monitoring the requirements for structural changes and of devising appropriate schemes to accomplish this. British organizations have, on the whole, been less inclined to treat reorganization as a continuing incremental process, probably as much by default as by a calculated preference for periodic comprehensive changes.

Broadly speaking, reorganization can be directed at bringing about improvements in efficiency or flexibility which enhance the organization's capacity to absorb risks—that is to *react* successfully to changes from the environment. It may also reflect a *pro-active* intention on management's part, namely to enhance the organization's capacity to take the risks which accompany an attempt to seize new opportunities: when, for example, diversification and growth are planned. It is possible to identify some of the environmental pressures for organizational change which have been active in recent years, as well as some of the strategic policies that can stimulate change.

1 Environment

For most organizations environmental conditions have in recent years been changing with increasing speed. Business companies have generally experienced heightened competitive pressures. In many industries, competition in product markets has increased along with the lowering of tariff barriers and the multinational spread of large companies' activities. Competitive pressures have sometimes been increased by a rising rate of product innovation, as in the field of electronics where micro-circuitry is a prime example.

Changes in world economic conditions have substantially shortened the time horizons up to which it is realistic to plan ahead. For example, commodity prices and supplies have fluctuated considerably and become more dependent upon political factors: in the case of sugar and cocoa beans market fluctuations have greatly increased the uncertainty of management in the confectionery industry. Violent changes in copper prices have had similar consequences for management in the non-ferrous metals industry. The rapid rate of price inflation experienced in the early 1980s also raised uncertainties about the behaviour of consumers, whose patterns of expenditure exhibited new peaks and troughs of demand in anticipation of and following major price rises. In the field of employment, legislation has also changed the conditions under which organizations can be managed.

These environmental changes are recognized well enough, but they do carry important implications for structural change. When environments become more volatile, with consequently shortened planning time horizons, adaptability becomes vitally important. This means that it is necessary for managers to secure more up-to-date intelligence about events in the outside world and to evaluate and co-ordinate the information more rapidly for the purpose of deciding how to respond to changing conditions. In structural terms, this implies that management may have to consider increasing its employment of specialists like market researchers, representatives to trade fairs and conferences, and commodity buyers, in order to improve its capacity to keep track of external developments. Specialists such as these also provide the expert advice required for management to respond creatively to the opportunities, or threats, which new developments bring. Even the use of outside agencies for some of this activity is unlikely to eliminate internal specialists, who have to serve as contact points and in a liaison role.

A complex and differentiated structure is more difficult to co-ordinate. Indeed, the external conditions described make it imperative for organizations to generate an increased capacity for integrating information across different specialized functions, and for transmitting the end result effectively to the point of management decision. Circumstances today often change too rapidly for management to be able to rely upon programmes, plans and referral of exceptions for top level decision. These traditional bureaucratic decision and planning mechanisms are likely to be too slow and inflexible. Events are liable to occur too frequently and to present too many novelties. In times of world economic stringency and pressures on cash flow, it is not sensible to build in flexibility for coping with greater uncertainty either through costly higher inventory or through delays, backlogs and other reduced standards of performance.

These limitations imply that, in the new conditions, organization structures have to be re-examined to see how well they facilitate effective communications laterally between units and functions; and whether full advantage is being taken of aids like planning staff and computerized information systems which improve the vertical flow of information. In other words, improved structural mechanisms for both lateral and vertical integration are called for. These might well include some regrouping of activities to reduce the complexity of communications and to strengthen links between those functions which need to work together in a particular area.

An example of thinking along these lines is provided by Ian Mangham and his colleagues (1972). When reviewing its objectives, the Petrochemicals Division of ICI recognized that in a period of increasing social and technical change one of its highest priorities was to improve the management and capabilities of its people. Success in coping with change was seen to depend on the contribution employees were prepared to make. The Division's management concluded that this not only required encouragement for individuals to take on greater responsibility, but also a reduction of barriers in the organization structure to increase contact between managers and employees, and the capacity of teams and sections to work in an integrated manner. In this way, the Division's evaluation of strategic requirements led it to embark on a major effort in the field of organizational change and development.

Competitive pressures provide a major stimulus for reorganization. Many companies in Europe since the mid-1970s have attempted to reduce staff and managerial overheads in response to a period of economic stringency. Appropriate reorganizations here might involve a reduction in the number of management levels, using a method of the kind described in Chapter 3. It may be feasible to centralize certain service functions such as purchasing and training, thereby gaining staff economies. Attention will almost certainly be given to improving the control of expenditure within the organization. This is often interpreted as meaning not only less expenditure, but less delegation of discretion on expenditure as well. In circumstances where a greater capacity to adapt is also required, this may be counter-productive to the longer-term success of the organization. It is usually more sensible to improve control by obtaining more accurate and up-to-date information on expenditure instead of referring more decisions on expenditure up the hierarchy, with inevitable delays.

The increasing intervention of government and its agencies is another significant change in organizational environments. In some countries from time to time, there has been regulation of prices and incomes. This has forced management to standardize and centrally regulate policies in areas where previously considerable discretion may have been delegated to local operating units. In the public sector too, a long-term trend towards centralization is observable. These centralist tendencies have occasioned the comment that some industrial societies are moving towards a corporatist state. If sustained, they are likely to put a brake on policies of devolution within organizations designed to facilitate a more flexible response to environmental change. Leaving aside social or political considerations, the inflexibility

which governmental regulation imposes on managerial policies is a disadvantage in terms of coping with environmental change, unless the State
itself can remove a substantial amount of uncertainty through effective
national planning.

2 Diversification

In the early stages of diversification into a new field of activity, managements quite often make only minor adjustments to organization structure.
A special 'co-ordinator' may, for example, be appointed to look after the
new operation and left to secure a commitment of time and resources from
functional departments as best he can. At a later stage, when the amount of
business in the new area builds up to a substantial proportion there are pressures to adopt a divisionalized structure which allocates resources to the
diversification as a major area of business within the organization. At what
point does an organization move away from a functional structure, or create
a new division out of an existing one? This is a particularly difficult question.
Indeed, there is always the option not to move to a fully-fledged divisional
structure, but instead, to graft a divisional-type split of certain departments
like marketing onto a basically functional structure. This type of mixed
structure needs to be complemented with clear policies on priorities, to
avoid the problem experienced by the manufacturer of specialist steels cited
in Chapter 4, where difficulties arose because of competing claims on a
single production function.

3 Growth

The successful pursuit of growth sets up a need for reorganization. Pressures
for reorganization arise when the top executive or the top team can no longer
maintain effective day-to-day control, and when the growth of the organization requires a broader range and greater specialization between management functions. Growth generally leads to extended hierarchies and
problems of communication. If it occurs on the basis of diversification into
many unrelated fields, it can generate serious problems of control and co-
ordination. In these various ways, continued expansion is a prime source of
pressures for reorganization. For this reason size has emerged in so many
studies as the major predictor of the type of structure adopted by organizations in practice.

Fisons Limited provides an example of how problems of growth, diversification and competitive pressure led its management to undertake a major
reorganization. During the 1940s and 1950s Fisons had diversified away
from its vulnerable reliance on a single industry product—fertilizers—into
other activities including pharmaceuticals, agrochemicals, industrial chemicals, food products, the assembly of industrial refrigerators and many other
products. By the mid-1960s, however, the results of diversifying into so
many largely unrelated products had proved to be disappointing. The company's strong position in its basic fertilizer business was being eroded by
competition, and difficulties were being experienced in the introduction of
new technology for manufacturing intermediate and end products. Profits

in other new areas were declining and the company was facing a cash crisis. This was the combination of pressures on Fisons to change direction at the time.

The company decided to clarify its prime corporate objective, which was continuous growth in earnings per share. It decided on a concept of its business, in which the connecting thread was health for humans, animals and plants. This signalled a determination that the company's future growth would come from related and mutually-supporting activities, and all activities which did not fit this concept were disposed of, thus solving the company's cash problem. The reorganization which was undertaken followed from these strategic decisions. In 1967 the company had as many as 53 wholly-owned subsidiaries, each with its own board, set of accounts, company secretary, accountants and other managers. The complexities of coordinating this collection of miscellaneous, largely unrelated businesses were forbidding and very wasteful of management energies. With the policy decision to concentrate on only three major activities—fertilizers, pharmaceuticals and agrochemicals—most of these separate companies were wound up, and a three-division structure substituted instead. Full profit, capital expenditure and cash flow budgetary responsibility was allocated to the director in charge of each division.

4 Technology

Chapter 9 described the very rapid growth of new technology applications and the relevance these have for changes in work and organization. New technology may be used to effect changes in other organizational contingencies, through, for example, economizing on manpower and on managerial overheads in order to arrest and perhaps reverse the inflation of organizational establishments. If new technology is applied to retain only a relatively small group of long-serving primary-segment employees, new possibilities arise for dismantling the bureaucratic structures erected in the days of large labour forces which identified less closely with managerial objectives. On the other hand, automation and computerization may enhance the numbers and significance of certain specialist groups such as systems analysts, electronics engineers and financial analysts. From a structural point of view, difficulties can arise in the integration of such specialists into line hierarchies, and Chapter 5 mentioned how many organizations have experimented with team structures designed to accommodate the problem. In short, developments in technology can be seen to provide a significant impetus to reorganization.

5 Personnel

Chapter 2 mentioned the long-term changes in educational levels, distribution of occupational skills, and employee attitudes which have together stimulated interest in work restructuring and participation. Although this interest has waned noticeably at the time of writing, it remains an aspiration and may return as a force to be reckoned with. At shopfloor and office levels, work restructuring and participation imply changes in the organization of work and in the role of junior management. Employees may take on responsibility for some of the detailed organization of the work, allocation of people to tasks, inspection and routine maintenance of equipment. The burden on the first-line manager is potentially reduced. His or her control of work could now involve more negotiation of output targets and less direct personal supervision. In these ways, the first-line manager can be relieved from having to deal constantly with immediate contingencies. In principle, this should give him the chance to devote more attention to opportunities for longer-term improvements in methods, layout, equipment and employee development.

In practice, it is doubtful whether this kind of change will be implemented swiftly or easily. Changes in organization at the operative level require modification in procedure, delegation, management style and so forth, at higher levels. Top managment has to hold a positive philosophy about work restructuring and participation, and to know what they entail, before any change in that direction is likely to succeed. Second, it is doubtful if all first-line managers are willing or capable of coping with the longer time perspective and the negotiating role described. Third, lengthening the time horizons of jobs lower in the hierarchies will increase the overlap between work done at adjacent hierarchical levels, unless there is increased delegation right the way down the management hierarchy. Even then, it may be decided to remove a level of management, which may be beneficial in the long term but provoke immediate resistance. None the less, these comments points to the difficulties of implementing change rather than to the inappropriateness of that change as a response to developments in the personnel field.

Formal factory and company systems of participation have been introduced in many European countries and are recommended by the European Commission. Judging by experience in Israel, Yugoslavia and elsewhere these developments also promote structural changes. Many processes of decision-making become more formalized and a sharper distinction is drawn between matters of policy and matters of executive management. Purely *ad hoc* policy-making through the medium of executive decisions tends to become less acceptable. Although the processes of participation can create delays, bringing decision-making into a more open and formalized arena may well result in better co-ordination of information and contributions from the different parts of the organization. The clear separation of policy from executive decisions could also relieve executive authority from much of the challenge it currently receives to its legitimacy, as Lord Wilfred Brown has consistently argued in his writings on organization. My strong impression, gained from visiting plants in Israel and Yugoslavia, is that affording workers the opportunity to share in policy making leads them to accept day-to-day executive authority with little demur. Worker participation in the discussion of policy appeared to give additional legitimacy to managers' authority in executing the policy.

There are clearly many developments, some long-term and some more immediate, which create pressures for structural change. How then can managers identify the need for change when it arises in their own organization? What are typical warning signals, and what guidelines may help to identify the nature of an organizational problem?

Identifying a need to reorganize

In general terms, when any of the above pressures for reorganization arise then it is timely to consider whether structural changes are called for. This planned approach to change will help to avoid a situation in which the performance of an organization actually declines before an inappropriate structure is identified as a contributory factor. A greater rate of environmental change raises questions of how to ensure adequate innovation in the organization's activities and how to avoid an overload in its decision-making capabilities. Competitive pressures may also require an innovatory response as well as ways of securing administrative economies. Growth and diversification should alert managers to the problem of avoiding deteriorating communication, control and speed of response, in an organization that is becoming more complex. Technological developments signal possible implications for the management of new specialist staff, for the role of middle managers and (in the case of integrated systems) for relations between hitherto separate departments. Work restructuring and participation indicate possible changes in the structure of operative level management and in managerial systems.

The need for organizational change does not necessarily arise as a consequence of a major strategic development. Nor is the change required necessarily large-scale. The continual incremental changes in operating conditions, size, technique, personnel and other features at any level down to the work group may generate problems that require modifications in organization. There are also situations where poor performance is found on further investigation to be rooted in a more fundamental behavioural failure, for which structure has to take some of the blame.

For example, the immediately obvious reason why a company is losing sales is its failure to honour promised delivery dates. Underlying this, however, may be inadequate integration between sales and production departments. Sales are perhaps forcing unplanned 'special' orders onto production. Production may be giving lead-time estimates based on standard runs knowing that delays can be blamed on Sales and their special orders. I have known such a situation, which had deteriorated so much that special orders were regarded by each party as an opportunity to discomfort the other. A structural development such as the SOLD system described in Chapter 5 would be one way to improve matters and to ensure that sales and production worked to agreed criteria and a common programming system.

A number of common problems can arise from structural deficiencies (see Chapter 1). Four specific examples are given here, to illustrate how such problems can serve as a warning that organization structure requires examination. They are managerial overload, poor integration, insufficient innovation and weakening control.

Warning signs of a structural problem

1 Overload   One common sign of overload among top management is the working of excessive hours. Another sign is a disjointed *ad hoc* approach to formulating strategy, betraying an inability to let go of details and to concentrate on the long-term and broad view of things. Hard work is not a necessary concomitant of good management. If it signifies overload, the likely consequences will be deteriorating quality of decision-making and slower communication with the rest of the organization. In most cases of overload, greater delegation is indicated with only the clearly strategic issues remaining reserved for top management attention. Achievement of effective delegation may require a series of further changes in structure, including the establishment of a framework of indirect controls, the personal development of subordinates, and possibly the establishment of more general management positions below the chief executive.

2 Integration   Conflict between managers or between their departments is also common. Although this can result from a clash of personalities, it is not unusual to find that it is a sign of structural inadequacy as well. Genuine differences of opinion between departments whose activities are interdependent, such as a conflict between engineers and buyers over the correct balance between quality and price in purchases, have ultimately to be resolved, since the purchases must be made. A structural mechanism, such as a regular purchasing meeting, would offer an opportunity for different opinions to be brought into open confrontation and resolved in a way that elicits the formal agreement of the parties concerned. The likely alternative is that the conflict continues to be dealt with on a basis of mistrust and mutual evasion.

Open disagreement between parts of an organization presents one of the more easily identifiable problems in the area of communication and integration. Less obvious but still very costly problems can include duplicated effort between units which are not exchanging information adequately, and poor morale among staff who feel they are not given enough information about changes planned for their areas of work. Supervisors often complain that their authority is undermined by this latter failing. It is true that a complaint about 'communication problems' is often used by managers as a euphemism for the presence of deep-seated conflicts, but it nevertheless remains the case that communication, in the sense of information processing, is often deficient. Such deficiency could signal the need for some reorganization such as reducing management levels, re-grouping activities or introducing new co-ordinative mechanisms.

3 Innovation   A little verse was once written about one of Britain's largest enterprises:

'Along this tree from foot to crown,
Ideas flow up and vetoes down.'

A failure to innovate and to be receptive to new ideas is often another sign of structural failure. Innovation of any kind involves a process in which ideas are generated, selected for further development, and adopted for regular use by the client or beneficiary. The type of structure an organization has can affect this process at any stage. For example, among the conclusions which emerge from studies of creativity and the generation of ideas is that both are enhanced by (a) freedom to communicate with other people who are a source of ideas inside and outside the research group and by (b) freedom to pursue research without too much distraction or administrative interference. Basically, the requirement at this stage is for the innovators to be able to consider every relevant possibility and avenue of advance. This speaks for a structure which is 'organic' in nature and to some degree self-contained from the everyday operational side of the organization. It also suggests, for instance, that the inventive productivity of scientists is increased when they are not expected to attend too many administrative meetings, which could be time-wasting and distracting for them.

On the other hand, a common reason why ideas once formulated fail to be recognized and applied, lies in the over-separateness of the 'ideas men'. They may be too removed from the level at which decisions on adoption of new developments are made, or lack a sponsor at that level, so the problem of 'ideas up and vetoes down' remains. The ideas men may not be integrated with members of the organization who are aware of customer or client needs, so that innovations tend to be rejected as impractical or economically unattractive. A well-designed structure can assist in the integration and control of the whole innovative process, and repeated failures in this field quite likely signify a structural weakness.

4 Control   If the planning and control process is to be effective, people should have a good idea of what they are expected to achieve. A very common complaint from employees and managers is that they have not been given a clear definition of what are their responsibilities or authority, or that they have not had the opportunity of establishing their work objectives in discussion with management. The classical approach to management, which is still reflected in standard personnel practice, would see this problem as primarily a failure of structural definition, which can be resolved by a clear statement of objectives, responsibilities and authority in job descriptions, manuals of procedure and the like.

Depending on the circumstances, other approaches might be appropriate but would still require some structural change. For example, job descriptions and other aspects of formalization can be self-defeating in rapidly changing or ambiguous situations. In these cases, it would be more appropriate to keep the definition of people's jobs open to adjustment. Employees, particularly professional and skilled personnel, may resent a managerial attempt to define methods of work to an extent which denies them personal discretion. In these circumstances, the type of structure required could well involve output control on the basis of mutually agreed objectives and performance criteria, and the provision of an adequate means for integrating individual efforts through, for instance, grouping all concerned into the same team.

Specific questions to ask

Through the use of these examples, I have been trying to make the point that common problems of management are often made worse by structural inadequacies. The presence of such problems serves to warn managers that some change in structure may be necessary. Of course it is not always easy to decide just where the root of the problem lies, to what degree it arises from poor structure, and at what stage it is worth undertaking the trouble of reorganization. It is impossible to offer any useful generalizations about these matters since they relate entirely to the particular problem and situation. It is possible, though, to suggest a number of questions which may help to sensitize a manager to the nature of an organizational problem, and so provide him with the rudiments of an analytical approach.

1 What is the scope of the problem?   Sometimes the performance of an organization will be poor along a whole range of dimensions—poor growth, low profit or high costs for services provided, lack of innovation and investment, and so on. In other instances the problem may be far more localized. In the event of poor overall performance, if the management's strategy appears to be sound then it is quite possible that the whole structural framework through which management is attempting to operate is ill-adjusted to prevailing contingencies, is internally out of balance, or is simply more costly compared to that of competitors. In these circumstances a great deal can often be learned about one's own organizational problem by making a direct comparison with more successful competitors. The airline study described in Chapter 8 was set up for such a purpose, and it led the sponsoring company to make constructive changes in its own organization.

2 What is the source of the problem?   Most localized organizational problems first show up in personal terms. That is, the problem appears to revolve around a particular person or around poor relations between two or more people. There is always a temptation to make a scapegoat for organizational troubles of the person who does not fit in. For example, in one company, which had diversified into a technically more sophisticated segment of its industry, the Production Director was blamed for failures in meeting delivery dates. He was a 'rough diamond' in a socially conscious senior management team and, not unexpectedly, reacted to criticism in a highly defensive manner which made no contribution at all towards resolving the problem. In fact, the trouble stemmed at least in part from a structural failing. When the diversification took place, a new sales group was established to market the new product lines. The production department was therefore faced with competing demands on its resources from two sales groups. No procedure was laid down to provide the production department with criteria by which to decide on priorities between producing the standard and the new lines, both of which required the same plant. No integrative mechanisms were established for collectively discussing problems of priority in scheduling. The need for these was all the more pressing because there were frequent technical failures in producing the new, more sophisticated products, and these affected delivery dates.

This is an example of where personal blame was attached to a man for failures which stemmed partly from structural inadequacy. It is well known that personal behaviour will tend to become erratic and even aggressive when someone is under strain. This means that a person's natural disposition can be substantially modified when he or she is placed in a stressful position because of circumstances which originate from poor structure or from some other feature of inadequate management. It is always worth while asking the question whether structure, management policies or other circumstances could be having an effect on the personal behaviour one first observes to be the problem. In any case it is extremely difficult to change personalities, and unreasonable to expect people to cope with a badly structured situation—it may be much easier to change organization instead. Personal style can create problems of its own which training and development may mitigate, and inter-personal hostility can be reduced through techniques of confrontation, teambuilding and training-groups. It is, however, important to warn that one should not expect too much from such efforts if there is an underlying structural inadequacy which is not also amended.

3 Is the problem temporary or permanent, unique or recurrent?   Considerable managerial time and effort is usually required to make a change in organization structure. It is therefore worth evaluating whether the problem to which one is thinking of applying a structural solution is only a temporary matter or a more basic problem. Similarly, one has to assess whether the problem is unique or part of a recurrent pattern. If the problem does seem to be temporary and one-off in nature, it will not be worth undertaking a substantial reorganization in order to deal with it. For reorganization can unsettle people and reduce effectiveness for a while, as Petronius Arbiter warned. This is the kind of decision managers face when choosing between setting up a temporary task force to bring together a range of contributions to tackle a problem, or establishing a more permanent team such as one would find within a matrix structure. On the other hand, there is always a temptation to regard a problem as being unique and temporary, in the hope that it will soon go away or be resolved! It is worth re-examining such problems to see if they do not turn out to be phases of a recurrent difficulty that has so far only been dimly perceived. In fact, if a manager finds he frequently has to deal with apparently unique problems, he may well be deceiving himself about their uniqueness and their temporary nature. In that case, reorganization could be called for.

4 At what level in the organization is the problem located?   For some purposes it is useful to think of organizations as systems of interdependent segments. This helps to remind us that not only are different departments interdependent through their contributions to the same activities and workflows, but so also are the different levels in an organization. We noted back in Chapter 6 how the concentration of decision-making at a high level in the management structure appears to affect behaviour lower down, promoting conformity and unwillingness to innovate. This is an example of how a problem which appears at one organizational level can have its source at another level.

Most organizations are hierarchical institutions in which it is accepted that those at a higher level have authority over those lower down. This means that employees and managers will take their cues on many matters from those at the next level above them. If a manager thinks that he has problems among his subordinates he should therefore consider whether he might be contributing towards the difficulty. Is he applying appropriate methods of co-ordination, control, objective-setting, assessment and so forth? Is he allowing his subordinates to define and carry out their roles in a way which meets their aspirations and capabilities? Has he assisted them to integrate adequately with other departments? A manager can structure the roles and behaviour of his subordinates in various ways, and so he is partly responsible when these characteristics become problematic.

Formal structural arrangements are an important part of the organization member's work environment. As such they are likely to affect his behaviour and performance by either facilitating or impeding the way he carries out his job and his motivation towards it. To a large extent structure is 'imposed' on the individual by higher management—the main structural parameters will appear to be established from above. For this reason, attempts to develop organizations that focus upon the individual and his immediate relation to other people and to technology often do not have as much effect as does a focus on the context of structural practices, policies and regulations. These structural features in turn need to be understood in relation to the organization's choice of overall strategy and to the contingencies this brings into effect.

Seen in this light, diagnosing the level of an organizational problem and deciding on the appropriate level for any planned change are vital requirements. If it is desired to modify the ways in which people behave and relate, or in which work is done, it may be ineffective simply to try to 'develop' the people concerned, *even* if all parties are agreed on the desired direction of change. A tendency to concentrate on people and to ignore the structural and contingent work environment deriving from a higher level, has been one of the reasons for the high rate of failure in the so-called 'Organizational Development' movement.

The practical importance of level in the analysis of requirements for change is illustrated in a paper by Robert Toronto (1975). He describes change programmes in two functions of a southern USA oil refinery. These were the shipping function, responsible for the handling of finished products, and a maintenance function, responsible for the maintenance of a portion of the refining facilities. Over a two-year period, the shipping function was subject to changes at the immediate operational level (what Toronto calls the 'system' level). There was no attempt to effect change at a higher ('suprasystem') level involving the wider department of which shipping was part. The trend of performance over this period was erratic. There was a temporary upsurge in the early stage of the change programme, when employees were expecting a significant change for the better. When their expectations were not met performance fell off, and after some subsequent improvement during the rest of the programme, it then declined sharply. Toronto concludes that 'a gradual improvement cannot sustain itself without supporting changes in the suprasystem' (p.152).

Maintenance was subject to changes at both operational and at higher levels. The exact nature of these changes is not specified. Judging maintenance performance in terms of reductions in minor maintenance costs, Toronto concludes that the improvement in that area was more consistent and sustained than in shipping. It was also found that a measure of effort given to teambuilding at the level of the function's top management was more closely related to the trend of cost reduction than was effort given to teambuilding at the foreman-employee level. Toronto's data do not permit a causal analysis, but they are highly suggestive in regard to the question of interdependence between levels in organizational change. As Toronto concludes, 'I believe that . . . holistic reasoning is the direction that organization theory and research must take in order to adequately understand and describe the complexity of organizational change' (p.156).

Problems of implementing reorganization

This book concentrates upon the diagnosis of organizational problems. For organization to make a full contribution, however, quality of diagnosis must be complemented by quality of implementation. Questions arise as to how managers might seek to implement proposed changes in organization, the time required to see implementation completed, and the role which third parties can play in the change process. I have space here only to draw attention to these issues; they are given detailed consideration in the further reading suggested at the close of the chapter.

1 Method of implementation

In the first edition of this book, written in the mid-1970s, I cited E. A. Johns (1973) who expressed doubts as to whether any change introduced without some measure of consultation would be successful. Two main considerations lay behind this view: first, the value of the contributions organizational members with skills and experience can make to the design of improved arrangements and, second, the capacity of members to resist change or to subvert its operation should they not be convinced of its legitimacy. At the same time, I made the point that a participative approach would be unlikely to further the implementation of change if a serious conflict of interests were involved such that one party would clearly lose from the proposal.

It is important to give careful thought to the circumstances in which consultation and participation are likely to facilitate the implementation of reorganization; there is also the question of what is ethically appropriate. It is likely that a participative approach will give its most constructive contribution to the process of change in situations where there is underlying agreement about the objective of the change but where (1) there are differing views about the best way to achieve it and (2) no one party has a monopoly of relevant knowledge or power. In this kind of situation there will be a shared motivation to enter into discussions and a reasonable prospect of forging an eventual consensus. In a second type of situation, however, where there is either total agreement on how to proceed or where management is sufficiently powerful to enforce its preferred solution, participation may well be dismissed as a waste of time. In a third type of situation, where there is an inflexible opposition to a proposed change based on a fundamental disagreement with the aims of its promoters, consultation and participation are likely to be used simply as opportunities for obstructing implementation.

The shift in the balance of power during the 1970s and 80s towards the buyers of labour is therefore significant because it brings into play the second type of situation just described. Many employers now see themselves having an opportunity to force through changes in manning and work organization more fundamental in nature and at a faster rate than would have been possible under a genuinely participative regime. Workers have often been presented with the stark choice of either accepting change or facing redundancy. This way of doing things has been justified in terms of economic necessity and as the price that has to be paid in order to secure the longer-term survival of the organization. At the same time, workers maintain that it could be building up trouble for the future in terms of goodwill lost among employees and in the community. A loss of goodwill can also impair the willingness of employees to contribute positively towards improved ways of organizing work through suggestions and high motivation in general.

Some public sector organizations have provided examples of inflexible opposition to reorganization. This is the other kind of situation which a participative approach to implementing change is unlikely to suit. If a customary mode of operation is sufficiently embedded, then the only way to change it is probably to attack unilaterally both its structure and ideology. In such situations, participation would tend to be used by the organization's incumbents simply to direct attention away from plans for action, and to delay their implementation. The British government's difficulties in effecting change in its civil service bureaucracy provide one example of the problem, but it has actually been much more comprehensively described for the United States governmental bureaucracy.

Donald Warwick (1975) documents the resistance of the US State Department to attempts at structural reform. This resistance was led by the Department's own senior career staff and was enhanced by their ability to mobilize external support in Congress. Warwick questions what he calls 'the sometimes facile advocacy of employee participation in decisions about change' (p.199) in cases like large public bureaucracies, where large size, rigid hierarchy and the intrusion of different political power groups all make unworkable the notion of moving towards a consensus solution through participation. Similarly, Nicole Biggart (1977) has drawn upon the case of the 1970–71 reorganization of the US Post Office Department to point out how the removal of old methods and structural forms can require drastic action. As with many long-established organizations, the majority of the staff were committed to preserving the existing structure and it took the imposition of a new structure by a coalition of external interest groups to effect a change. It is most unlikely in these circumstances that an approach which relied on the active participation of the organization's members would have successfully swept away the old in order to provide room for building the new.

A reorganization is therefore likely to meet with varying degrees of resistance. It is important that a manager understand the reasons behind this, because they will help him to appreciate how a change that he regards as rational and even of minor significance, may well appear unreasonable and far from trivial to the people directly affected. It is tempting for a manager who does not understand the reasons why people object to change to dismiss their opposition as simply 'bloody-mindedness'. Resistance to change is in fact a universal phenomenon among groups who feel that their interests are threatened. It is found at all levels of organization from boardroom to shop-floor and throughout history from handloom weavers in the early 1800s to motorway protest groups today.

People will resist reorganization if they believe it is detrimental to aspects of their work life and roles that they value. If the change breaks up established informal social groups, it is likely to be seen as a threat to their power and status within the organization. A change aimed at simplifying an organization structure, perhaps by reducing the number of hierarchical levels, will probably be seen by some as a threat to their job security and to their prospects of promotion. A change aimed at enriching the jobs of subordinates may be viewed by a manager as a threat to his authority. A re-allocation of functions will be regarded with alarm by some senior managers as a diminution in their territorial rights within the organization. Increased delegation may be received, at least initially, as just an extra burden by some subordinates. A specialist may regard the attempt to restructure him away from his functional department and into a production or product team, as a threat to his professional development and market value. The very process of change itself may be seen as an unwelcome disturbance and interference to a well-established routine.

Any decision within organizations is reached and implemented through a political process. Politics is about the use of power, and decisions are a formalization of that use, which will have to be reached through negotiation and compromise when power is spread among several parties. When the decision involves a major change, the political process leading up to it is likely to be all the more active. It is not too difficult to identify the probable major sources of resistance to a proposed change, if one understands the ideology and perceived interests of the groups concerned, and if one can estimate their awareness of their power to influence the change and their propensity to employ it.

The main areas of resistance to change in organizations are reasonably well known. Employees will resist changes which they perceive to affect their job security, payment and status differentials, working conditions and methods; on the whole these are the 'hygiene' factors singled out by

Herzberg as sources of dissatisfaction when threatened (see page 177). At the managerial level, a focal point of resistance to change lies in the relationship between specialists and the 'line' manager users of their services. Specialists such as operational researchers, management services staff and management development personnel justify their presence by the projects they contribute for improvement and change. They not only seek to promote change, but naturally this change is defined in terms of what is best according to their 'professional' judgement. Their clients often resist such proposals. There is a risk to the maintenance of their routine operations in accepting the disruption of something new. There may be resentment at the implied criticism of having specialists tell them how to manage better.

Because resistance to change is to be expected, and because it is in some degree predictable, Tom Lupton (1965) suggested the rudiments of a systematic approach for carrying out such prediction. He saw the management problem to be two-fold. First, how to minimize potential disturbances during the period of change. Second, how to move quickly to a new stable situation which will produce a satisfactory level of performance. He suggested that those planning the change should:

(a) List all the alternative ways of implementing a change, together with estimated time schedules.

(b) Identify all the sections of the organization, occupational categories or work groups affected by the change, however indirectly.

(c) Calculate the likely reaction of these groups in general terms.

(d) Calculate their likely reaction for specific issues such as wage rates, differentials, promotion prospects, retraining, working practices and redeployment. Securing data of reasonable quality on these issues involves obtaining the opinion of managers in close contact with all the groups, and even better the direct reaction of the people concerned.

(e) Conclude by estimating in a crude way the overall acceptability of the change and of each approach to the change.

Information gathered through applying an approach such as this clearly remains highly subjective. But it is systematically organized and in this respect better than the alternative, which is sheer guesswork. One major requirement in assembling information is to ascertain whether spokesmen and sources accurately reflect the views of the people they speak for. This is one of the main considerations in favour of adopting a participative approach in the planning and implementation of change.

If a proposed change is clearly contrary to the interests of those affected by it, there is no point in trying to plan it on a participative basis as a mutual problem. People who stand to lose their jobs are only concerned with finding ways to block the change or, if that fails, with negotiating the best possible severance terms. This, of course, raises the possibility of offering guarantees of no job loss in connection with reorganization as a basis for eliciting the cooperation of employees and their willingness to participate in designing and implementing the change. A no-redundancy policy incurs obvious risks and is best suited to conditions where the level of activity is likely to remain buoyant; it could also give rise to an inappropriate labour force profile and to difficulties in recruiting younger people with new skills. On the other hand, it is a policy which some managements have successfully pursued in combination with careful manpower planning and agreements on flexible deployment between jobs. They claim that it provides significant benefits in terms of promoting a climate in which employees identify with management's objectives and of facilitating the process of adaptation to new requirements.

Where zero-sum bargaining is not involved and an integration of interests is possible, the involvement of people concerned in the design and implementation of a change will normally offer the best chance of success. One reason is that participation provides an opportunity for the rationale behind the proposed change to be explained and critically examined. This can help to lessen people's fears stemming from a lack of knowledge and a feeling of powerlessness. If people contribute actively towards establishing the new development this helps to create among them a degree of commitment to the change and to making it work. It has been found in American companies, for example, that the probability of operational research projects being successfully implemented is much higher when user departments are fully involved in their design and feel some sense of ownership over them than in situations where this degree of participation was absent.

A second consideration is that a great deal of the information required as a basis for planning a change—data on present problems, work activities, decision points, time cycles, files, costs, personnel and so forth—will only be known in detail to the people who are affected. Their participation is therefore necessary if the reorganization is to have a grounding in the realities of the situation. The implementation of Mary Parker Follett's (1941) 'Law of the Situation' requires participation, as she realized. Thirdly, the process of employee participation should assist managers to learn about their employees' attitudes, values and perceptions, and this learning experience should assist them to plan further necessary changes in ways that provoke less conflict. Equally, the chance to influence and understand structural change should create employee awareness of the need for frequent reorganization, and perhaps eventually a desire to take the initiative in this field through more far-reaching participative mechanisms such as planning agreements.

A participative approach, then, can be appropriate in introducing organizational change, and it offers the best prospects of developing an 'adaptive learning capacity' in organizations. Many people, the writer included, would also maintain that it is ethically the correct procedure for planning changes which affect other people. One can, however, expect too much from it, and I have already indicated the kind of conditions under which it may not work. Participation is a way of confronting the political issues involved in change, not a means of avoiding or smoothing over them. If there is a deep-seated conflict of interest between the parties involved in a proposed change, participation will probably not turn up a mutually acceptable solution. Also, if hidden anxieties and hostilities are present it may be necessary to introduce a skilled third party, a social consultant, to bring these into the open where they can be confronted and dissipated. So long as anxieties and conflicts are present, and not totally recognized, participation is likely to prove an unfruitful exercise.

A participative approach can be difficult for other reasons as well. It is usually very time-consuming, the more so in a large-scale organization where participation has to cross many hierarchical levels to link decisions on change initiated at a senior level to the people affected at a junior level. In some circumstances time may simply not be available, when a quick reaction to an unexpected event is required. Managers also make the point that time spent in discussion is time lost to getting on with the job. These are genuine difficulties, though they are to some extent exaggerated by a failure to anticipate new developments in advance so as to allow time for their discussion, rather than having to react at the last minute.

A further problem that is often raised concerns the apparent lack of interest among employees in participation—an unwillingness to devote the effort and share in the responsibility. It is true that some experiments in adopting an American democratic management style have not evoked a positive response in European countries such as Norway, where one direct replication of an American experiment was made (French et al. 1960). However, this does not indicate employee resistance to participation so much as the fact that in Europe this has traditionally been undertaken by union officers and local elected departmental representatives, rather than through direct personal relations with managers. I know of no evidence to indicate that members of organizations do not desire to enter discussions on matters of immediate relevance to their jobs and work, be this direct discussion or via representatives. In short, the participative approach to handling change is not an easy one, and is not always functional. For management, the consequences of refusing to participate can be most costly where people are in a position to resist or even sabotage change, but where they would be willing to go along with it constructively if consulted.

If considerable resistance to a proposed change is anticipated, and if it is possible to introduce it first of all on a limited basis, then the use of a 'pilot project' may be helpful. In a pilot project it is agreed that certain specific changes will be made to the existing organization on an experimental basis. After a given period, the change is evaluated on the understanding that it will be withdrawn if it is unsuccessful or unacceptable. This approach can have a number of advantages. A favourable situation can be selected for the pilot scheme, perhaps enlisting volunteers. This contributes to the eventual success of the change by getting it over the early period of trial and error in favourable circumstances. Less committed and confident members of the organization may be more prepared to accept the change once the scheme is completed, including managers who may be wary of committing resources to any new development until they can assess its effect.

Pilot projects do, however, carry risks. They prolong the period of uncertainty that accompanies any change, and if this is a source of considerable anxiety the result may be to increase rather than lessen hostility to the change. If the pilot scheme is located in too favourable an environment, it may not be possible to replicate any success it has across other parts of the organization. A pilot scheme which excludes people who are less receptive to change may also exclude those with power. Employee representatives are likely to be particularly cautious about proposed organizational changes because they have a responsibility to work out every possible ramification for their constituents' interests. For this reason it may not be easy to secure the open approval of employee representatives for a pilot scheme. Yet, paradoxically, by running a change as a pilot scheme, management are in effect placing it on a conditional basis. A change which managers may believe is vital to the continued effectiveness of the organization is in this way made subject to a legitimate, formal veto. Finally, given the inter-connectedness of functions and levels, it will in many situations be impossible to isolate a proposed change in organization and to pilot it on a limited experimental basis.

2 Time required

The implementation of organizational change, because it usually involves a threat to someone's position, is characteristically a lengthy process which is often punctuated by crises between the parties involved. These crises can be quite positive in their consequences since they bring opinions out into the open and make everyone face up to the issues. The participative and dis-cursive approach to implementing change is often considered a time-wasting process, especially by those who maintain that it would be better to decide on a change, impose it and 'be done with it'. Quite apart from the ethics of this, we have seen that resistance to change is likely to attend this kind of policy where employees have some degree of power, since people will mostly not accept authoritarianism as legitimate unless there is a real and obvious emergency on their hands. Hugh Marlow (1975), who has had a long experience of reorganization working for a company manufacturing and introducing computer systems and subsequently for a major consulting firm, has pointed out that the successful introduction of any change within organizations will take a long time. In his view, changes take place in four phases. These phases can be identified and defined separately, though they tend to overlap in practice. Marlow's opinion is that where reorganization has failed, this has usually been the result of management attempting to shorten or eliminate one or more of the following phases.

Phase 1—Personal acceptance This phase can take at least six months. It involves gaining acceptance by the people who are responsible for introducing an organizational change. More than just personal acceptance is involved here; it also includes acceptance of the function they belong to (systems team, organization department, etc.) or of their company if they are outside consultants.

Phase 2—Expression of resistance to change During this phase, which may last a further six months or so, underlying fears, hostilities and sus-picions regarding the proposed changes are brought into the open. Until such views and feelings are expressed openly, no matter how much infor-mation is given by management, it will not be accepted at its face value.

Phase 3—Identification with the objectives of the reorganization   It is at the beginning of this phase that the underlying fears encountered in Phase 2 are resolved. The people affected by the change can now begin to see the objectives of the change programme as their objectives and not something imposed on them by higher management. Practical steps towards achieving the objectives of the change can now start to be taken. This phase of active mutual effort towards implementing the change may last for some two years or so in Marlow's experience.

Phase 4—Building into the organization a facility for continuous critical appraisal   At this stage the reorganization is completed and it is being evaluated. The monitoring of the change and subsequent adjustments should help all concerned to recognize that some organizational modifications have to take place continually. Instead of management waiting until it is forced to adapt to changed circumstances, there could now be a conscious positive effort to anticipate and plan for change. This may become institutionalized in the form of an organization planning or development team. If this stage is reached it is likely to be some three years or so after the original reorganization was first mooted.

This time scale is lengthy indeed, and many managers I have spoken to reject it as being unrealistically so. Their problems will not wait that long. In practice, a minor reorganization, perhaps establishing a new co-ordinative mechanism such as a regular meeting or a new communications procedure, will take nowhere as long to plan and implement. A major change such as divisionalization, however, could take as long as Marlow suggests. Of course, it might be possible to force through even a major reorganization much faster than this, but with greater risk of disruption (e.g. a strike) and of details not being thoroughly worked out. Once an organization has experienced a structural change, it should be possible to reduce drastically the time scale of receptiveness to change, so long as the process of critical problem examination and discussion of possible organizational solutions is maintained. While there is no sense in advocating change for change's sake, it will help a management facing the need for frequent adjustments of structure if it can make the process of adjustment and reorganization part of the accepted mode of maintaining long-term equilibrium, rather than introducing change as a relatively infrequent and therefore more traumatic experience. The former approach shortens the time it takes to implement reorganization and also offers a facility for identifying needs for organizational change earlier rather than later.

3 Use of third parties

The term 'third party' in the context of organizational change refers to any individual or group who assists in the process of diagnosing problems and implementing solutions, but who is not part of the organization system directly involved in change. Third parties could be outside commercial consultants, academic staff, or members of an organization's development team. The benefits which they can bring include the contribution of analytical technique and experience developed elsewhere, an ability to assist in the resolution of conflicting views by standing outside the conflict, and the acceptability of their advice by virtue of their image as experts and (especially in the case of academics) by virtue of their relatively neutral position with respect to organizational politics. For reasons such as these, third parties are frequently asked to assist in organizational changes.

The involvement of third parties can create certain problems. Commercial consultants are usually perceived by employees as being committed to top management interests alone, by virtue of their fee payment. There is also some temptation for consultants to apply a standard solution to organizational problems. This is partly because their experience lies largely in the application of standard techniques, and partly because the costs of consultancy can only be borne over a limited time so that a reasonably quick solution is called for. Standardized approaches, however, go against the contingency approach and they are unlikely to be in tune with the unique culture of a particular organization. If management is to engage commercial consultants in the field of organizational change it would be well advised to ensure that solutions are not decided upon at the outset, or to the exclusion of other groups concerned in the change.

The staff of management schools are potentially in a better position to enter into long-term collaborative relationships with organizations, and to extend this collaboration over the period of diagnosing and implementing change. It is easier for them to undertake the role of action researcher, which devotes some time to the formation of a consensus on the direction of change through research, feedback and mutual discussion. The typical sequence of events in an action research approach to organizational change would be: (a) research is carried out to provide data for problem diagnosis; (b) this is fed back to relevant management and employee groups; (c) the feedback is evaluated by all concerned; (d) there is then discussion with the researchers regarding options for action; (e) a decision is made on what action to take and a change is made. The effects of the change can then be further investigated by the researcher (possibly doing this together with people from the organization). There is further feedback, discussion and the cycle continues. The research and feedback stages of the cycle are likely to identify problems and create an awareness of their existence in people's minds—roughly equivalent to going through the first two stages in Marlow's scheme. Discussion of options for action is likely to promote a sense of 'ownership' of the change project and identification with the objectives of the change which are indeed being clarified by the discussion itself (equivalent to Marlow's stage three).

If the organization is large enough to employ its own internal organizational planning and development teams, or internal consulting teams, then they may be able to play the part of action researcher instead. They have, of course, to gain credibility and to be seen as performing a relatively neutral service role. They may also have to rely on outside help for advice on techniques such as those of survey analysis. Internal consultants will, however, enjoy considerable familiarity with the organization's background and management will find them easier to programme than outsiders.

Action research is a lengthy process, and careful control has to be retained over the programming of feedback reports and discussions if valuable time is not to be lost and expectations within the organization disappointed. Management school staff have other demands upon their time, and may not be able to provide the intensity of commitment that is required. Another point is that, while such staff with their professional academic standing are more likely to be seen as 'neutral' to the political issues within an organization, the price of this independence may be that the academic feels free to import values of his own into the organization. Managers and employees alike should ascertain what they are taking on when the third party is an independent academic for there is a considerable variation in their values and approaches. Some go so far as to see action research as a means of subverting what they believe are oppressive and exploitative bureaucratic institutions. Others appear to limit themselves purely to a top management perspective, which is also a limitation of their potential contribution as 'third parties' and facilitators of the organizational change process. Many management school staff are, on the other hand, sensitive to the difficulties of playing a role which inevitably brings them into organizational and industrial politics, but feel nevertheless that they have an obligation to offer their services as best they can and to apply their knowledge to practical use.

Bearing in mind that organizational change must gain the positive commitment and understanding of those who have to live with the new arrangements and make them work, it is appropriate that third parties adopt a role which facilitates this. In other words, they are not required to solve organizational problems. Rather, they are required to collaborate with the parties immediately involved in reaching their own solution through activities such as advising on surveys of attitudes, helping people to establish constructive working relationships and promoting the open confrontation of conflicts. Those with experience in this field have pointed out that there are situations in which progress can be made by the third party himself taking on the role of expert problem solver, when for instance a technical matter is concerned. It has even been suggested that a dominant role, backed by top management, can speed up the progress of change. While it is true that to be effective a third party must have some influence, the adoption of a leading or dominant role is unlikely to prove an effective general strategy. Apart from the ethical considerations of power without responsibility, such roles can engender an undue dependence upon the third party. A successful implementation of organizational change in the long-run requires that the people concerned participate actively in the process of working out the new arrangements both as a learning experience and as a basis for generating their personal commitment to the change.

The relationship between third parties and members of an organization is therefore not easy to manage. There may be a difference of values and language, different ways of working, different time perspectives. These are compounded when the technical training of the people concerned also varies, as with a behavioural scientist working with engineers on a change in job design, or an organizational expert working with accountants on a change in control procedures. Integration into an effective team can be difficult, but this difficulty is a price to be paid for bringing together the people best suited to doing the detailed work on a complex change which involves many different technical facets.

4 A summary of general considerations in implementing reorganization

Whatever the ethical and ideological attractions of participation, there are only some situations in which it is likely to succeed as a means of implementing organizational change. Managers will in any case tend to enter into participation with some reluctance because it can be slow and personally bruising. With this situational approach in mind, a number of writers have developed a contingency analysis in order to identify the conditions under which they would recommend managers to pluck up courage and embark upon a process of consultation and participation as the appropriate means for facilitating the introduction of change. Earlier in this chapter I commented briefly on the kind of situation in which the participative approach is likely to have a good chance of success. Combining the threads of this discussion with points which other writers have raised, it is possible to set out the following list of conditions which favour the use of the participative approach. Their absence will encourage managers to use a top-down directive approach instead:

(1) there is no definite time limit on when the reorganization has to be completed—the situation is not urgent and the organization's survival is not at stake;
(2) management anticipates that it will require information from members of the organization to help design the change, as well as their commitment in order to make the new organization operate effectively;
(3) the need for change is not widely or clearly recognized throughout the organization;
(4) the members of the organization expect to be involved in discussions prior to any change—this has become part of the organization's culture;
(5) some resistance to the proposed reorganization is anticipated but it is not likely to challenge the underlying objective of the proposal;
(6) the power of the initiator of reorganization is limited vis-à-vis other groups, without being wholly constrained.

On the basis of studies that have been conducted into success and failure in organizational and workplace change, it is also possible to offer some tentative guidelines to the operative factors. These assume that the proposed change will not simply be regarded by employees in zero-sum terms and implacably opposed. Given that assumption, it appears that reorganization has a better chance of success when the following conditions apply:

(a) The change has the support and understanding of top management, or at least of one influential manager if we are talking of a localized change only. It is therefore treated as a mainstream rather than a peripheral activity.

(b) The change is preceded by a careful diagnosis of the existing situation in order to ascertain the nature and level of the problem, and to isolate the organizational features which are contributing to it.

(c) There is discussion of the problem and possible lines of action with all groups who will be affected, and a willingness to adapt any plans in the light of this discussion.

(d) Partly based on the information gained from participation in discussions, there is an attempt to assess how receptive people are likely to be to the proposed change and to different modes of implementation. This assessment is allowed to influence judgement of how to proceed, and what direct effects or side-effects to expect at each stage.

(e) Training and personal development requirements connected with the change are satisfied before rather than after the event. The staff concerned with carrying through the change are adequately educated and equipped. Not least, senior management is given an understanding of the problems and duration of change so that it appreciates what is likely to happen, and can be quite clear as to the probable costs as well as benefits.

(f) A clear understanding is reached between all parties involved in discussion of the change and any third party, of what the latter's role is expected to be. The momentum of third-party contributions is sustained and these are treated as an integral part of the change process.

(g) Attention is given to a systematic monitoring and evaluation of the change and its effects. This is used as a basis for modification when necessary.

Suggested further reading

The Addison-Wesley Publishing Company's series on Organization Development includes what are still some of the most useful short volumes on the issues raised in this chapter: in particular, R. J. C. Roeber, *The Organization in a Changing Environment* (1973), Richard Beckhard, *Organization Development: Strategies and Models* (1969) and Paul R. Lawrence and Jay W. Lorsch, *Developing Organizations: Diagnosis and Action* (1969). E. A. Johns, *The Sociology of Organizational Change* (Pergamon 1973) provides a good coverage of research findings on problems of changing organization and is well illustrated with case studies. Newton Margulies and John Wallace, *Organizational Change: Techniques and Applications* (Scott, Foresman 1973) examine relevant techniques in some detail. Gerald Zaltman and Robert Duncan, *Strategies for Planned Change* (Wiley 1977) provides a good practical review, especially on resistance to change and on the role of change agent.

In recent years there has been a greater appreciation of the political processes involved in the negotiation of reorganization and in resistance to it. Ian Mangham, *The Politics of Organizational Change* (Associated Business Press 1979) develops a 'micropolitical perspective'. Tony J. Watson, 'Group Ideologies and Organizational Change', *Journal of Management Studies*, July 1982 analyses the way in which various interests were articulated and mobilized in the case of a major organizational change in an engineering company. In the public sector, Donald P. Warwick, *A Theory of Public Bureaucracy* (Harvard University Press 1975) provides an insightful analysis of successful resistance to change in the US State Department and in so doing enhances our understanding of the workings of bureaucracy. Nicole Woolsey Biggart, 'The Creative-Destructive Process of Organizational Change: The Case of the Post Office', *Administrative Science Quarterly*, September 1977 provides another example of the political process of reorganization in the public sector.

Peter A. Clark examines the role of behavioural scientists as third parties contributing to planned organizational change in his *Action Research and Organizational Change* (Harper and Row 1972). Lisl Klein, *A Social Scientist in Industry* (Gower Press 1976) records the experience of a behavioural scientist attempting to promote change within the large organization that employed her. Hugh Marlow, *Managing Change: A Strategy for Our Time* (Institute of Personnel Management, London 1975) draws upon the author's wide experience and in particular calls attention to the time scale of the change process.

Reference was also made in this chapter to Warren Bennis, *Organization Development* (Addison-Wesley 1969); J. R. P. French, J. Israel and D. As, 'An Experiment on Participation in a Norwegian Factory', *Human Relations*, February 1960; Tom Lupton, 'The Practical Analysis of Change in Organization', *Journal of Management Studies*, May 1965; Ian L. Mangham, D. Shaw and B. Wilson, *Managing Change* (British Institute of Management, London 1972), which is a practical guide with examples drawn from the ICI Petrochemicals Division; H. C. Metcalf and L. Urwick (editors), *Dynamic Administration: the Collected Papers of Mary Parker Follett*, (Pitman 1941); and Robert S. Toronto, 'A General Systems Model for the Analysis of Organizational Change', *Behavioural Science*, vol. 20, 1975.

BIBLIOGRAPHY

ABERNATHY, W. J., CLARK, K. B. and KANTROW, A. M. (1983) *Industrial Renaissance: Producing a Competitive Future for America*. Basic Books.

AGUILAR, F. J. (1967) *Scanning the Business Environment*. Macmillan.

ALLEN, S. A. (1978) Organizational Choices and General Management Influence Networks in Divisionalized Companies. *Academy of Management Journal*, September.

ARGYRIS, C. (1957) *Personality and Organization*. Harper and Row.

ARGYRIS, C. (1976) Single-Loop and Double-Loop Models in Research on Decision Making. *Administrative Science Quarterly*, September.

ARVEY, R. D. and IVANCEVICH, J. M. (1980) Punishment in Organizations: A Review, Propositions and Research Suggestions. *Academy of Management Review*, January.

BAILEY, J. (1983) *Job Design and Work Organization*. Prentice-Hall.

BAKER, J. (1978) Keeping Wheels Turning. *Accounting Age*, 24 February.

BANNON, L., BARRY, U. and HOLST, O. (editors) (1982) *Information Technology. Impact on the Way of Life*. Tycooly Publishing.

BARKDULL, C. W. (1963) Span of Control: A Method of Evaluation. *Michigan Business Review*, 15.

BECKHARD, R. (1969) *Organization Development: Strategies and Models*. Addison-Wesley.

BENNIS, W. (1969) *Organization Development*. Addison-Wesley.

BERG, M. (1980) *The Machinery Question and the Making of Political Economy 1815–1848*. Cambridge University Press.

BERRIDGE, J. (1980) Changing Complex Information Systems: Medical Records at Anersley Hospital. In *Systems Organization: The Management of Complexity*, Block 3 'Organizations'. The Open University Press.

BESSANT, J. (1982) *Microprocessors in Production Processes*. Policy Studies Institute, London.

BEYNON, H. (1983) *Working for Ford*. 2nd edition. Penguin.

BIGGART, N. W. (1977) The Creative-Destructive Process of Organizational Change: The Case of the Post Office. *Administrative Science Quarterly*, September.

BJORN-ANDERSEN, N., HEDBERG, B., MERCER, D., MUMFORD, E. and SOLE, A. (editors) (1979) *The Impact of Systems Change in Organizations*. Sijthoff and Noordhoff.

BLAU, P. M. (1955) *The Dynamics of Bureaucracy*. University of Chicago Press.

BLAU, P. and MEYER, M. W. (1971) *Bureaucracy in Modern Society*. 2nd edition. Random House.

BOSWELL, J. (1972) *The Rise and Decline of Small Firms in Britain*. Allen and Unwin.

BOWEY, A. M. (editor) (1982) *Handbook of Salary and Wage Systems*. 2nd edition. Gower Press.

BROWN, W. (Lord) (1962) *Piecework Abandoned: The Effect of Wage Incentive Systems on Managerial Authority*. Heinemann.

BRUNS, W. J. Jnr. and WATERHOUSE, J. H. (1975) Budgetary Control and Organization Structure. *Journal of Accounting Research*, Autumn.

BUCHANAN, D. A. and BODDY, D. (1983) *Organizations in the Computer Age*. Gower.

BURBRIDGE, J. L. (1981) Britain's Counter-productive Plants. *Management Today*, November.

BURNS, T. and STALKER, G. M. (1961) *The Management of Innovation*. Tavistock.

CADBURY, Sir A. (1983) Cadbury Schweppes – More than Chocolate and Tonic. *Harvard Business Review*, January–February.

CAMERON, K. S. and WHETTEN, D. A. (editors) (1983) *Organizational Effectiveness*. Academic Press.

CAPLAN, R. D. et al. (1975) *Job Demands and Worker Health*. US Department of Health, Education and Welfare.

CARLISLE, H. M. (1974) A Contingency Approach to Decentralization. *Advanced Management Journal*, July.

CHANDLER, A. D. Jnr. (1962) *Strategy and Structure*. MIT Press.

CHANDLER, A. D. Jnr. and DAEMS, H. (1979) Administrative Coordination, Allocation and Monitoring. *Accounting, Organizations and Society*, 4.

CHANNON, D. F. (1973) *The Strategy and Structure of British Enterprise*. Macmillan.

CHANNON, D. F. (1978) *The Service Industries*. Macmillan.

CHILD, J. (1970) More Myths of Management Organization? *Journal of Management Studies*, October.

CHILD, J. (1973) Predicting and Understanding Organization Structure. *Administrative Science Quarterly*, June.

CHILD, J. (1974) Managerial and Organizational Factors Associated with Company Performance. *Journal of Management Studies*, October.

CHILD, J. (1974) What Determines Organization Performance? The Universals vs. the It-All-Depends. *Organizational Dynamics*, Summer.

CHILD, J. (1975) Managerial and Organizational Factors Associated with Company

Performance – Part II A Contingency Analysis. *Journal of Management Studies*, February.

CHILD, J. (1978) The 'Non-productive' Component within the Productive Sector: A Problem of Management Control. In Fores and Glover (editors) (1978).

CHILD, J. (1978) The Myth at Lordstown. *Management Today*, October.

CHILD, J. (1982) Professionals in the Corporate World: Values, Interests and Control. In Dunkerley and Salaman (editors) (1982).

CHILD, J. (editor) (1973) *Man and Organization*. Allen and Unwin.

CHILD, J. and KIESER, A. (1979) Organization and Managerial Roles in British and German Companies. In Lammers and Hickson (editors) (1979).

CHILD, J. and KIESER, A. (1981) Development of Organizations over Time. In Nystrom and Starbuck (editors) (1981) vol. 1.

CHILD, J. and MACMILLAN, B. (1972) Managerial Leisure in British and American Contexts. *Journal of Management Studies*, May.

CHILD, J. and PARTRIDGE, B. (1982) *Lost Managers: Supervisors in Industry and Society*. Cambridge University Press.

CHILD, J. and TAYEB, M. (1982) Theoretical Perspectives in Cross-National Organizational Research. *International Studies of Management and Organization*, Winter.

CHILD, J., FORES, M., GLOVER, I. and LAWRENCE, P. (1983) A Price to Pay? Professionalism and Work Organization in Britain and West Germany. *Sociology*, February.

CLARK, A. (1972) *Organizational Design: Theory and Practice*. Tavistock.

CLARK, P. A. (1972) *Action Research and Organizational Change*. Harper and Row.

CLAWSON, D. (1980) *Bureaucracy and the Labor Process*. Monthly Review Press.

COREY, R. and STAR, S. H. (1971) *Organization Strategy*. Harvard Business School.

COUNCIL FOR SCIENCE AND SOCIETY (1981) *New Technology: Society, Employment and Skill*. CSS, London.

DALTON, G. W., LAWRENCE, P. R. and LORSCH, J. W. (editors) (1970) *Organization Structure and Design*. Irwin-Dorsey.

DANIEL, W. W. (1973) Understanding Employee Behaviour in its Context. In Child (editor) (1973).

DAVIS, L. (1979) Optimizing Organization-Plant Design: A Complementary Structure for Technical and Social Systems. *Organizational Dynamics*, Autumn.

DAVIS, L. and TAYLOR, J. (1972, 1979) *The Design of Jobs*. 1st edition Penguin, 1972; 2nd edition Goodyear, 1979.

DAVIS, R. C. (1951) *The Fundamentals of Top Management*. Harper.

DAVIS, S. M. and LAWRENCE, P. R. (1977) *Matrix*. Addison-Wesley.

DEWAR, R. D. and SIMET, D. P. (1981) A Level-Specific Prediction of Spans of Control Examining the Effects of Size, Technology and Specialization. *Academy of Management Journal*, March.

DICKSON, J. W. (1981) Participation as a Means of Organizational Control. *Journal of Management Studies*, April.

DONALDSON, L. (1979) Regaining Control at Nipont. *Journal of General Management*, Summer.

DONALDSON, L. (1983) Explaining Structural Change in Organizations. Unpublished paper, Australian Graduate School of Management, Kensington, N.S.W.

DONALDSON, L. and LYNN, R. (1976) The Conflict Resolution Process. *Personnel Review*, Spring.

DRUCKER, P. (1974) New Templates for Today's Organizations. *Harvard Business Review*, January–February.

DUBOIS, P. (1981) Workers' Control over the Organization of Work: French and English Maintenance Workers In Mass Production Industry. *Organization Studies*, No. 2/4.

DUNBAR, R. L. M. (1981) Designs for Organizational Control. In Nystrom and Starbuck (editors) (1981).

DUNCAN, D., GRUNEBERG, M. M. and WALLIS, D. (editors) (1980) *Changes in Working Life*. Wiley.

DUNCAN, R. B. (1973) Multiple Decision-Making Structures in Adapting to Environmental Uncertainty: The Impact on Organizational Effectiveness. *Human Relations*, 26.

DUNKERLEY, D. and SALAMAN, G. (editors) (1982) *The International Yearbook of Organization Studies 1981*. Routledge and Kegan Paul.

DYAS, G. P. and THANHEISER, H. T. (1976) *The Emerging European Enterprise*. Macmillan.

DYER, W. G. (1977) *Team Building: Issues and Alternatives*. Addison-Wesley.

ECONOMIST INTELLIGENCE UNIT (1982) *Chips in Industry*. EIU, London.

EDSTROM, A. and GALBRAITH, J. R. (1977) Transfer of Managers as a Coordination and Control Strategy in Multinational Organizations. *Administrative Science Quarterly*, June.

EDWARDS, J. et al. (editors) (1983) *Manpower Strategy and Techniques in an Organizational Context*. Wiley.

EDWARDS, R. (1979) *Contested Terrain: The Transformation of the Workplace in the Twentieth Century*. Basic Books/Heinemann.

EQUAL OPPORTUNITIES COMMISSION (1980) *The Impact of Telecommunications and Information Technology on Equal Opportunities*, EOC, London.

FAYOL, H. (1949) *General and Industrial Management*. Pitman.

FILLEY, A. C. (1975) *Interpersonal Conflict Resolution*. Scott, Foresman.

FILLEY, A. C., HOUSE, R. J. and KERR, S. (1976) *Managerial Process and Organizational Behaviour* 2nd edition. Scott, Foresman.

FLAMHOLTZ, E. (1979) Behavioral Aspects of Accounting Control Systems. In Kerr (editor) (1979).

FOLLET, M. P. (1947) *see* Metcalf and Urwick.

FORES, M. and GLOVER, I. (editors) (1978) *Manufacturing and Management.* HMSO.

FORESTER, T. (editor) (1980) *The Microelectronics Revolution.* Blackwell/MIT Press.

FRANKO, L. G. (1976) *The European Multinationals.* Harper and Row.

FRASER, R. (editor) (1968) *Work: Twenty Personal Accounts.* Penguin.

FREEMAN, C. et al. (1982) *Unemployment and Technical Innovation.* Frances Pinter.

FREEMAN, C. et al. (1972) *Success and Failure in Industrial Innovation.* University of Sussex Science Policy Research Unit.

FRENCH, J. R. P., ISRAEL, J. and AS, D. (1960) An Experiment on Participation in a Norwegian Factory. *Human Relations,* February.

FRIEDMAN, A. L. (1977) *Industry and Labour.* Macmillan.

GALBRAITH, J. R. (1973) *Designing Complex Organizations.* Addison-Wesley.

GALBRAITH, J. R. (1977) *Organization Design.* Addison-Wesley.

GEERAERTS, G. (1983) The Effect of Ownership on Organization Structure in Small Firms. Unpublished paper, University of Tilburg.

GERSHURY, J. and MILES, I. (1983) *The New Service Economy.* Frances Pinter.

GOGGIN, W. C. (1974) How the Multinational Structure Works at Dow Corning. *Harvard Business Review,* January–February.

GOODMAN, P. S., PENNINGS, J. M. et al. (editors) (1977) *New Perspectives on Organizational Effectiveness.* Jossey-Bass.

GRAICUNAS, V. A. (1937) Relationship in Organization. In Gulick and Urwick (editors) (1937).

GREENWOOD, R. G. (1974) *Managerial Decentralization.* Lexington Books.

GRINYER, P. H. and KESSLER, S. (1967) The Systematic Evaluation of Methods of Wage Payment. *Journal of Management Studies,* October.

GRINYER, P. H., YASAI-ARDEKANI, M. and AL-BAZZAZ, S. (1980) Strategy, Structure, the Environment, and Financial Performance in 48 United Kingdom Companies. *Academy of Management Journal,* June.

GULICK, L. and URWICK, L. (editors) (1937) *Papers in the Science of Administration.* Columbia University Press.

HACKMAN, J. R. (1975) On the Coming Demise of Job Enrichment. In *Man and Work in Society.* Van Nostrand Reinhold.

HACKMAN, J. R. and OLDHAM, G. R. (1980) *Work Redesign.* Addison-Wesley.

HACKMAN, J. R., PEARCE, J. L. and WOLFF, J. C. (1978) Effects of Changes in Job Characteristics on Work Attitudes and Behaviors. *Organizational Behavior and Human Performance,* 21.

HACKMAN, J. R. and SUTTLE, J. L. (editors) (1977) *Improving Life at Work.* Goodyear.

HANDY, C. (1982) Where Management is Leading. *Management Today,* December.

HARASZTI, M. (1977) *A Worker in a Worker's State*. Penguin.

HERON, R. P. and FRIESEN, D. (1976) Organizational Growth and Development. *University of Alberta, Edmonton, Working Paper*, March.

HERZBERG, F., MAUSNER, B. and SNYDERMAN, B. B. (1959) *The Motivation to Work*. Wiley.

HOFSTEDE, G. and SAMI KASSEM, M. (editors) (1976) *European Contributions to Organization Theory*. Van Gorcum.

INCOME DATA SERVICES (1980) *Changing Technology*. IDS Study No. 220.

INTERNATIONAL DATA CORPORATION (1983) The Impact of IT. *Management Today*, June.

INTERNATIONAL LABOUR OFFICE (1975) *Final Report on a Study of the Effects of Group Production Methods on the Humanization of Work*. ILO.

INTERNATIONAL LABOUR OFFICE (1979) *New Forms of Work Organization*. ILO.

JAQUES, E. (1956) *Measurement of Responsibility*. Tavistock.

JAQUES, E. (1976) *A General Theory of Bureaucracy*. Heinemann.

JOHNS, E. A. (1973) *The Sociology of Organizational Change*. Pergamon.

KELLY, J. E. (1980) The Costs of Job Redesign: A Preliminary Analysis. *Industrial Relations Journal*, 11.

KELLY, J. E. (1982) *Scientific Management, Job Redesign and Work Performance*. Academic Press.

KELLY, J. E. and CLEGG, C. W. (editors) (1981) *Autonomy and Control at the Workplace*. Croom Helm.

KERR, S. (1975) On the Folly of Rewarding A, While Hoping for B. *Academy of Management Journal*, December.

KERR, S. (editor) (1979) *Organizational Behavior*. Grid.

KERR, S. and SLOCUM, J. W. Jnr. (1981) Controlling the Performances of People in Organizations. In Nystrom and Starbuck (editors) (1981).

KHANDWALLA, P. N. (1973) Viable and Effective Organizational Design of Firms. *Academy of Management Journal*. September.

KHANDWALLA, P. N. (1974) Mass Output Orientation of Operations Technology and Organizational Structure, *Administrative Science Quarterly*, March.

KLEIN, L. (1976) *A Social Scientist in Industry*. Gower Press.

KNIGHT, K. (editor) (1977) *Matrix Management*. Gower Press.

KOLODNY, H. F. (1979) Evolution to a Matrix Organization. *Academy of Management Review*, 4.

KOTTER, J. P., SCHLESINGER, L. A. and SATHE, V. (1979) *Organization*. Irwin.

LAMMERS, C. J. and HICKSON, D. J. (editors) (1979) *Organizations: Like and Unlike*. Routledge and Kegan Paul.

LAWLER, E. E. (1971) *Pay and Organizational Effectiveness*. McGraw-Hill.

LAWLER, E. E. (1977) Reward Systems, In Hackman and Suttle (editors) (1977).

LAWLER, E. E. and RHODE, J. R. (1976) *Information and Control in Organizations.* Goodyear.

LAWRENCE, P. R. and LORSCH, J. W. (1967) *Organization and Environment.* Harvard Business School.

LAWRENCE, P. R. and LORSCH, J. W. (1969) *Developing Organizations: Diagnosis and Action.* Addison-Wesley.

LENIN, V. I. (1918) The Immediate Tasks of the Soviet Government. Reprinted in *On the Development of Heavy Industry and Electrification.* Progress Publishers 1962.

LENZ, R. T. (1980) Environment, Strategy, Organization Structure and Performance: Patterns in One Industry. *Strategic Management Journal,* July–September.

LIKERT, R. (1961) New Patterns of Management. McGraw-Hill.

LITTLER, C. R. (1982) *The Development of the Labour Process in Capitalist Societies.* Heinemann.

LITTLER, C. R. and SALAMAN, G. (1982) Bravermania and Beyond: Recent Theories of the Labour Process. *Sociology,* May.

LOCKE, E. A., FEREN, D. B., McCALEB, V. M., SHAW, K. and DENNY, A. T. (1980) The Relative Effectiveness of Four Methods of Motivating Employee Performance. In Duncan, Gruneberg and Wallis (editors) (1980).

LORSCH, J. W. (1970) Introduction to the Structural Design of Organizations. In Dalton, Lawrence and Lorsch (editors) (1970).

LORSCH, J. W. and ALLEN, S. A. (1973) *Diversity and Interdependence.* Harvard Business School.

LORSCH, J. W. and LAWRENCE, P. R. (editors) (1970) *Studies in Organizational Design.* Irwin-Dorsey.

LORSCH, J. W. and MORSE, J. J. (1974) *Organizations and their Members.* Harper and Row.

LOVERIDGE, R. (1983) Labour Market Segmentation and the Firm. In Edwards et al. (editors) (1983).

LUPTON, T. (1963) *On the Shop Floor.* Pergamon.

LUPTON, T. (1965) The Practical Analysis of Change in Organization. *Journal of Management Studies,* May.

LUPTON, T. and GOWLER, D. (1969) *Selecting a Wage Payment System.* Kogan Page.

MACHIN, J. L. J. (1979) A Contingent Methodology for Management Control. *Journal of Management Studies,* February.

MANGHAM, I. (1979) *The Politics of Organizational Change.* Associated Business Press.

MANGHAM, I. L., SHAW, D. and WILSON, B. (1972) *Managing Change.* British Institute of Management, London.

MARGULIES, N. and WALLACE, J. (1973) *Organizational Change: Techniques and Applications.* Scott, Foresman.

MARLOW, H. (1975) *Managing Change: A Strategy for Our Time.* Institute of Personnel Management, London.

MARTI, J. and ZEILINGER, A. (1982) *Micros and Money.* Policy Studies Institute, London.

MASLOW, A. H. (1970) *Motivation and Personality.* Revised edition. Harper and Row.

MCCAN, J. and GALBRAITH, J. R. (1981) Interdepartmental Relations. In Nystrom and Starbuck (editors) (1981).

METCALF, H. C. and URWICK, L. (editors) (1941) *Dynamic Administration: The Collected Papers of Mary Parker Follett.* Pitman.

MILLER, D. (1981) Towards a New Contingency Approach: The Search for Organizational Gestalts. *Journal of Management Studies,* January.

MILLER, D. (1982) Evolution and Revolution: A Quantum View of Structural Change in Organizations. *Journal of Management Studies,* April.

MILLER, E. J. (1975) Sociotechnical Systems in Weaving, 1953–70: a Follow-up Study. *Human Relations,* **28.**

MILLER, P. (1982) The Rewards of Executive Incentives. *Management Today,* May.

MINTZBERG, H. (1973) *The Nature of Managerial Work.* Harper and Row.

MINTZBERG, H. (1979) *The Structuring of Organizations.* Prentice-Hall.

MINTZBERG, H. (1983) *Structure in Fives: Designing Effective Organizations.* Prentice-Hall.

NEGANDHI, A. and REIMANN, C. (1973) Task Environment, Decentralization and Organizational Effectiveness. *Human Relations,* **26.**

NORTHCOTT, J. and ROGERS, P. (1982) *Microelectronics in Industry: What's Happening in Britain?* Policy Studies Institute, London.

NYSTROM, P. C. and STARBUCK, W. H. (editors) (1981) *Handbook of Organizational Design,* (2 vols) Oxford University Press.

OLDHAM, G. R. and HACKMAN, J. R. (1980) Work Design in the Organizational Context. In Staw and Cummings (editors) (1980).

OTLEY, D. T. (1980) The Contingency Theory of Management Accounting: Achievement and Prognosis. *Accounting, Organizations and Society,* **5,** 4.

OUCHI, W. G. (1977) The Relationship Between Organizational Structure and Organizational Control. *Administrative Science Quarterly,* March.

OUCHI, W. G. (1978) The Transmission of Control Through Organizational Hierarchy. *Academy of Management Journal,* June.

OUCHI, W. G. and PRICE, R. L. (1978) Hierarchies, Clans and Theory Z. *Organizational Dynamics,* Autumn.

PARKINSON, C. NORTHCOTE (1958) *Parkinson's Law or the Pursuit of Progress.* John Murray.

PENNINGS, J. M. (1975) The Relevance of the Structural-Contingency Model for Organizational Effectiveness. *Administrative Science Quarterly,* September.

PETERS, T. J. and WATERMAN, R. H. Jnr. (1982) *In Search of Excellence.* Harper and Row.

PETTIGREW, A. M. (1975) Strategic Aspects of the Management of Specialist Activity. *Personnel Review,* 4.

PFEFFER, J. (1978) *Organizational Design.* AHM Publishing Corporation.

PIPER, J. A. (1980) Determinants of Financial Control Systems for Multiple Retailers – Some Case Study Evidence. *Managerial Finance,* 6.

PORTER, L. W. and LAWLER, E. E. (1968) *Managerial Attitudes and Performance.* Irwin.

PUGH, D. (1979) Effective Coordination in Organizations. *Advanced Management Journal,* Winter.

REIMANN, B. and INZERILLI, G. (1979) A Comparative Analysis of Empirical Research on Technology and Structure. *Journal of Management,* 5.

ROBEY, D. (1977) Computers and Management Structure: Some Empirical Findings Re-examined. *Human Relations,* 30.

ROBEY, D. (1982) *Designing Organizations: A Macro Perspective.* Irwin.

ROEBER, R. J. C. (1973) *The Organization in a Changing Environment.* Addison-Wesley.

ROWBOTTOM, R. and BILLIS, D. (1977) The Stratification of Work and Organizational Design. *Human Relations,* 30.

RUMELT, R. P. (1974) *Strategy, Structure and Economic Performance.* Harvard Business School.

RUMELT, R. P. (1981) The Electronic Reorganization of Industry. Paper presented to the Conference of the Strategic Management Society, London, October.

SADLER, P., WEBB, T. and LANSLEY, P. (1974) *Management Style and Organization Structure in the Smaller Enterprise.* Ashridge College, Management Research Unit.

SALAMAN, G. (1979) *Work Organization: Resistance and Control.* Longman.

SCHOLZ, L. and WOLFF, H. (1981) *Limits of Conventional Theories and New Approaches for Theoretical and Empirical Investigations.* EEC Brussels, September.

SCOTT, B. R. (1971) *Strategies of Corporate Development.* Harvard Business School.

SHELDON, A. (1980) Organizational Paradigms: A Theory of Organizational Change. *Organizational Dynamics,* Winter.

SLEIGH, J. et al. (1979) *The Manpower Implications of Micro-electronic Technology.* HMSO.

SLOAN, A. P. (1967) *My Years with General Motors.* Pan Books.

STAW, B. M. and CUMMINGS, L. L. (editors) (1980) *Research in Organizational Behaviour* vol. 2. JAI Press.

STIEGLITZ, H. (1962) Optimizing Span of Control. *Management Record,* September.

STOPFORD, J. M. and WELLS, L. T. Jnr. (1972) *Managing the Multinational Enterprise.* Longman.

STOREY, J. (1983) *Managerial Prerogative and the Question of Control.* Routledge and Kegan Paul.

STRAUSS, G. (1962) Tactics of Lateral Relationship: The Purchasing Agent. *Administrative Science Quarterly,* September.

SUOJANEN, W. W. (1955) The Span of Control – Fact or Fable? *Advanced Management,* **20.**

SWEDISH EMPLOYERS' CONFEDERATION (English translation 1975) *Job Reform in Sweden.* Swedish Employers' Confederation.

SYKES, A. J. M. and BATES, J. (1962) Study of Conflict Between Formal Company Policy and the Interests of Informal Groups. *Sociological Review,* November.

THOMPSON, J. D. (1967) *Organizations in Action.* McGraw-Hill

THORSUD, E. (1976) Democratization of Work as a Process of Change Towards Non-Bureaucratic Types of Organization. In Hostede and Sami Kassem (editors) (1976).

TORONTO, R. S. (1975) A General Systems Model for the Analysis of Organizational Change. *Behavioural Science,* **20.**

TOWNSEND, R. (1970) *Up the Organization.* Michael Joseph.

TRIST, E. (1981) *The Evolution of Socio-Technical Systems.* Ontario Quality of Working Life Centre, Toronto, Occasional Paper No. 2. Also appears as Chapter 2 in Van de Ven and Joyce (editors) (1981).

UDELL, J. (1967) An Empirical Test of Hypotheses Relating to Span of Control. *Administrative Science Quarterly,* December.

URWICK, L. (1956) The Span of Control – Some Facts about the Fables. *Advanced Management,* **21.**

VAN DE VEN, A. H. and JOYCE, W. F. (editors) (1981) *Perspectives on Organization Design and Behavior.* Wiley.

VAN DE VEN, A. H., DELBECQ, A. L. and KOENIG, R. Jnr. (1976) Determinants of Coordination Modes Within Organizations. *American Sociological Review,* April.

VANCIL, R. F. (1973) What kind of Management Control Do You Need? *Harvard Business Review,* March–April.

VERNON-HARCOURT, A. (1982, Revised annually) *Rewarding Management .* Gower Press.

WALKER, A. H. and LORSCH, J. W. (1968) Organizational Choice: Product vs. Function. *Harvard Business Review,* November–December.

WARWICK, D. P. (1975) *A Theory of Public Bureaucracy.* Harvard University Press.

WATSON, A. J. (1982) Group Ideologies and Organizational Change. *Journal of Management Studies,* July.

WEBBER, R. A. (1969) Red Tape versus Chaos. *Business Horizons,* April.

WEINSHALL, T. D. (1977) Multinational Corporations. In Weinshall (editor) (1977).

WEINSHALL, T. D. (editor) (1977) *Culture and Management.* Penguin.

WHITAKER, A. (1982) *People, Tasks and Technology: A Study in Consensus.* University of Lancaster, Department of Behaviour in Organizations.

WHITE, M. (1981) *Payment Systems in Britain.* Gower Press.

WILKINSON, B. (1982) Managing with New Technology. *Management Today,* October.

WILKINSON, B. (1983) *The Shopfloor Politics of New Technology*. Heinemann.

WILLIAMSON, O. E. (1975) *Markets and Hierarchies*. Free Press.

WOODWARD, J. (1965) *Industrial Organization: Theory and Practice*. Oxford University Press.

WORTHY, J. C. (1950a) Factors Influencing Employee Morale. *Harvard Business Review*, January–February.

WORTHY, J. C. (1950b) Organizational Structure and Employee Morale. *American Sociological Review*, April.

ZALTMAN, G. and DUNCAN, R. (1977) *Strategies for Planned Change*. Wiley.

ZALTMAN, G., DUNCAN, R. and HOLBEK, J. (1973) *Innovations and Organizations*. Wiley.

ZIMPEL, L. (1974) *Man Against Work*. Eerdmans Publishing.

Index of Names

Index of Names

Index of Subjects